DUNBAR

A CRITICAL EXPOSITION
OF THE POEMS

DUNBAR

A CRITICAL EXPOSITION
OF THE POEMS

TOM SCOTT

OLIVER & BOYD
EDINBURGH
LONDON
1966

OLIVER & BOYD LTD

TWEEDDALE COURT
EDINBURGH 1

39A WELBECK STREET
LONDON W. 1

FIRST PUBLISHED 1966

PRINTED IN GREAT BRITAIN
BY OLIVER & BOYD LTD
EDINBURGH
SCOTLAND

THIS BIT BUIK IS DEDICATIT
TIL WILLIAM KERR SCOTT AND
KATHERINE BAILLIE OR SCOTT
FRAE THEIR SON THE SCREIVER O'T

Preface

THERE are many books to be written on Dunbar, and this
one seeks neither to compete with those already written
nor to discourage future work: on the contrary, this is
merely one contribution—the one most immediately necessary,
and which I am most able to do. But there is room for a small
work reviewing Dunbar studies up to date, as a guide to, and
clearing-house for, future work. I have tried here to do a sketch
of such a work in my bibliography: this is only an outline,
but space forbade any more exhaustive approach. Another
great need is for book-length studies of Dunbar's language
(long-overdue), his metric (still premature, pending more
evidence from phonetic studies), and of his imagery—the last
tracing its sources in the common stock of medieval culture,
rather along the lines of Isabel Hyde's valuable but too brief
study (see Bibliographical Review, Section E). These books
should, properly, have been written before the present one;
but what is desirable is not always practicable. Another work
of criticism can follow them, when the time is ripe.

My thanks are due firstly to Edinburgh University for
making the work possible; to the staff of the University library,
the National Library of Scotland, and Edinburgh Central
Library, Scottish Section; to my friends and supervisors
Professor MacQueen and the late Professor Butt for their help;
to my palaeography teacher Dr O. K. Schram; and finally
and mostly to those previous labourers in this thistle-field
without whose work this one could not have been.

TOM SCOTT

Edinburgh, December 1965

Contents

I

Within this Land

VERY little is known about the facts of William Dunbar's life. This is of small importance, for the poems tell us more about him than any list of dates and events would. Indeed, in some ways the less we know about a writer's life the better, for then we must concentrate on what is relevant, the work—and those who cannot or do not want to do that have less material to distract us with.

Dunbar lived in Scotland during the reign of James IV who reigned from 1488 to 1513. He had some connexion with the court, and some of his verse is of a semi-official courtly nature, and almost all of it in some way related to or aimed at a courtly audience. Some of his poems celebrate such state occasions as the marriage of James to Margaret Tudor in 1503 and the visit of the Queen to Aberdeen in 1511: others are direct appeals to the King for a benefice or pension or other relief of the poet's material poverty: many are satires of court life, or comic-satiric pieces meant chiefly as court entertainment. Some half-dozen of his poems were printed during his lifetime, about 1508, by Chepman and Myller of Edinburgh. There is evidence in some of the poems that he travelled abroad on some unspecified sort of court business, and also as a mendicant friar or novice. In August 1500 he was awarded a pension of £10 per annum for life, paid by the King, and subject to withdrawal if he should receive a benefice worth £40 a year.[1] In November 1507 this was increased to £20, and in August 1510 to £80, to cease if he were preferred to a benefice of £100 or more.[2] A reference to "the king's offerand

[1] See *The Poems of William Dunbar*, ed. J. Small, 3 vols., Scottish Text Society, Edinburgh 1889-93, Appendix to Introduction 1. cliii ff.

[2] These and other refs. to a William Dunbar, almost certainly the poet, are found in the Accounts of the Lord High Treasurer of Scotland, the Register of the Privy Seal of Scotland, and perhaps in Henry VII's Privy Purse Expenses, and other public records. For details, see the list given in *Poems*, ed. Small, 1. cliii ff.

at Maister William Dunbar's first mes", an offering of seven
French crowns, on 14 March 1503, suggests that Dunbar was
ordained priest somewhere about that time. Nothing certain
can be deduced from his flyting with Kennedy, because the
convention of lies, exaggeration, abuse, scurrility, forbid one's
treating such a source as reliable. Some of the material in
the "Flyting of Dunbar and Kennedy" has been proved to
have a factual basis from other sources, but this does not alter
the fact that the "Flyting" is not to be relied on as evidence
without such external support.

Dunbar is often called "Maister", and was probably a
Master of Arts. Yet there is no evidence which proves that
he was the William Dunbar who attended St Andrews
University (1477-9); and all else is mere conjecture.

Rather more is known, however, about the court of James
IV and the social life of the Scottish people during Dunbar's
lifetime, and this is of greater importance than mere biographical matter. Dunbar lived in an age and tradition which
made poetry a public virtue rather than a private vice; and
although Dunbar is the most personal of the Makars, even his
"persona" is a social one, and it is social life he writes about
mostly.

At the beginning of the fourth quarter of the fifteenth
century—James IV was born in 1473—Scotland was "even by
medieval standards an uncomfortable and uninviting country".[3]
The shaggy wastes of hill and moor were still haunted by
wolves, and "nature" was an object of dread rather than the
sentimental scenery of romantic nineteenth-century poets. The
garden was the symbol of the human, and over the walls lurked
the wild and dangerous realm of all that was not human.
Trade with the Continent was limited to the months of spring
and summer, from February till about October, because of
the dangerous sailing conditions at sea during the winter.
There were few walled towns, great churches, or large castles.
Of the Royal Burghs, only Perth and Edinburgh had battle-
mented walls: others had only ports and gatehouses at their
main entrances, and dykes at the foot of the long narrow
roods, strips of garden that sloped upwards to the fronts of

---

[3] R. L. Mackie, *King James IV of Scotland*, Edinburgh 1958, p. 3.

houses on the principal streets. Most of the houses were built of timber and thatch, with middens piled at every door of these main streets, which were deserted except on market-days. Cattle were driven through these streets every morning to the common ground outside, and brought back to the town in the evening. Agriculture was as primitive in the towns as in the remoter districts, and the twofold division of infield and outfield was wastefully customary everywhere. Only meagre crops could be reaped from the parsimonious soil, and a wet summer meant famine.

The peasantry shared their poor hovels with their cattle. Each peasant held land only on a lease of five years at most, and being liable to be turned out of his house every few years, had no incentive to build a house that would stand up to time and the weather. Under such conditions the poor had no sense of security even in poverty. The castles and towers built by the feudal knights also were meagre structures by the stand-ards of the time, usually only single towers enclosed by twenty-foot walls. The parish kirks were without aisle or transept, and had not improved since the twelfth or thirteenth century. Even St Andrews, the biggest cathedral in Scotland, was small compared with those of other countries, being only 357 feet in length.[4] The country was, in fact, seriously underdeveloped, although the fifteenth century had been a comparatively pros-perous one for Scotland. No English army had crossed the border since 1385, and there was considerable competition for Scottish trade on the Continent. Here and there the rise of new houses and kirks of a more ambitious sort began to appear, but the change was slow, and even that was to be ended by the English raids on the Forth and Tay in 1481-2.

The larger houses, even the palaces, were by no means sumptuous. No castle had more than one chair in the hall, and the floors were covered with rushes. The rooms were dark, with low raftered ceilings, and with small windows having only the upper half glazed, the lower being a wooden shutter. The ceilings were painted, however, and tapestries were hung on the walls of the principal rooms. Costly plate was common, there were log fires in the open fire-places. Bedrooms were

[4] York was 457 feet. See R. L. Mackie, *op. cit.*, p. 6.

bare of furniture other than the bed, but that might have its
canopy and arras and a huge feather mattress.

Disease was rife and life-expectancy short. Leprosy was
still common enough, and in the "Flyting of Dunbar and
Kennedy" Dunbar accuses Kennedy of living in a disused
leper house. Venereal disease in particular was common, and
there are gruesome descriptions of it in some of Dunbar's
poems, and of its cures. I have said that the houses in the
towns had middens at their doors, but it would perhaps give
a more exact impression if one said that the town streets were
public middens with houses in them. This filth was of course
a constant source of plague and disease. One outbreak of
plague hit Edinburgh and its neighbourhood in 1498, beginning in the villages of Currie and Swanston. The town itself
was barred to all incomers from these areas, under penalty of
death. By 1499 all schools were closed, children forbidden to
wander the streets, and merchants prohibited from setting up
booths and from holding markets. Special "cleansers" were
paid a shilling a day to perform funereal and similar duties.
This was a high rate for the time, and included "danger
money". The first four of these "cleansers" seem to have
died. Provisions were made for boiling and disinfecting clothes,
and for fumigating houses: but no provision was made for the
removal of the filthy refuse, and the festering sources of the
disease were therefore left to breed more horror. In 1502—
the year before James married Margaret Tudor—it broke out
again, and in 1505 we have the first sign of some suspicion
of the true cause: in that year Edinburgh Council entrusted
the bellman with "purgeing and clengeing of the hie streit . . .
of all maner of muk, filth of fische and flesche, and fulyie weit
and dry". But the old filthy state soon returned, and skinners
and furriers continued to hang their stinking goods in the High
Street. Such sanitary measures as were taken applied only to
the main streets, and not to the vennels and closes adjacent
thereto. These remained as before, to breed further death and
disaster. It has been said that the plague marched with the
men to Flodden, but it at least came back to Scotland un-
scathed. Henrysoun's poem *The Pest* speaks achingly out of
experience of the plague.

One of the worst of these disease-breeding middens was the kirkyaird, which was used as a general dumping-ground of offal and unwanted rubbish. As well as being the burial-ground of cast-off bodies, it was used for games and dancing, for pasturing cattle, sheep, and pigs, as a public lavatory, as a wenching-ground, and was the resort of beggars and outlaws. In 1606 the Burgh Council of Aberdeen granted permission to a man to build a ship in the kirkyaird. They agreed it was the best place for the work, and was only being used as a midden at the time.

As if the human body were not punished enough, merely for being, by nature and human ignorance, it had to bear also much of the burden of the ruling-class's vengeance for offences against its laws. The town's tolbooth was liable to be the scene of displayed limbs, nailed ears, scourgings and pilloryings, brankings and creelings, and of executions. Fines, it is true, were beginning to be used, whenever possible, instead of these outrages of the flesh, but not for any merely humane reason: they were pure profit, whereas the cost of executions and the like were a charge on the burgh. But for the poorest workers, exploited in every possible way by the ruling-class, the flesh had to pay; and the workman's body, which alone made it possible for the barons to live in idleness, gaming, and warring, had to bear this burden too.

According to Piccolomini, who visited Scotland in 1435, the workers, who produced the wealth for merchants to trade with, aristocrats to seize for their unproductive pastimes, the Church to mulct and spirit away to Rome while the parish kirks were scarcely even kept in decent repair, were poor and ragged and begged half-naked in the streets.[5] The merchants had almost complete, and corrupt, control of the burghs—they being able to juggle up finance for the King and nobles. They made a closed shop of the burgh and kept the craftsmen under their thumbs, while the ordinary people were slaves in all but name.

In "Eftir Geving I speik of Taking", Dunbar speaks of the peasantry being beggared of their harvest to pay for luxuries

[5] W. Croft Dickinson and G. Pryde, *A New History of Scotland*, 2 vols., Edinburgh 1961, I. 276.

for their landlords—themselves among the courtiers satirised by Dunbar in many other poems. This throws some light on the subject of beggars, of which we hear much in history of the period and of Scotland in both earlier and later times. These "beggars" were not criminal elements: they were the robbed, exploited, and disinherited people of the country victimised by their vicious ruling-classes. That many of them should have been driven to theft and actual crime is no cause for wonder.

Workmen were forced to labour as long as it was daylight in summer, and long before and after that in winter. A sixteen-hour day was normal. In 1469 an act had to be passed against too many holidays for the workers—they were bad for the "national economy". The slaves ought to be producing more for their masters, not indulging in idle religious festivities. The burghs were run by and for the burgesses, the bourgeoisie, which meant, in effect, the merchants and traders, whose patron by tradition was the god Mercury, the god of liars and cheats. Dunbar excoriates them too in his poems, particularly in the poem to the merchants of Edinburgh. This merchant class had achieved power, which was at a later date to make them the real ruling-class over even the landed gentry, by their usefulness to the Crown and nobility in raising money for ransoms, wars, and other costly indulgences of the gentry. The main struggle between the Crown and Rome during, before and after our period was a dog-fight over the rights of hogging the harvest, and the merchant class was useful to both. Indeed, in the Reformation settlement (1560), which finally resolved the issue in Scotland, the gentry used the religious fervour of such genuine reformers as John Knox to subvert the power of Rome, and thus completely trounced the "Kirk Malignant"; and the middle classes, especially the lairds, were the chief beneficiaries.[6]

The corruptions of the Church are well known and well-sustained, but too much has been made of this fact as a motive behind the Reformation. It was greed, not moral conscience, that motivated the gentry. Although it is a convincing picture

[6] The whole of W. Croft Dickinson's introduction to his edition of Knox's *History of the Reformation* (Edinburgh 1949) is relevant here.

of corruption that Lyndsay paints in *Ane Satyre of the Thrie Estaitis*, he exposes not only the Church, but also the gentry and the bourgeoisie, whose vices were merely increased by the Reformation. Dunbar himself exemplifies the state of feeling among the lesser gentry: he is motivated, in his tirades against the abuse of Church benefices and the like, not only by righteousness, but also by envy. He was angry with the parasites only because he was not one of them, and this motive behind so much of his work limits its ultimate value. But he is the voice of his class.

The reign of James IV has been widely represented as a Golden Age in Scottish history, and the King himself presented as a typical Renaissance prince—a great man, a patron of the arts and sciences, a man of culture and learning. This is a false picture. There are no "golden ages". There were stirrings of far-reaching changes in Scotland in our period, for better and for worse, as in other countries, but the pleasanter side of this has been over-stressed. Similarly, while James himself had many excellent qualities, there was another side to him, and that darker side was the dominant one. He was a man of impulsive and irresponsible character with little of the solider qualities necessary to kingship—prudence, judgment, patience, balance, and a cool grasp of reality. James was generous and personally attractive, genial and open, gay and active, with a quick if superficial interest in all that was going on in his time. But he was mercurial rather than stable, adventurous rather than wise, courageous rather than disciplined, a man of enthusiasms rather than of solid values. He had the temperament of a soldier rather than a governor, and as a soldier, that of a cavalry officer rather than that of a general. He was more fitted to the saddle than the seat of government. As a military commander he was disastrous. His tendency to rush headlong into a fight like some foolhardy youngster instead of sitting still and directing his men like a good commander was remarked by Pedro de Ayala fifteen years before this trait cost him his life at Flodden: and Ayala tried to emphasise all that was good and likable in James.[7] He saw himself not as the steady, wise governor of a kindgom—the sort of statesman

---

[7] Mackie, *King James IV of Scotland*, p. 84. The whole book is relevant here.

B

Robert Bruce became in his later years—but as a romantic
leader of a European crusade. He was, in fact, a bad king
unsuited to the life of an administrator-cum-judge, and this
combination of irresponsibility and power—the perennial
curse of hereditary kingship—brought his reign and his people
to the disaster of Flodden.

The same romanticising tendency among historians and
commentators of the period has given us also a false picture of
Dunbar as a sort of poet laureate of the court of this golden
age. In fact, despite one or two poems in the aureate style
in which Dunbar does celebrate a state occasion somewhat in
the manner later expected of poets laureate, the bulk of his
work is satiric, and the court of James comes under his savage
denunciation. In such poems as "Schir, Ye Have mony
Servitouris",[8] "Be Divers Wyis",[9] "Schir, at this Feist of
Benefice",[10] and other poems of petition, complaint or satire,
he shows James as encouraging the unworthy at the expense
of the worthy (chiefly, of course, the worthy Dunbar himself),
giving benefices to scoundrels, ignoring good advice, permitting
corruption of law and society, and generally being irresponsible
and indiscriminate. In "The Fenyeit Freir of Tungland"[11]
he rages against the promotion of a charlatan who actually
tried to fly from Stirling Castle, and who seems to have been
able to get support from James for all manner of quack enter-
prises.

One of the earliest of James's mistakes of judgment, if not
of downright folly, was his support of the pretentions of Perkin
Warbeck to the throne of Henry VII: he invaded England in
this cause in 1496, taking Norham and other castles. He allowed
himself to be used as a tool by Pope Julius II in his League of
Cambrai, directed against the state of Venice—it was in this
context that he allowed himself to dream of leading an all-
Europe crusade against the Turks. When Julius dropped both

---

[8] 17 ("Remonstrance to the King"). All such refs. are to *The Poems of William
Dunbar*, ed. W. Mackay Mackenzie, Edinburgh 1932. Many of the titles that
Mackenzie gives to Dunbar's poems are modern inventions; I have usually pre-
ferred to cite them by first line or refrain.

[9] 29 ("Aganis the Solistaris in Court").

[10] 11 ("Quhone Mony Benefices Vakit").

[11] 38. Same title.

the League and James, the latter turned to Louis of France and allowed himself to be drawn into a renewal of the Auld Alliance in 1512, and thence to Flodden. To that battle he marched despite the contrary advice of his elder statesmen, such as Elphinstone and Angus. Once in England, he wasted a fortnight in the game of castle-taking. When Surrey challenged him to fight a battle on the plain of Milfield, which he might well have won, he refused to descend from Flodden Hills, and then allowed Surrey to outmanoeuvre him. Instead of trying to head off Surrey's march north, he took up an exposed position on the forward slope above Branxton; but Surrey's artillery silenced his, and forced him to plunge headlong down into the low ground beneath it. Finally, he abandoned his command when the battle was being fought, and rushed forward into personal assault of the enemy vanguard, getting himself killed and leaving his army leaderless, not even having appointed a substitute commander.[12] This would seem to be the truth behind the legend which is or was well-known to schoolboys of the gallant Scottish king dying—suspiciously like the story of Harold at Hastings—at the centre of a hard core of his faithful knights, the last remnant of the Scottish army, pierced by an arrow through the eye. There is always a suggestion of foul play about being pierced by an arrow. It is a form of sniping, not a fair man-to-man combat. But Bruce had, in any case, scattered the archers of a greater English army with only five hundred cavalry, so the tale is a weak one. A Stewart king would surely be well versed in the military techniques of Robert Bruce, and if James had "stood" at all in the centre of his knights and discharged the duties of command though he might still have been defeated, yet he would most probably have been able to make an ordered retreat.

It is true that James showed great interest in building a navy, but little of lasting value seems to have come of it. The Great Michael itself seems to have been an expensive white elephant, and was eventually sold to the King of France. It is easy, of course, to be wise after the event, but surely that is a duty—otherwise the lessons of history go unlearned. James

[12] Cp. the study of the Battle of Flodden in M. McLaren, *If Freedom Fail*, London 1964, which completely supersedes all previous accounts.

was pioneering in the matter of naval power but the same cannot
be said of his military conduct. On the whole, we are left
with the impression that James was unsuited to kingship in his
time, and the anger of Dunbar against his many failings is
understandable and even perhaps justifiable. Yet one point
may be made, mere speculation though it be, in James's favour.
His guilt in connexion with his father's death, and the belt of
penance he is said to have worn for years after, is well-known:
was there perhaps an element of self-punishment or of atone-
ment in his impetuous courting of danger in battle? In any
case, if this were so, it would only bear out what we have
alleged against his competent wielding of the sceptre.

Dunbar's poems throw much more and other light on James.
In "Sanct Salvatour! Send Silver Sorrow",[13] he appeals to
the King to end the chronic malaise of his empty purse. In
"Musing allone this hinder Nicht",[14] he quotes "Gude James
the Ferd, our nobill king", as advising that all people should
do good and care not what others may say, because none can
escape criticism: but that was when the King was young, and
Dunbar seems to have neglected his own advice in later years.
In "Schir at this feast of benefice",[15] to quote its first line, he
tells us that the King does not share out benefices equally, but
gives many to one while some deserving people (including of
course the poet) get none. And in the companion piece "Off
Benefice, Schir, at everie Feist", he goes on to say that those
who ask most get most, while he, Dunbar himself, stands
"fastand in a nuke". The kind of people James does promote
do their parishes more harm than good. He complains, in
"This Waverand Warldis Wretchidnes",[16] of "The liell labour
lost and liell service", and of the small reward these bring,
adding that this is true not only of Scotland but of other
countries he has been in—France, Ingland, Ireland, Almanie,
Italie, and Spane. "Gude rewle is banist our the Bordour",
while wrong-doings and disorder reign. He alleges that the
son would disinherit the father; that churchmen's consciences
are so broad that you could turn a cart and eight oxen on them;
that while some have benefices, he, Dunbar, has none; that

---

[13] 1 ("To the King").   [14] 8 ("Of Deming").
[15] 12 ("To the King").   [16] 13 ("Of the Worldis Instabilitie").

stable-boys aspire to be cardinals, while he can't even get a
kirk "scant coverit with haddir". For all this only the King
can bring relief, and he appeals to him to do so. In "To
Speik of Gift or Almows Deid",[17] he refers to James as giving
to the rich who have no need at all, while the poor die of want,
unheard; and says that while he, Dunbar, is ignored, the King
gives to the charlatan Damian "That yisterday fra Flanders
flew". This whole poem is, in fact, a veiled complaint against
James's irresponsibility in respect of giving. In "Eftir Geving
I Speik of Taking",[18] he also complains that clerics mulct the
poor and care nothing for their souls; that the barons rob the
folk of their harvest and make them beg from door to door;
and that the merchants take illegal profit. Robbery and piracy
have no cure but the gallows. If some had as little fear of
men as they have of God, they too would rob their neighbours.
Men of power who rob the poor "Ar sett full famous at the
Sessioun", while poor ordinary robbers are hanged.

In "Schir, Ye Have mony Servitouris",[19] the complaint
against his evil dispensation reaches a new and daring height
of utterance. In it he lists the useful people whom James
patronises, those of every craft and productive pursuit, those
of the Church, the law, the court, of medicine, philosophy,
music, strategy, carpentry, masonry, and the like: these he
admits deserve their reward. But he himself, he claims,
though unworthy to be ranked with them, has done work which
will hold as long in mind "But wering, or consumptioun,
Roust, canker, or corruptioun, As ony of thair werkis all",
although he gets little reward for it. But there is a quite
different sort of person whom James patronises also, being,
says Dunbar of the King, "sa gracious" and "Meik". These
are feigners, flatterers, boasters, and all manner of worthless
hangers-on. When he, Dunbar, sees such useless wasters
rewarded, while he is ignored, "Than on this fals warld I cry
Fy". His heart almost bursts out of his breast with anger
that his eyes should see such abuses daily in the court, and he
must either wreak vengeance with his pen or die. He ends with

---

[17] 15 ("Of Discretioun in Giving").
[18] 16 ("Of Discretioun in Taking").
[19] 17 ("Remonstrance to the King").

a warning to James that if he does not watch out, if he does
nothing to cure Dunbar's rage, then the swelling of his anger
will spout out all its poison. This poem is a remarkable
comment on the "golden age", and on the "gallant" James
IV. There is no reason to doubt either Dunbar's sincerity or
the truth of his allegations. We certainly cannot disprove his
account of the state of James's court, however much apologists
may try to take the edge off Dunbar's biting truth.

Even in the lighter poems in humorous vein—among the
very best Dunbar ever wrote, for his humour had a sweetness
and wry pathos unique in Scots poetry—he keeps up the barrage
of complaint against James. In the poem in which he prays
that the King "war Johne (Joan) Thomsounis man" (i.e., a
hen-pecked husband), he says that the Queen knows Dunbar's
worth better than the King does, and he wishes the King would
be guided by her. But instead, James is "harde, dour, and
mercyles" to Dunbar. And in "This Hinder Nicht in Dunfermeling", [20] he reveals another aspect of James's irresponsible
character—his spoliation of his subjects' wives and daughters.
This does not affect Dunbar closely—he is no Rigoletto—and
he treats it humorously, but the picture of the husband or
father's anguish is grim enough under the surface. An ordinary
man had no redress against a monarch in such matters.

The main note of his complaint against the King is, however,
a more strident one; and in "Complane I wald" [21]—a com-
panion-piece to "Schir, Ye Have Mony Servitouris" [22]—he
again vilifies the hangers-on at court and James, by implication,
for patronising them. He asks him "to auld servandis haff
ane E". And in "Exces of Thocht Dois me Mischief", [23] he
complains of his long years of service to the King, years that
have gone unrewarded although lesser men have been paid
for lesser services. He renews his plea, not of right, but begging
for mercy. He points out that although in childhood he had
been brought up to think of himself as a bishop-to-be, now in
auld age he cannot even obtain a vicarage, and Jok, once a
cattle herd, possesses a string of benefices. Dunbar is no

---

[20] 27 ("The Wowing of the King quhen he wes in Dunfermeling").
[21] 19 ("Complaint to the King").
[22] 17 ("Remonstrance to the King").   [23] 20 ("To the King").

democrat and would have scorned Burns's "A man's a man for
a' that", and his social snobbery is typical of the gentry of this
and much later periods all over Europe: indeed, it is a salient
characteristic of European culture.

The complaint against James goes on in " Quhom to sall I
Compleine My Wo",[24] this time on a moralistic level; virtue
is despised at court while rogues prosper. All good-breeding,
all nobleness, have gone from rank, and there is no pity in
princes. Flattery wears a furred gown, and falsehood conspires
with nobility, while truth stands barred at the door and honour
is exiled from town. Here we have the elements of Lindsay's
great satire, when the Reformation tide was in full flood. Fair
words, say Dunbar, are in every mouth, but deception is in
every heart: demure looks come from every eye, but few good
deeds come from the hands. He turns from life to death for
his reward, looking beyond the grave for it. In more humorous
vein, he complains in "Schir, Lat it Nevir in Toun be Tald"[25]
that he has grown old in the King's service without reward,
and must now beg for even a new coat for Christmas or be
ridiculed in court and in town.

The lighter side of court-life is touched on in such poems as
"Sir Jhon Sinclair Begowthe to Dance"[26] and those on James
Doig, the Queen's wardrobe-master.[27] These suggest that he
had an intimacy with the Queen which was both homely and
broad. The poem on Norny, the court jester,[28] and even more
that on the negress at court,[29] suggest that Dunbar shared the
brutal insensitive humour of his age. But in "The Fenyeit
Freir of Tungland"[30] he turns his savagery on his courtier
enemies, exposing the pretentions—which took in the gullible
James—of the alchemist and quack mediciner John Damian.
Indeed, Damian becomes something of a scapegoat for all that
Dunbar most hates at court and in the King himself. Damian
is an obvious peg to hang this hatred on, but the man did have

---

[24] 21 ("None may Assure in this World").
[25] 22 ("The Petition of the Gray Horse, Auld Dumbar").
[26] 32 ("Of a Dance in the Quenis Chalmer").
[27] 34 ("Of James Dog, Kepar of the Quenis Wardrop") and 35 ("Of the Same
James, quhen he had Plesett Him").
[28] 35 ("Of Sir Thomas Norny").
[29] 37 ("Of ane Blak-Moir").   [30] 38 (same title).

the sincerity to put his notions on the possibility of human flight to the test, breaking his leg in the process. It is possible to see in him an early, groping scientific experimenter, and there probably were much worse elements at court much more favoured by the credulous and unjust King. Damian is also attacked in "Lucina Schynnyng in Silence of the Nicht",[31] in which Dunbar complains that he will never be well-off until two moons are seen in the sky, or an abbot flies above the moon.

Dunbar bears witness against not only the court of James IV, but also against town life and life in general in Scotland. In "Renunce thy God"[32] it is the life of the burgh that comes under his flail. Craftsmen of all sorts are given to swearing impossible oaths, most of them also blasphemous, and all of them lies. The goldsmith swears, on pain of Hell, that he loses in all his work. The merchant swears that no finer silk than his ever crossed the ocean. The tailor swears, by the Devil, who is listening with grim contentment to all this, that there are no better-shaped gowns than his. The shoemaker swears, by the Devil, that no better boots are made of better leather. The baker says, may God forsake him if any man saw better bread than his. The butcher swears, by God's wounds, that better beef or mutton than his cannot be. The taverner likewise swears by his wine, the brewer by his malt, the smith that he can't make threepence in ten days—and so on. To all of them the listening Devil whispers grimly: "Renunce thy God and cum to me". They have all sworn themselves into his power already, and he merely claims his own.

The law-courts are satirised in "Sic Tydingis Hard I at the Sessioun".[33] No man can trust another, says Dunbar, offenders are better off than their victims, flatterers, hypocrites, and confidence-tricksters abound there. Some neglect their lands while a decision is pending; some prosper at court through influence; some complain of partiality; some see their suits postponed; some win, others lose; some rejoice, while others are done out of all they possess. Some cut throats or pick purses; some go in procession to gallows to be hanged;

[31] 39 ("The Birth of Antichrist").   [32] 42 ("The Devillis Inquest").
[33] 43 ("Tydingis fra the Sessioun").

some bless the judge, others damn him to Hell. Religious men come to wench women, both Carmelites and Cordillers, so that more friars may be engendered, the elder men of God instructing the younger. Strong young monks have their pleas granted by all merciful women. This is the kind of news one hears of the Court of Session. Much of all this, of course, is common medieval literary stock, and Dunbar is, as always, even at his most personal, seldom straying far from convention: but the conventions arose to meet a real need, and the pressure of truth behind so much of this conventional stock was a main cause of the Reformation. The fact that in medieval poetry it was conventional to joke about friars and the religious orders is not in itself a reason for doubting the truth of much that was alleged. The Church itself acknowledged the state of corruption into which it had fallen by gratefully accepting the Society of Jesus.

Edinburgh life also comes under Dunbar's penetrating eye. In "Quhy will Ye, Merchantis of Renoun",[34] he reproaches the merchants of Edinburgh with allowing their town to get a bad name, for "laik of reformatioun"—surely a significant word indeed here. The stink of fish at the town gates puts people off entering at all—the stink of fish and the cries of old women and brawls and scurrilous railing in front of strangers of every rank. The "stinking style" overshadows the parish church. Front staircases darken the houses as in no other country. At the High Cross, milk and curds are sold, not gold and silk; at the Tron, whelks, cockles, puddings, and haggis. The town minstrels know only two tunes—*Now the Day Dawis* and *Into Joun*. Clowns have better men for servants. Tailors and shoemakers and other lowly craftsmen, he says, filthy the fairest streets, and merchants are crowded into the Stinking Style like bees in a hive. The burgh is a nest of beggars clamouring without cease, molesting honest people with pitiful cries and lamentations. No provision is made for the poor. Profit gets bigger daily as good deeds get less and less, and one may not pass through the streets for the cries of neglected blind people and cripples. If Court and Session have to leave Edinburgh because of the burgesses' failure to repair

[34] 44 ("To the Merchantis of Edinburgh").

these faults, then the whole town will decay. Therefore, he says, strangers should be well-treated and not overcharged for their needs, and the merchants should be careful not to be extortionate, but should keep order and look after their poor neighbours. But their own individual profit has made them so blind that the profit of the community as a whole lags far behind. All this should cause them to feel shame so to allow their name to be dishonoured. This homiletic note is Dunbar at his most genuinely religious. Could not a minister of the Reformed Kirk have said much the same at any time after 1560—even today? Some indeed of the worst abuses have gone or been ameliorated, but have they all? This is relevant, for in such poems Dunbar is still very much alive for us, and has contemporary significance.

By contrast, there is an "official" poem on the Queen's visit to Aberdeen—"Blyth Aberdeane".[35] The poem is a deliberate and stately compliment to the burgesses of the town, and while the panegyrist sings the praises of the town and its folk, the satirist looks the other way. The Queen is met by the richly dressed burgesses, with four strong young men to bear the crimson velvet pall above her head. Artillery salutes her. A procession meets her at the Port, led by a pageant of the Virgin and Child accompanied by the Magi: other figures in it are Adam and Eve and Robert Bruce and former Stewart royalty. Then twenty-four young maids dressed in green and playing on timbrels meet her. The streets are all hung with tapestry and pageants are played while lieges are received by the Queen. The Cross runs wine "aboundantlie", says Dunbar, but this delirious vision of affluence is sobered somewhat by a figure given for a similar occasion in Edinburgh: the wine run at the cross amounted to only one puncheon.[36] The Queen is conducted to her lodging and presented with a costly cup. He ends by advising the Queen to be thankful to Aberdeen for her reception:

Thairfoir, sa lang as Quein thow beiris croun,
Be thankful to this burcht of Aberdein.

---

[35] 64 ("To Aberdein").
[36] W. Croft Dickinson, *A New History of Scotland*, 1. 242.

In "A General Satyre"[37] he tells how he dreamed about the plight of his country. Nobility and responsibility have gone, and hunger and cowardice are rife. The prelates are proud and ignorant, surrounded by rogues, and they are unknown in their abbeys. Priests dress in secular clothes, and very few are able to conduct themselves. He describes scholars and clerks as wasters. Scotland has never seen so much anger, so much venereal disease, so many foolish Lords, so much treason, so many partial judgments, so much public neglect, so many thieves, boasters, and brawlers, so much litigation, so little justice for the poor, so much cheating and profiteering, so many rich merchants, so many poor tenants, so much vanity of dress. Wherever he looks, he sees decay and degeneration of the old ways and morals.

Other poems, too, add their comment on social abuses. In "Thir Ladyis Fair",[38] he tells of women who come to plead causes instead of their menfolk, and trade themselves to the judges in the oldest form of bribery. In two days they accomplish more than their husbands in ten, so all husbands should dress up their wives and send them to court to do the pleading. In less than two hours, in some quiet spot, they can buy some grace from the judges, and at no material cost— their evidence is completely endorsed. Such wise women are to be prized. The poems on the regency of Albany may not be by Dunbar, but they reflect the despair of the people and the gentry after Flodden, and the worthlessness of the Regent who absented himself for four years in France, leaving Scotland in chaos and disorder. Dunbar takes the view that this disaster was rather the work of God's wisdom than of human folly, and begs God to stay his punishing hand before the whole kingdom is lost. In "Of Covetyce",[39] he complains that generosity, honour, and nobleness, fair wages, manhood, happiness, and good-breeding are now regarded at court as vices. All virtue is changed into vice, all healthy sport into gambling, and true servants are put away and replaced by accomplices in vice. Burghs are decayed, farmers have no beasts except cats and mice. Honest yeomen are now lousy

[37] 77 (same title).   [38] 48 ("Of the Ladyis Solistaris at Court").
[39] 67 (same title).

and ragged, while lairds go in silk that their tenants had to sell their harvest to buy, so that they now have to dig roots for food. The charitable are held to be fools, and robbers are considered wise men. All this is because of the sin of avarice.

In giving this outline of the social background, in part, of Dunbar's age, I have drawn largely on its greatest authority —Dunbar himself. It is customary to speak of that age as one of transition. Every age is an age of transition, and in our period great changes were going on in Scotland and elsewhere, and those changes were gathering momentum. Feudalism was giving way to capitalism, the rule of powerful land-grabbers to the coming one of a moneyed merchant-class. Trade was becoming a more powerful and valuable economic activity than land-owning; and one might symbolise it by saying that the ship was proving to be a more potent source of wealth than the baronial tower, and money or movable goods a more valuable and resilient form of wealth than mere territory. This transitional trend, deep, slow, and far-reaching, was less dominant during our period than the one soon to be consummated by the Reformation of and around 1560— namely the change-over from Church-ownership of large parts of the country to secular seizure of Church lands. Indirectly this increased the power of the bourgeoisie: directly it created an augmented class of smaller lairds, of lesser gentry, which soon began to assert itself, in and through the growing power of Parliament, as an increasingly influential factor in Scottish life. Thanks to the growing power of Parliament, James VI failed in his attempt to make the power of the monarchy absolute in Scotland; and in 1603 he and his court set the pattern for succeeding generations by deserting Scotland for England, which, having a firmly established monarchy and episcopal Church, seemed to promise well for James VI's monarchical ambitions. In 1688 it was Parliament which ended the rule of the Stewarts; in 1707 it was Parliament which betrayed Scottish independence to the Auld Enemy. As a by-product of the land revolution, the age was also one of transition from Catholicism to Presbyterianism. In art, the romantic and chivalrous tradition of the feudal period gave way more and more to the growing realism of the lower classes

—the *fabliau* began to oust the romance from its supreme position: this is clearly seen in the work of Dunbar. The small, compact Kingdom of Scotland, in which the Crown had never really succeeded in establishing itself over the feudal anarchy of the nobles, was itself in process of being liquidated. The task of monarchy was to make the nation-kingdom an integrated whole. In achieving this task, the English monarchy had developed a parliament founded on the commons as representative of the whole nation, and used it against the anarchically ungovernable nobles. The Scottish monarchy did not succeed in developing an effective parliament, or even, like France, in imposing an absolute monarchy on the aristocracy: and its failure destroyed the kingdom, which was sold out by the nobles.

The great medieval harmony, the world of the Church in which everything had its proper place and all life had meaning at every level, the world of Aquinas and Dante, was breaking up, perhaps for ever in that form. The great harmony of Henrysoun's tales, a moral harmony in which good and evil were easily known and accepted, gives way to Dunbar's short-poem views, his world of doubt and anxiety, his sense of impending doom. By comparison with Henrysoun's, Dunbar's vision of life is fragmentary, disintegrated and bitty, its proper form the short poem, for there is no wholeness to sustain a long one. The Babylonian captivity and the great schism both undermined the authority which, partly by their own unaided effort, but largely with the help of the Carolingian and German Emperors, the Popes had so laboriously built up; the central foundations of Western Christendom had crumbled; and, although some ancient kingdoms were lucky enough to be able to arrest the resulting disintegration by turning themselves into nation-states, others, like Scotland, fell among their own nobles, either to lie there permanently weakened, or later to be taken over by other kingdoms.

Out of that age the present one was being born, the age of capitalism, of "science", of the increasing mastery over the physical world of "nature", of real social progress, of stressing the centrality of mankind rather than that of God—and God was the old word for Reality—the age of doubt and anxiety, of spiritual agony and material comfort. The great dream of an orderly intellectual universe given incomparable expression by the sublime Alighieri proved to be only a dream—mankind, in Tennyson's words, was to come "ravening down the centuries to burst into the desolation of reality". But if much was lost, much was gained. The human predicament may never change from age to age—conception, birth, pain, disease, accident, eating, drinking, breathing, sleeping, certain death, are all eternal conditions of human life—but the social environment can be and is constantly being changed, materially for the better. Material progress in this respect is real, and valuable. It is impossible to look back on the sufferings of the medievals in this regard without pity. The oppression of human suffering revealed in their poetry is almost unbearable. They suffered more through ignorance than sin, having no real understanding of their social plight. The headache that stopped Dunbar writing on one famous occasion could today have been dispelled by a cheap pill. A modern fireman's hose, properly applied, would have done much to prevent the ghastly ravages of plague which they, in their ignorance, abominably attributed to a punishing God: in itself a denial of Christ's teachings on forgiveness. A swift descent into the Middle Ages—so-called: the Feudal Ages really is what we mean—is the best corrective for that fashionable cynicism common today, that sneering at social progress affected by many "educated" people and "intellectuals", that treason of the intelligentsia which so disfigures the present age. We are reminded how much we owe to the scavenger who empties our buckets and incinerates the contents; to the engineers who simplify existence for us; and that no civilisation is any better than its sewage system, no culture higher than its lowest "menial". In the material sense, we might be forgiven for feeling that the medievals wrote so incomparably of Hell because it was where they lived.

James gave Scotland vigorous government, but not good government, for he was unable to grasp the real tasks of kingship in his time—like all the Stewarts except the first James. Dunbar may have seen only part of the truth—no man can do otherwise—but his indictment of the age was true, and no mere " poetic " fiction.

II

Off Every Study, Lair, or Disciplene

THE greatest single influence on medieval poetry was *Le Roman de la rose*. Of the two parts of that poem, the first by Guillaume de Loris and the second by Jean de Meung, the first part was the most influential on love-poetry. This part was translated by Chaucer into English, and is the main embodiment of the doctrine of *amour courtois*. An understanding of this medieval phenomenon is essential to an understanding of the poetry of the time, and of much later poetry.

During the eleventh century, in the south of France, a certain ruling-class culture flourished: a culture founded on life in isolated castles and towers. The owner of each castle or tower led, with his guests and retainers, a life of military and field sports, of jousting, duelling, weapon-practice, riding, and sword-play, and of hawking, hunting, and the like. These strenuous open-air sports were of course masculine ones, like the great game of war, for which, largely, they were rehearsals and training. But life for women was very different, shut up in lonely castles and towers, with only the needle and the spindle for work and exercise. The more laborious work of the lord's womenfolk was done by servants, and their social outlet was confined to presiding at the lord's table over junketings more robust than refined: even this was occasional, as the lord would be away for long stretches at a time, leaving only a handful of old men and boys to carry on the needs of castle-maintenance, care of women and children, food provision, and even emergency defence. Life must have been somewhat dull for the women, and for their retainers, during long periods of loneliness. Young squires and minstrels bore the weight of the duty of entertaining them. This dullness of existence was intensified by the fact that love was no part of feudal marriage, which was a contract between land-owners involving the exchange of women as part of the land-deal.

Therefore no deep love of husband was likely to sustain the lady of the castle during her lord's absences. On the contrary, his absence was more likely to be a source of temptation. Love, which was unnecessary and even undesirable in marriage, had perforce to live outside the law.

In such conditions the elaborate game of *amour courtois* grew up. The rules of it were determined by the "ladies" themselves—notably by Eleanor d'Aquitaine and her daughter Marie de Champagne.[1] This game of love was the main inspiration of the songs of the troubadours, that unique school of lyric poets who invented most of the lyric forms used in European poetry ever since. Even Burns's favourite stanza, the staple of Scottish eighteenth-century poetry, was first used and probably invented by Guillaume of Poitou in the eleventh century. *Amour courtois* seems to have begun in the south, but when Eleanor became Queen of France, the game was spread and encouraged in the north, where she and her daughter actually held mock courts of love in which points of etiquette and technique in the game were decided. From Marie de Champagne, in particular, this cult seems to have come into the Arthurian romances through Chretien de Troyes, and to have become through succeeding poets a stereotyped pageantry regressively degenerating into depths of monotony and artificiality. Earthier and more masculine though it was, Ovid's *Ars amatoria* was one of the literary ancestors of this type of poetry: but it was widely translated into French, and widely read, and may at least have influenced the literary side of the cult, not only in poetry, but in *De Arte honeste amandi*.

In this handbook of the game, Andreas Capellanus sets out the following main laws and principles of *amour courtois*:

1. *Amour courtois* is sensual, and aims at physical consummation; but it has to be approached through an elaborate play of etiquette, designed partly to bring out the finest qualities in the *ami* (lover), as seen from the feminine angle, but chiefly to heighten the preliminary love-play for the woman.

[1] W. G. Dodds, *Courtly Love in Chaucer and Gower*, Harvard 1913, p. 1. I am indebted to this book and to several others, notably C. S. Lewis; *The Allegory of Love*, for much of the material used in this brief outline.

2. It is illicit, indeed illegal, and adulterous, in direct
   conflict with the teachings of the Church and the exac-
   tions of the law. Andreas reports that Marie laid it
   down that love cannot exist between husband and wife,
   because she is his inferior, and also his body-slave. By
   the same rule, a woman could not plead marital fidelity
   as an excuse for denying the *ami*. Notice here the
   supremacy of the female in all this game—the lover
   moulds himself to her ideal. This is the opposite of the
   reality of feudal marriage.

3. Since the nature of the courtly love-affair is adulterous,
   secrecy is of the utmost necessity. No sin that the *ami*
   can commit is greater than that of making the slightest
   mention of any favour that the *dame* ("lady") may have
   bestowed on him. The fear of spies and of betrayal
   is a constant source of anxiety to both parties. Love
   cannot survive discovery—even the lovers themselves
   may not survive discovery, as in the case of Paolo and
   Francesca in Canto V of Dante's *Inferno*. The *dame's*
   reputation must, at all costs, be safeguarded, for while
   it is no violation of the code to commit adultery, it is
   an unforgivable offence against it to be found out. This
   is not because of any sexual jealousy that the husband
   may feel—for since the husband cannot "love" his
   wife, he cannot be sexually jealous of her; but the
   husband is jealous of his rights of property in the lady,
   and the laws and the Church support him. In Hell
   Dante meets Paolo and Francesca only: he does not
   meet the husband who murdered them.

4. It is of the essence of the game that love should be
   difficult, fraught with danger, hardship, inaccessibility.
   The *dame* is high-born or high-placed or both, and carefully guarded, while the *ami* is in an inferior position.
   He may be a knight, but more usually he is a servant or
   minstrel, a person of inferior social rank—and perhaps
   younger than his *dame*. This social class-division between
   them contributes to the invariable idealisation of the *dame*.
   She is out of reach, far above the lowly male who aspires
   to her favours, hard to get because of her husband's

c

wealth and position, and her own exalted rank. This idealisation of the *dame*—always the "lady", never the "woman"—neatly inverts the masculine tradition of patriarchal society, which relegates the female to an inferior social position; and in the *ami* the ensuing collision between his patriarchal tradition and his courtly love breeds an emotional and moral conflict productive of symptoms resembling those of neurosis or even insanity.

Some of these symptoms are: solitary mourning and moping; blushing and going pale; going hot and cold alternately; self-forgetfulness, dumbness, and motionlessness; restlessness when absent from the *dame*; an insatiable longing for sight of the beloved; self-torture, self-reproach, and remorse—particularly over an opportunity missed through timidity; secret lingering approaches to the *dame's* dwelling; loss of speech in her presence, accompanied by trembling, blushing, and paling alternately; agonies of sleeplessness at night; happy dreams of the beloved, followed by anguished awakenings; secret visits to her dwelling in the small hours of morning; lurking in her precincts at all hours and in all weathers; pining and wasting and growing thin and ill. These are the marks of *amour*; and they appear throughout the poetry of *amour courtois*, and linger on even today not only in literature but in life, and in feminine fantasies. They are so well-known that Polonius thought he recognised them in Hamlet,[2] who indeed seemed almost to caricature them. Polonius may have been nearer truth than we realise: but with Gertrude, not Ophelia, as the object of *amour*. Certainly the conditions set out above are those typical of mother-son incest: the older woman already married and in a superior position of authority, the fear of the husband, the secrecy and guilt. This kind of love manifestly is not procreative: the *ami* is in typical son-relationship to both the *dame* and her husband, and a lasting union is not in question. It is essentially a relationship of dependence on the side of the *ami* and of power on the side of the *dame*.

To all the symptoms already mentioned may be added the

---

[2] *Hamlet*, I. 2.

even more alarming ones of loss of appetite, fainting, going mad, and even dying. Yet *amour* is supposed, in the code, to "ennoble" the *ami* to inspire him to deeds of high idealism, to raise him from vulgarity to chivalry, to make him a man of "culture", as conceived by the code—in a word, to make him "courteous". Courtesy is the great virtue cultivated by chivalry and *amour courtois*—the quality of behaving like a perfect courtier. Spenser's *Faerie Queen* was one of the culminating romances of a long and exhausted tradition; Sidney one of the last of the courtier-heroes, on this side of the Channel.

This code is almost an inversion of the marital ideals of the Church and the realities of feudal marriage: yet this profane romantic cult is paralleled in religion by the rise of the cult of the Virgin and of Mariolatry. There is more than a hint of pagan goddess-worship in it—but a sick version of the old robust fertility cult—fertility being precisely what the cult utterly lacks. This phenomenon is not, in fact, a culture in any real sense: it does not embody a total way of human life. On the contrary, it is lopsided, obsessively narrow, concerned with only a small part of life. It is, moreover, dependent on a fuller, more real way of life, however brutal and barbarous, for its very existence. It is a cult of the sensibility rather than of the intellect; of feeling rather than of thought; of the part rather than the whole; of art rather than religion; of fantasy rather than active living. We may see in it a rather crude emergence of a corrective feminine sensibility from under the lopsided weight of patriarchal society and religion. Certainly it is a product of castle life, with its few women and many men, and the high isolation thus accorded to the "ladies". Each castle tended to resemble an outpost of empire with its regiment of unmarried men, the colonel's wife and daughters the only women except for native servants, and the colonel himself often absent from base conferring with the governor or other superiors. *Amour courtois* did not and was not likely to appear in village or town life, where life was real and natural, men and women living and working together in normal community. This normal life gave rise not to romance, but to another great type of medieval literature, the *fabliaux*: comic-satiric tales which often ridiculed the high-flown fantastic romances. They were the Sancho Panzas to the Don Quixotes of the romances.

The centrality of the castle tempts one to suggest that in fact the castle itself was the true object of desire, the *dame* merely symbolising it in the power-fantasy of a young and landless squire, minstrel, or wandering knight. But she also symbolises the garden, the small patch of cultivation in the surrounding wilderness, and as such has a genuine cultural significance. Further, in her lord's absence, the lady of the castle became in a very real sense his chief mate, with delegated male power: whereas there were no ambiguous lady "Lord Provosts" in the towns. Part of the essence of this love-game is precisely that it is not a "woman" who is the object of love, but a "lady", a fiction. This is why love is said to be impossible in marriage, for the "lady" is no more than a woman to her husband, and is so used—or abused, as an inferior in the patriarchal tradition. In "The Frankeleyn's Tale", Dorigen tries to bring Aurelius to his senses by pointing out that she is no "lady", but the body-servant of her husband, who can use her any time he likes:

> What deyntee sholde a man han in his lyf
> For to go love another mannes wyf,
> That hath hir body whan so that him lyketh? [3]

Another corollary to this "love" dictum is that, given the opportunity, a knight might rape a peasant woman: but since she can never be a "lady", he can never "love" her. The "lady" is a phenomenon of the castle: towns and burghs have to make do with mere "women".

The masculine attributes of the *dame* as her lord's lieutenant reveal themselves in the code. The term "midons" by which she is addressed by the *ami* actually means "milord", and is transferred from the husband to the wife. The feudal relation itself, between lord and man, although non-sexual, was often of a deeply passionate nature—homosexual in all but deed. Love, if it could not exist between man and woman in the marital relation, could and did exist between men in the feudal one. Love is one thing, sexual activity another. The

[3] Chaucer, "The Frankeleyns Tale," Group F, ll. 1003-5.

code of courtly love at least tried to bring love and sex both into the one heterosexual relationship. It is interesting to note this, not only because of the nature of feudal marriage, an impersonal land-contract, but also in the light of the teachings of the Church. Celibacy was enjoined on the priesthood, condemning it to an unnatural life. Sexuality was held to be of its nature sinful, and only redeemed, not by love, but by the purpose of procreation. Monks and nuns also were committed to celibacy. Love, as distinct from sex, was admitted only in the disembodied form of Pauline *caritas*. Virginity was idealised and marriage relegated to the lower "worldly" orders of souls. The Church itself was appalled when the Albigenses took this to its logical conclusion and condemned even procreation. Is it surprising that so perverse a creed as *amour courtois* should have grown up as a third aberration to the other perversions of feudal marriage and clerical asceticism? All three were unsound and unhealthy abuses of sexuality.

Amour courtois was, indeed, something of a heresy, a rival cult to the religious teaching of the Church. Erotic love, sinful in the orthodox teaching, is the supreme virtue in the other—is deified as Eros, Amor, in fact. The ambiguous Cupid-Venus relationship is deified in the code of *amour courtois*. The god Amor has his retinue of angels, his Devil with a retinue of fiends, and these make up the mythology to be found in the romances from *Le Roman de la rose* on: we meet some of them in Dunbar's "Goldyn Targe", and in one or two other poems of his, which will be discussed in their due place.

Amour courtois, then, was a cult which expressed certain aspects of castle life among the ruling-class landed gentry in the late Middle Ages. It seems to have begun in Provence and spread north to France and other northern states, and (at least in its literary manifestations) across the Channel to England and Scotland; and south to Italy and Spain. It had a marked influence on such Italian poets as Guido Cavalcanti, and Dante wove its influence into his *Commedia*. Some of his *canzoni* are almost pure examples of the cult, and his Beatrice owes much to the cult of the *dame*, however much she was identified with Thomist theology. But the cult itself was native to territory now part of modern France.

If *amour courtois* influenced much of the content of poetry and romance in the later Middle Ages, the device of allegory influenced much of its structure. As developed in the Middle Ages, allegory seems to have been essentially of Roman origin.[4] Its main feature is a dramatised type of thinking and feeling, with emotions and abstract qualities such as lust, anger, greed, and patience, friendship, reason, and so on, personified. This device of personification seems to have developed from the decay of Roman religion into mythology—the gods, no longer really believed in as such, becoming mere personages of the mythopoeic imagination, and not the dominant powers they had been to Homer, or even to Virgil. In their poems the twin themes of war between gods aided by men, and of the long voyage or journey of a hero, still have the power of religious significance: yet they have an allegorical aura, too, and appear in later allegory proper. Bunyan's *Holy War* is a descendant of the *Iliad*, and his *Pilgrim's Progress* is an heir of the *Odyssey*. The same may be said of Milton's two epics, and even of Dante's *Commedia*. The difference may be that whereas the pagan originals were forces beyond the control of men, the figures of allegory are mental counters very much controlled by the human mind: on the one hand we have dynamic forces with absolute and arbitrary power over men, and on the other we have abstractions manipulated by the human intellect. Allegory is essentially a didactic and intellectual device by which an intellectual doctrine or system of ideas can be presented to the imagination with more emotional force, through imagery and dramatisation, than by abstract argument. Like the Hebrew form, parable, it is an essentially poetic way of putting across abstract ideas: but not in itself a form of poetic creation.

In the romantic poetry of the Middle Ages it is used to put across the doctrine of *amour courtois*, which is expressed through the machinery of an *amant* in search of a "rose" in a garden, the difficulties and dangers that confront him, and the "persons" who help or hinder his quest. The "rose" is not merely a vague female symbol, but specifically the favours of a married woman. The figure "Jalosie" specifically is the

---

[4] C. S. Lewis, *The Allegory of Love*, Oxford 1936, p. 48.

husband's right of possession, and a danger to the *amant*. The garden itself is the garden of mirth, of sensual pleasure, a sort of materialist Heaven or caricature almost of the Earthly Paradise. It is always summer there, and only the young can inhabit it, the old being kept outside its walls. The figure "Vekke" is the female go-between, the nurse or duenna or chaperon of the *dame*, and the *ami* too has his "Friend", the one only person in whom he may confide his case, and who is bound by the code to help him as go-between—as pandar, in fact. Other figures in this allegorical drama are: "Popeholy", or chastity; "Beautee", which is self-explanatory; "Suete-loking", which is the handsomeness of the boy lover; and "Franchyse", "Largesse", "Curtesye", "Felonie", "Villanie", etc.—all obvious enough. Time is kept outside the Garden, Idleness guards the Door, the Hedge of matrimony surrounds the Garden, and so on. The whole machinery is too much to be considered here, and the use that Dunbar specifically makes of it will be discussed in relation to specific poems. It is a huge and elaborate dream of eternal youth in pursuit of the unattainable, a materialist parody of the religious life, and at bottom is the longing of landless adolescent squires and suchlike to possess the power and castles of their overlords. It is a fantastic cult which reflects the fantastic actuality of feudal life, in this particular aspect. One cannot read far into it in this century without hearing the ribald laughter of Cervantes over the shoulder. Don Quixote with his Dulcinea are implicit, somehow, in the whole cult and its literature, so that Cervantes seems more of a discoverer than a creator.

Allegory in the Middle Ages of course was not confined to the poetry of courtly love; it was a basic mode of thought, developing slowly from late Latin via such works as the *Anticlaudianus* of Alanus de Insulis to its triumphant culmination in Dante's *Commedia*. Only an age which believed that all fundamental questions were already solved could have used it: it can only be used to convey belief, and never as an instrument of discovery. When men began to look at the real world around them, allegory began to die: it can only give answers, not ask questions. Allegory and dream were to the Middle Ages what scientific hypothesis and experiment are to ours, and the theological doctor of that time was what a nuclear physicist is to ours. The structure of intellectual belief gave a sense of spiritual or psychological security to the medievals at the expense of appalling ignorance of material reality. Theirs was an intra-psychic world, all essential relations being between aspects of the mind, and not between mind and external reality. There is nothing vague about allegory—everything is over-intellectualised and detailed—specific, clear, exact. It is the opposite of what we call "symbolism" in certain poets of the last hundred years or so: in them a lamp-post in the dark may "suggest" many things at many levels of reality, but in allegory (religious allegory in particular), if lamp-posts had existed, they would have a precise and exact intellectual meaning or set of meanings. Literally, it would mean a lamp-post; morally, it might mean virtue; allegorically, it would mean some specific use of light-plus-vision; and anagogically it would mean the Light of the World. It is necessary to insist on this fixity and exactness of allegory, for the modern mind is apt to think of allegory as vague and wambly, not the hard intellectual structure it really was. The trouble with the medieval mind was not that it was vague and wambly, but that it was not vague enough in the right way; it confused thought and knowledge, believing it knew when it merely thought. A knowledge of its own ignorance would have been salutary: but its thought as such was intellectually superb, however unreal; and thought which is not adequately related to facts, or ignores them, is dreamlike, a spontaneous function of the psyche.

The dream has a place in medieval literature second only to that of allegory: it is often used, in fact, to introduce an allegorical subject, either as a dream proper or a waking vision. It always, for the medieval poet, was a sign that something important was coming, and typically, when he says "I woke up" or the like, he means that he has fallen asleep, and *vice versa*. This is a matter of value: the material world is of no value, therefore to go to sleep to it is to awake into the world of dreams, which is valuable. When Dante says at the beginning of the *Commedia* that he "came to himself" beside a dingy wood, he means that he woke out of the sleep of material reality into the daylight of psychical reality. The poet of *Le Roman de la rose* begins by telling us of a dream he had, in which gradually the matter of the poem is revealed. Dunbar uses the dream in this way, and also in a much more realistic way, as in "This Nycht, befoir the Dawing Cleir".[5] The dream is more important than reality, from which it is freed—freed from mere sensation into abstraction, where the psyche can live its own life without interference from awkward actualities. The dream to the medieval was more real than reality, for his stand-point was psychical, not physical. The depreciation of physical reality and the exaltation of the psychical—"spiritual" —life was at the heart of medieval thought. It is not that they were confused, these two worlds—at least not habitually. That is the state of obvious lunacy. They were held distinct, but the psychical was preferred and accorded higher value. The poets, and Dunbar in particular, knew perfectly well that brick walls were brick walls and couldn't be walked through, and that men could not in fact fly, much less go on Dantesque wanderings among the stars in outer space: they were fundamentally sane. But in literature the imagination made the dream one of its most powerful tools.

This dichotomy between physical and psychical runs through the whole of medieval thought. With formidable logic, but in utter contempt of mere facts, men of intellectual genius dreamed up philosophical systems of incomparable complexity, even (if the term is not inappropriate) of great beauty. Perhaps the greatest of these men was Johannes Erigena, John the Scot, a ninth-century Irishman. John was deeply read in the Greeks, and was influenced by Platonic idealism—which itself tended to depreciate the material in favour of the conceptual. John saw reality as of four kinds: the uncreated creating—God; the created creating—the "ideas" or forms; the created uncreating—the created physical universe; and that which is neither created nor creates—God as consummation. On this basis he constructed a theory of nature, *De Divisione naturae*, with a sublime indifference to the scientific verificatory processes of, say, a Darwin, tidying up the whole world of created things into a vast system of interlocking parts, all having

[5] 4 ("How Dumbar was Desyrd to be ane Freir").

meaning, everything having a place, and everything in its place, which is too vast to go into here. He interpreted Scripture with a similar freedom, seeing Genesis as allegory rather than truth—a modernistic idea, for allegory was not for the medieval mind proper, opposed to truth. Bertrand Russell says of John that his thought, his speculations, were extraordinarily free and fresh.[6] Implicit in his work there was a pantheistic vision; and partly for that reason the Church condemned his work.

Scholasticism itself—which produced the climate of ideas in which Dunbar and his contemporaries had their being— seems to have been born out of the fumblings of the nominalists and realists. This was a much humbler approach to a world-theory than that of Johannes Erigena, and was concerned with the question whether universals were real substances or merely names—such as, for example, "humanity", "life", "virtue" —of abstractions. Is humanity a substance which individual people partake of, or is it merely a quality manifested by individuals? The nominalists held that universals were but names: the realists asserted that they were real substances. If one held the nominalist point of view, then the Trinity was not one but three; if the realist, it was not three but one. This led to an outcry against the nominalists by the Church, and logic itself was questioned. Anselm came to the defence and set himself to try to show that a reconciliation was possible, and his attempt succeeded well enough to mark the beginning of an effort to put theology on a rational basis.[7]

Schools of dialectic grew up out of the controversy, and the debate and dialectic form began to invade theology itself— and even poetry, later—or at least the teaching of it. Peter Abelard tried to find a middle way between the heretical nominalists and the teachings of the Church, finding that universals are neither things nor names, but concepts predicated of particulars. Setting out from the position of intellectual scepticism which he maintained with regard to matters of faith, Abelard evolved his own theories. Under the influence

[6] Bertrand Russell, *History of Western Philosophy*, London 1946, p. 423.
[7] I am indebted here to *The Legacy of the Middle Ages*, edd. Crump and Jacob, Oxford 1926: in particular to the article by C. R. S. Harris, pp. 227 ff.

of the fanatical mystic Bernard, the Church condemned them. Yet they provided scholasticism with its foundations. Philosophy began to transform theology, and at Chartres a school of thinkers (which had already tried to solve the problem of reconciling the code of courtly love with orthodoxy) attempted to harmonise the teaching of the Church and Plato's *Timaeus*. The theory which Plato had expounded in the *Timaeus* was essentially an organic cosmology; it saw the universe as a great organism pulsating with life through all its creatures—a pantheistic theory, in fact.

Early in the twelfth century, scholars began to make more and more use of Aristotle's logic: and, true to the synthesising impulse of the age, it, too, had to be reconciled with Plato and Church teaching. They held that the universal had a three-fold existence: that before Being—the Idea; that in Being—material form; and that after Being—abstract concept. But as the great works of Aristotle began to exert their full weight of influence, the problem became more and more that of reconciling his work with orthodoxy. This was attempted by Alexander of Hales, but by confusing philosophy with theology he marred his work. Albertus Magnus and his pupil Aquinas accepted the division of theology and philosophy as being on the one hand divine revelation and natural reason on the other. It was enough for them that while theological matters could not be "proved" by reason, neither could reason show them to be false. But in fact Aristotle and orthodoxy simply cannot be reconciled. Despite the fact that he possessed a prodigious gift for synthesis and system, Aquinas himself could not achieve the impossible; and the realisation that he had failed seems to have been one of the main factors which precipitated the collapse of scholasticism. I write as a layman in these matters, but it would seem that the physics of Aristotle make personal survival impossible, and this is of course totally irreconcilable with the teachings of the Church. Faced with this problem, Aquinas appeals to faith and contradicts Aristotle by asserting the immortality of the soul, as a separable essence. But if, as Aquinas himself asserts, form is universal and can only be individualised in matter, it follows that the survival of particular forms is absurd; therefore Aristotle and orthodoxy are irreconcilable. Similarly, it is impossible to reconcile the ideal man of piety and humility held up by the Church with the Aristotelian ideal of the magnanimous man—they are as irreconcilable as Alexander of Macedon and Yeshu of Nazareth. But to the medievals inclusiveness was more important than consistency, and the theory of the corruption of human reason as a consequence of the Fall made it possible to posit that the contradiction may only seem to be so because of the fallibility of human reason. Aquinas was criticised by later and contemporary thinkers—notably by Duns Scotus, who tried unsuccessfully to achieve a subtler synthesis by asserting the supremacy of will over the intellectualism of Aquinas. The influence of Averroes seems rather to have brought out the discrepancies between the two truths—so-called—of orthodoxy and Aristotle. The voluntarism of Scotus was developed by William of Occam and seems only to have stopped short of a scepticism which threatened to deny faith altogether—and which brought William into collision with the Church. The dream of a synthesis died away, being too obviously born of the wish, and was to become the laughing-stock of Renaissance humanists.

The method of medieval thought was deductive reasoning, and the syllogism its main figure. The instrument of inductive reasoning working upon the data of experimentation, which dominates our own age was as yet almost unknown. Thought by itself can only create fantasies: only when it combines with actualities either sensual or *a priori*, as in science or mathematics, can its constructions stand the test of reality. And when fantasies become objects of faith, it makes no difference how much subtlety, how much intellectual brilliance they possess; they run up against the arch-heretic—truth. For this reason scientific curiosity, rare in itself in the age of faith, was positively discouraged as heresy—Galileo is the most famous example. Truth, reality, are irreconcilable with even the most logical of dreams.

With all its defects, scholasticism was a rigorous intellectual discipline, which exerted a powerful influence on all educated men, and therefore on literature itself, both in terms of ideas, and, more important, in terms of logic, debate, rhetoric, and other formal aspects of discourse. Dunbar was an M.A., and universities concentrated on logic, grammar, and rhetoric (the Trivium), particularly logic, rather than on arithmetic, astronomy, music, and geometry (the Quadrivium)—a strongly dialectical bias. Yet Dunbar was not as "intellectual" a poet as Henrysoun, Douglas, or Lyndsay; both in terms of knowledge and of leading ideas, their learning flows easily through all their work: but, to judge by the scanty evidence of Dunbar's learning (as such) that his work provides, it was often erratic. But Dunbar had a powerful practical intellect, an artist's shaping intellect, which had been ground and sharpened in these disciplines: not only the disciplines, but the climate of ideas they worked in, had a formative influence on his technical power and the content of his poems. He is less "philosophic" than these other major poets, but among them he is the supreme artist, the Makar *pur sang*: and the practical intellect of the artist owed much of its edge to its work in the metaphysical workshop of the schoolmen.

Philosophy was not, however, the basic interest of the medieval mind. Theology had already answered most of the questions, and life was more a matter of pious observance of Church teaching than of thought; life was a cross to be borne rather than a "problem" to be solved—a matter of action and endurance, not of thinking. The basis of life was mystical, and the great mysteries were so because they were beyond the grasp of reason. What was impossible to reason was possible to faith, and this was more fundamental to the age than the attempts to rationalise theology. Abelard could not stand against Bernard, and faith ultimately triumphed over mere reason. It was an age of poetic imagination, and its most perfect expression, its greatest achievement in art, is the *Commedia* of Dante Alighieri—a supreme work of art, a synthesis of thought and belief which will not bear the touch of science. In Dunbar, there is more evidence of this orthodox piety—despite his equally evident irreverence in many poems— than of the thought of the schoolmen: but no man of his time could escape their influence.

These are the main influences in Dunbar's background, as far as his poetry is concerned. The great influence of Boethius's

De Consolatione philosophie, which coloured so much of medieval literature—Chaucer and Henrysoun, for instance—touched him but little, and that only indirectly in the "moral" poems. The fable epic of the fox, *Le Roman de Reynard,* which strongly influenced the more humorous Henrysoun, shows in Dunbar's "This Hindir Nicht in Dumfermeling",[8] but otherwise affected his work very little. The formal influence of the *fabliau,* however, is very strong in his work—notably in "The Tretis of the Tua Mariit Wemen and the Wedo".[9] The *fabliau* influence is there in poems remote enough from the form—as a vein of comic, irreverent, realistic, or earthy wit. These *fabliaux* are a contrast to the literature of romance, and are of peasant origin, and of the burghs and towns rather than of the castle. They seem to have derived from the Middle East, and may have been brought to western Europe by merchants or returning crusaders. This type of robust tale was the forebear of many of the *Canterbury Tales,* and of Boccaccio's *Decameron.* It also foreshadows the novel of middle-class life.

Dunbar's so-called "aureate" poems were influenced by the works of the French school of poets known as "Les Grands Rhétoriqueurs"[10]—not only in the direction of "aureation", but also of the use of heraldic symbolism, as in "The Thrissill and the Rois".[11] This tendency in Dunbar was also strengthened by his reading of Lydgate, particularly, and of Chaucer, but the fashion came to them from France, and Dunbar had direct contact with France not merely through his travels, but in the court. All Scotland at the time was part of the general European culture: and European culture was predominantly French. The Auld Alliance ensured that Scotland was in closer touch with France than England, which probably is part of the reason why Scots poets of the fifteenth century were so much better than their English contemporaries.

This French influence shows itself also in the metrical forms used by Dunbar, which were almost all French lyrical forms. The only poem ascribed to Dunbar for which a tune is extant

[8] 27 ("The Wowing of the King quhen He was in Dumfermeling").
[9] 47 (same title).
[10] Cp. Janet M. Smith, *The French Background of Middle Scots Literature,* 1934, p. 62, and throughout.
[11] 55 (same title).

is "Welcum of Scotland to be Quene".[12] It is quite likely that many others had tunes, already standard at court, to which they were composed, and musical researchers may yet be able to identify some of them. Dunbar was less helpful in this regard than Burns.

The sermon was as important in medieval life as it was after the Reformation, though less exclusively so, and the homiletic note is obvious in some of Dunbar's poems: notably in "In to thir Dirk and Drublie Dayis",[13] "I that in Heill wes and Gladnes",[14] and other pieces in similar vein.[15] Preaching was part of Dunbar's work as a cleric, and he probably did as much of it as he did making "sangis" and "ballatis" "undir the byrkis". This influence was not merely a didactic one of tone: it was a highly imaginative one and many of his striking images and forceful expressions stem from it rather than from original genius. "Off Februar the Fyiftene Nycht"[16] is almost entirely traditional in this sense.

Mention of that poem reminds one that many different strands of tradition and influence were woven into one poem on occasion, for in it is also pageantry, drama, or at least a strand drawn from the mysteries. The influence of law, so deftly used by Villon, is in "I Maister Andro Kennedy",[17] blended with the goliardic drinking-song, which is strongly there also in "This Lang Lentern Makis Me Lene".[18] The more philosophical-academic vein blends with the homiletic in "Dunbar at Oxinfurde".[19] Indeed, in some degree the warp and woof of medieval life not merely are present in all his work, as in that of other medieval poets; they are, in fact, its subject-matter. To track down the precise correspondences would be a life's work, and would fill volumes, or at least one concordance.[20] Dunbar's originality was a matter of treatment

---

[12] 89 ("To the Princess Margaret").   [13] 10 ("Meditatioun in Wyntir").
[14] 11 ("Lament for the Makaris").
[15] I am indebted in general here to G. R. Owst, *Preaching in Mediaeval England*, Oxford 1926, and *Literature and the Pulpit in Mediaeval England*, Oxford 1933.
[16] 57 ("The Dance of the Sevin Deadly Synnis").
[17] 40 ("The Testament of Mr. Andro Kennedy").
[18] 46 ("The Twa Cummeris").
[19] 53 (same title).
[20] Thus in a single poem, 83 ("The Tabill of Confessioun"), Dunbar sums up the whole essential Roman Catholic Doctrine of the age.

rather than of content—indeed he looks much more original
to us in this century than he did to his contemporaries, who
admired him more because, in Lyndsay's phrase, he "langage
had at large" than for his thought. Originality of thought,
indeed, would have probably seemed heretical: a charge
which Dunbar did not escape at least from Kennedy.[21] A
medieval poet made his poems out of the wisdom (and the
folly) of the ages, not out of his own ephemeral personal
experience.

Dunbar's greatest poem is "The Tretis of the Tua Mariit
Wemen and the Wedo"; and many strands of tradition are
woven into it. Later we shall fully discuss these; here, however,
we are concerned with the whole position of women in the
Middle Ages. Theory and practice are at variance here, for
while the woman was denied equality with the man in the one,
she quite often had real equality with him in the other. In
theory, woman was the *dame* in the code of *amour courtois*: the
Church tended to see her as temptation, as Eve, who caused
the Fall, and at the same time, as Mary the Virgin Mother of
God; while the reality of woman was somewhere between these
and the Wife of Bath. Her reality was the eternal one of wife
and mother, and general manager of the household. The
ruling-class "lady" managed not only a household, including
the whole castle, but the estates of her husband when he was
away at the all-important male business of "war". She fought
law-suits (Dunbar gives us some inkling of how successfully in
"Thir Ladyis Fair"),[22] doctored the sick, directed labour, and
often commanded the castle in the withstanding of a siege. If
her lord was captured, she had to raise his ransom, squeezing
the last drop from tenants and dependents—so-called. She
was able, in fact, to add much of the male role to her own.[23]
Her ability was such that one suspects that the legend of male
superiority is a defence against the fact that women are the
better-adapted sex in reality. The Wife of Bath found peace
at last, and accorded it to her last husband, when ". . . I hadde
geten unto me/By maistrie, al the soveraynetee . . ./ After

---

[21] E.g., 6 ("The Flyting of Dunbar and Kennedy"), l. 524.
[22] 48 ("Of the Ladyis Solistaris at Court").
[23] Article by Eileen Power, in *Legacy of the Middle Ages*, pp. 401 ff.

that day we hadden never debaat": in other words, when she wore the trousers. [24]

Among the "aristocracy" marriage was almost the only occupation for women, the only alternative being the nunnery. The brides of Christ were mainly drawn from the "aristocracy", together with their dowries—for "Christ" was as much in need of the wife's portion as a medieval landlord. Women of the lower classes could be absorbed into many kinds of work, although among the bourgeois *nouveaux riches* it became fashionable to put their unmarried daughters into convents too—keeping up with the Messires Joneses. The bourgeoise also had to be the able manageress of a large household, family, servants, perhaps help run the business, and be a thorough professional manageress. Only the working-class women were expected to do, and did, almost everything their men-folk did, with the possible exception of heavy ploughing. They and their husbands were the props that kept the medieval heavens in their place, the beasts of burden, the slave-class all the other classes battened on, hosts to the lordly parasites. These "immortal souls", made in the image of God, were treated like the domestic animals they shared their hovels with. But literature was little concerned with them.

The contrast between the patriarchal theory of woman's inferiority and the obvious fact of her immense competence and grasp of reality is at the heart of much of the realistic satire on woman: this is particularly true of Dunbar's. Medieval man might dream of his patient Griselda (a most sadistic and brutal tale), or of his inaccessible "ladye": but fortunately for him, it was the reality caricatured in the Wife of Bath that he had to live with.

[24] Chaucer, "Wife of Bath's Prologue," Group D, ll. 817-22.

D

III

The Scheld of Gold so Schene

THE question of women and their social position in a patriarchal society brings us at once into Dunbar's poems. Dunbar could not be called in any sense a "love" poet, but it is remarkable how many of his poems are concerned with women and sexual relationships, directly and indirectly. In "The Goldyn Targe"[1] woman is treated as the idealised *dame* of the courtly-love romances, and the poem is written for a ruling-class audience. In the "Tretis of the Tua Mariit Wemen and the Wedo"[2] woman is seen as the amoral vicious bitch of the *fabliau* tradition; and whatever audience is aimed at, the women are middle-class. Between these polar opposites are poems in which women are written of as more or less close to one pole or the other, but rarely—perhaps only once, in "Now of Wemen this I say for Me"[3]—as they really are, somewhere close to the centre between.

"The Goldyn Targe" is the first poem to be considered here, for a number of reasons. It is his supreme performance in the aureate style: it is a poem not merely *in* the romantic tradition of *amour courtois*, but about that tradition and its incompatibility with reason; it belongs to the older poetry of the feudal ruling-class, whereas the poems of the satiric and *fabliau* tradition lead on to Burns and beyond: and it is his most celebrated poem. This last brings me to my chief reason for considering it first. It is largely on this poem and "The Thrissill and the Rois"[4] that the conventional view of Dunbar as a sort of Scots poet-laureate of the court of James IV is founded, and I want to show that this is a false and misleading view, Dunbar being in fact one of the most devastating critics a court ever had, and that the bulk of his work is of a satiric, abusive, irreverent, and mocking nature. It was obviously not

[1] 56 (same title).
[2] 47 (same title).
[3] 45 ("In Prais of Wemen").
[4] 51 (same title).

his first written poem, being far too masterly for that, but it
may have been his first bid for influential attention. Certainly
in it he explores deliberately the poetry of *amour courtois*,
demonstrates his mastery of the *genre*, but at the same time
dismisses it as incompatible with reason, and as leading to
unreality and madness. The poem is almost a parody by a very
great parodist, and is certainly at least highly critical of the
genre it uses, and which it ends by rejecting in favour of realism.
This argues an early date for the poem, both in time and in
terms of development—not always coincident. It was published about 1508 in the Chepman and Myller prints, but was
almost certainly written long before that.

The structure of the poem falls into seven parts, the first
being a prologue of five stanzas (ll. 1-45) which set the scene
in aureate terms, but with naturalistic detail rather than the
conventional romantic properties. The description in ll. 28-36
of the light reflected on the river being refracted to the over-
hanging boughs is classical in feeling—almost Homeric or
Virgilian. This is landscape painting of a high order, despite
the rather overlarded effect of such aureate writing as "goldyn
candill matutyne" and "stern of day" for the sun. The poet
is walking on a May morning in a rose-garden, listening to the
birds and feeling the almost sexual glamour of May. All this
is typical of the tradition of *amour courtois*, but the sheer realism
of the description is at odds with that tired convention: even
the crystal tears of "Aurora", hanging on the boughs as
"Phoebus" and she part, take on a comparative concreteness
in the setting.

Having sketched in his scene, the poet uses the next seven
stanzas (ll. 46-108) to develop the action. He falls asleep as
he lies on "Flora's mantle", lulled by the magical harmony,
and dreams he sees a ship approaching. A hundred "ladies"
descend from it—dream-girls with long bright tresses and white
breasts above waists like willow-wands. Using the figure
"occupatio", he tells us that he is unable to describe them,
those white lilies with which the fields were brightly painted—
not even Homer, he says, nor Cicero (!), those famous aureate
bards, could do that. He sees among these beauties Dame
Nature, Venus, Aurora, Flora, Juno, Apollo (a goddess most

strange), Prosperina, Diana, Clio (whom he seems to confuse as a poetic muse with Erato, Melpomene, Thalia, and Calliope), Thetis, Pallas AND Minerva, Fortune and Lucina—the last surely another name for Diana.   Dunbar's knowledge of classical mythology is either very shaky or he is pulling our legs: compare this with Henrysoun's similar catalogue[5] in the *Testament of Cresseid*, which combines great descriptive writing with sound classical learning.   Among these figures are May's sisters, April and June.   All these are mere personifications, empty counters totally lacking the weight of the pagan originals. These "ladies" come into the garden where the poet lies hidden by leaves, and they are saluted by the singing of the birds.

The third part of the poem is two stanzas (ll. 109-26) which introduce another court in the train of the "ladies"—that of Cupid attended by Mars, Saturn, Mercury, Priapus, Phanus, Janus, Neptune, Bacchus, and Pluto. The fourth and main part is the next eleven stanzas (ll. 127-225) in which the poet, guarded only by the golden targe of reason, fights a losing "psycho-machia" against the attacking "ladies".   It opens with Venus discovering the hidden poet and sending her archers against him—typical of the poetry of *amour courtois*.   He is attacked by figures translated directly from the *Roman de la rose*: Beauty, Fair Behaving, Fine Portraiture, Pleasance, and others. Reason, personified as a goddess, comes to his defence with her shield of spotless gold, valiant as Mars himself.   He is then assailed by Tender Youth, Green Innocence, Shameful Abase-ment, Dread, and Humble Obedience: but these irresistible creatures are too timid for violence.   Sweet Womanhood has no such inhibitions and attacks him with a world of artillery. She hurls against him Nurture, Good Fame, Continence (an odd charmer for such company), Patience, Discretion, Stead-fastness, and another rather unlikely one for such a purpose, that ravishing lovely Soberness.   Reason, of course, springs valiantly to the defence and fends them off.

Now High Degree comes to the attack, a formidable "lady" who is aided by such powerful allies as Estate, Dignity, Honour and many others—but they fly their shafts at him in vain while

---

[5] *Testament of Cresseid*, ll. 145-343.

Reason wields the golden targe. Seeing this, Venus brings up her reserves and orders Dissimulation, Presence, Fair Saying, and Cherishing to the attack. Still the great warrior Reason holds the fort until Presence, ruthless as a commando, casts a powder into the eyes of Reason, who reels about like a drunk. The poet is then wounded nearly to death, and Beauty, who seems far lovelier now that Reason is blind, takes him prisoner. Hell seems to him like paradise now, and gracelessness is merciful. He is delivered over to Depression (Hevynesse), and things look bad for him indeed until, suddenly, a blast from the bugle of Eolus brings the cold wind of (Scottish?) reality to his aid.

The fifth part of the poem is two stanzas (ll. 226-43) describing how this cold wind lays waste the garden—as if the rose of Provence could not survive in Scotland—and the "ladies" all disappear into the ship. The ship itself crowds on all canvas and makes off, firing its guns as it does, and thus waking the poet from his dream. The sixth part is a beautiful stanza (ll. 244-52) in which the reality scene is re-established, with real birds singing in the sunshine of the real May morning, the concrete detailed harmonies of nature restored, the abstractions of dream swept away. The dream had become a nightmare and the poet happily wakes to sweet sanity and health. The seventh part is a coda, unnecessary and unconvincing, of three stanzas (ll. 253-79) in which he addresses his poet-teachers Chaucer, Gower, and Lydgate, with more humility than truth, more flattery than critical awareness, and bids his little book be always obedient, humble, submissive, etc., before the faces of men of learning.

Within this formal structure there are four changes of scene in the poem. First, reality: May morning, in a real garden, full of concrete actualities, but, like one of Van Gogh's paintings, deeply and powerfully charged with the spirit of fertility. Then, secondly, concrete reality dissolves in sleep; the world of waking life is transformed into the world of dream; and with the entry of the goddesses and their attendants, the spirit of fertility takes over. Thirdly, the dream-paradise turns into a nightmare—Hell, which menaces the poet; and suddenly the cold wind of reality changes the summer garden into a winter wilderness. Finally, like one recovering from an illness, a mental breakdown, the poet rediscovers the actual world and real May morning in the real garden. Dunbar is not indulging in any pretty-pretty dream allegory here—he is exploring a poetic mode, and his comment upon it is that the thing is fundamentally insane. For Dante, the "coming-to" himself beside the "*selva oscura*" meant taking leave of the actual world of concrete reality for the more important one of allegory: Dunbar reverses the process, his "coming-to" himself being an awakening from allegory—admittedly, only the weak and fantastic "allegory" of *amour courtois*—to concrete actuality. For him, reality is sensuous and concrete, not ideal and abstract. The battle in the poem is between reason and insanity. The golden shield is to Dunbar, faced by a descent into madness, what the golden bough was to Aeneas faced with a descent into Hell. The comparative "lightness" of the Dunbar poem and the weight of the Virgilian one should not blind us to this very real correspondence. Dunbar—disciplined in the rationalism of the schoolmen—knows precisely what he is doing. His targe of reason is no mere poetic figure: he has already decided against the poetry of *amour courtois* as being irrational to the point of madness: his poem says quite clearly that only a man who has lost his reason is in danger from such crazy fantasies—and he makes sure that he gets his reason back. Many a poet has wandered off into the mists of dream and never come back. Keats recorded the danger in his "La Belle Dame sans Merci"; and Holderlin is almost the type of the victim. But Dunbar identified himself with reason, perhaps a bit too cannily so, and condemns the poetry of abstraction and of romantic love in favour of a poetry of the concrete and actual.

The very title announced this allegiance to a rational poetry, and the strange conflict of the allegory of *amour courtois* with realistic descriptive detail running through the poem resolves itself in favour of the latter. In him the old allegorical type of poetry is yielding to the new concrete type, the poetry of the ruling-class giving way to the realism of the middle-class type. Romance is obsolete and dangerous, unhealthy, and Dunbar sets his face against it, even in the act of using it. In the very act of using the old convention, he strikes one among many blows in a battle between romance and realism, the final and triumphantly realist one being struck by Cervantes in Don Quixote. In this poem, in fact, we hear one of the earliest notes of the Renaissance in Scottish poetry.

This conflict between two styles and modes, the one a mere shuffling of obsolete coin, the other a vital mint-fresh currency, is best demonstrated by taking two stanzas out of their context and simply juxtaposing them. Compare, for instance, this:

> Thare saw I Nature and Venus, quene and quene, 73
> The fresch Aurora, and lady Flora schene,
>   Juno, Apollo, and Proserpina,
> Dyane the goddesse chaste of woddis grene,
> My lady Cleo that help of makaris bene,
>   Thetes, Pallas, and prudent Minerva,
>   Fair feynit Fortune, and lemand Lucina,
> Thir mychti quenis in crounis mycht be sene,
>   Wyth bemys blith, bricht as Lucifera.

with this:

> Doune throu the ryce a ryvir ran wyth stremys, 28
> So lustily agayn thai lykand lemys,
>   That all the lake as lamp did leme of licht,
> Quhilk schadowit all about wyth twynkling glemys;
> That bewis bathit war in secund bemys
>   Throu the reflex of Phebus visage bricht;
>   On every syde the hegies raise on hicht,
> The bank was grene, the bruke was full of bremys,
>   The stanneris clere as stern in frosty nycht.

The rhyming of "lemys" with "glemys" in ll. 29 and 31 stanza above may be a fault in terms of perfection, but it is a very slight one that goes unnoticed in the general excellence of the whole. The one stanza is a dull parade of properties, with no imaginative force, and the other is reality visualised in imagination, and cast into superb verse. Real imagination is imagining what really is: unreal imagination is fantasy. In this poem the two interplay, but Dunbar is never really happy with the fantasy element, and the end of the poem is, despite

the coda to his "reverend" masters, his farewell to the poetry
of romance and espousal of the muse of realism:

> And as I did awake of my sueving   244
> The joyfull birdis merily did syng
>   For myrth of Phebus tendir bemes schene;
> Suete war the vapouris, soft the morowing,
> Halesum the vale, depaynt with flouris ying;
>   The air attemperit, sobir and amene;
>   In quhite and rede was all the felde besene
> Throu Naturis nobil fresch anamalyng,
>   In mirthfull May, of every moneth Quene.

The aureate style is still there, and the convention of "mirthfull
May", but it is the real May, "of every moneth quene", not
the May of *Le Roman de la rose*: the air is no longer the cloying,
syroppy air of dream, but "attemperit, sobir and amene".

This is not to say that having written "The Goldyn Targe"
Dunbar was finished for ever with that style of poetry. There
is nothing so crude or revolutionary as a clean break: but of
the two great strands of abstract allegorical poetry and concrete
realistic, he has shown preference for, and greater ability in,
the latter. He was too much the man of his time to make a
revolutionary innovation—he knew how to let the greater
supra-personal hand of tradition guide his merely personal
one—but for him at least, by temperament and by choice,
the way was to be the way rather of realism than of romance,
and therefore, of the plain style that bites and connects rather
than the high rhetorical ornate style of "aureation". He has
been most celebrated as an "aureate" poet, but in fact, having
explored that passing craze, he did very little in it. The bulk
of his work is of very different style. The golden shield of
reason did save him, after all, from the temptations of the
allegory of love: and in turning from allegory to sensuous,
objective fact, he turns from the medieval toward the modern
world.

In aureate style, but of very different content, is the semi-
official poem "The Thrissill and the Rois". It, too, is written
in an elaborate stave, but not the five-stress nine-liner of the
"Targe": it is in the stanza used by James I of Scotland in
his *Kingis Quair*, and was a favourite stave of Chaucer's. This

is commonly known as rhyme-royal, and has been popularly supposed to derive this name from its use by James I. In fact, however, the name is merely a translation of the French "chant-royal", and it is from the French that both Chaucer and James derived it.[6] The poem is very much in the French mode of Les Grands Rhétoriqueurs—aureate, full of the "garden" properties and flavour, rhetorical, heraldic, and conventional.[7] The symbolism is heraldic rather than allegorical, and suggests the influence of the Burgundian court poet Chastellain as well as the Rhétoriqueurs.[8] This influence is really very slight (fortunately) in Scots poetry, but it was an influence in the direction of artificiality, Anglicisation, false gentility, and unhealthy "smoothness" and sweetness, and so weakened language and expression that it can only be regarded as a disease of Scots, the true nature of which sings vigorously in Barbour and Henrysoun, in the alliterative poems, the folk poetry, and in the best of Dunbar. But even in this contrived poem Dunbar's realism illumines the stiff brocade and breathes some life into the moribund courtly conventions. For instance, while

> Quhen Merche wes with variand windis past,   I
> And Appryll had, with hir silver schouris,
> Tane leif at nature with ane orient blast;

is courtly enough, yet one feels that the "orient blast" has more than a touch of Scottish nor'-easter in it, that "nature" here is more real than personified, and the phrase "Tane leif at" is good racy Scots, not merely literary.

There are many different French traditions woven into this poem, different conventions or styles of poetry, as C. S. Lewis has pointed out.[9] James and Margaret (the poem is in honour of their marriage in 1503), for instance, are presented as the *ami* and the *dame* of romance, in the tradition of *amour courtois*. The device of the "garden" is also used. The King and Queen are presented also as heraldic beasts or flowers—

---

[6] J. Schipper, *History of English Versification*, Oxford 1910, p. 328.

[7] Chaucer's *Parlement of Foules* and Lydgate's *Mutability of Human Affairs* are other examples of the *genre*.

[8] Janet M. Smith, *French Background of Middle Scots Literature*, p. 63.

[9] C. S. Lewis, *English Literature in the Sixteenth Century*, Oxford 1954, p. 91.

he as lion and eagle, for instance, and also as the thistle, and she as the rose. "Nature" as a goddess presides over the proceedings, as in the work of Alanus ab Insulis, and the style is aureate. Lewis goes on to say that this *pot-pourri* of conventions "enables the poem to remain recognisably occasional and yet at the same time to become almost 'pure' poetry".[10] It does no such thing; it remains recognisably very impure poetry indeed, being corrupted by the decadence of the court poetry of the time—regressive and morbid instead of progressive and vital. The thing is forced, contrived, unreal, unconvincing, spurious, and Dunbar would not have written it off his own bat. It is indicative of the values obtaining among the ruling-classes of his age that this sort of thing was demanded of him, that he may have been rewarded for this "service", whereas better work in the same vein was neglected or ignored: we have Dunbar's own word for his neglect at court.

It is instructive to consider what this poem is actually celebrating. Margaret Tudor was the daughter of Henry VII, and was a girl of thirteen at this time. James was already middle-aged, a habitual libertine, and as such would be lucky to be free of venereal disease. She was traded in marriage by her father for what political advantage he hoped to get out of James by the match. No true poet could "celebrate" such an occasion without his tongue in his cheek, and "pure" poetry does not come when the Muse withholds her blessing. It is a poetry—if "pure poetry" means anything at all other than pure nonsense—of musical delight in phonetic harmonies to the neglect of clear sense, content, and meaning. These things are accidental to the "lovely noise" of verbal music. This delight is the distinguishing mark of the poet: without it a man may be ever so great a writer of prose, or even of verse, but can be no poet. But no truly major poetry is musical and nothing else—"purity" in this sense is the mark of minor work. One finds it in Shakespeare's and other Elizabethan lyrics, but not in his major dialogues and speeches, where the "music" of the verse enhances the import of what is being said. Edgar Allan Poe had a gift of "pure" poetry, but Browning and Hardy almost totally lack it, not to mention

---

[10] C. S. Lewis, *English Literature in the Sixteenth Century*, Oxford 1954, p. 91.

Donne, Pope, and even Milton. The "purest" poetry in English
is the first stave of "Jabberwocky". Dunbar himself comes
near it in "Hale, Sterne Superne!":[11] but even here the music
is subdued to the effect he wants—that of a peal of joyful bells.
Dunbar is one of the most "impure" poets, one of the most
adulterated, social, critical, didactic, moral, propagandist even,
but always audience-conscious, committed, professional, deliberate, unspontaneous, as impure as reality itself—in fact, a
Makar and a Bard. Not for him waiting for the troubling of
the waters, the waiting for the Muse. He was more like to
take her by the hair of the head and rape her. Inspiration
gives herself only to those who are strong enough to take her
in battle, and not to passive dreamers. Dunbar is a very
different kind of poet from such comparatively "pure" ones
as Keats and Tennyson at their most mellifluous. Lewis is on
safer ground when he compares him, in the same place, to that
other impure, virile, massive-ranged, professional courtly poet,
John Dryden—a most valuable comparison. Both might well
have echoed Strafford's "Put not your trust in princes". The
real Dunbar shows in the later stanzas in which he sermonises
at the King, warning him to keep faith with his "rois" and
not go whoring after vile nettles, wild weeds, or any other
flower, as this:

> And, sen thow art a king, thow be discreit;   134
>   Herb without vertew thow hald nocht of sic pryce
> As herb of vertew and of odour sueit;
>   And lat no nettill vyle, and full of vyce,
>   Hir fallow to the gudly flour delyce;
>   Nor latt no wyld weid, full of churlichness
>   Compair hir till the lilleis nobilnes.

He knew his James: but this is one more example of the extraordinary freedom of speech and criticism allowed court bards
by Scottish kings. It is hard to imagine an English poet
addressing, say, Henry VIII in such terms without forcing his
soul to forgive the executioner.

The action of the poem, if it may be called that, is as
follows: One morning in May, Aurora wakens Dunbar, and

[11] 82 ("Ane Ballat of Our Lady").

bids him get up and write something in her honour, rousing
his weak poetic courage to sing of love. Dunbar replies that
tears would be more appropriate, the weather has been so
foul lately. He complains of the cold wind—a significant and
recurrent property of his poems—and its boisterousness. She
prevails, however, and he goes out into the garden after her
to find summer in full early bloom, all flowers and green leaves
and singing birds. Nature curbs the usual turbulence of the
Scottish wind and wave (Eolus and Neptunus in the poem)
and orders Juno to keep the heavens mild, then commands
that all fauna and flora appear before her. They all obey,
with the "Lyone" first among them, powerful and brave,
red of colour, standing (*i.e.*, rampant) on a field of gold lavishly
encircled by fleurs-de-lys. Nature makes him King of Beasts
and protector of woods and groves, and all the others fall
humbly at his feet. Then she crowns the "Egle" King of
Birds and bids him keep one law for eagles and wrens: and
calls in the flowers next. She examines the terrible "Thrissil",
with his barricades of spears, and perceiving him to be a warrior,
charges him with defence. She then admonishes him in the
stanza already quoted, to keep faith with the "Ros", which she
now crowns Queen of Flowers. All the birds sing her praises
with such a din that Dunbar wakens out of the sleep he has
been in and writes down the poem, it being the ninth of
May.

The thing is light-weight compared to "The Goldyn
Targe", even as an aureate poem. The threefold presentation
of James as Lyone, Egle, and Thrissil is apt to look like a case of
multiple personality to the post-heraldic mind, but it is his
offices which are symbolised, not the man. The Lyone
represents him in his role of Government: the Egle in his role
as law-giver, justice: and the Thrissil in his role of war leader,
responsible for the defence of the realm. Thus understood, the
heraldic symbolism has considerable poetic power, being itself
of an essentially poetic nature, having deep roots in the racial
psyche going back at least as far as totemism. This deepens
and intensifies the barbaric display evident in its element of
pageantry, its rich and glittering surface.

Underneath the surface glitter, the true and sterner notes

of Dunbar are struck here and there, not only in the stanza quoted above, but in various other injunctions of Nature. For instance, the injunction to the Egle to treat all birds equally before the law is a jibe at the nobles, and a note we hear again and again in the satires. Crowning him King of Birds, she

> . . . bawd him be als just to awppis and owlis   122
> As unto pacokkis, papingais, or crennis,
> And mak a law for wycht fowlis and for wrennis . . .

The peacocks, popinjays and cranes are dealt with unmercifully in "Schir, Ye have Mony Servitouris". The Lyone, too, is instructed to see to it that no large animal tramples on small: no wild ox is to oppress the meek plough-ox, but go peaceably in the yoke beside him. We know how peaceably the Scottish ruling-class went in the yoke with the peasantry—or with the King, for the matter of that.

The same note of conflict between convention and reality is heard in this poem as in the "Goldyn Targe". Dunbar's objection to being called from his bed in the opening stanzas sets this note at once. The Scottish weather is unwholesome and makes the country no place for flower-festivals; the birds have more cause to weep than to sing. This is the peculiarly Scottish note in poetry, the centre of the Scots tradition. It is sheer folly to try to transplant the frolics of the soft south to the harsh Scottish climate, which calls for a very different set of attitudes. A nation is what its geography and history makes it, and to try to behave as if your geographic and historic conditions were something else is folly. Take five million people out of the South of England and swop them for the five million Scots: in a few generations the transplanted English will show the typical characteristics of Scotsmen, and the Scots will show those of southern English. This is why it is of the utmost importance for each country to give priority to the cherishing and developing of its own culture. Dunbar knew more of the wintry drip at the nose than of sunshine on the vineyards, and the poetry of Provence is proper only *to* Provence. This is one reason why the craze for aureation never really took root in Scotland, and why our literature is so different from the English. The influence of this kind of writing did linger on as far as

Burns and his imitators in their more "flowery banks" and
"blithe nature arrays" vein, and it is this I suspect which
led T. S. Eliot to remark that Burns is in fact a decadence of
the great Scottish tradition.   But there is nothing decadent
about the central Burns—the Burns of the satires and epistles,
for example.   These are in the central Scots tradition, and as
vigorous and lively as similar work in Henrysoun, Dunbar,
and Lyndsay.   Mr Eliot did not remark that the aureate
tradition was never anything else but decadence.   Dunbar
does not tell us in this poem what the peasantry had to suffer
in pillage of their meagre produce to support the revels of
the marriage—though he does tell us of similar pillagings in
other poems.   But these, being solid gold, do not need to be
gilded.

There is only one other poem of Dunbar's which can be
properly associated with these, and that is "Sen that I am a
Presoneir".[12]   Less aureate than the other two, it is more
purely in the tradition of courtly love than either of them,
although once again he ends by rejecting courtly love—this
time in favour of married love.

The poet tells how he has been taken prisoner by the Lady,
and first bound and handed over to Strangeness, who takes
him to Comparison.   He is thrown into a dungeon, watched
over by Langour, and the jester Scorn often shakes his bauble
at him.   Good Hope whispers to him to write boldy to her,
and he and Lowliness will send the note by Fair Service.
His case is taken up by Pity and Thought, who besiege the
dungeon, aided by Lust and Diligence.   Strangeness is burned
in his porter's lodge, Scorn has his nose pierced with thorn,
Comparison is buried alive, and Langour leaps down from
the wall and breaks his neck.   The Lady, who is Seemliest, is
in danger, and her hand-maid is chased by Lust.   Good Reputation is drowned in a sack, and the Prisoner ransomed.
Slander and Envy hear of this and attack the prisoner, but
Matrimony, that noble king, chases them to the west coast
(among the Gaels?) and endorses the bond between the Prisoner
and his Lady.   The heir of Good Reputation comes of age

---

[12] 54 ("Bewty and the Presoneir").   This is a misleading title, for the lady
has many personified attributes, not only beauty.

and enters his inheritance at court, where Matrimony reigns. He is confined in all that belongs to his mother and stays at court in his own right.

The poem, despite its allegorical rigging, is light and misty —again it is as if Dunbar's heart was not really in it. Here and there the poem is so obscure that one feels it must be corrupt. For instance, in the third stanza, in which Strangeness is at once described as the porter, and then as handing over the Prisoner to the porter, at the same time addressing him as the Lover—which is strangeness indeed. Here it is:

> Thai had me bundin to the yet,   17
>   Quhair Strangenes had been portar ay,
> And in deliverit me thairat,
>   And in thir termis can thai say,
>   "Do wait, and lat him nocht away";
> Quho Strangenes unto the porteir,
>   "Ontill my lady, I dar lay,
> Ye be to pure a presoneir."

The poem is complete only in Bannatyne's manuscript, in which it is anonymous. Two verses of it appear in Reidpeth's, in which they are ascribed to "Dumbar". I personally doubt whether it is by Dunbar at all, but having no solid ground on which to reject the attribution in the Reidpeth, I accept it, with these reservations, as his. It lacks Dunbar's polish, his vitality even in dull stuff, his mastery of rhythm and technique, and, above all, his clarity and precision and subtlety of cadence.

The most remarkable thing about it is the place assigned King Matrimony. This is totally at odds with the tradition of *amour courtois*, which was declaredly adulterous and banished love from the marriage relationship as an impossibility. This was a real problem with which poets were occupied in the later Middle Ages. It is the central problem of Chaucer's "The Frankeleyns Tale", the theme of which is married love as *fait accompli* confronted by the tradition of courtly love. Arveragus and his wife Dorigen are in love with each other— this is given. The reason why it is possible is that Arveragus treats Dorigen with the love due to the Lady of romance—

that is, he swears

> That never in al his lyfe he, day ne night,
> Ne sholde up-on him take no maistrye
> Agayn hir wil, ne kythe hir jalousye,
> But hir obeye, and folwe hir wil in al
> As any lovere to his lady shal;
> Save that the name of soveraynetee
> That wolde he have for shame of his degree.[13]

The problem was that love could not exist in feudal marriage because of the man's "maistrye," his domination over his wife as a master over a slave. It was this that gave rise to *amour courtois* as an extra-marital affair. Chaucer in this poem resolves the problem by removing the cause—"maistrye". But Dorigen is beloved by Aurelius, who claims his rights by the canon of *amour courtois*, which states that marriage shall not be offered as an excuse by the *dame* to refuse her *ami*. This is precisely what Dorigen does, being in love with her husband and having no desire for extramarital relations. The working-out of the problem (Aurelius sees the light and spares her) is the main action of the tale, ending in the triumph of married love at the expense of both feudal marriage and *amour courtois*. How much weight is to be given to Chaucer's achievement here I cannot say. Was he reflecting enlightened opinion, or was he the first to suggest the solution? In any case the solution seems to have been generally accepted by Dunbar's time, and Spenser idealised it in the *Faerie Queen*, in the next century, or later in the same: the actual date of this poem is not known. Dunbar was as distant in time from the eleventh-century origins of *amour courtois* as we are from Dunbar, quite apart from geographical distances. No troubadour or poet of *amour courtois* could have written:

> Syne Matremony, that nobill king,   97
> Wes grevit, and gadderit ane grit ost,
> And all enermit, without lesing,
> Chest Sklander to the west se cost,
> Than wes he and his linege lost,
> And Matremony, withowttin weir,
> The band of freindschip hes indost,
> Betuix Bewty and the presoneir.

---

[13] Chaucer, "The Frankeleyns Tale", Group F, ll. 746-52.

One other poem has some slight claim to consideration here, being a debate between physical love of the *amour courtois* type and spiritual love of the religious, Agape, type—"The Merle and the Nychtingaill".[14] But it is really a religious poem and is best considered as such.

[14] 63 (same title).

IV

Now of Wemen this I say for Me

DUNBAR's poems about women, or involving the sexual relationship, move from the highly romanticised worship of the *dame* conventional in *amour courtois*, through a more realistic appraisal of women, to the gross satirisation of them in "Tretis of the Tua Mariit Wemen and the Wedo".[1] Between these poles is the whole world of his social poetry, by far the bulk of the whole, as distinct from poems in more religious or philosophic vein.

"Now of Wemen this I say for Me",[2] seems to have been written for an audience of women, and is a blatant piece of flattery. In the poems addressed to the Queen, and in "Schir, for Your Grace",[3] and the fact that he accompanied her on visit to Aberdeen, there is abundant evidence that Dunbar was something of a favourite of the Queen: this poem therefore may have been written for her and her ladies. It is in the five-stress couplet, seventeen of them, and praises women above all earthly creatures, to be respected and honoured by men as such, since men "Of Wemen Cumin all ar". A man brings great dishonour on himself by disparaging women:

> Wo wirth the fruct wald put the tre to nocht,   9
> And wo wirth him rycht so that sayis ocht
> Off womanheid that may be ony lak,
> Or sic grit schame upone him for to tak.

They bear us in pain, and fed by them we repair to bed in their breasts. He makes much of the suffering of childbirth— always a matter of something like awe for the man—and of suckling. No man may be half as dear to another as a woman

---

[1] 47 (same title).
[2] 45 ("In Prais of Wemen").
[3] 18 ("To the King: That He war Johne (Joan) Thomosounis (*sic*) Man").

is. She is our very nest of nurture, and the man who says anything against them is like a bird—an early example of this common saying—that fouls its own nest:

> In lak of thame quha can say ony thing,   22
> That fowll his nest he fylis, and for thy
> Exylit he suld be of all gud company . . .

No wise man should listen to such an unintelligent person. Christ had no father in human form, therefore the more we should honour women, who bore the King of Kings. The tone is forced, but there is a ground-bass of sincerity and genuine appreciation of women in the poem. But, if there was not some disparagement of women inherent in the male attitude as Dunbar knew it, would it be necessary to praise women at all? He protests too much, and we deduce that his real appraisal of women is not quite so high as all that. This is a pre-Burnsian toast of "the lassies, God bless them"—but it is only recently, and still not the general rule, that women have been allowed into Burnsian junketings at all, except as table-maids.

The piece is slight and of little worth in itself. It strikes a note common enough in Scottish poetry of later date, and is not original. Yet it is the earliest example of a separate poem in Scots on this subject.[4] The line "Wo wirth the fruct wald put the tre to nocht" is good and forceful, but the twist given to the nest-fouling proverb is a bit unsavoury, crude with a crudeness not uncommon in Dunbar, a tell-tale indelicacy under the sentimental veneer. Flattery is at best a form of exaggeration, and at worst a dishonourable attempt to corrupt its object; and this poem is flawed by its very purpose.

"Sweit Rois of Vertew and of Gentilnes"[5] is Dunbar's most perfect lyric, and one of the supreme lyrics in Scots and English. The three five-line stanzas move with exquisite grace and smoothness of rhythm, no word, no syllable superfluous or misplaced, no phrase awkwardly turned, no image or

---

[4] Dunbar of course was the first Scottish poet to show a preference for lyric over narrative form.

[5] 49 ("To a Ladye").

thought jarring the mood.   It is a simple complaint, in the
romantic style, of his lady's cruelty, and is so short that one
may quote it in full:

> Sweit rois of vertew and of gentilnes,   I
> Delytsum lyllie of everie lustynes,
>   Richest in bontie and in bewtie cleir,
>   And everie vertew that is «held most» deir,
> Except onlie that ye ar mercyles.
>
> In to your garthe this day I did persew,
> Thair saw I flowris that fresche wer of hew;
>   Baith quhyte and reid moist lusty wer to seyne,
>   And halsum herbis upone stalkis grene;
> Yit leif nor flour fynd could I nane of rew.
>
> I dout that Merche, with his cauld blastis keyne,
> Hes slane this gentill herbe that I of mene,
>   Quhois petewous deithe dois to my hart sic pane
>   That I wald mak to plant his rute agane,
> So confortand his levis unto me bene.

If there is an imperfection, it is in the awkward move from
final z to initial s in "Hes slane"; but I am not sure that this
is not almost appropriate here in the context.   The poem is
in the tradition of the poetry of courtly love, but transcends it.
One of the last distilled drops of May-dew from that tradition,
it is one of the earliest and purest love-lyrics in Scots or English.
The syllables rise out of and melt into each other without
jerking or tripping, the emotion of the poem (whatever may
have been life-emotion, if any, behind it) is single, convincing,
unforced—sweet and gentle.   This is pure singing;   and if some
musical researcher were one day to discover the tune to which
it most likely was composed, the world would be a richer place
for his life, if he did nothing else.   Without the tradition of *amour
courtois* it could never have been—the whole hundreds of years
of that cult are here exonerated if not justified in leading to
such a distillation—yet here, too, is struck the characteristic
note of Dunbar's Scottish realism.   "Merche with his cauld
blastis keyne" makes his lady harsh and unyielding.   There
may even be a subtle hidden meaning here: Dunbar was sib
to the Earls of March, the Corspatricks.   Is he saying that the

lady cannot yield to his own rougher nature? Or is there a reference to another lover, a kinsman perhaps, who comes between them as in *amour courtois*? These speculations are not wild: but it is unlikely that the poem springs from so personal a source. It is more likely that it was written deliberately and professionally—or re-written from an original—to a favourite tune. Dunbar here is the opposite of boisterous or cold. The poem reveals through its syllabic harmonies, its dignified pace, its varied speech-song rhythms, the mellifluous sweetness of its utterance and feeling, a deep and true tenderness. It is quite the tenderest of Dunbar's poems, and its naturalness indicates that this is deep in his nature. Under the fretted surface of the abused court bard was a hypersensitive and gentle nature which, precisely because it was tender and vulnerable, could be soured and hurt to madness and violence by injustice and abuse. It is the finest and gentlest natures who are most affected by outrage, and whose response is the most outrageous. It is tempting to see in this poem evidence of a real love: but while Dunbar was the most personal of Renaissance poets in Scotland, he was also the most formal, traditional, and stylised. He is writing in a convention, and the freshness of his work is not to be confused with originality in the sense of invention. Even this poem, as with most of Dunbar's, is more of an artefact, a thing made, than necessary utterance. The tenderness of the poem is not to be confused with a personal one: we are entitled merely to deduce that only a fine sensibility could have produced it.

In contrast to this poem is the humorous poem in the tradition of *amour courtois*—"My Hartis Tresure".[6] The seven seven-line stanzas mock the ravings of the *ami* and guy his symptoms. He addresses the *dame* as his heart's treasure and convinced enemy, the ender of his life, the cruel breaker of his heart, and he cries her mercy a thousand times. What has he done that she should murder him? Such deadly swoons have a hundred times passed over his heart that his spirit runs in sheer terror. Death rages furiously in his breast, and without her mercy he will die—where, alas, is her womanly pity? He implores her to look on his hideous pallor, his deadly passion,

[6] 50 ("Quhone He List to Feyne").

his moaning and supernatural mourning with sorrowful tears. How could any gentle heart bear "to se this sycht on ony creature"?

> Quhyte dow, quhair is your sobir humilnes?   36
>   Swete gentill turtour, quhair is your pete went?
> Quhair is your rewthe? the frute of nobilnes,
>   Off womanheid the tresour and the rent;
>   Mercie is never put out of meik intent,
> Nor out of gentill hart is fundin petie,
> Sen mercyles may no weycht nobill be.

Even when his tongue fails to speak, being worn out, he will still importune her for mercy in his mind; and when death eventually overtakes him, he will wish her well.

The note here is openly satirical, the golden shield of reason matched by the cutlass of wit, the jibe of mockery. Yet, just as there is an undertone of realism, of counterpoise to the exaggerated romantic attitude of the more serious poems in the tradition of *amour courtois*, so here there is a curious undertone of seriousness under the mockery—as if he were laughing or mocking at feelings of which he disapproved but still actually felt. One cannot pinpoint this—it is something which comes over from the whole poem, but is difficult to locate. It may be that, in order to make his comedy the more effective, he underplays: or it may be something subjective in me projected on to the poem. He may jest at scars, but he has felt a wound—only he who *has* felt a wound can jest at scars. The young Queen must have had her attractions, and Dunbar would be sensible of them. We have his own word[7] for it that a Mistress Musgrave among the Queen's attendants had roused his attentions; and he obviously enjoyed dancing. That he rejected *amour courtois* is obvious: that he still was under its influence is equally obvious: might it be that in rejecting courtly love, he found himself without any alternative discipline of love by which to educate and express his sensibility?

In "Quha will Behald of Luve the Chance"[8] he creates a mood of disillusionment and bitter disappointment in love.

---

[7] 32 ("Of a Dance in the Quenis Chalmer"), ll. 25 ff.
[8] 51 ("Quhone He List to Feyne").

Love has a sweet, dissembling face, is inconstant and holds no
continuous service:

> Quha will behald of luve the chance,   1
> With sueit disayving countenance,
> In quhais fair dissimulance
>   May non assure;
> Quhilk is begun with inconstance,
> And endis nocht but variance,
> Scho haldis with continuance
>   No serviture.

Discretion and thought are both outwith her behaviour, for
which reason its short pleasure cannot last. She is so fond of
new acquaintance that she forgets old ones: therefore he gives
up bothering about love. To live in such an intemperate way
is ignorant, since time misspent is of no use to anybody. It
is as foolish to take love seriously as to bid a dead man dance
in his grave.

The "luve" spoken of here, of course, is *amour courtois*, and
again Dunbar's attitude is negative: but the mood is that of
the *ami* in his depressed state. Even in rejecting it he cannot
do without it; he has no other way of saying. The tone of
the poem is personal; one feels he is talking out of experience;
yet the mode of expression is conventional and formal. This
blending of the personal and the conventional is typical of
Dunbar. He invents nothing new in form, but he makes the
familiar forms reverberate with a new voice, the tired conventions glow with real feeling. One cannot miss the force of
the last bitter comment:

> In luve to keip allegance,   21
> It was as nys an ordinance
> As quha wald bid ane deid man dance
>   In sepulture.

Women are fickle by nature and not to be taken seriously,
being incapable of fidelity. Here, as so often in Dunbar, some
personal emotion seems to break through the decorum, the
conventionality of the form. For a moment the polite, urbane
mask slips and reveals the face of real pain underneath the
assumed one. Yet it lacks the note of deep suffering and passion

which distinguishes Alexander Scott's best love-songs. Indeed, mention of Scott makes one realise that, whereas Scott writes vivid, partisan reports from the heart of the battle, Dunbar really is only an onlooker at the war of the sexes. It is an impoverishment of Dunbar's nature that he never had the experience which allowed Scott to write these songs and Mark Alexander Boyd to write his magnificent "Sonet" on Cupid and Venus. A man of his passion and sensibility really needed a deep and lasting experience of woman to mature his feeling: it is the lack of this as much as any lack of an alternative discipline for sensibility which keeps him tied to the wooden tradition of *amour courtois*: and it is his clerical status which committed him to celibacy. Scott found his alternative in real experience of woman in marriage, and it is out of married love that he writes.

Since it was Dunbar's fate to be starved and deprived in respect of deep sexual love—that is of such lasting and whole relationship as marriage—it is odd to find him giving advice to young lovers. But "Be Ye ane Luvar" is mere convention. The very form of the poem is gimmicky, with its play on "be":

> Be ye ane luvar, think ye nocht ye suld   I
>   Be weill advysit in your governing?
> Be ye nocht sa, it will on yow be tauld;
>   Bewar thairwith for dreid of misdemyng.
> Be nocht a wreche, nor skerche in your spending,
>   Be layth alway to do amis or schame;
> Be rewlit rycht and keip this doctring,
>   Be secreit, trew, increasing of your name.

So it goes on through the three stanzas of the poem. We are in danger of seeing more originality in Dunbar, in many of the poems, than is really there because so much of the poetry of the period has been lost—probably much of his own, including plays. But here there is no danger—the form is ballade, though without the *envoi*, and the corsets of convention creak in every line. This homily is addressed to a young courtier—whether real or imaginary—instructing him in gallantry. The worst thing of all, he goes on, is to be a liar—and a gossip is just as bad. If you tell tales, you fall from grace, so never again be slave to such vices. Don't be talkative when you ought to be silent, and keep the heid—self-control. Don't be depressed by slander, nor too proud, be wise so that others may learn from you, and—is he laughing at himself?— don't preach about your lady.

It is unlikely that this mask of Dunbar as a Polonius had much effect on anybody—and he was too intelligent to imagine it would. It is therefore, for all his avuncular sermonising— and if he had been born three or four hundred years later, what a "meenister" he would have made!—only a piece of entertainment. It may have been read (or sung) to the court, among other pieces, for amusement. If this was the kind of thing that "sanct Francis" had in mind, when, in "This Nycht, befoir the Dawing Cleir",[9] he reproached Dunbar for having "Lang Done Venus Lawis teiche", then he must temporarily have mislaid his sense of perspective.

In contrast to this homily is the comic poem "In Secreit Place this Hyndir Nycht".[10] The poem is a typical piece of eavesdropping comedy, and is a burlesque of the garden situation. He is in a secret hiding-place eavesdropping on two lovers—but their talk is not quite according to the rules of Courtly Love. The man protests that his "huny" won't give him "comfort", and that she will break his heart, in the traditional style: but his handsome beard is stained with kail soup. He is both sophisticated and hare-brained, and he caresses her and kisses and clucks, "as with the glaikis he wer ouirgane", yet his appearance makes it clear that "he wald have fukkit". His loins are so full of love for her that (like a ghost!) he frowns and groans. His "huny" answers modestly:

> "Tehe!" quod scho, and gaif ane gawfe,   22
> "Be still my tuchan and my calfe,
>   My new spanit howffing fra the sowk,
>   And all the blythnes of my bowk;
>   My sweit swanking, saif yow allane
>   Na leyd I luiffit all this owk;
>   Fow leis me that graceles gane."

He replies with similar endearments, bidding his sweet sheeps-head broth be warm-hearted and not "ewill willie":

> Your heylis, quhyt as quhalis bane   33
> Garris ryis on loft my quhillelillie;
> Ye brek my hart, my bony ane.

Then she bids her unweaned giant, her soft sumph with mother's milk still in his "mychane", her "slawsy gawsy", etc., be of good comfort, for his thinking aloud would melt a heart of stone. He replies happily to his kid, his capercailzie, his curds and whey, assuring her that

> Quhone that our mouthis dois meit at ane
> My stang dois storkin with your towdie;
> Ye brek my hart, my bony ane.

This makes her even more ecstatic, and she assures her stuttering steer that she is agreeable to his wishes. He gives her a ruby-red apple:

> And thai twa to ane play began   59
> Quhilk men dois call the dery dan;
> Quhill that thair myrthis met bayth in ane,
> "Wo is me!" quod scho, "quhair will ye, man?
> Bot now I luif that graceles gane".

So at least one *ami* did not die unrequited by his *dame*. The fun is in the ridiculous names the "lovers" call each other, the clearly insincere verbal flattery with its ulterior motive not in the least hidden from either. Speech is the human specific, and even lust has to pay its tithe to this fact. Dunbar is simply burlesquing the extravagant prattle of lovers. The note is one of genuine good-humoured comedy—a rare one in Dunbar, whose laughter is apt to have the bite of an arctic wind in it: but this is the hearty belly-laughter of a Rabelais or a Boccaccio. It is at the opposite end from the prurient sick pornography of our own times, in the decline of western capitalism. It takes the genteel middle-class culture, with its veiled hypocrisy which equates "morality" with "chastity", and finds the *Lysistrata* obscene rather than the war which the women in the

play find obscene, to produce filth. Dunbar here is as healthy
as Aristophanes, earthy and innocent, vigorous with the
vitality of the peasantry. There is a quality of permanence
here, of timelessness, which is one of the qualities of art at its
best. The peasant experience of life is timeless and permanent
—of all humans the peasantry live closest to basic human
reality—and its vitality, rooted in the cycle of the seasons, in
the basic realities of ploughing, sowing, and reaping, the eternal
song and dance of the cultivation of the soil, is a gift to art.
The poetry of *amour courtois*, on the other hand, is a mere
fashion, and has neither permanence nor timelessness. It
partakes of the necessary evanescence of any ruling-class
fashion: ultimately unreal and inferior.

This eternal comic vision of the peasantry enlivens also
"This Lang Lentern Makis me Lene".[11] This poem is an
irreverent joke about Lent: the kind of thing was common in
the Middle Ages precisely because it was an age of faith. It
takes a religious age to have that sense of security of faith
which can permit irreverence and self-mockery. The two
neighbour-women sit drinking wine together early on Ash
Wednesday. One of them, as she relishes the wine, complains
to the other that the long fast of Lent makes her skinny. She
sits on a couch beside the fire, huge and fat, but pretending
to be feeble, and asking her neighbour to agree that the long
fast of Lent makes her skinny, too:

> "My fair, sweit cummer," quod the tuder,   11
> "Ye tak that nigertnes of your muder;
>   All wyne to test scho wald disdane
> Bot mavasy, scho bad nane uder;
>   This lang Lentern makis me lene."

She inherited her scrawniness from her mother, who disdained
all wine but Malmsey, and could abide nothing else. She
further advises her friend to resign such long fasting, and be
blyth both night and day, though she had to beg and borrow
for it, and let her husband bear the pain. This sentiment
finds willing acceptance. She goes out of her way to annoy

11 46 ("The Twa Cummeris").

her husband anyway, for he isn't worth a bean in bed—so fill
up the glass and drink my health, she says.   And so:

> Off wyne owt of ane choppyne stowp   26
> They drank twa quartis, sowp and sowp,
>   Off drowth sic exces did theme strene;
> Be than to mend thay had gud howp
>   That Lentrune suld nocht mak thame lene.

"Rycht airlie on Ask Weddinsday . . ."   Ash Wednesday is
the first day of Lent, and it has only just begun—"rycht
airlie"—yet here we have these two women complaining,
as they steep themselves in wine, that this long Lent makes
them thin.   The disparity between idea and reality, the
hypocrisy of paying lip-service to social *mores* while actually
indulging the eternal realities of the natural flesh, has always
been the stuff of comedy.   Dunbar is playing an old tune which
is for ever new: but—subject always to the qualification of the
Lost Literature—the instrument is new in Scottish verse.   It
is not merely that the women seek to deceive others, but that
they seek to deceive themselves and each other, which amuses.
For the human soul men and saints make impossible rules
which women and sinners break in the interests of the human
body—but the strength of public opinion or the power of the
priest, or other social sanction, make it necessary to disguise
this under a mask of pious observance, and even to deceive
themselves in order the more effectively to deceive others.
Reality for women is predominantly biological—copulation,
gestation, birth, nursing, tending of physical needs.   The male-
dominated patriarchal social systems have used this fact to
keep women even more tied to the biological than nature
enforces, and thus subject to the male.   The Judaeo-Christian
religious tradition is heavily patriarchal, and its rules and regu-
lations evolved chiefly for the benefit of the male.   Woman,
therefore, is apt to see them from another angle than man, as
male impositions against which she inwardly rebels, but to
which she must pay lip-service because of her subjection.
Language, like other social forms, is also male-dominated, and
has less relevance to and value for women: but to this, too,
lip-service must be paid.   All this is going on in the mere

thirty lines of the poem. The women accept a totally double
standard—to them all talk is double talk. So long as they are
pious in speech, they have rendered all necessary and appropriate tribute from women to male customs: their bodies can go
on, as usual, following the course of nature, not that of men.
And if this is not enough, let the husbands do the fasting for
their wives, since it's their nonsense anyway: if they like self-
torture and unnatural behaviour, let them get on with it, while
the women behave like sensible daughters of the great goddess
disowned by men, Nature. The underlying rebellion against
the male world slips out quite naturally in "All is to tene him
that I do". The poem is a minor comic masterpiece, a great
subject treated lightly and easily, with good humour, and with
great depths under the smiling surface. The comedy of
husband and wife is a *genre* that was very popular among the
producing-classes in the Middle Ages—and in all ages—and
perhaps among other classes, too, for it smacks of the eternal
and the universal. The poetry of "This Lang Lentern Makis
me Lene" lives for us today and will always live, when the
whole tradition of Courtly Love is hopelessly dated.

A somewhat similar poem is "Kynd Kittock".[12] There is
no authority for attributing this poem to Dunbar, as the
manuscript leaves it anonymous. Is it the sense of property
that accounts for the desire to father the "illegitimate"
children of "Anonymous" with some respectable adopted
father? In any case, not only is this poem not claimed for
Dunbar, it is unlikely that Dunbar wrote it. The poem is
good folk-poetry in the form and manner of the "Gyre Car-
ling", a much rougher and coarser-grained art than Dunbar's
polished technique. I have no authority to consider it here,
for all its worth.

A most unusual poem—unique, in fact, and in my view
uniquely bad—is "Lang heff I Maed of Ladys Quhytt".[13]
He tells us that he has long written poems about white women,
but now he will write about a black one who has recently
been landed from a ship. He wishes to describe perfectly "My
ladye with the mekle lippis". She is spout-jawed like an ape,

---

[12] 85 ("The Ballad of Kynd Kittock").
[13] 37 ("Of ane Blak-Moir").

gapes like a toad/beggar/vagrant (gloss uncertain), her cat-like nose perks up, and she shines like soap. When she dresses in fine clothes, she glints like a tar-barrel. The sun endured an eclipse when she was born, the night willingly fighting her cause. Whoever for her sake proves mightiest in the field with shield and spear shall kiss and copulate with her, embrace her, and henceforth command her love:

> And quhai in felde receaves schaem,   21
> And tynis thair his knychtlie naem,
>   Sall cum behind and kis hir hippis,
> And nevir to uther confort claem:
>   My ladye with the mekle lippis.

This poem is the first we have yet considered in which we get a glimpse of the actual court of James IV, and is clearly about a real event. The barbarity of that court is already apparent, not only in the fact of the cruel enslaving of a negress as an object of amusement, but in the fact that Dunbar could write such a poem about her for a court audience. It is brutally inhuman and insensitive, the humour unworthy of civilised persons, and the skill of the poet merely bringing out the cruelty underlying the poem.[14] One cannot plead "the age" as an excuse—the age is some fifteen centuries after the coming of the light, the gospel of the sanctity of personality. It needs little imagination to guess the inner feelings of this wretched creature torn out of her natural and proper environment where she might have fulfilled her life with some humanity and dignity, subjected to this kind of treatment, and meeting God knows what kind of end. But merely as humour, as literature of the humorous *genre*, the poem is unsatisfactory: real humour is laughter at one's self, not at others—and Dunbar is not remarkable for it.

Moving further away from the romantic view of women, or even a realistic appreciation of them, and in direct contrast to the poem in praise of women, is "The Beistly Lust, the Furious Appatite".[15] It appears in Bannatyne's and Reidpeth's

---

[14] Dunbar's conscious purpose of course is to burlesque the romance tradition tournament: but his bad taste is still scunnersome.

[15] "Ballate against Evil Women", in *The Poems of William Dunbar*, ed. J. Small, S.T.S. (1889), II. 266-8, III. 355-6.

Manuscripts, but only the latter ascribes it to Dunbar. There is therefore an element of doubt about its authorship. Mackenzie omits it from his edition, but Small includes it in his. I see no reason to ignore the authority of the Reidpeth, and none why it should not be regarded, technically, as by Dunbar. It seems to me a most likely poem for him to have written. It is not an attack on women in the round, but only— the point is important—on women of whom their own sex disapprove. There is no reason why it should not have been addressed to the Queen and her ladies. The only reservation I have is that the first stanza seems to lack a predicate—it is one sentence. It makes sense only as an exclamation: but this may be due to corruption.

He rails against the beastly lust, the insane appetite, loss of reputation, and vile joys of those women who care nothing for the blame of God or man, so disordered are they by their fearless desires, Cupid their only God. So a randy bitch will take the foulest cur in her lust, the mare some misshapen nag. The most beautiful woman devised by nature you may see, in contempt of becoming suitors, stoop to take a deformed creature. It is their fate—so who can blame them? Wise writers have warned us against wicked women and the harm they do. If it were possible to combine in any one body the wit of Solomon, the learning of Aristotle, the stamina of Samson, and Hector's virility, yet (some) women would render these virtues powerless. If you want to learn about inconstancy, follow them and learn from their envy and spite. Men should shun treacherous whores. He ends with a prayer to the Saviour to save him from his own sensuality, for reason and spirituality persuade his conscience to repent.

The poem is a mixture of accusation, sermonising, confession, and repentance. The sermon is perhaps the strongest influence on it, but again, as so often with Dunbar, the conventional and the personal are confused, the personal bitterness breaking through the convention. He begins by preaching against some women, goes on to confuse them with women in general, and ends up with a personal confession. Is the reference to the taking of unworthy lovers born of personal jealousy? These factors make the poem unsatisfactory—but there is no reason why Dunbar should not have written an unsatisfactory poem. The themes, the tone, the betrayal of pain, are quite in keeping with Dunbar in his mood of disillusionment with love, and his conflict between his "sensualitie" and "spiritualitie." The underlying theme would seem to be that, having risked his affections with some woman or other, he was rejected in favour of someone else, turns from women in disgust, and seeks refuge in his religion as a protection from sex. This is expressed in the disguise of a moral lecture to women. I am not sure that the very unsatisfactoriness, the conflict and confusion of aims in the poem, do not argue Dunbar's authorship—who else has quite that combination of complexities? The very technical faults of the poem suggest a breathless tirade, passion breaking through mere form: and occasionally technique and passion come together in a powerful stanza:

> So quhone the biche is jolie and on rage,
>   Scho chesis not the grewhund in the hour,
> The foulest tyk quhill scho hir lust aswage;
>   Rycht so the meir forsaikis the cursour,
>   And takis a crukit aver and a dour,
>   Evin so women wairis their virginitie
>   On thame that maist ar holdin onworthie.

Why the word "virginitie"? In the sermon tradition would one not have expected rather "chastitie"? It runs more smoothly with the metric, moreover: does this hint at a personal reason for the use? The tension between traditional material and personal experience is typical of Dunbar, though it must be admitted that the technique is below his average level, let alone his best.

For reasons which will become evident, I leave "The Tretis of the Tua Mariit Wemen and the Wedo", the greatest of Dunbar's poems on women, to a later chapter: and the last to be considered here is "Thir Ladyis Fair".[16] This poem is more of a satire on men than on women, but the very nature of it makes it an appropriate one to lead over into consideration of the satirical poems. It is one of his best and wittiest pieces,

---

[16] 48 ("Of the Ladyis Solistaris at Court").

light yet devastating, and above all, well-controlled. These
fair ladies, he says, who frequent the law-court will do more
in three days to end a dispute than their husbands can do in
ten. With little trouble they can settle a matter once for all,
quietly, in the evenings, with their mild, demure manners. It
may involve a little kissing and trysting, but so what?—their
business is achieved. They are very understanding advocates,
true as steel, and nothing noticeably missing when they come
home. Lairds are very lucky to have such ladies to dare the
dangers of the bar for them. Therefore, he counsels, if you
have any plea or case to plead, send your ladies all gaily dressed.
They can defend up to the hilt a thing pressed forward—and if
they do give anything away, it won't be property.

> In quhyet place,   33
>   Thocht thay haif space
> Within les nor twa howris
>   Thay can, percaice,
>   Purches sum grace
> At the compositouris.
>   Thair compositioun,
>   With full remissioun,
> Thair fynaly is endit,
>   With expeditioun,
>   And full conditioun,
> And thairto seilis appendit.
>
>   Alhaill almoist,
>   Thay mak the coist
> With sobir recompens,
>   Richt littill loist,
>   Thay get indoist
> Alhaill thair evidens.
>   Sic ladyis wyis
>   Thay ar to pryis,
> To say the veretie,
>   Swa can devyis,
>   And none suppryis
> Thame nor thair honestie.

The play on the sexual innuendoes to be got out of legal
language is worthy of Villon himself, the great master of the

F

genre. The real target is the middle-class landed gentry, the small lairds, and their like: the men of property. The whole poem turns on the fact that these men care more about their property than the honour of their womenfolk, and their women are ready enough to fall in with this scale of values. The dancing quick-step of the metre suits Dunbar very well—he is essentially a lyric poet, whose art resembles that of a dancer, simple, sure, quick-footed, and he is always at his best in rhythms like these. Narrative was not his *forte*; and the larger stanzas, in which Henrysoun had been so triumphantly at ease, sometimes compelled him to force his Muse a bit. I believe James Kinsley was the first to make the critical point of the importance of dance in Dunbar's work.[17] Dunbar shows less mastery of *Largo* than of *tempo di ballo*; and his work in the roomier stanzas is mostly aureate work, laboured and artificial. But in the poem about the ladies soliciting at the law he is at his rapid, easy, deft, witty, subtle metrical best.

The "Tretis of the Tua Mariit Wemen and the Wedo" should, in terms of the subject, be treated here among these poems of women. But as that poem is of such greater dimensions, being indeed Dunbar's finest work, and including almost every "kind" of poetry he wrote, every technique he explored or mastered, it has seemed to me most fitting to postpone discussion of it until certain other poems have been discussed. In any case, this poem demands a chapter to itself.

[17] William Dunbar, *Selected Poems*, ed. James Kinsley, Clarendon Mediaeval and Tudor Series, Oxford 1958, introduction (summing-up).

V

Think Ye Nocht Schame?

THE complaint against the lady solicitors in court was
aimed more at their men than at the women themselves.
In "Sic Tydingis Hard I at the Sessioun"[1] this vein of
complaint opens out into a more general satire on the corruptions of the law. The opening of the poem is unusually
narrative-dramatic for Dunbar, more like the opening of a
novel or story, or even a ballad, than a satiric poem. We
almost see the man arrive home from the Session, tie up his
horse, answering a neighbour eager for news as he does so:

> Ane murlandis man of uplandis mak   I
> At hame thus to his nychtbour spak,
>   "Quhat tydingis gossep, peax or weir?"
> The tothir rownit in his eir,
>   "I tell yow this undir confessioun,
> Bot laitly lichtit of my meir
> I come of Edinburgh fra the Sessioun."

He has just got down from his mare, having been to the Court
of Session, and his neighbour goes on to ask what news he
heard there. Confidentially he replies that no man there
trusts another. A common criminal gets on better than many
law-abiding people—such is the news he heard at the Session.
There are confidence-tricksters, hypocrites telling their beads
as they plan exploitation, falsely humble folk, people who have
pawned their lands while awaiting a decision, bankrupts
relieved of worries, and people who have won their cases
through bribery. Some complain of partial judgments and
how enmity and favour drive away justice, some people sue,
and others defend, while some attend merely to learn legal
jargon. Some cases are adjourned, others are lost and won:
the winners rejoice in wine, losers are deprived, and some

---

[1] 43 ("Tydingis fra the Sessioun").

people live on credit. Some curse God and abandon Him.
Some are foxes in skins of lambs, others wear their humanity
on their tongues, while others cut throats and pick purses.
Some go in procession to the gallows; some bless the bench,
others curse themselves. Some come merely to indulge their
sexuality—the religious orders:

> Religious men of divers placis   43
> Cumis thair to wow and se fair facis
> Baith Carmelitis and Cordilleris
> Cumis thair to genner and get mair freiris,
> And ar unmyndfull of thair professioun;
> The yungar at the eldar leiris:
> Sic tydingis hard I at the Sessioun.

The youngest of these monks are so touchingly humble in their
coming-between that all merciful women grant their requests:

> Thair cumis yung monkis of he complexioun,   50
> Of devoit mynd, luve, and affectioun,
> And in the courts thair hait flesche dantis,
> Full faderlyk, with pechis and pantis;
> Thay ar so humill of intercessioun
> All mercyfull wemen thair eirandis grantis:
> Sic tydingis hard I at the Sessioun.

The poem is condensed—in fact, he tries to get too much
into its fifty-six lines. We would have liked to be told rather
more about these goings-on, but Dunbar is, as so often, merely
following the catalogue tradition and listing wrongs and complaints rather than analysing or elucidating them in detailed
instances. There is an element of world-weariness in the poem,
and in its type, as if this were all so commonplace, so consequent
on that great scapegoat, Original Sin, that one merely piles
up the evidence against the world instead of anatomising the
disease. Is it not strange that this cleric should save his heaviest
condemnation and satire for the comparatively minor offences
of the monks? Is it because it is mere convention, or because
he has greater knowledge of this, having himself been a wandering monk? Or the feeling that there is less excuse for the
religious? Or simply because it seems to him to be the graver

evidence of human depravity? If so, his values are question-
able: the sexual impulse is a natural one, and the ideal of
celibacy inhuman: but for a judge, for instance, to be accessible
to bribery is neither natural nor moral, and is evil by any
standard.

These last two stanzas in fact are an important modulation
of the mood of the poem from satire to something nearer
comedy. The opening set a mood of oppression, the two
neighbours gossiping in whispers lest they be overheard, so
that the paranoiac sense of the law as an awesome, omnipresent
evil is conveyed and sustained for five stanzas. But with the
lines "Baith Carmeleitis and Cordelleris Cumis their to genner
and get ma freiris" the mood suddenly lightens. We laugh
at the idea of friars coming to beget more friars, and the mood
of Kafkaesque oppression is broken. Did he intend this
particularly, or did it just happen? The key to the poem is
that the "Law" makes it impossible for one man to trust
another—suspicion and secrecy, as of a country under enemy
occupation, predominate and pervade life. But the introduction of the religious element at the end does something else:
it exposes the humbug of confusing the laws of men, mere
expedient rules of a transient ruling-class, with the moral law,
the Law of God, with reality itself, dismissing the claims of
both Church and State as so much humbug: both are corrupt,
deserving contempt, not respect, This is his real purpose in
introducing these stanzas, and the modulation to comedy is
unintentional—or at least, for Dunbar it was not strong enough
to cause the anti-climax we may feel in it.

Dunbar is first, last, and all the time a moralist, and a
Catholic moralist at that.[2] The horror and disgust he feels
at sight of this corruption is deep and strong, and for him the
joke is carried away on a flood of repulsion. We are more
distant from that reality which was so present to him, and the
wry joke looms larger for us. The destruction of the monasteries swept away the friars: but the law-courts are still with
us. Besides, no reader of history can view the destruction of
the monasteries without mixed feelings: they were the maternity
hospitals of some of the best features of such civilisation as we

---

[2] This is perhaps a bit exaggerated, but is substantially true.

have yet managed to achieve, and whatever evils they bred are minor compared with the evils which their loss helped to bring about. Therefore we regard the peccadilloes of the monks with more charity than Dunbar could do, whereas we dare not tolerate legal corruption. There is, too, a conventional aspect of the monk passage—they had been for centuries such Aunt Sallies of the poets and satirists that the sport has palled. The weakening influence of these last stanzas, though fine in themselves, is the more to be regretted because one of Dunbar's sleekitest hits is in the last three lines—the law, too, is a merciful woman to those who butter it up in the right way: the law is a whore.

Edinburgh is the scene of the satire in the above poem, and in case we think that only the law-court is corrupt in that town, we need only look at another poem Dunbar left us "Quhy will Ye, Merchantis of Renoun".[3] The town is run by the merchant-class, and a fine mess they make of it.

> Quhy will ye, merchantis of renoun,   I
> Lat Edinburch, your nobill toun,
> For laik of reformatioun
>   The commone proffeit tyine and fame?
>   Think ye nocht schame
> That ony uther regioun
>   Sall with dishonour hurt your name?

Note that ominous word "reformatioun", and the sly way in which he tries to engage bourgeois interest at the start by mention of "proffeit". The appeal to pride, "Think ye nocht schame", is less obvious, but he must have known his audience. Edinburgh, as the capital city, with its pretentions to superiority over "ony uther regioun", has its pride to keep up. Having baited his hook, he assumes the fish has bitten and he strikes home. Nobody can pass through the main gates or thoroughfare because of the stink of haddock and skate, the cries of old women, quarrels and offensive scoldings that go on before all manner of strangers. The kirk (of St Giles') is blocked from the light of day by the stinking style.[4] The staircases of houses make them dark as in no other country.

---

[3] 44 ("To the Merchantis of Edinburgh").
[4] "Scull" in MS., but "styll" almost certainly meant.

The high Cross ought to have gold and silk, but instead there is nothing but milk and curds, and the Tron has nothing but cockles and whelks, tripes, Jock-and-Jamie puddings, etc. The town minstrels have no tunes except (such threadbare stuff as) *Now the day dawis* and *Into June.* Better skilled men serve Saint Clown and never claim any other trades—are you not ashamed to keep such jokers in your pay? Tailors and shoemakers and other low trades defile the loveliest streets, and at the Stynkand Styll merchants swarm like bees in a hive. The town is a nest of beggars, big lazy fellows who won't stop shouting, and molest honest people with their piteous clamour. Dunbar, being no economist, does not see that "beggars" are the creation of an unjust economy: but he does see that they are a social symptom. The merchants' profit, he goes on, increases daily, but their godly works get less and less. Their lack of elementary charity makes it impossible for people to use the streets without being importuned by the cries of the malformed, the lame and the crippled and the blind, who, he implies, ought obviously to be looked after by their more fortunate brethren. It behoves the citizens of Edinburgh, since the royal court and Court of Session, the main governing bodies of the country, meet there, to be ready to correct all blameworthy faults. All foreigners and King's liegemen should be treated decently and not stung for every penny: the merchants should be discreet and honest so that no charge of extortion is brought against them. Individual profiteering so blinds the merchants that the benefit of the community as a whole, being left to look after itself in the cut-throat world of commerce, is neglected. He prays the Lord who died in Jerusalem to find the remedy and make them ashamed, so that they may recover reason and a good name. The last stanza, with its almost contemporary attack on immoral commercialism, has a lacuna in the last line:

> Singular proffeit so dois yow blind,   71
> The common proffeit gois behind;
> I pray that Lord remeid to fynd,
>   That deit into Jerusalem
>   And gar yow schame
> That sum tyme ressoun may yow bind
>   For to   yow guid name.

Something like "keip to" is missing: or perhaps, "purches to."

An Edinburgh student asked me, "Why should *I* have to read Dunbar at all? " Clearly he only did so because he had to, but I replied, "Because he has so much to say to us today— the evils he complained of are still with us either in kind or degree, or under another guise, and his scheme of values is in many ways superior to our own, so that we can learn from him to be better people: and finally, even if that were not so, he would be worth reading for his poetic quality". I should simply have said: "Go and read the 'Merchants of Edinburgh', then take a walk down the Grassmarket and a look at the morning paper: and if you don't know then why you should read Dunbar, don't—it would be pointless". The "beggars" are still with us, though not so many nor so importunate. Road-hogs howl from the columns of newspapers for the removal of statues and even the beautiful gardens of the New Town to make room for them and their murderous tanks, while slum property gets worse and worse and slum-clearance schemes move about as fast as a penny-farthing bicycle locked to a lamp-post. The Merchants of Edinburgh are still with us, and they still have the same mentality: "Singular proffeit so dois them blind. The Common proffeit gois behind". Dunbar at the dawn of the capitalist era, and we at its murky end, look out on much the same world. The skates and haddocks may be gone, but there are worse smells still with us. The town is no longer exploited merely by its own merchants, but by bands of international profiteers as well. The royal court is no longer with us, Holyrood is a coffin in which only the dead bones of Scotland may be seen, and the Parliament House, which once rang with such voices as Fletcher's of Saltoun, is inhabited now only by draughts and ghosts of the past. The Court of Session still sits—a much improved one since Dunbar's time—but it sits as the last guardian of Scottish independence. All over Scotland, instead of listening to Dunbar, the merchant class went from bad to worse, until the whole country was sold down the river to the Auld Enemy.

Why should we read Dunbar? Because we can still find

in him a sense of real values, already menaced by the filth of commercialism, which we today, so corrupted we are by the very things Dunbar warned us against, find much harder to come by than he and his contemporaries did. The evil of the merchant triumphed over the good of the poet, and the God Dunbar was taught to reverence and understand at St Andrews University became the Devil of the expanding capitalist society in which we still live. Dunbar helps us to understand the evil in which we live, and the good, the "common proffeit", which still calls to us to turn from our wickedness and live. "Schame" is the word Dunbar uses of the state of Edinburgh, and the whole age from Dunbar up to date is an age of shame, of Scotland's shame, and of mankind's. Between the feudal age, before Dunbar, and the socialist one now being born throughout the world is an age of shame, a human jungle of economic anarchy which has brought the race to the brink of extinction after centuries of unparalleled waste of life and culture and civilised values in appalling capitalist wars, a wasteland of profit and loss, spirit expended in a waste of shame, lust of profit in action.[5]

In this and other poems Dunbar is still working very much in the whole medieval tradition of complaint and satire: the flaying of vice was a common feature of a great mass of literature in Latin and the vernaculars—Chaucer and Langland in English, and Henrysoun in Scots were full of this denunciatory preaching—but in Dunbar there is a new urgency and stridency, a personal note, an intolerance and demand for change which seems to me to be the note of the Reformation. In Scotland it came to full literary flower in the satire of David Lyndsay, which, though it grew out of the medieval tradition from at least the twelfth century on, was essentially Reformation satire. There is a sense in which the Reformation itself—the genuine religious movement, not the middle-class revolution which used it and betrayed it—was implicit in much of the medieval religious satire.

Tradition itself is a dialectical process—it moves by a

---

[5] "Active evil is better than passive good", says Blake (*Proverbs of Hell*); and this paradox is borne out by the fact that capitalism also brought, for a time, social (and spiritual) benefits.

conservative principle on the one hand, and a revolutionary or
reform one on the other, and it is not always easy to see which
is truly which at a given point in time. The picture is complicated by the fact that within the conservative principle
there is also a revolutionary or reform one, and within the
revolutionary one is a conservative element. In this very poem,
for example, Dunbar is a reformer in his attack on the monastic
vices: but he is a conservative in his defence of Christian morality
menaced by the tide of immoral commercialism. This is a
perennial condition of human life, which, being relative more
than absolute, is constantly having to choose not between good
and evil so much as between good, better, and best, or more
often, between bad, worse, and worst. A revolution—or a
reformation—is not so much something new in itself as something old reasserting itself against corruption. The upheaval in
Europe which we call the Protestant Reformation was not so
much the supplanting of the old Catholic values by a new set
as the reassertion of those values against the corruption which
had brought the Church so low. Not only Protestantism but
Catholicism itself was saved by this upheaval.

Like most good poets, Dunbar does not so much invent
new tunes as play variations on old ones. But there is an
increase in intensity of satire from, say, Henrysoun, through
Dunbar, to Lyndsay. Tradition, like the seasons, is cyclical,
a process of birth, growth, maturing, decay, death, and rebirth: but unlike the seasons, as we know them, the cycle of
tradition is on an ascending spiral, as far as social development
is concerned. Each new revolution, or reformation, is a rebirth out of the decayed and dead: but it also takes us a little
nearer the goal of the good society: it brings the Kingdom of
God a little nearer existence on earth. This perception of
progress is one of the great and distinguishing insights of the
Judaeo-Christian tradition in which Dunbar was steeped:
though Dunbar shows little sign of it as such. For Dunbar the
problem is essentially a moral one, and morality is not a
relative thing to be decided relatively, in the concrete, each
case on its own merits, but an absolute already established by
the great doctors of the Catholic Church centred on Rome.
But I anticipate the religious poems.

The eleven septains of the poem are further evidence of
Dunbar's happiness in the short line and dancing rhythm.
The stanza itself foreshadows the type of verse which became
so popular in the eighteenth-century Scots revival as "Standard
Habbie."

If Edinburgh is in such a shameful state, how much worse
is Scotland as a whole: and in "Renunce thy God"[6] Dunbar
turns his moral eye on one general aspect—the vices of tradesmen: and in "Doverrit with Dreme"[7] the whole country
comes under review.

The first of these poems is in the dream convention. Dunbar
is startled in his sleep by a vision of the Devil tempting the
people with dreadful oaths, saying as he passes through the
market-place, "Renunce thy God and cum to me". The
people are swearing such blasphemous, lying oaths, that they
are in danger of damnation. Thus, a priest takes in vain the
name of the very God he has just received at the altar, and the
Devil tells him, "Thow art my clerk". A courtier swears out
of pride by the bloody and wide wounds of Christ and by His
hurts when torn upon the cross, and the Devil says, "Renunce
thy God and cum to me". A goldsmith says may the Devil
take him if his gold be not so pure that he loses all his profit
from his work, and the Devil says, "Thow art myne". The
common people curse and swear, in his dream, blaspheming
the majesty of God:

> Dremand me thocht that I did heir   21
> The commone people bane and sueir,
>   Blasfemiand Godis majestie;
> The Devil ay rownand in their eir,
> "Renunce your God, and cum to me."

The merchant swears many oaths that no man ever saw better
cloth, that no finer silk had come over the sea—"Be not loath
to swear", says the Devil, "I will have you to sell MY mer-
chandise". The tailor says he gives himself freely to the Fiend
if there be a better gown in the whole city:

> "Grant mercy, talyour", quod Mahoune,   34
>   "Renunce your God and cum to me."

---

[6] 42 ("The Devillis Inquest").   [7] 77 ("A General Satire").

So it goes on through all the trades—shoemakers, bakers,
butchers, taverners, maltmen, brewers, smiths, minstrels,
fishwives, and other crafts. Even the gamesters and thieves
and courtiers—all are damned for the same sin of blasphemous
swearing:

> To bane and sweir na staittis stud a   101
> Man or woman grit or sma,
>   Ryche and pur nor the clargie;
> The Devill said then, "Of common la
> All mensworne folk man cum to me."

They all reveal the same psychological machinery: they tell
others the opposite of what they know to be true, and knowing
the truth, try to bolster up the lie by sensational oaths to
impress their truthfulness on the customer. Thus they reveal
not only their contempt of moral truth but their religious
blasphemy. What Dunbar does not, and could not, bring
out, is the desperation which brings men, brought up in the
full consciousness of the moral code of the Church, to such
risking of their eternal souls. The natural man always puts
the life of the body before the life of the psyche, and an empty
belly will steel him to dare eternities of metaphysical torment
for bread for his children. This is life's ultimate sanction
against moral codes. Therefore, if we want people to be good,
if we want to save their eternal souls and bring them to God
and life more abundant, we had better see to it that their
bellies are full. Only saints can be hungry and good at the
same time, and saints by definition are not ordinary men:
and it is ordinary men that Christ claimed to have come to
save—not saints, but sinners. The "Devil" in the poem is
their own consciousness of the state of truth. These people
are not to be thought of as not believing in either God or Satan:
they believe passionately in both. But under pressure of what
we now call "economic necessity", they willingly sell their
souls to the Devil for advantage in trade. "Le père de famille
est capable de tout."

This poem is pure satire, unmixed with the note of complaint which runs through so much of Dunbar's satire—and
other medieval satire—and introduces an element of appeal

not to be found in satire proper, which merely flays vice.[8]
Not persons but the age here is satirised, and Dunbar himself
is, for once, not personally involved. An interesting feature of
the poem is that the Devil is an *agent provocateur*—an interesting
inversion of our own time when *agents provocateurs* are devils—a
sort of policeman or government official provoking his victim
into a breach of the law for which he is going to report him.
He is tempter, accuser, and jailer combined. The Devil, in
fact, is a moralist who knows the code better than any other
being except God, with whom he has such an intimate
relationship that they seem to be head and tail of the same
coin. The casuistry of the one is the casuistry of the other.

Dunbar here is at his priestliest, preaching a sermon on
the text "Swear not", and the work is entirely traditional.
The figure of the Devil in the poem is very convincingly
created—a grim sinister shadow moving unnoticed, but
noticing everything, through the market-place, which is a
symbol of ordinary life. He is learned, a man of higher
intelligence, omniscient as God Himself, amused by the weakness of mere ordinary mortals and how they play into his
hands—but always grim, fanatical, earnest. This is not the
jolly peasant "Deil" of Robert Burns, a friendly figure
infinitely more likable than Holy Willie, almost a drinking-
companion. This one is not merely interested in such minor
sins as wining and wenching—the main sins of Protestant
morality—but with the real mortal sins of the market-place,
economic evils, the sins of usury, profiteering, and exploitation
which are the normal commercial "way of life". This argues
a great decline of moral consciousness from Dunbar's time to
that of Burns. Protestantism concerned itself more with sins
of pleasure, conviviality, than with the greater social evils
condemned by Catholicism.[9] Therefore, while Dunbar's
Devil is a grim moral conscience haunting the market-place,
Burns's conducts a dance of witches in the place of kill-joy—
the kirk. Love, dance, song, *camaraderie*, were the immoralities

---

[8] I am indebted here in general to J. Peter, *Early English Satires and Complaints*,
Oxford 1956.

[9] Despite the fact that the Church was itself the greatest medieval land-owner
and business power.

of puritanism—all of them leading to a putting of the community before the individual. Capitalist individualism had to repress these things. On the other hand, usury and profit were not sins to it but virtues: individual self-seeking at the expense of the community—always the major sin in any religion—was now seen as a good, as the supreme virtue. Dunbar's Devil became the capitalist God, and Dunbar's God of *caritas*, love, community, became the Devil of the Protestant Burns—no wonder the Devil in Burns is a sympathetic figure. Dunbar had a stronger grasp of real values than Burns had, and this is a matter not merely of personal difference but of the quality of consciousness of their respective social backgrounds. Even Burns's concept of "freedom" is suspect: the "freedom" which the French Revolution aimed at was freedom of the market-place: and freedom of the market-place is freedom from God, freedom from moral values. To Dunbar it would have meant the freedom claimed by Satan.

As in "Quhy will ye, Merchantis of Renoun",[10] what we find here in fact is a moral analysis of capitalism and the perception of it as essentially anti-religious and immoral. Dunbar saw the evil before it had come to its present domination, and in this, too, he is a contemporary of ourselves, however different his vocabulary. We cannot read him without realising that whatever we have gained materially since his age is offset by a loss of consciousness of true religious values—which is to say, of community, the knowledge that morality is a matter of economic conduct in society, not merely of sexual conventionality. What Dunbar does here is an early analysis of sales talk.

In "Doverit with Dreme"[11] the attack broadens from trades (mostly) to the whole social scene. Again the technical device is that of the dream, and in half-sleep Dunbar muses on the state of the country which, once guided and provided for by many noble men, is now the scene of such hunger, cowardice, and distress as never before.

So much "pryd with prellattis", so few to preach and say prayers, such "hant of harlettis", both by night and by day, with men who should have God always before their eyes, but

[10] 44 ("To the Merchantis of Edinburgh").
[11] 77 ("A General Satire").

flaunt such "nyce array", and are such strangers to their abbeys, "within this land was nevir hard nor sene". The gimmick of "Sic" or "So mony" this and tother, "Within this land", etc., goes on through sixteen stanzas. The device is too rhetorical for close analysis: but priests, graduates, clerks, swaggering youths, lords who are born fools fitted more for ballgames than ending the misery of the poor, all are put into the black list.

> So mony maisteris, so mony guckit clerkis,   16
> So mony westaris to God and all his warkis,
> So fyry sparkis of dispyt fro the splene,
> Sic losin sarkis, so mony glengoir markis
>   Within this land was nevir hard nor sene.
>
> So mony lordis, so mony naturall fulis
> That better accordis to play thame at the trulis,
>   Nor seis the dulis that commonis dois sustene;
> New tane fra soulis sa mony anis and mulis
>   Within this land was nevir hard nor sene.

So much treason, so many unjust legal decisions, so little ex-hortation to promote common welfare that all the laws are despised, so many flaws in title-deeds pretended, so many walls in disrepair—the catalogue goes on. Thieves and pil-ferers are defended by lords who share their spoils, and the problem is faced by too few people. The nobles are always promising to do something about it, but spear and battle-axe are no good when they are not wielded by courageous purpose. The familiar complaint about "beggars" comes up again. There have never been so many boasters, brawlers, and brag-garts, all degenerate, nor so many retailers to exploit the poor, so many traitors and robbers. Too many judges and lords are being made: there are too many excuses to beat down the poor, too many highwaymen, and too few people caring for the common good. Judgments are reversed to win possessions and familiarity or charity from powerful families. Nothing that makes profit is thought to be sinful—how well we know it, five hundred years after Dunbar's birth, we who see cigarettes still advertised, and youth encouraged in the habit, although it has been proved to be a main cause of lung cancer. Even

Dunbar did not see, could not have seen, the enormities that
were to come of this same evil: he saw only the first shoots of
the weed among the grain, and not the full, choking horrible
growth.

> Sa mony merchandis, sa mony ar mensworne,   61
> Sa peur tennandis, sic cursing evin and morne,
>   Quhilk slayis the corne and fruct that growis grene;
> Sic skaith and scorne, so mony paitlattis worne,
>   Within this land was nevir hard nor sene.

Even tennis, which seems to have become a craze, is flailed
and the players condemned as worthless. Women's dress and
such also are attacked:

> Sic fartingaillis on flaggis als fatt as quhailis,   71
> Facit lyk fulis with hattis that littill availis,
>   And sic fowill tailis to sweip the calsay clene,
> The dust upskaillis; sic fillokis with fucksailis
>   Within this land was nevir hard nor sene.

> Sa mony ane Kittie, drest up with goldin chenye,
> Sa few witty, that weill can fabillis fenye,
>   With apill renye ay schawand hir goldin chene;
> Off Sathanis senyie sic ane unsall menye
>   Within this land was nevir hard nor sene.

Thus he ends the poem. A remarkable feature of it is the
half-line rhyme scheme, which raises the question of whether
it is written out in its true form, or whether it ought more
properly to be written thus:

> Sic knavis and crakkaris   56
>   To play at cartis and dyce,
> Sic halland shakkaris
>   Quhilk at Cowkelbyis gryce
>   Ar haldin of pryce
>   Quhen lymmaris dois convene,
>   Sic stoir of vyce
> Sa mony wittis unwyce
>   Within this land
> Was nevir hard nor sene.

The scheme is the same throughout the poem—the halves of
ll. 1 and 2 rhyme, and the halves of ll. 3 and 4 rhyme with the

end-rhymes of ll. 1 and 2 and with each other, and also with
the end-rhyme of l. 4, which rhymes with the ends of ll. 1 and
2. It is an extraordinarily intricate stanza, and I will have
more to say on the subject in the chapter dealing with Dunbar's
metric. But it is worth drawing attention to it here, because
whereas Dunbar usually gains in power and freedom the more
tightly he corsets his verse, again like a nimble professional
dancer, here the poem suffers from too tight a form, too strict
a discipline. It heightens the catalogue effect, which becomes
a bit boring, and reduces his freedom to develop a fuller
analytic case against the evils under consideration. The poem
is all nouns and adjectives, and mostly nouns, and the language,
therefore, is not sufficiently active, not sufficiently lubricated
with verbs, not sufficiently innervated with thought.

Some of these more intricate stanzas of Dunbar's may be
innovations of his own, and he certainly had a marked preference for them: he had learnt that, as far as verse goes, "freedom is the consciousness of necessity": but the vice attendant
upon this virtue is gimmickiness. There are two main aspects
of any poem—utterance and artifice. In a perfect poem they
are perfectly married: but in an imperfect one, either utterance or artifice predominates. In Dunbar, there is a tendency
for artifice to predominate over utterance: too strict a frame
inhibits utterance, dictates to thought, and leads to over-
simplification.

This poem can, I think, be charged with this fault. A less
cruelly restrictive form might have resulted in a more complex
and realistic statement. A satirist scores rather by showing
the reader the vices he castigates in action, than by merely
denouncing them as vices. Besides, no human beings are either
wholly good or wholly evil, but a varying degree or mixture
of both: to show us the vices in the round, in action, would
add humanity, and at once increase the satiric force by showing
the good with which it is mixed, and thus, by a process of
attraction and recoil, further isolate the vice condemned from
the sinner—who is to be forgiven. Dunbar—it is the fault of
all cataloguists—is far too flat here, and in many other poems.
In this, Chaucer is vastly his superior. Henrysoun, too,
excels here, and there is more rounded satire in the *Fabillis*

G

than in the bulk of Dunbar's work—Henrysoun being the only
one of the major Makars who is really Chaucerian in his
breadth of mind and largeness of soul. It is the great merit
of "The Tretis of the Tua Mariit Wemen and the Wedo"
that Dunbar does show us their vices in the round, with the
result that the grimness of the satire is relieved by a saving
element of comedy. But that must wait till a later chapter.
Length, of course, is relevant, but Dunbar's choice of form
also implies a choice of taste and capacity, and the lesser mind
chooses the lesser form.

The attack on the displacement of real values by commercialism which he saw going on around him is given even
more specific expression in the poem "Of Covetyce".[12] Values
are being turned upside down because of the greed of gain—
at court, generosity, honour, nobleness, courage, manhood,
laughter, and good-breeding are now considered to be vices.
All welfare, wealth and fun are changed to misery, and sport
is little valued. Gambling replaces healthier sports:

> Halking, hunting, and swift hors rynning　　　　　9
> Ar chengit all in wrangus wynnyng;
> Thair is no play bot cartis and dyce;
> And all for caus of covetyce.

Honourable households are all brought low, and lairds keep
company only with low flatterers who encourage them in evil
ways, for the sake of greed. The decadence affects burghs and
towns, and farmers who had large granges with cattle and
corn in plenty now have no beasts but cats and mice. Self-
respecting peasants, once well-clad, now go in rags, because
of the lust of gain. Lairds go in silk from top to toe which
"their" tenants have had to sell their own stores of meal for
the summer to obtain, themselves living on roots under the
bushes, because of avarice.

> Quha that dois deidis of petie　　　　　　　　　33
> And leivis in pece and cheretie,
> Is haldin a fule, and that full nyce;
> And all thruch caus of covetyce.

---

[12] 67 (same title).

The Christian virtues of good deeds, charity, and peaceful community life are now considered sheer folly, because they are incompatible with avarice. Economic individualism, grabbing all you have the power to grab at the expense of the community, is now the ideal:

> And quha can reive uther menis rowmis,   37
> And upon peur men gadderis sowmis,
> Is now ane active man and wyice;
> And all thruch caus of covetyce.

Dunbar's standpoint is inevitably the religious one, and he ends rather weakly by a conventional appeal to "Man" to please his Maker and be gay, setting not a cherry by the world, and work for the place of Paradise, where no avarice reigns. St Francis is said to have shamed a wolf out of its prey, but Dunbar was no St Francis, and he might as well have appealed to the fox to give up hen-stealing and become a vegetarian as ask the propertied classes to stop preying on the poor. He disarms himself by his last line, "For thairin ringis na covetyce". If avarice doesn't reign in Paradise, then Paradise is Hell for the worshippers of Mammon. Had he painted a picture of Heaven as a sort of glorified stock-exchange or bingo-hall for those who sacrifice their greed on earth, he might have turned a few tenderer souls from the pursuit of personal fortunes at the expense of the community.

Dunbar could not know that he was witnessing the beginning of a new era in history, in which the ruling classes worshipped Plutus six days a week, and paid lip-service to God only on the seventh. His standpoint is much the same as that of Dante some two centuries earlier. Dante saw the avaricous merely as sinners of incontinence, and punished them in the fourth circle of his Hell as being "squint-eyed in mind".[13] That avarice was to prove the most tremendous force in history, throwing up great powers of good as well as evil, and lead to undreamt-of material triumphs of man over his environment, with whole vast colleges of immensely learned men teaching it and its ways as a way of life, while philosophers of genius elevated it to a science of economics totally free of mere

[13] *Inferno*, Canto VII, ll. 40-1.

moral considerations, with gifted poets singing its praises as "freedom", neither Dante nor Dunbar—nor Chaucer, Henrysoun, nor Langland, for the matter of that—could have foreseen. They saw it merely as a "squint" of mind, an aberration which distorted men's sense of real value. Dunbar, it is true, in this poem, sees the process at a later stage than Dante: he speaks not of a mere squint which distorts the otherwise wholesome vision, but as promoted to the place of supreme virtue—the squint has become the whole vision, good has become evil, and evil has become the supreme good. They would have shuddered to see this heathen creed pose as Christianity and call itself the Christian way of life.

The most "modern" mind cannot expect that Dunbar should have been able to see the new monetary barbarism as the emergence of economic "laws" from under the old cloak of assumed human moral responsibility. He is concerned with values, being a poet, not a scientist, and what he sees in the changes going on in his time is not "progress" or "historical necessity", but the corruption and degeneration of human values. These values were some of them identified with the old ruling class, the landed gentry, and with feudalism (for want of a better word)—generosity, honour, nobleness, chivalry; but others are more lasting and are eternally the genuine Christian ones—charity, love, community feeling, reverence for life and personality, the belief in exalted spiritual values transcending material life.

Yet this standpoint of Dunbar's does limit the force of his work: the "age" dominates him too much, permeating his work and his mind to saturation-point. Dunbar's satire runs to breadth rather than height or depth, his vision is shallow compared with other great medieval poets, his greater predecessors such as Dante, Chaucer, Langland, and Henrysoun, and his poetically lesser successor David Lyndsay, whose satire surpasses Dunbar's. The poem is not satirical enough—it is more a complaint than a satire proper. He does not see the rise of the bourgeois to power as a dawn in which it is good to be alive: but neither does he see it as a dusk in which it were better to de dead; he does not, indeed, see it at all as such, but merely as a conventional moral evil, the answer to which is to be found in the Church's teaching of other-worldliness. A greater poet would have seen deeper, but Dunbar, major poet though he is, lacked that transcendent quality which only the few really great ones have. Even in his most powerful criticism of his age—and that means elsewhere than in this minor poem—he is still the prisoner of his age, of time itself. He did not see life *sub specie aeternitatis*, but only as an intelligent man of his day saw it. This is enough to make a major poet, but not a maximal one.

Mention of the court in this poem—the corruption of the former courtly virtues by the lust of avarice—brings us to the bulk of Dunbar's work. This is his satire and complaint about life at court, and his own in particular. Many of these poems are addressed directly to James IV; many others indirectly angled at him. Some others are addressed to the Queen. The law-courts, the town of Edinburgh, the merchant class, the trades people, the country at large, he knew only at remove. But the court was the special bit of Hell in which he was cornered, and it is the court which drew forth the bitterest of his attacks, which must now be considered.

VI

Schir, Lat it nevir in Toun be Tald

"**B**E Divers Wyis"[1] gives us a good introductory view of the court of "James the Ferd". By various ways and works, Dunbar tells us, men make their solicitations in court: some by service and diligence, some by continual residence; some by living on their means until fortune provides for them; others by singing or dancing or telling stories, some merely by sitting up at night till dawn. One trifles, another pretends, yet another tries flattery. One man, by the wall, looks as if nothing would please him. Some stand in corners and whisper secretly together, while others almost swoon with envy and avarice, and yet others conduct themselves as if they would go mad of feverish desire for the world's goods. Some leave all devotion at mass to labour busily for promotion, others have advocates in the private chambers. Dunbar himself lacks the guile to do other than rely humbly on the King's grace:

> My sempillnes amang the laiff   21
> Wait off na way, sa God me saiff,
> Bot with ane humill cheir and face
> Refferis me to the Kyngis grace:
> Me think his gracious countenance
> In ryches is my sufficance.

This coy meekness, in the light of the savagery of later or other poems on his own position at court, suggests that it is an early one. He is soon disillusioned of "the Kyngis grace" and of "his gracious countenance", and does not find these by any means "In ryches is my sufficance". What he lacks in guile he makes up in outspoken querulous demanding.

It is a slight piece, only twenty-six lines of it, but it is surely an example of the guile he disclaims having. Certainly it is

---

[1] 29 ("Aganis the Solistaris in Court"). Not to be confused with 48 ("Aganis the Ladyis Solistaris—at court").

a study in, and example of, hypocrisy. What he is in fact saying is that his method of hanging-on, relying, like Uriah Heep, on "bein' 'umble", is superior morally to the methods used by other hangers-on. For a hanger-on at court is precisely what he was—the most distinguished one in Scottish history. Yet even this is a simplification, for what he hung on for was the benefice that would make him independent of the court and let him keep as far from it as possible. The final couplet is a dishonest shy glance at James's purse.

His own purse he speaks of in more honest mood in "Sanct Salvatour! Send Silver Sorrow",[2] which is addressed to the King himself. He asks the Saviour to send money to the Devil because it worries him both night and day, chasing all charity from him and causing him to pawn all happiness, so tormented he is by a purse full of nothing but pain. It even prevents his writing poems:

> Quhen I wald blythlie ballatis brief, 6
> Langour thairto givis me no leif;
>   War nocht gud howp my hart uphie,
> My verry corpis for cair wald cleif;
>   My panefull purs so prikillis me.

When he addresses himself to sing or dance or attend pleasant pastimes, thinking of his poverty tears these things from his mind, his "panefull purs so prikillis" him. When wealthier men go to drink or eat, he must put on a pious disguise and say he will fast till noon—the real reason being that he can't afford to join them. His purse is made of a skin that no coin stamped with the cross can endure to stay in—coins flee from it as from the Devil, win or lose. If he knew any man of any nation who could cast such a spell on it as to force money to be in it always, the Devil should have no power to make it torment him with pain. He ends up with an appeal to the King:

> I haif inquhyrit in mony a place 31
> For help and confort in this cace,
>   And all men sayis, My Lord, that ye
> Can best remeid for this malice
>   That with sic panis prickillis me.

---

[2] 1 ("To the King").

This is pure complaint with no hint of satire in it—personal, appealing, touching. "Sanct[3] Salvatour"—Christ himself— is the patron saint of the college Dunbar is said to have attended at St Andrews. Here the address is mere imprecation. The poem is remarkable for its sincerely-felt, finely-expressed presentation of the case against poverty. Poverty, so far from being good for the soul (involuntary poverty, at any rate), makes one mean, uncharitable, miserable, lonely, and isolated, unable to work, apathetic, and listless. It causes fear and worry which disintegrate the character, unless hope comes to the rescue. It makes pleasure in life impossible, prevents sociability with other men, and causes hypocrisy by pretence that pious asceticism, not simple poverty, is one's reason for being unsociable. Dunbar, in fact, cannot afford to keep up the minimal standards of a courtier. We must bear this in mind as we listen to the innumerable complaints to or at the King—not utter and abject poverty is complained of, but the chronic state of hardupness that prevents him living according to the standard expected of his status as a courtier. Mere common sense supports the view that if you expect a man to behave and conduct himself in a highly cultured manner, you had better see to it that he has the wherewithal to do so. Dunbar's position at court is so painfully ambiguous that we hear him beg again and again for a church so that he can retire from ostentation and pageantry into a quiet country life.

It is interesting to note that "Poverty" was the "bride" of St Francis who desired Dunbar elsewhere to become a Franciscan. No man was less suited, surely, to such a vocation. Is there perhaps a sexual innuendo in the "panefull purs" refrain? James is being put in good humour by a joke which, presumably, is to his taste. The purse is the scrotum, the coin is sperm, and the "pain" presumably either venereal disease or randiness. The point cannot really be proved one way or the other, but the reader does well to bear it in mind.

There is more of the element of satire in "Quhome to sall I Compleine my Wo",[4] in which, in more religious mood, he exposes the vices of courtly patronage. He does not know, he

---

[3] Here "sanct" probably simply means "holy."
[4] 21 ("None may Assure in this Warld").

says, to whom he can complain of his sadness and anxieties;
he knows not friend from foe, for in this world none can be
sure of anything. He has served long in court and received
no payment, his death is near, his past life irrecoverable.
Falsehood often rides out in high-ranking procession, while
Truth walks round on foot, spurred on by lack of means, so
that one is uncertain of how properly to behave. Only the
rich have good reputation: the poor are oppressed, the just
injured, so blinded are reason and intelligence.

> Vertew the court has done dispys   21
> Ane rebald to renoun dois rys,
>   And carlis of nobilis hes the cure,
> And bumbardis brukis benefys;
>   So in this world may none assure.

All good breeding, all high-ranking nobility have passed from
the ruling class, generosity is taxed, there is no charity in
princes. There is no armour against trouble, nobody can be
healthy long in a sick world. Flattery wears a fur gown,
Falsehood conspires with the lords, Truth stands barred at the
door, Honour is exiled from town.

> Fra everie mouthe fair wordis procedis;   41
> In everie harte deceptioun bredis;
>   Fra everie E gois lukis demure,
> Bot fra the handis gois few gud deidis;
>   Sa in this warld may none assure.

Tongues are now made of whalebone, hearts of flint, and though
eyes are sky-blue, hands are hard as diamond, as unyielding.
Yet heart and hands and the whole body must answer Death
when he calls to account before the coming Judge. He goes
on to discuss death, to rail at the whore Fortune whose false
promises roll away like the wind.

> O! quho sall weild the wrang possessioun,   61
> Or gadderit gold with oppressioun,
>   Quhone the angell blawis his bugill sture,
> Quhilk onrestorit helpis no confessioun?
>   Into this warld may none assure.

What use are seven lordships in Hell? He asks for no earthly
benefice, but to be received into God's Kingdom. The roll

of the Latin speaks with the voice of the Church in the last
stanza:

> Lord! sen in tyme sa sone to cum   81
> *De terra surrecturus sum,*
>   Rewarde me with na erthlie cure
> Bot me ressave in regnum tuum.
> Sen in this warld may non assure.

This poem is a late one, and the deep note of meditation
and religious resignation resound in it: in some ways it might
better have been considered among the meditative or religious
poems. But the main drive is not so much against the world
at large as at the court of James IV, and the personal note and
private experience keep coming through: it is his personal
plight that sets him off, not knowing friend from foe, lacking
reward for long service, lamenting his wasted time at James's
court: "Truth" at the door looks rather like William Dunbar,
and the just and the poor are his oppressed relations. It is
his own virtue that is despised, his own prince who lacks
charity. Therefore I have chosen to place it here among the
courtly complaints: it sets a polar opposite to the first two poems
mentioned in this chapter. They are the poems of the young
courtier, the one naively self-effacing, the other naively self-
demanding. This one is the old man disillusioned, bitter, and
turning in despair to thought of reward in another world.
Between these two extremes the bulk of the poems of courtly
complaint have their being.

The poem is one of his best, heavy with experience and the
load of Catholic tradition. There is no gimmicky versification
here, but the mighty roll of the elegiac verse weighted down
with the wisdom (and the folly) of the ages. Particularly
effective is the quotation from Matthew vi, 23, in the fifteenth
stanza:

> *O quante sunt iste tenebre!*   74

which was echoed also by Dante in the *Inferno*, and in our time
by T. S. Eliot in *The Waste Land.*[5]

In most of the poems of complaint about the court, however,

[5] See ll. 60-5.

Dunbar is neither content to live on the King's grace, nor to look to another world for his reward. In "Complane I Wald" we find him in very different mood. "Complane I Wald", he says, "wist I quhome till", or to whom his account should be rendered, whether to God the Creator, or to the Virgin, or to worldly prince. He would complain of wrongs and great injuries that nobles endure in these days, and men of virtue, skill, intelligence, wisdom and conduct who can get nowhere at court by being loyal, loving, or serving long and well. On the other hand:

> Bot fowll, jow-jowrdane-hedit jevellis,   15
> Cowkin-kenseis, and culroun kevellis;
> Stuffettis, strekouris, and stafische strummellis;
> Wyld haschbaldis, haggarbaldis and hummellis;
> Druncarts, dysouris, dyvowris, drevellis,

misguided limbs of Satan, misshapen mandrakes of mastiff strain, cravens, cowards, and thieves of all kinds, miminy-mouthed pansies with nattering cheeks, heavy-faced thieves with mucky trousers, chaff-midden yokels descended from scavengers—such gentlemen of the court do very well indeed. One, for no reason at all, gets himself a cowl and entices a great convent into evil ways, being himself an example of vice, ordained for his possessions instead of for piety, and the Devil himself is delighted by the appointment. Another importunes a surplice out of the King, thus destroying "ane dastart", while another, who gets a parsonage, thinks it is a present for his page-boy and is not content until he is called "milord". But content or not, the learned son of some earl or lord takes pity on this ruffian and clothes him in uniform to run his errands and such, and he behaves like a master native-born before his elders, with three times as much cunning to possess a dignity, talking hateful ignorance, counterfeiting a prelate's face, and sitting high above one at meals, though he used to clean out the stable. The abuse goes on in much the same vein, denouncing the fact that pickpockets are promoted to higher rank than men of ruling-class blood: Dunbar means, but does not say, "like myself". He ends up, however, with a direct address to the king which leaves us in no doubt about where the extraordinary rage comes from:

> Thairfoir, O Prince maist honorable,   67
> Be in this meter merciabill,
> And to auld servandis haff ane E,
> That lang hes lipnit into the;
> Gif I be ane off tha my sell,
> Throw regiones hes bein hard tell,
> Off quhilk my wrytting witnes beris;
> And yete thy danger ay me deris:
> Bot eftir danger cumis grace,
> As hes bein herd in mony plece.

The anger is real enough, but it has been exaggerated in the tradition of flyting, which, strangely to us, makes it more acceptable: it is supposed to be funny. Dunbar is up to something more sophisticated than would seem. He tried many ways of approach to James, hoping to move him by one of them. He tried flattery, denunciation of his enemies, reproach of James, humble appeal, rage and vituperation, flyting, and much else. Here, he is trying the approach of outraged virtue expressed in ingenious flyting—many of the terms are inexplicable, and probably always were, having only onomatopoeic value. The anger is perfectly "sincere"—the real sincerity of a poem's emotions need not be personal at all—in the personal sense, but it is much more controlled, and indeed contrived, than it looks. The "anger" is expressed in the rigmarole of abuse, the particular troops he deploys for this particular assault on James's fortified heart; but Dunbar is the commander sitting in the rear and conducting the campaign.

It is not a "pretty" poem, not even a good one. The syntax is often obscure or garbled, the predicate of a subject implied rather than stated—the list of rogues in the second paragraph, for example, has nothing definite predicated of it, but is an exclamation, with the predicate implied. It is ugly with the ugliness inseparable from the flyting tradition. One of the least pleasant aspects of it, quite apart from its scurrility, is the snobbery that runs through it. There is no inherent reason why a stable-boy should not become a bishop or a lord:

one wonders, indeed, whether to regard it as promotion or
demotion: all that matters is why he does so and how he
uses his rank. A stone-mason saved Athens—and some would
say, therefore, the whole of what is called "Western Civilisation"—at the battle of Salamis. Socrates himself was a mason,
and the founder of Dunbar's Church was a carpenter and son
of a carpenter. There is something repellent about a flea
which despises the dog it feeds off, and the non-productive
classes are fleas of the dog that produces the world's goods.
Those of us who are privileged to develop our talents in other
ways should honour the workers who make it possible for us
to live our lives, and for whom, indeed, we labour in our own
ways.

This false pride of Dunbar's in being descended from a
family of land-robbers and traitors runs through much of his
work—Kennedy makes unmerciful use of Dunbar's descent in
the "Flyting"—and leaves a nasty taste in the mouth. To
say that in this Dunbar is merely a man of his time brought up
in a revolting tradition of so-called "aristocracy"—the true
"best" of the Middle Ages were seldom found outside the
monasteries and universities—is merely to accentuate his
limitation as a poet, and as a Christian. The age is no excuse.
One of the better traits of James IV (as of his father before
him) was a willingness to promote men for their ability rather
than for irrelevant ancestors. That he often made mistakes
was obvious: but Dunbar's case was best founded on his merit,
not his "noble" blood, nor his hereditary "rights". The
basic elements of human goodness are inherent in reality, and
there they have been perceived and put into words, even
reduced to principles, by great prophets and teachers since the
dawn of consciousness, and there is no excuse for not knowing
them in any age. All normal humans are born with a direct
sense of this moral law which inheres in reality, as animals
are born with instincts appropriate to their species: education
is (or should be) the process by which this moral sense is led
out into full consciousness and put under linguistic control.
And Dunbar was a highly educated man of genius, highly
trained in a tradition of religion which holds that the meek
inherit the earth.

In "Schir, at this Feist of Benefice",[6] Dunbar tries the "sweet-reasonable" approach. The King should consider, at this feast of benefice-giving, that a little goes a long way, and that fair shares for all should content men of reason: but where some get all and others nothing, nothing can please.

> Schir, quhiddir is it mereit mair   6
> To gif him drink that thristis sair,
>   Or fill a fow man quhill he brist,
>   And lat his fallow de a thrist,
> Quhilk wyne to drynk als worthie war?

It is no happy carousal, he goes on, where one makes merry and another is depressed; where one drains the cup and another thirsts. Therefore the King should let the cup go round everybody once, thus earning the good-will of the whole company. This little poem of fifteen lines states his case very well, and is another reminder of the man's reasonableness when not outraged by injustice and neglect. The lines on the relative merit of giving a thirsty man to drink rather than filling a full one till he bursts have Biblical force and prophetic authority. Here again the Catholic tradition asserts itself powerfully, and poetically, in his work, and the poetic as well as the religious influence of the sermon-form makes itself felt. It is no coincidence that the great English religious poet, John Donne, was also a great writer of sermons: the two arts are born of the same Father by different mothers.

There is a whole parable condensed in the verse quoted above, and it has the stamp of a truism, an incontrovertible piece of invincible reality. This contact with "reality", as distinct from " realism", is something we keep running up against in Dunbar, as in most Scottish poets of any stature, and to a more intense degree than is usual in poets of other European nations. The "realism" is there, too: Dunbar's Muse is never happier than when writing on the subject nearest his heart—his own material needs. It never enters his head that the whole business of giving benefices at all—the right, to put it bluntly, of sorning off the peasantry under the guise of caring for their souls—is a racket. Nor does he question

---

[6] 11 ("Quhone Mony Benefices Vakit").

the King's authority in "spiritual" matters: there is a tacit acceptance of the fact that this is a matter of economics and not "spiritual" at all, although elsewhere he does denounce clerical incompetence. Dunbar's attitude to benefices throughout is not one of morality so much as expediency: he is motivated not by righteousness but indignation. Yet this envy, too, exists in a normal framework, like everything else in Dunbar. It is merely that his ethic is not deep enough, searching enough, thorough enough. Dunbar was faced with the perennial problem of the poet in society, and his approach to it is not that of the hardworking independence of Burns, whose hard life brought him to an early grave. Burns would have despised the ignoble fawning and whining of Dunbar, dependent on a king and court clearly unworthy of him. We may not do so—at least to the same extent. So long as society fears and hates the poetry to which it pays lip-service, the basic duty of a poet is to keep alive somehow in a world which prefers him dead: and Burns failed in this basic duty to his work. Would that he had done some fawning and whining himself, if that would have left us even more of his incomparable work! Yet the nasty taste of Dunbar's degradation at the court, and open avowal of it, remains. Poets are not saints, but with the advantages Dunbar had of genius, education, and connexion, one wonders whether some better solution could not have been found.

In similar mood, but with greater depth of vision, is "Off Benefice, Schir, at everie Feist".[7] Every time benefices are to be given out, he complains, those who already have the most demand the most, and if they get less than everything, they think that the king wrongs them. The burden of their tale is always—give us the spoil to divide among us.

> Off benefice, Schir, at everie feist,   I
> Quha monyast hes makis maist requeist;
>   Get thai nocht all, thai think ye wrang thame:
> Ay is the ouir word of the geist,
>   Giff thame the pelffe to pairt amang thame.

---

[7] 12 ("To the King"). Is it a sequel to 11 ("Quhone Mony Benefices Vakit")?

Some eat duck and swan, while Dunbar stands in a corner
with nothing to eat—he is constantly giving us a picture of
himself as a quiet, envious, suffering bystander—until they
have seized for themselves the greater part, leaving him
standing with a most piteous look on his face as they part the
spoils among them. At certain high feasts of glorious saints,
patronised by the lairds, he has often sung to them (as priest
of the mass) *Caritas pro Dei amore*, but got no charity from them.
Thus always the blind world pays its debts—the rich set snares
for the poor, spread nets to catch them, and are privileged to
fish in all waters. He who has nothing, gets nothing, but sits
always like a cipher among them. So long as they control the
Church, they care little about its welfare, nor for its books,
nor for those who ring the bells, and so long as they have the
spoils to part among them, they give no thought to the poor
of the parish. But—here he rubs in the lesson drawn from the
lairds' blasphemous interpretation of "To him that hath shall
be given"—when the dragon Death stings those who could
never have enough of the world's rent, they will have the most
penance to do in Purgatory, with the largest share of sin to
part among them:

> Quha maist hes than sall maist repent   29
>   With largest compt to pairt amang thame.

With that, I'm afraid, the lairds would be well content.

In this poem the personal complaint of Dunbar is widened
into satire of the court in general, and that satire is universal-
ised into an eternal statement of the relationship between
exploiter and exploited, the turning of real values upside down.
Yet the note of self-pity is still there, and muffles the force of
the poem. His poetry is, at its best, a poetry of reform: in
this he is the father of David Lyndsay: but true reformers
want a better world for other people, for their own children
perhaps, not for themselves. The self-sacrifice which is the
bread and water of the life of a reformer is incompatible with
self-seeking. Dunbar—it is perhaps my most fundamental
judgment of him—missed the greatness of a national reforming
poet which his gifts thrust upon him, and allowed himself to
be turned aside by pettiness into a merely personal one.

He is at his best when the edge of his prophetic wrath is tempered by the breadth of meditation. The supreme example of this is "This Waverand Warldis Wretchitnes",[8] in the beautiful elegiac stanza he used also in "I that in Heill wes and Gladnes".[9] The theme is still his own ill-treatment at James's court, but the meditative vein universalises it, rising above the merely personal. He speaks of the pain of thinking about the misery of this unstable world, the activity that fails and gets no reward, the time mis-spent, the loyal service given in vain, the slippery joys, the brief happiness, the pretended love, the false comfort, the pleasant tarrying, the cunning snare—all these "For to consider is ane pane". The sugared mouths with minds absent, the fine rhetoric with two faces, the pleasing tongue with the insincere heart; the loyal work and loyal service gone for nothing, the long effort in humble manner, and the little reward it receives, are painful to think about. He speaks not only about Scotland:

> Nocht I say all be this cuntre,   17
> France, Ingland, Ireland, Almanie,
> Bot als be Italie and Spane;
>   Quhilk to considder is ane pane.

The world changes from weal to woe, the good old customs have gone from hall and bower, from town and country. Faith is dependent, trust doesn't last long, appointments are fleeting and courts are changeable—purpose changes like wind or rain.

> Gude rewle is banist our the Bordour   29
> And rangat ringis bot ony ordour,
> With reird of rebaldis and of swane;
>   Quhilk to considder is ane pane.

The people are so wicked in their habits that the fruitless earth bears witness to it, and the air is infected and profane (this is the note of Greek tragedy). In order to seize the temporal goods of his father, the son would disinherit him and abuse him as a bankrupt. Churchmen are so holy and good that eight oxen and a cart might turn round on their consciences,

---

[8] 13 ("Of the Warldis Instabilitie").
[9] 7 ("Lament quhen He wes Sek").

H

so spacious and crude they are. He returns to his favourite
subject:

> I knaw nocht how the kirk is gydit,   45
> Bot benefices ar nocht leill devydit;
> Sum men hes sevin, and I nocht ane;
>   Quhilk to considder is ane pane.

> . And sum, unworth to browk ane stall,
> Wald clym to be ane cardinall,
> Ane bischoprik may nocht him gane;
>   Quhilk to considder is ane pane.

Among others, Dunbar's unworthy self desires a church and
can't get one, although some people have access to a score.
Benefices come through King or Queen, but they are always
so far away from Dunbar that none could shoot an arrow
across the gulf between. A benefice, in fact, might come in
shorter time from Calcutta and the New-Found Isle, or from
the deserts of India across the great ocean. One might have
come from any quarter, from Paris, from the Far East, from
Africa. One is so long coming to Dunbar that he fears it will
be used up, or returning on its course: meanwhile he has got
financially involved on the strength of it, and people are asking
when it will come. He knows it will be provided for him, but
his heart breaks and his brain bursts with the weariness of waiting for it. Not that he wants much:

> Greit abbais grayth I nill to gather,   85
> Bot ane kirk scant coverit with hadder;
> For I of lytill wald be fane;
>   Quhilk to considder is ane pane.

The King may rest assured that Dunbar's soul is in no danger
of damnation for having so many cures in various places
through James. His experience is so dispiriting that he
despairs of the world—the only hope he has left is the King:

> The formoist hoip yit that I have   97
> In all this warld, sa God me save,
> Is in your Grace, bayth crop and grayne,
>   Quhilk is ane lessing of my pane.

There is something weak in his whole attitude here—the "philosophic" approach is a rather negative one. He hovers between "hoip" and a defeatist "resignation"—resigned to defeat of hope, that is. There is no true philosophic resolution and acceptance of the problem, much less any decision on a course of action. Even the vision of evil, the universalisation of his private-cum-social sufferings, is a weak thing compared, for instance, with what that great sufferer Baudelaire made of the vision of evil. The suffering is not sufficiently transformed into a universal work of art: it is still too personal. Even Villon, whose circumstances were much worse than Dunbar's, made greater art out of greater sufferings in such poems as his "Ballade of the Hanged". Villon was welcome at the court of Charles d'Orleans—a more enlightened ruler than James IV —but did not find it to his taste. In fact Villon wrung greater sweetness and humanity out of the stews and gutters of Paris than Dunbar ever got out of the court of his royal master.

The most devastating of these poems of complaint at court life—though not the best—is "Schir, Ye Have Mony Servitouris".[10] It is a well-constructed poem, but one in which his anger, at least once, touches true greatness. Dunbar addresses the King:

> Schir, ye have mony servitouris   1
> And officiaris of dyvers curis . . .

churchmen, courtiers, fine craftsmen, doctors of law and of medicine, diviners, rhetoricians, philosophers, astrologers, artists, and orators, soldiers, knights, musicians, minstrels, dancers, carpenters, shipbuilders, masons—the catalogue throws interesting light on James's court—shipwrights, glaziers, goldsmiths, stone-cutters, painters, and apothecaries. All these are skilful in their craft and satisfactory and honourable to His Highness, very convenient for him to have beside him, most worthily deserving his gratitude, reward and succour.

[10] 17 ("Remonstrance to the King").

Dunbar himself is unworthy to be counted among them—
and yet:

> And thocht that I amang the laif,   25
> Unworthy be ane place to haif,
> Or in their nummer to be tald,
> Als lang in mynd my wark sall hald,
> Als haill in everie circumstance,
> In forme, in mater, and substance,
> Bot wering, or consumptioun,
> Roust, canker, or corruptioun,
> As ony of thair werkis all,
> Suppois that my rewarde be small.

But, he goes on, James is so gracious and mild that a very
different set also attends upon him, worthless and despicable.
Pretenders, flatterers, criers, boasters, gossips, spongers,
sharpers, gunners, Frenchmen, gourmets, beggars, thieves,
cattle-rustlers, scandal-mongers in corners, sorners of free
meals, etc., who have no shame, cannot lay claim to any skill,
knowledge, or craft other than to crowd in his doors, eavesdropping on councils, not learning culture from any man.
Among them are silly engineers in alchemy who can greatly
"alchemise" in folly, rather than in gold or elixirs, fantastic
fools, greedy and false, liars of tongue and ill-working of hand.
They daren't show themselves in the market-place for fear of
prosecution.

No reasonable man would object to the first sort he mentioned getting reward: but when this second sort of silly fools
who feasted at Cockelby's Sow are all rewarded and he is not,
then his heart nearly bursts with anger, he cries "Fie! on this
false world", and can't bear to see such great abuse daily in
court going on before his eyes.

Despite this, he desires yet more penance, for if he were
rewarded among the rest, it would satisfy him and reduce his
melancholy, causing him to overlook many a fault which now
stares him in the face. His mind is so set on scolding (flyting)
that he can write nothing else; either his heart must break or
he must avenge with his pen. He ends up with an extraordinary
direct threat to the King:

> And sen the tane most nedis be, 83
> In to malancolie to de,
> Or lat the vennim ische all out,
> Be war, anone, for it will spout,
> Gif that the tryackill cum nocht tyt
> To swage the swalme of my dispyt!

The poison will all burst out if James does not medicine him at once.

There is a quite deliberate intellectual construction in this poem. In the first paragraph, of twenty-four lines, Dunbar acknowledges and catalogues those dependants of the court whom he deems worthy of patronage. In the second, of ten lines, he humbly associates himself with these worthy men, and even asserts his equality with the best of them, rising to greatness in his true assessment of his own poetic merit, which he knows as surely as a brigadier knows that he is a brigadier. In the third paragraph, of twenty-six lines, he denounces and catalogues those dependants whom he deems to be worthless. In the fourth, of twelve lines, he expresses his rage at the sight of these rogues being rewarded by the King when he himself is slighted: and in the fifth and last, of twenty lines, he lets loose uncontainable rage at the injustice done him by the King.

I would give all these poems of complaint to James, except only "Schir, Lat it Nevir in Toun be Tald", to see the poem he would have written—perhaps did write—letting "the vennim ische all out". It would have been some piece, if this is just a hint of what might be, as he seems to suggest. The flyting tradition is in evidence throughout the poem, and, as always, it tends to debase and bore. The claim for his own merit is remarkable in that not only does he prove the accuracy of his awareness of his own poetic rank, he states the main source of his rage. Genius, or talent, is its own authority; it is authorised by nature and by God. But unless it wins social recognition, is further "authorised" by society (and society in this case is the Crown), then it is outlawed as crime or heresy, or despised as a form of madness or aberration. Dunbar speaks out of the intense suffering not merely of poverty, but of the artist in a society in which there is no correspondence between real value (talent, virtue, any sort of real gift) and the arbitrary

perversions of value conferred by fashion. Society's values are
relative and temporary, but the value of powers-for-good is
absolute and eternal. Dante Alighieri is another poet who
startles us by an accurate assessment of his own poetic rank,
when he aligns himself with the great poets of antiquity—
especially with Virgil and Statius.[11] Dante, too, knew suffering
and, in his case, exile, but the reasons were at least partially
political, and his poetry as much as his birth and status made
him welcome in a more enlightened society: Can Grande was
a worthier patron of Dante than James IV was of Dunbar.
Dante's claim is an easy assumption of his simple right:
Dunbar's is forced from him by injustice, and it is made with
confused timidity and stridency—but with a self-consciousness
of which the sublime Dante was quite innocent.

The sincerity and depth of feeling in this poem, its pathos
and pain, its sense of moral outrage, are unequalled even in
Dunbar. He speaks with the bitterness of Shylock to Antonio.
The utterance breaks through the artifice too painfully here
and there, and this intrusion of real emotion into the emotion
of the poem is the main flaw in it—apart from the boredom of
the catalogue and flyting techniques. Yet we are convinced
of the essential rightness of his case. This power of Dunbar's
to convince us by a hard core of reason and sound sense of
values under the torrent of rage is the main reason why his
witness against his age and James's court is so damning: he
speaks as a witness, a martyr who bears witness of truth: and
we know that fundamentally he is right. This power of being
right, of telling the truth, however unpopular it may be—and
truth is always unpopular—is the supreme mark of the major
poet, as of the prophet. It is the main reason for their un-
popularity with establishments. Did anything else come out
of James's court of anything like the value of Dunbar's poems?
Dunbar, therefore, does not overstate his case, in his claim to
merit. James lives here as nowhere else, and it is his fate that
he is seen as an inadequate ruler by the man who might have
been his Virgil—had he been an Augustus. Yet it is remarkable
that such a poem could be addressed to any monarch: this

---

[11] Cp. *Purgatorio*, Canto XXI. Dante errs slightly on the side of understatement.

suggests that bards may have had some such licence at court
as jesters had.

Despite the tediousness of the catalogue device and the
weakness of the flyting, the poem has dignity—not always a
feature of Dunbar in his satiric-querulous mood—and structure:
it has nobility, manliness, courage, and the outspoken assertion
of the rights of real merit.   These are no minor virtues in any
poem by any poet.   It rises above the merely personal—always
the mark of minor or negligible poetry—into an assertion of
values which make for life more abundant.   It is not merely
Dunbar who is abused at James's court but the gifts of God
lodged in Dunbar for the benefit of mankind.   He denounces
false values and bad government and asserts true values and
the role of justice.   He speaks out of his own outraged sense
of reality, his deep intuition of the real needs of life and of the
society which is the vehicle of the furtherance of human life.
A society which abuses its poets is a sick society on the brink
of catastrophe.   In this, and in other poems of Dunbar exposing
the state of James's court and the country at large, the catastrophe of Flodden is already implicit.   This reflects not merely
on James, but on government by kingship—it is too much for
any man born of woman, even if he be an elected king, there
by virtue of his outstanding abilities: and James was merely
an ordinary man put in office by that purblind god Heredity.
When art is abused, true value is lost, and the guilty society
floats on to meet the doom floating to meet it.   Dunbar here,
in airing a deep-felt personal grievance, transcends the merely
personal and utters a prophetic warning not only to his own
bad society but to all such at all times.

In all these poems we hear only the voice of Dunbar complaining: we infer from the number of complaints that they
fall on deaf ears: but there is one poem in which the King
replies in an affirmative voice to the plea.   That poem is
"Schir, Lat it nevir in Toun be Tald".[12]   Now that Christmas
is approaching, "lufferis cummis",[13] he says, "with larges
lowd"; and since young mares will be combed and decked
to be ridden by both noble and commoner, why should not

[12] 22 ("The Petition of the Gray Horse, Auld Dunbar").
[13] I.e. "Liveries."

palfreys also be proud? He asks that the King should never
let it be told in town that Dunbar got no new gown from his
master at Christmas—that he was a Yule-tide jade, a worn-out
and thrown-out old horse. When he was young:

> Quhen I was young and into ply   7
> And wald cast gammaldis to the sky,
> I had beine bocht in realmes by,
>   Had I consentit to be sauld.
> Schir, lat it nevir in toun be tauld
> That I suld be ane Youllis yald.

When he wants to eat with well-bred horses, a whip is laid
on him, and he must jump to coal-heavers who are scabby,
lame, and rheumy with cold. Even if he were an old hackney
jade shot out over the hollows to squash the clover, he would
be housed at Christmas; and though he is not dressed in stall
like silk-clad coursers, yet he would be housed anew against
the Christmas cold.

> I am ane auld hors, as ye knaw,   31
> That ever in duill dois drug and draw;
> Great court hors puttis me fra the staw,
>   To fang the fog be firthe and fald.
> Schir, lat it nevir in toun be tald
> That I suld be ane Youllis yald.

He has this long time run out in the field on pastures bare
and stripped: he should be taken in now from old age, his
"bekis" are sticking out bold and high. His mane has turned
white, as the King well knows, and when other horses had
bran to eat, he got only grass, no matter how much it pained
him in the stomach. It was never his lot to be petted in the
stable, his life has been so miserable that he is willing to offer
his skin for some badly-cleaned straw to tear. He asks the
king, should he die in the King's possession, although his lot
has been so meagre, not to let the shoemakers get his skin to
chew with their ugly gums. The court has worn him out:

> The court hes done my curage cuill   61
> And made me ane forriddin muill;

> Yett, to weir trapperis at the Yuill,
> I wald be spurrit at everie spald.
> Schir, lat it nevir in toun be tald
> That I suld be ane Yuillis yald.

Then there follows the four couplets of the King's "Responcio":

> Efter our wrettingis, thesaurer,   67
> Tak in this gray hors, Auld Dumbar,
> Quhilk in my aucht with service trew
> In lyart changeit is in hew.
> Gar hows him aganis this Yuill,
> And busk him lyke ane bischoppis muill,
> For with my hand I have indost
> To pay quhatevir his trappouris cost.

The hand may indeed be the hand of the King, but the voice
is the voice of Dunbar: James must have been a good mimic.
It is quite likely that Dunbar wrote it as a sort of postscript
after getting his request from the King. We have the James
Dog poems to show that he was as apt at acknowledging the
granting of a request as at demanding. But there is of course
no reason why James should not have had this much competence in verse as one of his many accomplishments. Wisdom
he lacked more than ability.

This is one of Dunbar's very finest poems, despite its rather
limited and personal subject. The reason for this is that it is
a sustained imaginative paralleling of the life of the poet and
that of a horse, in masterly verse in which imagination and
verbal expression, utterance and artifice, are perfectly blended.
The point, of course, is not the "horse" metaphor in itself
(though that gives the unique wry humour, the mellow pathos
which is so endearing), but the sustained imagination. This
is the mark of the major, and even of the maximal poet.
Any minor poet can produce metaphors and similes, use his
imagination in his verse: but the ability to sustain and tease
out an image is the mark of the man of higher gifts than a
lyric demands. This imaginative power takes a mere image
and, instead of merely throwing it on the page, traces out all
its implications and relations, its levels of meaning or suggestion,
until the subject is as nearly exhausted, as completely expressed,

as the man can make it. Shakespeare does this kind of thing
again and again in his poems and speeches: but the supreme
master is Dante. Dunbar is not to be compared with these
maximal poets, nor is this poem to be compared with any of
their works: but this is a major poem and the work of a major
poet. It is not merely that the poet shows some superior
cleverness, ingenuity, in being able to tease out an image: it
is that the more an image will bear teasing-out, the greater
the degree of its rightness—the ability to stand up to such
sustained examination is the proof of its authenticity. The
more an image will bear teasing out, the greater is its poetic
validity: and the more the poet is able to tease it out, the
greater is his poetic ability. This is why the great allegory of
Dante—his life compared to a journey through Hell, Purgatory,
and Paradise—is the supreme poem of European culture, and
why it has such incomparable power: seeing the metaphysical
and physical, the spiritual and the historical, the psychological
in the actual in the one supreme imaginative vision. The
flaw in Dante's poem is that the theology of which his poem
is woven is obsolete, though it still holds, and will always
hold, values permanent in human life. Before a greater poem
can be written, a poet will have to arise who can make an
integrated vision of human life in terms of verifiable scientific
discovery—perhaps out of Darwin's theory of evolution, which
would give one term for a great poem on human adaptation
of and to life and environment.

There is a "theology" inherent in reality itself which has
an authority that transcends any merely speculative one, and
that theology is yielding its secrets unwillingly to science. The
book of the cosmos, for the man who can read it, contains
religious truth that will make all the Holy Books in the world
look like the fantasies of children. But here in Dunbar's poem
we are concerned not with the image of the human soul as a
progress through the evolution of species, but with the image
of William Dunbar's life compared with that of a horse. The
comparison in itself sets the poem's tone as humorous because
the greater (human) term of the metaphor is compared with
the lesser (a horse). The horse is a particularly sympathetic
symbol for humans, not only because it has been the most

important working animal in human life, but because its
qualities of grace, intelligence, strength, patience, meekness,
and even affectionateness, make it a particularly appealing
one. Swift, we know, ended his *Gulliver's Travels* by asserting
the superiority of horses over men, and the Greek legend of
Pegasus has identified the horse with inspiration and creative
energy. Dunbar, by comparing himself to a horse, by one
stroke wins the imaginative sympathy of the reader—more
importantly of the hearer, for James clearly was, for once,
touched by one of Dunbar's appeals. Moreover, the horse is a
humble, unselfconscious, and totally unassuming creature, and
Dunbar by thus humbling himself struck at a part of James's
nature which would not be moved by the outpourings of even
the sublimest poetic ire.

The metaphor is sustained, of course, not merely by holding
to the Dunbar-horse image, but by seeing the other courtiers
in the same terms.   He is the old gray horse, the jade, the
worn-out aver: but the young women of the court are mares,
combed and decked—and (sly innuendo) they "ridden ar
baith with lord and lawd".   Other courtiers are well-bred
horses, while he is a whipped coal-horse: and so on.

What he is doing here is making a new use of the medieval
fable tradition—as in Henrysoun for instance—giving it a
humorous personal turn.   Again his instinct led him right, for
the fable is a particularly appealing *genre*, at once making use
of human sympathy with animals and showing a simplified
vision of human life.   Beginning with Aesop, as far as we know,
the *genre* is still very much alive today in the work of Walt
Disney and his imitators.   This animal vision is essentially
comic, though in the hands of a Swift it takes on very different
and darker significance.[14]   In this poem by Dunbar, the native
comic genius of the *genre*, given a new and surprising twist by
his own genius, flowers anew as his finest comic poem.   The
little pathetic touches are very appealing indeed—he has
never been petted in stable; his mane is now white; suppose
he were an old hackney jade squashing the clover; he is an
old horse whom great court horses drive from the common
feeding-stall; he has only grass to eat while other horses eat

[14] Cp. also George Orwell's *Animal Farm*.

bran. In the image of his youth as casting "gammaldis" to
the sky, we have another happy reminder of his love of dance.
The image of his skin being chewed by his old enemies—or
Aunt Sallies—the shoe-makers, is at once comic and grisly.
All these correspondences combine in an integrated imagery
rare in his and any poetry, and giving very high poetic delight.
It is one of his very best poems, and certainly the best of the
complaints to the King, the tone mellow and meek with long-
suffering, the dark streak of melancholy running under the
wry humour reminiscent of Villon. So close is the affinity
between Dunbar and Villon that it would be nearer the truth
to call Dunbar a Scottish Villonian: but this too is inadequate,
for he is likest Villon not in his resemblance to him but in his
equal uniqueness among Renaissance poets. Yet it is true that
Villon might have written "Schir, Lat it nevir in Toun be
Tald", and Dunbar might have written at least certain parts
of the "Testament"—whereas Chaucer could not have
written either, nor either Dunbar or Villon any of Chaucer's
major work. Both Villon and Dunbar were writing mainly
in the French lyric tradition of form and metric, and both were
using this tradition in an entirely individual way: perhaps
"entirely" is too strong, for the individuality of Dunbar is
deeply Scottish—as much national as personal, and influenced
by a native tradition of wry, wintry realism, at once cold and
warm, like a sunny winter day, which runs through the whole
of Scottish poetry from Barbour and even earlier poets, up to
date.

Not only is the poem a rare blend of utterance and artifice,
it is a blend also of two poetic gifts to which these correspond—
genius and talent. Genius is the manifestation of a new or
fresh vision of life which makes the genius specifically a man
with something different to say in his medium, some new value
or order of values to reveal for the first time in his particular
medium; and talent is a gift of being able to use some particular
medium or artistic expression. The "inspiration" of talent
is a technical one: that of genius is visionary, coming from a
vision of life which has no necessary connexion with any particular art-form at all. Wordsworth's nature-mysticism, for
example, might have expressed itself just as easily in paint as

in verse, and he is an obvious example of a man whose genius
exceeds his rather uneven talent.

"Schir, Lat it Nevir in Toun be Tald" is, though not
quite perfect as we have it,[15] one of Dunbar's most original
and authentic contributions to poetry.

Another poem complaining of his plight in old age after
years of unrewarded service is "Exces of Thocht Dois me
Mischeif".[16] He asks the King to remember again, as he did
previously (this must be a reference to some past relief—
perhaps a direct reference to the "Gray Horse" incident),
how his youth has all been spent in his service in pain and
sorrow: good conscience, therefore, calls out for payment—
he is hurt by excess of worry. The King's clerics everywhere
have their needs attended to, yet Dunbar must cry out like a
kestrel that has no freedom to reach its prey because of moulting
plumage. The falcon race are always forgotten:

> Foryhet is ay the falcounis kynd,   11
> Bot ever the myttell is hard in mynd;
>   Quhone the gled dois the peirtrikis preiff,
> The gentill goishalk gois undynd;
>   Exces of thocht dois me mischeif.

but the shrike is remembered: when the kite tastes the partridge,
the well-bred goshawk goes without dinner. The magpie, with
its piebald coat, pretends to sing notes like a nightingale, but
she cannot strike the high note for the harshness of her churlish
voice. Birds from distant lands—here he has another jibe at
the hated Damian, who tried to fly from Stirling castle—
always have the most attractive feathers; although they may
have no song but yells (a reference perhaps to Damian's

---

[15] There is a corrupt rhyme in the text at l. 58, where "gnawin" appears where
we would expect "gnawed," to rhyme with "tauld" and "yald". The poem appears
in both Maitland's and Reidpeth's MSS., but is incomplete in each, the total poem
as we have it being an amalgam of the two fragments. Maitland's MS. contains
ll. 23-46, excepting ll. 30, 36, and 42. In Reidpeth's the poem occurs as fragments
in these different places: ll. 23-55, excepting 11, 30, 36, 42, and 48; then ll. 55-65,
excepting l. 60; and ll. 1-24, excepting ll. 6, 12, and 18. It follows that these
missing lines have no real textual authority. In all except l. 58, however, the
missing lines are part of the refrain; l. 58, therefore, is only in Reidpeth: where
did Reidpeth get it?

[16] 20 ("To the King").

breaking his thigh in his attempted flight), they sit in places of honour in silver cages; familiar native nests hatch only owls. Why does the King, the eagle, allow this:

> O gentill egill, how may this be?   26
> Quhilk of all foulis dois heast fle,
>   Your leggis quhy do ye nocht releif,
> And chirreis thame eftir thair degre?
> Exces of thocht dois me mischeif.

There is a rather clumsy pun there—"leggis" is at once "legs" and "lieges". He goes on to complain that when the needs of all other men are attended to, both well-bred and low-born of every clan, relatives of colliers and bailiffs even, Dunbar can get nothing: yet he, too, having no virtues to parade at court, is born of Adam and Eve and must live. If it were not an offence to God, he would prefer to live like a flatterer, for they want nothing in this world. In some respects he blames himself, for he is such a child that he can only make ballades, while others flatter and pretend. He agrees that his service is a slight one (one of the few references, this, to the fact that his services are poetic rather than politico-religious[17]): so he asks out of charity, not of right, for some relief. None can remedy his illness so well as the King:

> With ane benefice ye may preiff,   58
> And gif I mend nocht hastalie,
>   Exces of thocht lat me mischeif.

He was called by his nurse "Dandilie, bischop, dandilie," and now in age can't even be a simple vicar. A false card up the sleeve can make a cattle-boy worth more than a poet:

> Jok, that wes wont to keip the stirkis,   66
> Can now draw him ane cleik of kirkis
>   With ane fals cairt in to his sleif
> Worthe all my ballattis under the byrkis:
> Exces of thocht dois me mischeif.

Even uncouth Mitchell has two or three cures and a bundle of dispensations for his neglect of them, although he, too, has

---

[17] A point raised by M. P. McDiarmid: see Bibliographical Review, Section E (below, p. 378).

only quite recently left off tending cattle: he takes all at a
throw of dice, and Dunbar gets nothing. How should he live,
having no hereditary lands, and no benefice? He does not
mean to upbraid the King, though he admits he comes close
to it. Like a soul in Purgatory, living in pain but with hope
of salvation, so is he now in hope of the King's succour.

This poem has some features in common with "Schir, Lat
it Nevir in Toun be Tauld", notably the theme of his age and
the likeness to an animal—in this case a bird. The bird
metaphor is sustained only through the first thirty of the eighty-
five lines, but it is well-sustained at that. The tradition behind
this is the heraldic device of bird-species as symbols of rank,
as used in " The Thrissill and the Rois", and in Chaucer's
Parlement of Foules. There is also here the more specific use of
allusions to falconry: Dunbar himself is like a kestrel in moult:
the shrike seems to have been used as a lure in falconry.[18]
But as in "The Thrissill and the Rois", he soon tires of the
allegory—rather stiff, in this case. He was never happy with
the bird-device used seriously, and soon opens out into straight
complaint about the distorted values at court. Again we have
more of the ironic humility of Villon, the self-depreciation,
instead of the fiery arrogance or at least self-assertion more
common in Dunbar: more of the mellow pathos of age than
the angry wounded pride of youth. The reference to the
"slightness" of his service at court, being obviously how the
King thought of it, is far more damning of James than any
outpouring of rage could be, for Dunbar was the one courtier
he had whom posterity does not willingly forget. There is a
touching gnarled honesty, as of an old man at once querulous
and yet deferential, in the remark that while he does not intend
to upbraid the King, no doubt he comes very near doing so.
Compare that with the outburst in "Schir, Ye Have mony
Servitouris",[19] threatening the King with the eruption of his
bile. The fact is that James is shown up in a worse light in
this poem, because of its understatement, than in any other.

The verse here is assured, and occasionally rises into major
poetry, as in the fourteenth stanza ("Jok, that wes wont to

---

[18] *The Poems of William Dunbar*, ed. Small, S.T.S., III. 177.
[19] 17 ("Remonstrance to the King").

keip the stirkis . . ."). The ease with which thought flows into
excellent verse is the result of long use and mastery of his craft,
so that it has become habitual. One of the freshest things in
the poem is the honest self-analysis, self-revelation, and confession of state of mind: it is unusual in degree and intensity,
and in itself is evidence of the sense of uncertainty, doubt, and
insecurity he complains of—and in more than the material
sense. To what extent this *malaise* is temperamental and to
what extent circumstantial—personal or social—cannot be
gauged.

When relief does come, it is almost as much to the reader,
whose sympathies have been harrowed and oppressed, as to
Dunbar. "Welcom, my awin Lord Thesaurair",[20] is a whoop
of joy for benefits about to be received. Dunbar has long
longed for the time when a certain lord would come home and
meet his material desires:

> His name of confort I will declair,   3
> Welcom, my awin Lord Thesaurair!

He welcomes him above all ranks in this country, under our
"roy of most renoun", with even more might than he has.
He has responded to Dunbar's plea by promising to come to
Edinburgh without delay:

> Ye keipit tryst so winder weill,   13
> I hald yow trew as ony steill;
> Neidis nane your payment till despair;
> Welcom, my awin Lord Thesaurair.

Yet Dunbar had been somewhat afraid until the Treasurer
had taken the directest route from Stirling to the itinerant
courts: if he'd had to wait till Christmas for his pay, this
writing would have been all in sorrow, though he now sings
out with heart free from pain. Then we learn the wonderful
extent of his cause for joy:

> Welcum, my benefice, and my rent   25
> And all the lyflett to me lent;
> Welcum my pensioun most preclair;
> Welcum, my awin Lord Thesaurair!

---

[20] 24 ("Welcome to the Lord Treasurer").

Not only the longed-for benefice, but rent from a living and
a most beautiful pension: no wonder he signs himself as the
Treasurer's "man" and personal servant!

Over his shoulder we see the shadow of Flodden, and
remember that the records show no more payments to him
after that event.   Did he lose the benefice and living as well
as the pension?   He is old, white-haired, worn-out—we have
had the evidence in other poems which must have preceded
this one—and death itself is not far off.   We note also, with
sadness and doubt for his hopes, that the stanza in which he
sings his paean of joy for material reward is also the one in
which he sang his darkest despair:

> I that in heill wes and gladnes   1
> Am trublit now with gret seiknes
> And feblit with infermitie;
>   Timor mortis conturbat me.

And listen to it echo a grim reply to his hard-won material
security:

> No stait in erd heir standis sickir;   13
> As with the wind wavis the wickir
> Wavis this warldis vanite;
>   Timor mortis conturbat me.

His moment of pathetic joy was to be short-lived, but for the
moment joy is his, and his simple sincerity is very moving.
Reward has come too late to be of much use to him, as it
usually does to writers and artists whom society, having failed
to persuade them to stop being nuisances and die, at last
rewards out of sheer relief at seeing their death from old age at
last in sight.   Dunbar's cross was poverty and neglect: in our
own time he would probably have had exile and oppression
to add to its weight.   James felt secure enough not to fear the
truth: today we know no such security.

This poem is one of Dunbar's most personal and innovatory
ones: but it is also one of his most minor and least important
as far as poetry is concerned—and for much the same reasons.
Poetry is only maximal, or even major, when the poet creates
far beyond his own little borrowed time into eternity, and from

I

experience far greater than any mere individual can ever have —creates with the consciousness of the race behind him, singing not only as a man but as mankind, or some representative part of it.

Money is not the sole cause of Dunbar's complaint of his treatment at court. In "Schir, I Complane off Injuris",[21] he takes up what must be the most original complaint ever made to any king by a poet: he wants redress against a courtier who has "magellit my making":

> Schir, I complane off injuris: I
> A refing sonne off rakyng Muris
>   Hes magellit my making, throw his malis,
>   And present it in to yowr palis:
>   Bot sen he plesis with me to pleid,
>   I sall him knawin mak hyne to Calis,
>   Bot giff yowr Henes it remeid.

Dunbar will denounce him as far as Calais unless the king does something to compensate him for the injuries. That idiot Mure has chopped his metre to bits and poisoned it with vicious talk ("Strang salpeter"), with very defamatory talk about lords—which is utterly discordant with Dunbar's own nature and habit. Such cruel slander deserves death, telling lies in Dunbar's name—and he asks the King for justice. Mure has added to certain writings of Dunbar verse in his own hand which contain both treason and slander. He lacks nothing of a mad fool out of reason except a shaved head—for he has lost both reason and intelligence. And it is as a fool Dunbar would have him punished:

> Punes him for his deid culpabile   22
> Or gar deliver him ane babile,
>   That Cuddy Rig, the Dumfres fuill
>   May him resave agane this Yuill,
>   All roundit in to yallow and reid;
>   That ladis may bait him lyk a buill,
>   For that to me war sum remeid.

There is no evidence that any of the kind of slanderous gossip in verse which he complains of being interpolated into

21 5 ("Complaint to the King aganis Mure").

his work by Mure having come down to us. It may be there,
in some of the wilder attacks on the courtiers in certain poems,
but it is unlikely, and we cannot prove it. This poem suggests
not merely the sort of general satire against unnamed "types",
but specific slander against named persons: there is little of
this in Dunbar's work, and that usually "comic", as in the
"Flyting",[22] and about lowlier persons than "lords". None
of it is in "magellit making", or "dismemberit meter": and
if any scholarly sleuth could make out a case for this line or
that line, it would be of no importance to criticism as such.
The worth of Dunbar's—of any major poetry—is in spite of
many imperfections of many different kinds. The poem is too
personal to be of much value, but it does bring out again
Dunbar's professionalism and pride of craft, besides throwing
interesting sidelights in little *genre* pictures on the place of
poetry in court, of jesters, and of such "characters" of the time
as Cuddy Rig, and the garb and tonsure of fools.

The main exception to the rule that Dunbar satirises
"types" rather than persons (flyting is not satire) is John
Damian—"The Fenyeit Freir of Tungland".[23] This longish
poem (128 lines) is in one of Dunbar's favourite dancing
metres, fast and sure of foot. He begins once again in the
dream-convention, and tells:

> As yung Aurora with cristall haile   I
> In orient schew hir visage paile
> A swevyng swyth did me assaile
>   Off sonis of Sathanis seid;
> Me thocht a Turk of Tartary
> Come throw the boundis of Barbery,
> And lay forloppin in Lumbardy
>   Full lang in waithman weid.
> Fra baptasing for to eschew,
> Thair a religious man he slew,
> And cled him in his abeit new,
>   For he cowth wryte and reid . . .

Having thus become a friar, when his feigned character and
his whole accursed behaviour became known, he fled for fear

---

[22] 6 ("The Flyting of Dunbar and Kennedy").
[23] 38 (same title).

and came to France with a little Lombard learning.   There he
pretended to be a doctor, to the eternal regret of many a man,
for he left neither sick nor wounded unkilled before he went:
he cut veins very cleanly, and when so many died of his
incision, he fled again.

He came the directest way to Scotland to practise his skill,
and the demonstration of his art was no joke to some people
there.   He caused great pain as an apothecary and murdered
many with medicine;   the magician was a great genius and
born of a race of giants.   As a physician he was a murderer.
For one night's attendance his fee was a horse and the skin
of the man whom he killed, so great were his resources.   His
instruments were as crude as any rafter, and he had many of
them in his portmanteau.

> He cowth gif cure for laxatyve   41
> To gar a wicht hors want his lyve,
> Quha evir essay wald, man or wyve,
>   Thair hippis yeid hiddy giddy.
> His practikis nevir war put to preif
> But suddane deid, or grit mischeif;
> He had purgatioun to mak a theif
>   To dee without a widdy.

This prelate went to no mass at the sound of consecration bell
or tocsin: his head was begrimed like a blacksmith's by striking
at the anvil;   and though he came home a new-made canon,
he had dispensed with matins and neither stole nor maniple
ever came upon him because of the smoking of the smiddy.

As it seemed to Dunbar in his dream, he tried various ways
to make the philosopher's stone elixir, and failed;   and when
he achieved nothing, he took a coat of feathers on him and
prepared to fly to Turkey;   and when he mounted on high,
all the birds that ever saw him wondered what he could be.
Some thought he was Daedalus, others the marvellous Minotaur,
and yet others took him for Mars' blacksmith, Vulcan, or
Saturn's cook.   The wood-pigeons tore him, the ravens tore
him, the hooded crows pulled out his hair—he was unable to
enjoy the sky.   The hawk and hen-harrier took him for the
horned owl, and sat upon him giving him blow for blow.   The

cuckoo, the cormorant, and the kite biffed him with blows till
he bled. The sparrow-hawk hastened to the fight, as fierce as
flint fire. The peregrine tiercel gave him tug for tug, a kestrel
hung on each ear, the magpie pulled out his feathers, the stork
laid on always without ceasing. The buzzard, busy without
check, was so clever with her talons that he might no longer
enjoy the use of his testicles, for she seized them at one
stroke.

Dunbar, by this time off on a flight of his own, revelling
in the fun, goes on:

> Thik was the clud of kayis and crawis   89
> Of marleyonis, mittanis, and of mawis,
> That bikkrit at his berd with blawis
>   In battell him abowt.
> They nybbillit him with noyis and cry
> The rerd of thame rais to the sky,
> And evir he cryit on Fortoun, Fy!
>   His lyfe was in to dowt.
> The ja him skrippit with a skryke
> And skornit him as it was lyk;
> The egill strong at him did stryke,
>   And rawcht him mony a rowt.
> For feir uncunnandly he cawkit,
> Qhill all his pennis war drownd and drawkit,
> He maid a hundredth nolt all hawkit
>   Beneth him with a spowt.

This is Dunbar at his most eldritch, delighting in sheer
fantasy dancing with superb mastery among words, the
syllables a wild onomatopoeic accompaniment to the flying
fantasy and dancing rhythm. Working up to a crescendo in
the last stanza, he tells us that Damian tears off his beautiful
feathered cloak, slips out of it up to the eyes in mud in a bog.
The birds all strike at the feathered cloak as if at a monster
among them, till all the feathers spring out of it into the air,
and he lies plunged in the bog as long as any raven roars.
The crows seek him out with anxious cries, and if he had been
discovered by the rooks, they would have torn him to pieces
with their claws. For three days he lies hidden among the

ducks, and the air becomes so dark and full of angry birds that
Dunbar wakes up with the din:

> The air was dirkit with the fowlis   121
> That come with yawmeris and with yowlis,
> With skryking, skrymming, and with scowlis,
>   To tak him in the tyde.
> I walknit with the noyis and schowte
> So hiddowis beir was me abowte;
> Sensyne I curs that cankerit rowte
>   Quhair evir I go or ryde.

This ending reminds us of the awakening in "The Goldyn
Targe", in which it is the noise of the cannon of the departing
ship which wakens him, and of the same device of a gun firing
waking him from "This Hinder Nicht, Halff Sleiping as I
Lay",[24] more opposite still is his awaking to the noise of birds
singing in praise of the Queen in "The Thrissil and the Rois".
In "This Nycht, befoir the Dawing Cleir",[25] it is the "stynk
and fyrie smowk" and the feeling that he takes the "hous end"
with him as the Devil disappears, that wakes him: but always
the device is the same, and is psychologically valid—some
event in the dream comes so near reality that it wakes him up.
We all at some time have this experience of waking from
dream, and the authenticity of the device lends authenticity
to its poetic use. The verse here is not unlike the quatrain of
the Standard Habbie, which was the staple of eighteenth-
century Scots verse: compare with any quatrain quoted above
such a Burns quatrain as this:

> 'Whare I kill'd ane, a fair strae death,
> By loss o' blood or want o' breath,
> This night I'm free to tak my aith
>   That *Hornbook's* skill . . .

from a poem very much in the same tradition as this one of
Dunbar's—"Death and Doctor Hornbook".[26] Whereas the
fourth line of Dunbar's has three stresses, the fourth line of

---

[24] 60 ("The Dream").
[25] 4 ("How Dumbar was Desyrd to be ane Freir").
[26] *The Poetry of Robert Burns*, edd. W. E. Henley and T. F. Henderson, London
1896, I. 191-200 (391-3).

Burns's has only two: but, that apart, the metres are closely related and seem to have appealed to something deep in the Scottish poetic character—swift, wild humour. Dunbar makes up his stanza by running on from one quatrain to the next; and the quatrain is his fundamental unit. Burns completes his stanza by adding two more lines:

> . . . Has clad a score i' their last claith
> By drap and pill.

And by appending these riding lines he achieves a very different, end-stopped effect. But both staves are out of the same stable. The basic element of both is the swift four-stress triplet followed by a shorter rider, which makes for a verse full of running energy and exuberant vitality. Dunbar uses the same type of verse in "Off Februar the Fyiftene Nicht",[27] and similar types in other poems (it is used also in "Harry, Harry, Hobbill schowe",[28] which may be by Dunbar).

John Damian, the "hero" of the ballat, was an Italian who practised alchemy and was able to impose on the gullible James for help in his impossible efforts to make gold. James made him Abbot of Tungland, to Dunbar's disgust. On 27 September 1508 he tried to fly from Stirling Castle, promising to be in France before the Scottish ambassadors who left on that date. He fell and broke his thigh, but made the excuse that "thair was sum hen fedderis in the wingis, quhilk yarnit and covet the mydding and not the skyis".[29] Dunbar sees in him a symbol of the corruption at court, particularly with regard to benefices, and his disgust at so obvious a piece of criminal folly on the part of James is mixed with envy and scorn. The poem is in many ways a comic poem, but the savagery of the satire and its implications make it overwhelmingly a satiric one. It is almost impossible, though popular with scholars, to range Dunbar's poems in kinds, because in his work the kinds invariably overlap, and any one poem might be considered as belonging to any one of several

---

[27] 57 ("The Dance of the Sevin Deadly Synnis").

[28] 86 ("The Manere of the Crying of the Play"). In *The Bannatyne Manuscript*, ed. W. Tod Ritchie, S.T.S. (1928), II. 315, this poem is entitled "The Littill Interlude of the Droichis Pairt of the Play."

[29] John Leslie, *History of Scotland*, Bannatyne Club 1830, p. 76.

kinds. This cataloguing is convenient to the classifying tendencies of some scholars, but bears little relation to reality. Really, there is only one kind in Dunbar—Dunbar's kind.

This poem is a case in point, like so many others considered in this chapter, and I have chosen to deal with it as court satire and complaint because that is its predominant characteristic. Dunbar hits at Damian in other poems, too; and clearly the man symbolised for him the whole injustice and distorted values of his experience of court life. Damian, too, was a materialist; and, while Dunbar was materialistic in outlook, his basic consciousness as a cleric was that of at least a nominal spirituality. It is possible for us to see in Damian an early experimental scientist—for science grew out of magic. The magical view of life is at odds with the religious one, for whereas religion sees life as in the hands of an almighty Power who may be placated but cannot be controlled, magic sees it as subject to natural forces which men can learn to influence and control by their own efforts. The religious attitude sees God's power— or the gods' power—over men: the magical one sees the potential power of men over nature, or even over the gods. Magic is essentially a materialist code, and it has had great successes since the rise of capitalism, so that men now have an unprecedented control over the natural environment.

To us today it is easy to see that magic can have a place within a religious outlook: it is the will of God that men should have a limited control over their environment, and magic (now science) is the gift by which God makes this possible. Moreover, magic, being limited by its very nature to material reality, unlike mysticism, lives in the realm of the provable. Theologians may argue about how many angels can dance on the point of a pin, but they cannot put it to the test of proof: but a group of scientists who think they can split the atom can, and have, put their theory to the test of proof and proved that they are incontrovertibly correct by doing the thing they said they could do. But to Dunbar, magic was simply a contemptible heresy which no educated man (and all education was religious) could regard as other than dangerous lunacy. That James should prefer such a heretic to the learned man of genius, and—in the light of what has been said above—promote such

an enemy of religion to an abbacy over his highly qualified
head, was an outrage to God and nature. This comes out
clearly in the poem: nature is outraged by the pretentions of
Damian, and expresses this by sending the birds against him.
The air is the appointed element of the birds, according to
Genesis, as water is for fish, and earth for men: for men to
try to extend their empire over the element of air is a blasphemous outrage, a crime against the law and order which
God instituted in nature throughout the universe.

It is from this belief that Dunbar draws the power of his
attack on Damian, and the result, under the guise of wild
comedy, is a deeply serious theological poem. Dunbar could
not foresee—but perhaps Damian did—the time when a poet
could write of an airman:

> He will watch the hawk with an indifferent eye
> Or pitifully,
> Nor on those eagles that so feared him, now
> Will strain his brow . . .[30]

Damian was not an out-and-out charlatan: he seems to have
had the inordinate self-confidence and impressive personality
of one, but he was serious enough in his ideas of flying to put
them to the test at his own risk. This at least argues a modicum
of good faith, which is precisely what get-rich-quick peddlers
of quack medicines totally lack. A history of the development of
flying, having begun probably with the legend of Daedalus
and Icarus, might well go on to consider such attempts as
Damian's, and similar ones made almost into our own time.
Real "bird-men" have done astonishing glides in our own
time, and more than one of them has met his death as a result.
But Damian's fault was not so much in what he tried to do,
but in the claims he made, and the deliberate playing on
credulity to which he resorted. This is as much a criticism of
his age, and of James, as of himself. A more modest approach
would have been met by a more modest degree of support from
James. It is unlikely that Damian himself believed that hen's
feathers had anything to do with the failure of his flight: his
excuse is the measure of the credulous fools he made it to.

[30] Stephen Spender, *Poems*, London 1931.

Dunbar was no such credulous fool, but a highly educated man, and not to be imposed upon: but what then was James IV? Was a king so much worse educated than a minor cleric at that time? We are told that James was a highly educated man, and we have the "Responcio" to the Gray Horse to suggest that he was able enough to imitate Dunbar. It is true that there seems to be a split in medieval life between an educated clergy and an illiterate secular body: it is one of the tragedies, surely, of the Catholic Church that the vow of celibacy robs mankind of the progeny of a whole class of its most highly developed men: but surely royalty was exempt from secular ignorance? The evidence is not strictly relevant here, but it shows clearly that James VI, Mary Stewart, and Elizabeth Tudor were all very highly educated (and therefore so their forefathers would be). We can only surmise, therefore, that James saw the positive side of Damian's experiments, and had a vested interest in helping to make them succeed: whereas Dunbar, as a cleric, had his own bias against their succeeding. It is common to dismiss such conundrums by an appeal to the age, but apart from the fact that such appeals are always false— the age is apt to become the innocent scapegoat for so many facts awkward to scholarship—one can say that only the secular illiterates of the age were likely to be taken in by Damian. The educated clergy were not so gullible: as the critical but balanced attitude of the Church to such men as Copernicus and Galileo seems to show.

The point is that James did in fact favour Damian, who was a mixture of naive primitive scientist and plausible crook, and grossly neglected the finest poetic genius of his time; and that matters enough to be worth at least some speculation. At any level it reflects adversely on James and his court, and the shortcomings of this monarch affected not merely the personal welfare of one poet, but the whole realm. We who see that chemistry had its beginnings in alchemy, astronomy, in astrology, and medicine in leechcraft, may look back with more sympathy—and more understanding than Dunbar had— but the charge against James's sense of value remains. One gets from Dunbar a sense of the court as being hopelessly unreal and corrupt: something is desperately wrong in it, and Dunbar

cries out again and again, not merely as a major poet suffering
personal neglect, but as a minor prophet treated as a voice in
the wilderness. The end of it all in Dunbar's own time was
Flodden, and that was followed by the revolution and reformation of 1560, the deposition of Mary, the desertion of James VI,
and so on, to the sell-out of the kingdom in 1707. "Where
there is no vision, the people perish." The vision was there,
but it was rendered ineffectual by bad government under a
series of bad or inadequate monarchs. A Scotsman today
cannot look back at the rule of James IV and the romantic
idiocy of Flodden without feeling quite as bitter as Dunbar
did about James IV. Flodden was not the only disaster
Scotland suffered on the road to its defeat in 1707, nor perhaps
even the worst, but it was a peculiarly significant and unnecessary one.

All this would seem to show the poem in a more original
and personal light than is in fact true. Dunbar, as usual, is
working within a well-established tradition, but doing something more realistic and personal with it, and something more
technically excellent than the usual run of such poems. But
the satire on leechcraft, alchemy, friars, and witless credulity
was a commonplace of the Middle Ages, and also in later ones.[31]
Damian therefore fits into a stock figure of medieval literature,
but with the advantage of being an authenticated historical
personage. Dunbar writes with the full power of mastery of
a long tradition behind him, plus the intensity of a personal
and actual hatred of this particular man. What we are apt
to miss—and must not miss—is that Dunbar is flying at higher
game than Damian: it is James himself who sinks in the mud
under the outraged birds. The whole scene of the battle in
the air reads like an anticipatory parody of the war against
Satan in *Paradise Lost*, Book VI, with the outraged birds of
nature parodying the angels, Damian cast as Satan, and the
mud of the bog as the bottomless pit into which Satan is hurled
by the triumphant Messias and his angels. It would be absurd
to press the parallel too close, but it is there and should be
noted: it bears out my remarks on the underlying theological
nature of the poem, and of Dunbar's hatred of Damian.

[31] See, e.g., Henrysoun's "Practysis of Medicine", and Holland's *Howlat*.

The theological note is even more evident in the companion poem to this, "Lucina Schynning in Silence of the Nicht".[32] The poem has almost apocalyptic force as a vision of the impending birth of Antichrist, and the surface comedy should not blind us to the real depth and seriousness of the poem. It is one of Dunbar's most profound and prophetic insights, given his angle of vision as a Catholic poet and cleric. The device is much the same: the moon shining in the silence of the night and the heaven full of bright stars, he goes to bed, but is unable to rest, being so sorely oppressed by heavy thoughts that he longs for the painful light of day. He complains heavily of Fortune—who has power over all beneath the moon, we remember—because she so contrariously stands against him. At last, after much tossing and turning, a gentle sleep of sheer weariness comes over him and he falls into a state of dreamy fantasy:

> Me thocht Dame Fortoun with ane fremmit cheir   11
> Stude me beforne and said on this maneir,
>   Thow suffer me to wirk gif thow do weill,
>   And preis the nocht to stryfe aganis my quheill,
> Quhilk every warldly thing dois turne and steir.

She turns very many men up to the heights, she says, and causes as many to land very low down. Before you mount upon my treddles, trust well that your trouble is almost over, seeing these tokens—wherefore mark them correctly:

> Thy trublit gaist sall neir moir be degest   21
> Nor thow in to no benefice beis possest
>   Quhill that ane abbot cleith him in ernis pennis
>   And fle up in the air amangis the crennis,
> And as ane falcone fair fro eist to west.

He shall ascend a horrible griffin, a she-dragon shall meet him in the air; these terrible monsters shall copulate and, in the clouds, beget the Antichrist, while all the air is infected by their poison. Beneath the fiery region of Saturn, Simon Magus and Mahomet shall meet the Antichrist, and Merlin shall be awaiting him at the moon, and Janet the widow riding on a broomstick with a strange garrison of witches. And then they

[32] 39 ("The Birth of Antichrist").

shall descend with smoke and fire and preach the empire of
Antichrist on earth, by which time the end of the world will
be near. With that Fortune leaves him frustrated both asleep
and awake. When he woke up, his dream struck him as so
extraordinary that he was afraid to tell anybody about it, as
if it were vicious, until he heard that an abbot intended to fly
up into the sky, as many truthful men told him, with a coat of
feathers made wholly by artifice. At this:

> Within my hairt confort I tuke full sone;
> "Adew," quod I, "My drery dayis ar done;
>   Full weill I wist to me wald nevir cum thrift,
>   Quhill that two monis wer sene up in the lift,
> Or quhill ane abbot flew aboif the mone."

These were the signs given by Fortune—he would never get
a benefice until an abbot flew above the moon, and now that
time is at hand, so his "drery dayis ar done". The bite of
the irony is too sharp for comedy—there is no real humour
in it, but only the wry grimace of one who says, "My poverty
will end, now that the Greek Kalends are about to come".

The poem is heavy with a brooding apocalypticism under
the surface comedy, a deep half-inarticulate prophetic intuition
of the strange new power of science, with its threat not only
to his own values but to Christian values as he understands
them. It is the old antagonism of magic and religion: it is
significant that Merlin the magician is associated with the
Antichrist of the poem. Dunbar here is at grips with a greater
truth than he can cope with: a greater poet, experiencing
this vision of the Antichrist rising up in him from the depths,
would have stopped to ponder and wrestle with it, and might
have wrung from the experience a greater poem than Dunbar
or any man of his time ever wrote, hammering out new technique to fit it as he went. But this was impossible to Dunbar:
he is content to look at the monster as it surfaces from the deep,
and to tell us that he saw it: he is not compelled to attack it
and capture or kill it. The minor personal theme of his own
benefice is allowed to dominate the major universal one of
science and religion. It is his personal limitation which always
prevents him from transcending the bounds of even a major

poet and soaring into the sublime heights and depths of true greatness—as Dante, Shakespeare, Milton (despite his present puny denigrators, the one truly colossal figure straddling Europe between Shakespeare and Goethe), and Goethe. Dunbar lacked the ultimate higher dimension which makes the difference between good and the best.

The hardest lesson a poet has to learn is the tautological proposition that the poetically unimportant is poetically unimportant, though it may mean life or death to the poet personally: and that the poetically important, really is so even though it is of no personal concern to the poet whatsoever. The theme which really was challenging Dunbar in "Lucina" was his vision of magic-science as Antichrist:[33] if he had unreservedly given himself up to it, his poem might or might not have succeeded, but he would have anticipated Marlowe and Goethe in dealing with the most important problem in European culture since the schoolmen wrestled to reconcile the Church and Aristotle, which was the poetically important theme. The chief theme that he actually expounded was the question of his own benefice, which was poetically irrelevant. As a poet, Dunbar's main flaw is that his professionalism had its shadow-side: being professionally so competent, he tried to make poetry serve him instead of him serving it: by thus "saving his life" he lost it. Who lives by the personality dies by the personality, for poetry is not an expression of mere personality. Dunbar was more concerned with his own "heid-ake" than the great *malaise* which was racking all Europe. The poem itself is evidence that the Muse was trying to say far greater things through him—the apocalyptic vision is there, powerfully, unmistakably, and genuinely. But the poet was unprepared and did not grasp the demands being made of him to let go of his own precious ego and dare the heights and depths in pursuit of the inarticulate.

"To each is given what defeat he will", said Laura Riding.[34] Dunbar for once had a really great theme knocking for entrance, and he failed to rise to it. In Damian and

---

[33] This of course is the author's own opinion and reading: other opinions are possible.

[34] "Nor is it written", in *Collected Poems*, London 1938.

the theme of the alchemist magician he was on the threshold
of the Faust legend, the central problem of Renaissance
Europe. The problem is by no means resolved even today—
perhaps especially today. Robert Graves—one of the most
accomplished writers of prose and verse now living—has
revived the whole problem in *The White Goddess*, in which
he rejects all claims of Apollo, the god of science, to patronage
of poetry, and claims that poetry is ruled over solely by the
Muse, the "white goddess". Poetry he defines as the religious
worship of this goddess to the exclusion not only of the god
of science, but of all patriarchal gods. Now this seems to me
to be a counsel of despair for poetry, since it means that the
whole human experience of science is to be rejected by the
poet as unusable: and since science is the most important
experience in modern life, this is equivalent to saying that
poetry cannot and will not deal with the most important experience in modern life: which is poetic surrender. The real
need is to bring it under the control of the human values
written, like the Tables of the Law, imperishably into all
poetry worth the name. Mr Graves's imitators are becoming
more and more influential among us now in 1964, giving us
Graves-and-water instead of wine. The point for us here is
that Dunbar's poem is by no means a poem about a closed
issue and of no relevance to us today. It is still very much
alive for us today: Goethe by no means said the last word
on the problem of magic-science and religion. He has only
made one great contribution to the poetic—and therefore the
human—resolution of the problem.

Dunbar reveals only a dim awareness of this huge problem
in the poem. His intuition grasps that faith as such—and he
was living at the end of an age of faith—is menaced by a vast
shadow of doubt, as his own life is over-shadowed by Damian.
The Middle Ages regarded theology as the "queen of the
sciences": the time was at hand when men would study God
(under the new name of Reality), not through the books of
the prophets, but through the book of reality itself as revealed
in nature, with astounding results: so that for the modern
mind it might be said that science is "the queen of theologies",
the truest revelation of God in his cosmos. The poem is

gloomy and foreboding, the comic passages peculiarly humour-
less—Dunbar's humour is apt to be unsmiling—and an undercurrent of dread runs through the poem: it is too grim—like
so much of Dunbar's humour—to be funny.

"My Heid did Yak Yester Nicht"[35] owes its success as a
minor poem precisely to the "personality" which spoils
"Lucina Schynnyng in Silence of the Nicht".   In this little
poem of only fifteen lines, he complains to the King that last
night he had such a bad headache that today he cannot
compose anything, and that owing to the migraine which
pierces his brow like an arrow, he can scarcely look on the light:

> And now, schir, laitlie, aftir mes,   6
> To dyt thocht I begowthe to dres,
>   The sentens lay full evill till find,
>   Unsleipit in my heid behind,
> Dullit in dulnes and distres.

He rises very often in the morning while his heart still lies
sleeping, for neither mirth nor minstrelsy nor sport nor merriment nor dancing nor revelry can arouse him in any way.
There is no mention in the poem that this may be due to the
lack of a benefice, though we constantly wait for the perennial
theme to sound.   It seems, though couched in the complaint
tradition, to be rather an apology for not managing to compose
something he had promised the King.

This is further evidence that writing poetry was at least
one of the court duties expected of him.   This point is worth
making because there is no proof that the rewards of various
sorts mentioned in the records as paid to Dunbar were for
poetry alone or for poetry at all.[36]   It is a slight piece, excellent
of its kind, and one of the earliest and most intimate of intimate
poems in the Scottish language—though here as always one
must qualify such a statement by adding "as far as we know",
for we know from Dunbar himself, in "I that in Heill wes and
Gladnes", that a great mass of poetry known to Dunbar has
not come down to us.   This makes any assessment of originality
in Dunbar a very chancy business—we almost inevitably

---

[35] 3 ("On his Heid-Ake").
[36] See "Matthew P. McDiarmid", Bibliography, Section E.

overestimate the individual talent of Dunbar at the expense of the tradition, because the tradition has not adequately been preserved for us to judge by. But even so, the poem speaks with his personal voice, freshly, unmistakably, and with startling simplicity and directness, the pre-Flodden poem speaking to us with contemporary force, so universal is the experience, so effective the expression.

Another poem addressed to the King but not of complaint is "In Hansill of this Guid New Yeir"[37]:

> My prince in God gif the guid grace   1
> Joy, glaidnes, confort, and solace,
> Play, pleasance, myrth and mirrie cheir
> In hansill of this guid new yeir.

May God give the King blessed fortune and all abundance of virtue and grace always to persist—good prosperity, good luck, happiness during earthly life! May God help him to rule and defend his realm and guide it in peace and justice, giving bliss wherever he goes, sending him many French crowns, high generous heart and willing hands!

The five short stanzas are what they say they are—a gift to handsel James's New Year, which one we do not know. The poem has the mark of a rather early one on it—it is gay, fresh, hopeful, and the reference to French crowns is the only hint we have of his personal designs on James's purse: he himself hopes to benefit from the French crowns (gold coins common in Scots use at the time) and the "hie liberall heart and handis not sweir". The note of disillusion has not yet set in, and the poem probably dates from his earliest days at court. In his edition, Mackay Mackenzie gives the first line as "My prince, in God gif the guid grace", supplying a comma after "prince". This is meaningless, and if a comma is to be supplied at all[38] for the convenience of the modern reader (in the Reidpeth Manuscript, from which it is taken, there is none) then it should be after "God": "My Prince in God, gif the guid grace", etc. This is a simple opening in which Dunbar wishes his divinely appointed king good grace, joy, gladness,

---

[37] 26 ("A New Year's Gift to the King").
[38] In fact Mackenzie should have let well alone.

K

etc. Only then does he go on to wish that God should add
the other desirable things. To make sense, Mackenzie would
have had to delete the word "in", which metrically is impossible.

Another intimate poem of address is "My Lordis of
Chalkir",[39] this time on his perennial theme of the empty
purse.

> My lordis of Chalkir, pleis yow to heir   1
> My coumpt, I sall it yow mak cleir
> Bot ony circumstance or so«u»nye;
> For left is nether corce nor cunyie
> Off all that I tuik in the yeir.

They need not tire their thumbs by counting his rents and livings,
nor to make their counters rattle nor spend ink or paper in
the receipt of Dunbar's sums. He got a sum of money from
the Lord Treasurer for subsistence; he can't say how it was
spent, but knows well that it is all gone—which he considers
too sore an account. He expected to have long enjoyed it in
town, but has no trouble now in carrying the remains. He
has no proof to offer except his empty purse, which cannot lie
to them under examination.

This poem strikes obvious links with the similar one to
the Lord Treasurer—are they close sequels? Is this all that
came of the great benefit he was to have from the Treasurer?
The note of irony struck in the mention of his rents and livings,
whereas he tells us that all he got was "Ane soume of money
for to wair", makes us wonder whether perhaps the poem to
the Treasurer is not ironical also, with its reference to his
pension, living rents, etc. Had he his tongue in his cheek?
Was the simple joy of it too simple, and hiding a satirical
grimace? We cannot know, since we cannot tie these two
occasional poems to one occasion: but we can be aware of
the problem.

Another minor poem touching on his poverty and lack of
benefice, though under the guise of a piece of meditative
"moralising"—so many poems of Dunbar which seem to be
something else boil down to satire or complaint about his

---

[39] 25 ("To the Lordis of the Kingis Chalkir").

penury—is the little poem "Four Maner of Folkis ar Evill to
Pleis "[40]:

> Four maner of folkis ar evill to pleis; I
> Ane is that riches hes and eis,
> Gold, silver, cattell, cornis, and ky,
> And wald have part fra utheris by.

Another is a great and powerful lord of land and rent but is
unable to govern or guide, and yet would have more from
"utheris by", other people besides. Another is of noble
blood, well-married to a good and beautiful woman, but is
not content and wants more from other people besides. The
fourth kind of people ill to please are those who drink as much
as they can hold, but still would have more from their neighbours besides. Dunbar sees no man in the world so fortunate
in material goods that he would not have more if he could
from his neighbours. But of all this wealth, whoever has it,
he Dunbar does not, for it all goes from him to other people
besides; especially so at this Christmas, he says, Sir Gold gives
not to Dunbar but to other people besides. Even if we did
not have Reidpeth's authority for attributing this poem to
Dunbar,[41] the complaint about his poverty contained in the
last two stanzas unmistakably stamps them as his. No other
known poet has quite that note of wry self-pity about his lack
of monetary appreciation. The poem is well-made and well-
up to Dunbar's level of competence without being a masterpiece.

There is another group of poems, all related to each
other, which also fall between the categories of moralisings
and complaints. As they are all on the theme of his experience
at court, and addressed either directly or indirectly to James,
they belong in this chapter. These are "Musing Allone this
Hinder Nicht",[42] "How Sould I Rewill Me",[43] "Off Every

---

[40] 23 ("Of Folkis Evill to Pleis").

[41] Bannatyne's manuscript leaves this poem anonymous: the version in Maitland's is lost, but Reidpeth obtained his version from it; and he attributes the
poem to Dunbar. Small does not include it in the S.T.S. edition: but on Reidpeth's authority (and by implication Maitland's) Mackay Mackenzie rightly
accepts it as his.

[42] 8 ("Of Deming").

[43] 9 ("How sall I Governe Me").

Asking",[44] "To Speik of Gift or Almous Deidis",[45] and "Eftir Geving I Speik of Taking".[46] The first of these is angled at James, and is a veiled defence against Dunbar's detractors at court, and ends by quoting the King himself against them, and even warning James that he himself is not exempt from the detractions of these defamers. The poem opens:

> Musing allone this hinder nicht   1
> Of mirry day quhen gone was licht,
>   Within ane garth undir a tre
> I hard a voce that said on hicht,
>   May na man now undemit be.

For though I should be a crowned monarch, the voice goes on, yet I shall not escape adverse criticism—some would call me good, but others would call them liars, and yet others would pray to God to end my reign. If I were a lord and not ostentatious enough, then every thief and pickpurse would say "Land would be better bestowed on me", even though he was unworthy to lead a dog. If I happened to be a fresh and comely lady, with gentlemen paying attention,

> Than will thay say, baith scho and hie,   18
> That I am jaipit lait and air;
>   Thus sall I nocht undemit be.

Were I courtier or knight, dressed as becomes my rank, they would call me full of pride—but may God send them a strong halter!

> Be I bot littill of stature,
> Thay call me catyve createure;
>   And be I grit of quantetie,
> Thay call me monstrowis of nature;
>   Thus can I nocht undemit be.

And if I am elegant in my speech, then the kitchen-maid says I am so stiff and affected that I do not speak like the household servants, though her own mouth needs leeching to take the

---

[44] 14 ("Of Discretioun in Asking").
[45] 15 ("Of Discretioun in Geving").
[46] 16 ("Of Discretioun in Taking").

poison out of it. But if these people knew how their gossip
seems to others, those who condemn their neighbours, their
vicious words and pride and gossiping tongues that pour out
everything, some of them would give up condemning. Were
it not for the fact that it would make matters worse, the voice
goes on, I would certainly cause the death of many, and many
cowards to end their life in sorrow. " Gude James the Ferd,
our nobill king", said very wisely when he was a young man,
"Do good, and put no trust in judging by others, for no man
shall escape judgment". And so by God's grace, the voice
ends, I shall keep his (James's) commandment in this matter,
always entreating the holy Trinity that I may have a place
in Heaven, for there no man shall be condemned.

The word "Deming" simply means "judging". But in
this poem it has the *nuance* of "condemning". It is interesting
to find Dunbar complaining of this vicious trait; for although
it is common enough in any human community, the post-
Reformation Scots have raised it almost to the status of a virtue.
The denunciation of "sinners" was a duty of Calvinist con-
gregations, and what was reported to the minister and elders
would be published before the whole congregation at a service,
and the offender "disciplined" before the whole congregation.
Burns sings jocularly of having to sit on the cutty stool before
the whole congregation, because he had been denounced as a
fornicator.[47] Whatever may be said in favour of this encour-
agement of gossip and tale-telling in relation to sin, amongst
the Scottish people it also fostered an atrabilious attitude of
denigratory prejudice in general; and, reinforced by ordinary
human weakness, and by those negative aspects of democracy
which find expression in the indignant protest that one man's as
good as another, and in the automatic dismissal of merit with
the cutting remark "Him? I kent his faither!" or "I mind
the time when he hadnae a pair o' shuin to his feet", that has
produced the negative reductivism which still is one of the
blackest traits in the Scottish character.

This poem of Dunbar's—is it not itself, like so much of

---

[47] In "The Rantin' Dog the Daddy o't", for example. Burns and Jean Armour
sat in the "creepie-chair" as fornicators in the summer of 1786, two or three
Sundays running.

his work, an example of the very thing he preaches against?—
suggests that we may be wrong in attributing to Calvinism so
much that is regarded as characteristically Scottish. It may be,
not that the Calvinist Kirk produced the dour Scot, but that
the dour Scot produced the Calvinist Kirk in Scotland.
Certainly the democratic temper inherent in Presbyterianism,
in its positive side, is also already evident in Dunbar's attitude
to the King. This reminds us that, although the Stewarts
were rulers "by divine right", they were still much closer to
the people than kings of other countries such as France or
England ever were, before their respective revolutions. The
Stewarts had a tradition, not merely of being accessible to
ordinary people, but of going among them incognito and
"keeping their ear to the ground". Some of them even wrote
folk-poetry—that is, were so much of the people that they
still inherited the great oral tradition as well as the literary
one.[48] The Scot is by nature gay, passionate, turbulent, quick
to rouse, quick to avenge, but also quick to forget and make
up: he is also dour, suspicious, parsimonious with the prudence
learned of long grim poverty, and saturnine. It is interesting
to find all these traits in Dunbar—the Knox and the Burns
sides of Scottish character—long before the triumph of Presbyterianism. Dunbar lived amidst the earliest rumblings of
the coming Reformation—his own satiric work was itself one
of these rumblings—and the Reformation had not become
objectively articulate in him. He confused social and personal
issues, taking general wrongs of his age as personal affronts
because he was not aware of or committed to the big leading
ideas of the Reformation, which would have given his satire
an objective frame of ideas. In the next generation, David
Lyndsay did identify himself with the broad sweeping current
of reform, and thus found such objectivity. But while this
limitation of Dunbar's robs him of a certain large force of
direction as the voice of a great movement, what we find in
him is all the more reliable as personal witness. And he bears
witness to the fact that all the traits of Scottish character were
there already. What the Reformation resulted in was the
suppression of the gay, passionate, sensual side—the Burns

[48] "Of Peblis to the Play", by James I, for example.

side—by the dour, solemn, prudent, grimly realist side—the
Knox side—so causing a split between them. In Dunbar they
co-exist in a loose integration, and much of his work is the
product of a conflict between the two—between the poet of
sensation and the priest of intuitive piety. It is a rich conflict,
and only a rich nature, national and personal, could have
experienced it. The type of conflict is common in poets, and
two major examples of this struggle in later times than Dunbar's
are Donne and Manley Hopkins.

These speculations are a digression from the poem, but they
do raise issues which previous reading has been forcing upon
us, and this was a good place to draw some of these inferences
towards an interpretation of Dunbar and his significance. But
now I return to the work of descriptive criticism. The satirical
element is bitter and vehement, the personal involvement, as
always, ruffling the surfaces of the verse from underneath, and
threatening the composure of the argument and even of the
verse. It does not quite do this: the argument is strong and
well-handled, the verse effortless and masterly with that easy
assurance which Dunbar always displays when he is working
in a four-stress or shorter line and close-rhymed stave. He
finds his greatest freedom in the tightest bonds, when he is at
his best: but any slackening of poetic energy and prophetic
ire makes him the captive of his form, and this typically shows
in the last stanza. His final stanzas are often weak and trite
in this way, and would be better struck out—would have been,
since only the poet can do so.

Here, as always, the use of a refrain gives the poem focus
and keeps him from wandering too much, and expending too
much spirit in the waste of corruption under review. He uses
refrains rather like a minister of later times preaching on a
text, expounding, illustrating, coming back to, interpreting,
applying to contemporary cases, turning it on the assembled
audience or congregation, with sly digs here and there to this
one and that one, knowing precisely whose withers are going
to be wrung at just this point, and deliberately looking in
another direction as he utters it. The rhythm is sure and
subtle—his main innovation in Scottish poetry in succession to
Henrysoun was the introduction of subtler rhythms, more

personal involvement and vehemence, and the use of a wide
range of lyrical forms with shorter lines in place of the traditional five-stress narrative line in which Henrysoun had worked,
and had achieved his best work. There is something almost
presbyterian about the poem, Dunbar in a ministerish mood,
sober, polite, sometimes even unctuous and ingratiating,
sentimental-pious, but critical and even waspish, and knowing
his audience so well that he knows just whose hide will be
pierced by just what dart, exactly how many birds will be hit
by exactly which stone. It is uncanny, and a bit chilling.
The last stanza, too, which I have said is trite and weak, is
rather like the minister ending up his sermon with a hurried,
muttered, conventional "And now may the Lord make His
Face to shine upon you ". . . while the congregation look pious,
preparatory to loosening the tension with the odd cough, sigh,
rustle of hymn book, and surreptitious glance round to see
whether you gave yourself away over that bit about cheating
the grocer.

"How sould I Rewill me" goes on dealing with the same
subject as "Musing Allone this Hinder Nicht", and is obviously
a companion to it:

> How sall I governe me or in quhat wys,   1
> I wald sum wyse man wald devys;
>   Sen I can leif in no degre,
> Bot sum my maneris will dispys,
>   Lord God, how suld I governe me?

Dunbar has been much admired for his "wide range", and
justly: but equally remarkable is the narrow harping on one
topic, wringing it dry, hammering us with it—or more properly
hammering James IV with it—and not letting anyone forget
it. This is as it should be in a satirist: as long as the injustice
remains, so long must the attack go on. This subject of
"deming" is a case in point. Dunbar goes on to say that if
he is cheerful, gallant, and gay, then people will say that he
is out of his mind, or somebody has been charitable to him.
If he is sad and depressed, then they will say he is insane and
does nothing but mope as if he wanted to die; so both man
and boy will "deme" him. If he is generous, well bred, and

humane, they will say he is out of his mind, although he is of
a noble line. If he is gay, they will say he has a mistress, or
is proud and haughty, or that his gaiety is ill-gotten. On the
other hand, if he is not presentably dressed, they will say he
is up to no good—you can tell by his clothes.

> Gif I be sene in court our lang,   31
> Than will thai quhisper thame amang,
>   My friendis ar nocht worth ane fle,
> That I sa lang but gwerdon gang.
>   Lord God, how suld I governe me?

But if then he earns reward in court, they have malice and
envy and lie about him secretly and privately slander him.
How should he organise his conduct? If he is thrifty, he is
despised; if he is courteous, noble, and generous, then he is
counted a squanderer. Since everything is condemned, both
good and evil, and he is unable to halt any man's tongue, he
will make up his mind to do his best, let everybody say what they
will, and the gracious God may govern him.

Thus again he ends on the godly note, but this time with
more force and appositeness than in the poem previously
considered. How to get by without guilt is the question that
should never be asked, being impossible. Imperfection is not
a problem to be solved, but a cross to be borne: and in so
far as the carping of other people is not entirely malicious, the
answer is charity. If I am not mistaken the reference to the
court in the stanza that I have just quoted is another sly dig
at James, and at the same time insinuates that his enemies
consider the King not worth "ane fle". This is typical of
Dunbar's subtle, multiple-take shafts: he reminds James that
he is neglecting Dunbar, suggests that because of this people
think he is not worth a fly/flea, and at the same time exposes
his own enemies to the King's anger. His barbs are explosive,
wounding not only the man they hit but the people around
him as well. Dunbar is vengeful, deeply self-centred and ego-
centred, and no man could say with more accuracy "*Nemo me
impune lacessit*"—the Scottish national motto. He is prickly
and defensive, easy to wound, slow to heal, and savage as a
wild beast when wounded and cornered. Being a passionate

man, his passions run to evil as well as good, to the negative
as well as the positive, to destruction as well as creation. If
frustrated, such a man is a fiend—Iago was such a character—
but, fulfilled, may be as generous and open as Shakespeare
himself.

Is there another reason for this chip-on-the-shoulder of
Dunbar's? Is it solely his neglect at court he complains of:
or is there some deeper, undeclared motive, such as his small
stature, or illegitimacy, or sexual frustration, or the harsh lot
of a younger son? It was so deep set that psycho-analysis
could not have reached it, but he does give the impression
of a man who has lost not only his present due for services
rendered, but his heritage also. Has this perhaps a sexual
connotation—had his celibacy begotten in him an unconscious
feeling of being castrated? The note of failure is struck in
the love-poems, if they may be so called—the poems on women,
anyway—and the bitterness and savagery of some of his denunciation of them is too intense to be other than subjective.
The conflict over celibacy in a man of Dunbar's rich and
sensuous nature may be enough to count as cause, but one
senses a deeper *malaise* than that. It is not only "sex" that
is at issue here: the Church was charitable enough over lapses
in this direction: but marriage and children. Dunbar had
great tenderness in him, and such a man needs children almost
as a woman does. Not only his sexual drives were frustrated,
but also his paternal ones. The prime heritage of every born
man is to be a father of children: priests of true vocation can
sublimate this paternal drive into "fathering" of the flock:
but Dunbar seems never to have had a true vocation to the
priesthood, and so got the worst of both worlds. This question
of vocation I will return to when considering "This Nycht,
befoir the Dawing Cleir":[49] but when considering the deep
melancholy revealed here and there in the court satires and
complaints, one should be aware of these questions and should
wonder whether there is, under the monetary complaint, a
more painful one still at a deeper emotional level.

The heritage of a man is manhood: a man may lose all
his property, and still be a man: but the loss of his procreative

[49] 4 ("How Dumbar was Desyrd to be ane Freir").

function robs him of his minimal heritage as a man. Did
Dunbar feel this castration of the spirit? In any case, we do
feel in his work the deep and chronic complaint of a man who
has been robbed of his heritage, and as much in these two
poems as in any of the others.

The three poems of "Discretioun" are outwardly moralisings, like the above: but they are in fact on the same theme
of his ill-treatment at court, and are full of complaint and satire.
He generalises from the particular of his own case, and the
milieu of the poems is the court of James IV. In "Off Every
Asking"[50] he says:

> Off every asking followis nocht   I
> Rewaird, bot gif sum caus war wrocht;
>   And quhair caus is, men weill ma sie,
> And quhair nane is, it wilbe thocht:
>   In asking sowld discretioun be.

A fool, whether he has good reason or not, always cries in a
droning voice "Give me!" while he who always drones like
a bee should have a hearer as deaf as stone. One asks more
than he deserves, one less than he serves, and the like of Dunbar
himself is ashamed to ask but starves totally without payment:
(this argues that the poem is quite early, for he does not long
remain too ashamed to ask). To ask for payment without
giving service is bad for the reputation; but to ask payment
for service given is not culpable, for to give service and live in
beggary is shameful to both master and man. Some may
spoil the best of service by boasting and by begging at very
inopportune moments—few words are enough for the wise.
There is no need for man to be dumb; without some words
one gets nothing; not speed but diligence is what matters, for
nothing comes of speed alone. Requesting should be done at
appropriate time in appropriate places, with leisure and room,
without haste or thronging of crowds, without self-abasement,
and without careless speech. Some people who might, with
a little care, have been told yes, through too great labour get
the answer "No", because they can't wait for the right time,
thus losing both need and honour. He ends up with a

[50] 14 ("Of Discretioun in Asking").

philosophic shrug which, if admirably reasonable, he obviously found too hard to live up to:

> Suppois the servand be lang unquit,   41
> The lord sumtyme rewaird will it;
>   Gife he dois not, quhat remedy?
> To fecht with fortoun is no wit:
> In asking sowld discretioun be.

The years of being "lang unquit" soon soured that super-human resolve.

This poem, like its companion pieces, is one of the best, most objective, measured, argued, and organised, of the begging poems—for begging poem is essentially what it is. It is a rather prim, school-marmish essay, perhaps to be read at court, but in the King's presence, and looking to him, as to a headmaster, for approval—and of course giving him many a nod and hint as to who are most deserving, and to one most deserving in particular. The clear intelligence, the subtlety and complexity of mind and feeling, the quality of temper and of thought, are evidence throughout of his remarkable gifts. The poem is traditional, influenced by the admirable debating schools, and by his study of rhetoric and logic: but, as always, Dunbar uses the traditional forms and material not as ends in themselves, art for art's sake, but as weapons provided by God for him to carve his way with in the world. It is this shameless utilitarianism of Dunbar's use of traditional forms that gives his poems their extraordinary freshness, vitality, and personality. He is not just doing exercises: he is fighting a campaign, and the conventional weapons are hot with the fire of battle.

"To Speik of Gift or Almous Deidis"[51] is, logically, the second of these poems. It opens:

> To speik of gift or almous deidis;   I
> Sum gevis for merit and for meidis;
>   Sum warldly honour to uphie
> Gevis to thame that no thing nedis;
> In geving sowld discretioun be.

---

[51] 15 ("Of Discretioun in Geving").

Some give out of pride and vain glory, some grudgingly as if
it hurt; some for the supply of their needs, and some for only
twice as much in return.   Some give out of gratitude, some out
of fear, some out of wealth give money and others give food,
while some give only promises (a jibe at James?).   Some give
nothing at all.   Some (and here surely comes William Dunbar)
have to wait so long that their gratitude is exhausted and
wasted:

> Sum is for gift sa lang requyrd,   16
> Qhuill that the crevar be so tyrd
>   That, or the gift deliverit be,
> Then thank is frustrat and expyrd:
>   In geving sowld discretioun be.

One gives too little so niggardly that his gifts are not valued,
he is regarded as a miser, and the whole world cries "Fie"
upon him.   Some are so generous in giving that they overload
a barge and cause vice and prodigality to crush out honour.
Some give (a perpetual complaint against James) possessions
to the rich who might easily do without these further gifts, and
though a poor man should die of want, his cry is not heard by
them (compare with the poems directly addressed to James).
Some give (here he takes yet another kick at his *bête noire*
Damian) to strangers with new faces who have just flown in
from Flanders, and have no desire to take notice of old servants
(this surely is the final proof that James is the target, and that
the poems belong in this section), no matter how great their
virtue might be.   Some give to those who can complain slily,
others to those who can flatter and dissemble: but some give
to men of probity and disdain all gossip-mongers.   Some give
fine clothes and gifts to men for swearing that all their patrons
say is true, though they well know the contrary to be the case:
there are many such in these days, he adds, reminding us
again of other poems, "A General Satyre" in particular.   One
gives to good men for their qualities, another to deceivers and
scolds; some give authority to rogues of whom but few are
found worthy of office.   Some give parishes right and left,
churches dedicated to St Bernard and St Bridget, that they
might teach, rule, and supervise, although they are unfit by
lack of intelligence even to govern themselves.

This poem is much the same as "Off Every Asking", but is much more openly angled at James, and lets us see the cards in the poet's hand. Dunbar was a typical extravert, finding it difficult to hide anything: he is one of the frankest and most outspoken writers of any sort in any age, and though he has the subtlety and sophistication for the studied deceit, he has no temper for this approach; and his natural impatience with sly sophistry, although it was the staple of courtly intrigue, keeps breaking through. Dunbar cannot "distance" his work as Henrysoun and Chaucer could: he is the least detached of poets apart from Villon, and this is at once his main achievement and his chief limitation.

The third poem of the group is "Eftir Geving I Speik of Taking".[52] He tells us himself that this one follows the poem on giving:

> Eftir geving I speik of taking,   I
> Bot littill of ony gud forsaiking.
>   Sum takkis our littill awtoritie,
> And sum our meikle, and that is glaiking:
>   In taking sowld discretioun be.

Some, he says, take benefices by brawling, some from Peter and some from Paul, but so long as they get their rents they don't care whether the Devil takes every last soul of their flocks. Barons take from the poor tenants all the fruit that grows in the field, and by money-rents and grass-taxes raised too high force the poor to beg from door to door (compare with other poems, particularly "Of Covetyce").[53] Merchants take unlawful profit, which often makes their packs very meagre; by their heirs one may see that illgotten gains don't enrich the kin. Some take other men's leasings and oppress the poor, and never remember that they must die for it, until the gallows stretch them. Some take by sea and land and can never hold their hand from taking until they are tied up to a tree, which forces them to understand. One, if he could, would take all his neighbour's possessions, if he had as little fear of men as he has of God. If Dunbar himself stood in no more awe of man than of God, then he would be able to take both

---

[52] 16 ("Of Discretioun in Taking").   [53] 67 (same title).

odd and even, a bit of everything he might see—such justice is not worth a clod.

> Sum wald tak all this warldis breid   41
> And yit not satisfeit of thair neid,
>   Throw hairt unsatiable and gredie;
> Sum wald tak littill, and can not speid;
>   In taking sowld discretioun be.

Great men are made very famous at Court of Sessioun (see "Sic Tydingis hard I at the Sessioun" for comparison) because of robbery and oppression, while poor thieves are hanged, and their forebears and heirs (unlike the kin of baronial land-grabbers) shamed for ever.

This poem has more satiric content than the other two, being yet another exposure of the vice of the society of his time, and the villainies, hiding behind law for the most part, committed by the ruling and middle classes against the producers of wealth—the working-classes. All three estates (the working-class, the "fourth" and largest estate, as it would have been, had no representation in the Scottish Parliament), the clergy, the land-owners (to give them their correct designation and deny them the ludicrously inappropriate title of "nobility", which quality they conspicuously lacked), and the merchant-bourgeoisie are all attacked in the first four stanzas, and throughout the poem. Again, the material is traditional: Dante had crowded out his Hell with the same classes for committing similar outrages already in the early years of the fourteenth century: but Dunbar, as usual, gives it a fresh turn by writing out of his own actual experience of these crimes, and shows them to be on the increase. The Edinburgh of Dunbar's time was two hundred years further gone in economic "freedom" from morality than the Florence of Dante (1265-1321). Dunbar here is preaching again in the sermon tradition: but there is another side to this preaching: he is also teaching the King, educating him in his duties, helping to sharpen his perception, informing his mind, and above all teaching him to make balanced judgments of value—which clearly was a lesson James never did learn.

This role of teacher of kings was of course one of the

traditional functions of bards of the first order; and, after
Dunbar, Lyndsay bore an even more tutorial relation to James
V, and George Buchanan (not only a great scholar, but the best
Latin poet of his day) had the schooling of the wretched James
VI in his rigorous and punishing hands. This is worth mentioning, because we hear so much from Dunbar about the degradation of his position at court that we are apt to forget that this
is relative to a previous high status traditionally accorded to
Scottish poets at court, and that even in his own degraded
position Dunbar obviously has an extraordinary licence to
speak out and denounce royal and other courtly shortcomings,
however ungratefully this might be received.

There is another fault with which Dunbar might have charged
James, but doesn't: a reluctance to pay liberally for the rod
that beats him. Dunbar must have been a rather uncomfortable person to have around, like a personal gadfly, an upsetter
of royal complacency, a professional contradictor to tell you
your favourite pastimes are crime, your wisest moves sheer
folly, your friends unmitigated scoundrels, your ebullient
romantic nature sheer irresponsibility. It is the duty of a poet,
or any writer worthy of the name, to be an irritant in society,
constantly criticising, carping, raging, refusing to play the blind-
man's bluff of politics, of pretending that everything is all right
when it obviously isn't—indeed never can be, before the coming
of the millennium; the duty to be an eternal opposition with
no intention ever of becoming the government and without
knowing what to do with power if he had it.

To glance, for once, at the problem from James's eyes, to
have a professional and highly competent busy-body always
poking his nose into his affairs and exposing his weakness and
folly, instead of flattering him as his surrounding sycophants
did, must have been very uncomfortable. So much so, that
this may have been why he hit back at Dunbar, as society
does at poets and writers today, in the only way he could
without earning total contempt from the civilised minority of
the world—through his pocket, and through his status. It is
wicked, but human. From a tactical point of view it is sheer
incompetent folly, because, whereas a poet's mouth may be
stopped by excess of food and drink, starving never did anything

but make the dog bark louder than ever: witness William Dunbar. A dog may bite the hand that feeds it, but not so ferociously as it bites the hand that refuses to feed it.

There are a few more of these poems chiefly of complaint angled at the King—this chapter surely makes it clear that they bulk larger than any other *genre* in Dunbar—before we pass on to other courtly poems. The most unusual of these is "This Hinder Nicht, Halff Sleiping as I Lay",[54] which is a complaint in the form of an allegory: yet one more example of the impossibility of confining any of Dunbar's poems to any one "kind", with a few exceptions. In this poem he tells us how

> This hinder nycht, halff sleiping as I lay,   1
> Me thocht my chalmir in ane new aray
>   Wes all depent with mony divers hew,
>   Of all the nobill storyis ald and new,
> Sen oure first father formed was of clay.

It seemed to him that the sky brightened all over with lamp-light, and many vigorous people entered, some old, some young, variously dressed, singing, dancing, or playing on instruments, or disporting with light hearts. He thinks, what a wild tumult this is—or does his intelligence waver?—a good company: and if he is wrong and it is a "feindly fantasie", then may Jesus and Mary defend him.[55] Neither their pleasant song, tune, nor joy overflowed into his heart, for it seemed to him that the dreary damsel Distress and her sorry sister Heaviness (Depression) lay heavy as lead above him in bed. Languor sits at the head of his bed playing mournful songs on dead instruments, so that an hour seemed a year to him. Ladies come dancing in, Nobleness in front, saying with benign and womanly manner that she sees an oppressed man lying in bed, and asking her sisters to help him obtain grace.

> With that anon did start out of a dance   31
> Twa sisteris callit Confort and Plesance,
>   And with two harpis did begin to sing,
>   Bot I thairof mycht tak na rejoseing,
> My heavines opprest me with sic mischance.

---

[54] 60 ("The Dream").
[55] Reidpeth's manuscript shows "freindly" and is copied by editors: but Reidpeth must have misread "feindly", essential to the meaning.

L

They saw that he grew no happier; and a lady called Perceiving says that Heaviness so weighs on him that he is not pleased to hear the melody, she and her sister Distress so grieve him. Nobleness asks how he can escape them. Then Discretion answers, and says that if they do as she directs, she will make him sing and dance and drive Languor away long before night. Wit backs her up, saying if they don't follow Discretion, they won't follow her either, and Discretion goes on to say that she understands his malady, and that Nobleness can cure him.

> Or evir this wicht at heart be haill and feir,   51
> Both thow and I most in the court appeir,
>   For he hes lang maid service thair in vane:
>   With sum rewaird we mane him quyt againe,
> Now in the honour of this guid new yeir.

Consideration wishes them well, and promises to keep the dance going. Then a man called Blind Affection says he will go before them, as he has authority over the whole court. Reason says, that is true, but that the time is now come when he alone should distribute everything, as men have always blamed the deeds of Blind Affection. It is time that Dunbar had something, he who has long been a servant to the King and has never been able to flatter or feign in all his life, but has humbly complained in verse and patiently endured his torture. Reason advises him to be merry and jocular, for Nobleness will find his remedy. Discretion approves, saying Reason would be worth many a pound to this Kingdom if he sat with the Lords of Session. Then Inopportunity speaks, and says they will need his help, for he always stands before the King's face deafening him or making himself hoarse, and must be served before Dunbar. The King, he says, will sooner favour one busy asker than two servants loyally about his business; and an asker loses nothing whereas a servant loses long service— no joke. Then comes a mighty shoulderer of clerical responsibilities:

> Than com anon ane callit Sir Johne Kirkpakar,   86
> Off many cures ane michtie undertaker,
>   Quod he, "I am possest in kirkis sevin,
>   And yitt I think thai grow sall till ellevin
> Or he be servit in ane, yone ballat makar."

Then Sir Beat-the-Church says, "So that I may prosper, I have four or five busy servants directed all to various holdings, and waiting for the deaths of churchmen from whom I hope to hear some news soon". Reason says, this is an odd imbalance, that one man should have seven churches, whereas seven as good as he have none; this world is overcome by greed, and sufficiency and moderation live only in Heaven. Temperance says, this is not blameworthy, for while he may hold the balance, the King will choose wrongly and upset it—"Quha best can rewll wald maist have governance". Patience tells Dunbar to take heart and wait upon the King with humble countenance, for the King has noble intentions. He has no desire, even for a bishop's rents, that Dunbar should go unrewarded for half a year. Then, like phantoms, they rushed to the door and fired a gun which made such a rude noise that all the air roared; and it seemed to Dunbar that the gun broke asunder on Leith sands, and he awoke at once with the noise.

Thus ends the hundred-and-fifteen-line poem with the gun device mentioned elsewhere, reminiscent particularly of "The Goldyn Targe", with which this poem has also allegorical affinities. The reference to James "not for ane bischopperikis rent" letting Dunbar go unrewarded for half a year would seem to suggest that James himself drew rents from such sources before making a new appointment—bishoprics returning to the King under the laws of "*sede vacante*" on the death of a bishop. The invitation to abuse is obvious, and Dunbar here seems to be referring to some particular seat held by James for several months without making an appointment, but meantime drawing its rents. The mixture of conventions here—the dream-plus-allegory used for a satirical-cum-complaint theme—is unsatisfactory. The allegorical machinery is too cumbersome for the subject, which, being personal, concrete, and direct, should have that kind of treatment. Dunbar's best poems of this type are the ones so treated. The impersonal, abstract, circumlocutory nature of the dream-allegory is at odds with the theme, and the result is a weakening of the impact of the complaint. This, however, is yet another approach to James, another experiment in finding an approach that will stir his sympathy. Allegory of its nature demands a high and universal subject, and the pettiness (comparatively) of the theme here gives the poem the appearance of a rather bad joke, as of a rather distasteful burlesque. The high idealism of the allegory is mocked by the earthy materialism of the subject, like a clown aping a hero: at best it has something of the comic pathos of Don Quixote emulating a knight of romance. Dunbar is never very happy in the five-stress-line stanza, but here it moves well enough, though tending to diffuseness, slackness, lacking the taut springiness of his work in shorter lines: he walks less surely than he dances. The poem is more of a curiosity than an achievement.

All these poems of complaint and satire on court-life might be described as "negative"—attacks on bad behaviour at court. But there is one poem in which Dunbar sets out positively what he considers to be good behaviour at court, for the courtier. In "To Dwell in Court"[56] we find Dunbar playing the unusual role of tutor to a young friend new to court life—Dunbar as a sort of prating avuncular Polonius. If you want to live in court, my friend, he says, envy no rank for its gift of fortune (strange advice from the poet we have been considering); look about you and listen, giving your tongue a rest, for too much talk is an attribute of vanity. Never force yourself to lie out of malice, nor bother yourself, my son, to rule others who will not be ruled—he rules well that can conduct himself well.

> Bewar qhome to thy counsale thow discure,   9
>   For trewth dwellis nocht ay for that trewth appeiris:
> Put not thyne honour into aventure;
>   Ane freind may be thy fo as fortoun steiris:
>   In company cheis honorable feiris,
>   And fra vyle folkis draw the far on syd;
>   The Psalme sayis, *Cum sancto sanctus eiris*:
>   He rewlis weill, that weill him self can gyd.

One should be patient, although possessing no lordly rank, for exalted virtue may establish itself in low estate. Be content, and you will have no need of anything more; but if you are not, then

---

[56] 41 ("Rewl of Anis Self").

desire will create strife for ever, until death says "Checkmate". Though everything in the world were yours, who can resist the serpent of envy and malice? Flee from the company of those who are in bad repute, from all false tongues full of flattery, and from scolds who may put you to shame; for your own reputation will depend on the company you keep. Flee dangerous stories founded on envy, never argue with self-willed men, my son, for no reason may convert nor pacify them. Do not be a whisperer in a corner (this image of whisperers in corners is a favourite one with him: see, for example, "Be Divers Wyis"),[57] for nobody will trust you if you do. Don't be a scorner, for it will recoil on you, and beware of counselling anybody too far gone in pride. And since you see so many things changing, do all your work with whole heart and carefully. Rely on God as your friend faithfully, and He will stand by you in bad luck: and be not in any way contemptuous of the poor, nor wrong any man.

This poem, of course, is in the moralising vein, but the particular courtly material and the implied criticism of court life merits its inclusion here. That Dunbar himself may have tried to live by these precepts is possible: that he failed to do so is evidenced by poem after poem in which he breaks most of his own rules. The poem may be a piece of quite innocent hypocrisy, and it is well that Dunbar himself did not succeed in taking his own advice to be respectable and prudent and quiet and not tramp on anybody's toes nor envy other men their good luck—we would have had nothing out of him but poems as dull as this one. One should not, however, press the charge of hypocrisy, for a man may quite genuinely advise a younger man not to make the mistakes that he himself has made and can't help making. One thing, however, stands out: Dunbar is one of the most self-conscious of poets, always seeing himself as others see him, or trying to: this, perhaps, is the reason why he is so concerned about whisperers in corners. Are they whispering about *him*? This is not the same as the audience-consciousness of the bard, of any artist who knows he is trying to express something for his people rather than solely for himself. Barbour, Hary, Burns, and other Scots

[57] 29 ("Aganis the Solistaris in Court").

poets have this kind of audience-consciousness, as have Shakespeare, Dante, Villon, Marlowe, Milton, Chaucer, as had Homer and Virgil, as have all major poets. But this thing of Dunbar's is a different kind of thing altogether, being self-centred, fearful and unhealthy.

The last poem to be considered in this chapter—but by no means the last poem of court life—is "Schir, for Your Grace".[58] This too is a complaint to the King, but leads over to another person central to Dunbar's life at court—the Queen. Johne Thomsoun, or Joan Thomson, is a popular name for the eternal husband-dominating wife. Dunbar wishes that the King *would* allow himself to be dominated by his wife:

> Schir, for your Grace bayth nicht and day, 1
> Richt hartlie on my kneis I pray,
> With all devotioun that I can,
> God gif ye war Johne Thomsounis man!

If this were so, it would be well for Dunbar, he goes on. He would not be without benefice, his hard fortune would be ended. Some pity would rest in James, if only for her sake, the fairest and best in Britian since it began. It would do no sort of harm if one so fair and good as the Queen won such honour by her virtue. Dunbar would give all that he ever had if the King would vow to the Swan to be Joan Thomson's man for one year.

> The mersy of that sweit meik Rois 21
> Suld soft yow, Thirsill, I suppois,
> Quhois pykis throw me so reuthles ran;
> God gif ye war Johne Thomsounis man.

> My advocat, bayth fair and sweit,
> The hale rejosing of my spreit,
> Wald speid in to my erand than;
> And ye war anis Johne Thomsounis man.

> Ever quhen I think yow harde or dour
> Or mercyles in my succour,
> Than pray I God and sweit Sanct An,
> Gif that ye war Johne Thomsounis man.

---

[58] 18 ("To the King that He war Johne Thomosunis (*sic*) Man").

The reference to the "Swan" is to the medieval custom of
swearing solemn vows over the swan or peacock at a royal
feast (the swan being royal game).[59] This poem tells us clearly
that Dunbar had hit it off with the child Queen (which may
add some force to my remarks on Dunbar's tenderness and its
importance in a parent-child relationship). The poem is, of
course, addressed to the King, but can one really imagine it
making a very good impression on him? It is even a little
despicable, certainly pathetic, that a major poet should be
thus dependent on a young girl. But despite its address, may
it not have been really meant for the Queen's eyes, saying
about her to somebody else—as it would seem—what could
not be said about her to her face? Dunbar would be courting
quite serious dislike and even danger in claiming too much
through being a favourite of the Queen—or did his white
"mane" privilege him? These speculations admittedly are
of little help, but the questions are there to be asked. The
poem remains a curiosity, well-turned, pathetic, with a rather
weak humour. But it leads over into poems in which the Queen
herself is the direct object of address, or is involved in some
way, rather than the King.

I have here quite deliberately put the case—and it is
Dunbar's own case—against James and his court: the opposite
case has been put *ad nauseam* by previous critics. Dunbar, of
course, like all men, had a complex motivation—moral,
personal, social, and unconscious—now one uppermost, now
another. Much of his criticism of the Church is a medieval
convention, though he adds to it from his own sharp vision.
But if it be said that I am unfair to James because of what he
did for Dunbar, I must answer, what *did* he do for Dunbar?
And how late?

---

[59] *The Poems of William Dunbar*, ed. Small, S.T.S., III. 298, par. 19; the feast
need not be "royal".

VII

Madame, Ye Heff a Dangerous Dog

In the most successful of his petitionary poems Dunbar managed to get a new coat for Christmas out of the King. In "Madame, Ye Heff a Dangerous Dog",[1] his efforts to get a new doublet out of the Queen are frustrated by her wardrobe master, who is too strong a personality to be managed by the child Queen (she was thirteen when she married James in 1503). Dunbar, however, invokes the Muse as well as the Queen against him:

> The wardraipper of Venus boure   1
> To giff a doublet he is als doure
> As it war off ane futt syd frog:
> Madame, ye heff a dangerous Dog.

When Dunbar showed him the Queen's seal and order, he, Dog, turned on him and barked as if he were worrying a pig. When Dunbar showed him the Queen's own hand-writing, Dog snarled, so that Dunbar was afraid he might be bitten—he wishes him a heavy beam round his neck. When Dunbar spoke to him in a friendly manner, he barked like a midden cur chasing cattle through a bog. This powerful mastiff is strong enough to keep her wardrobe overnight from the great Sultan Gog-ma-gog himself, but too big to be the Queen's lap-dog:

> He is owre meikle to be your messan   21
> Madame, I red ye get a less ane,
> His gang garris all your chalmeris schog:
> Madame, ye heff a dangerous Dog.

This invocation of the power of the bard against the wardrobe-master has its effect, bringing Dog to heel with alacrity, to Dunbar's satisfaction. In the sequel, "He is na

[1] 33 ("Of James Dog, Kepar of the Quenis Wardrop: To the Quene").

Dog; He is a Lam",[2] also of twenty-four lines, he tells her that James is in fact no Dog, but a Lamb:

> O gracious Princes, guid and fair,   1
> Do weill to James your Wardraipair;
> Quhais faythfull bruder maist freind I am:
> He is na Dog; he is a Lam.

Though Dunbar joked about him in a ballad, he spoke no word in malice, but only to amuse her ladyship.

> Your Hienes can nocht gett ane meter   9
> To keip your wardrope, nor discreter
> To rewle your robbis and dres the sam:
> He is na Dog; he is a Lam.

But Dog's wife, who would willingly break his shins with the tongs, should be drowned in a dam. The wife who would make a cuckold of Dog should be well battered both back and sides with a barrow-shaft. Dog has so well obeyed Dunbar that he prays no such sufferings should ever make him sad.

"In malice spack I nevir ane woord", says Dunbar, "Bot all, my dame, to do your gam". Certainly the poems are light-hearted enough, but to amuse the Queen in the manner of the first one was very likely to be a bit too serious for good clean fun to the wretched Dog, striking, as it did, at his very job. Dunbar never hit one target, when he could possibly hit two with the same shaft; and the more targets he could hit the better. It seems clear that, under cover of fun, he was also showing the Dog the whip, and making it quite clear that, so good was Dunbar's standing with the Queen, so barbed his poetic arrows, that Dog had better keep in with him for his own good. The marked change in the second poem shows that Dog was not too dim-witted to take the point. Certain things stand out from these little poems: the closeness of Dunbar's relation to the Queen, and the mixture of lightness, tenderness, and respect with which he addresses her, are most notable. He treats her as a commanding figure, matriarchal, queenly; and, at the same time, lightly as a child who needs to be amused and also protected: as one who likes her fun, needs a mastiff to protect her clothes, but even more needs a

[2] 34 ("Of the Same James quhen He had Plesett Him").

lap-dog to fondle. Dunbar, in fact, is playing the role of a nice old daddy-figure who at once treats the child as if she were a grown and commanding woman, yet subtly meets her in her real immaturity. Girls are apt to love such a person: they are flattered by the attentions of the fatherly man at once treating them as if they were great motherly women, yet at the same time having a father's tender affection, undemanding, light, not leaning too heavily on them, not being too exacting of responsibility. The "Gray Horse, Auld Dumbar", would be just such a figure to the young Queen: and this may account for the good relationship he clearly had with her. An elderly poet would be particularly well-equipped for the role of good-daddy.

Another point is that he need not, for all her youth, be shy of talking of such things as cuckoldry to the young Queen. Other poems will bring out that, in fact, he could talk the most outrageous language to her without the least danger of shocking her—and indeed, since he sees himself in the role of entertainer in her duller moments, she must have relished a pretty coarse strain of talk. Lastly, there is quite a strong affection for James Dog running underneath the banter, revealing another side of Dunbar—the capacity for friendly loyalty. There is a homeliness about these poems, almost a cosiness as of the paterfamilias at his own fireside, which we do not easily associate with Dunbar, that disconsolate haunter of chilly courts. They are little *genre* pieces, Flemish[3] interiors, clear, realistic, warm, and unforced. We see Dog clearly before our eyes, a large, shambling, heavy creature with a saturnine grumbling face, heavy jowl, and probably rather bloodshot eyes, gruff but not unkindly, his "bark worse than his bite". His tread "garris all your chalmeris schog" with its massive lumberingness. Yet he is "bruder" to Dunbar, the small squat poet with the quick eye and mind. We know him better than almost any character in Dunbar's work—from the outside at least. We don't know him from the inside as we get to know "The tua mariit wemen and the wedo". These poems are among the best of Dunbar's minor pieces.

[3] The possible Flemish influence on Dunbar has been remarked, but never fully explained.

Another interior piece is "A Mirrear Dance Mycht Na Man See".[4] Again we have the lightness and gaiety, Dunbar in his warmest and most engaging mood as a happy dancer, the cosiness of the Queen's chambers, not the cold Hell of the King's court with its whisperers in corners and various corrupt factions. In the Queen's company Dunbar seems to melt and unbend into a suppler, tenderer, warmer person. In this poem he tells how Sir John Sinclair led off the dance (no doubt with the Queen herself), he being newly arrived from a French mission: but no matter what he might do, one foot always went against the other and would not agree with it. Somebody said, "Take away the Queen's knight". No man is likely to see a merrier dance.

> Than cam in Maistir Robert Scha: 8
> He leuket as he culd lern tham a;
>   Bot ay his ane futt did waver,
>   He stackert lyk ane strummall aver,
>   That hopschakellt war aboin the kne:
>   To seik fra Sterling to Stranaver,
>   A mirrear dance mycht no man see.

Then the master almoner comes in, a clumsy awkward shuffler like a steer staggering among the rye. His hips made a hideous noise many a time, and the jester, John Bute, said, "Woe's me, he's dirtied himself—Fie, fie!" But after these incompetents comes a *real* dancer:

> Than cam in Dunbar the Mackar;   22
> On all the flure thair was nane frackar,
>   And thair he dancet the dirrye dantoun;
>   He hoppit lyk a pillie wanton
>   For luff of Musgraeffe, men tellis me;
>   He trippet quhill he tint his panton:
>   A mirrear dance mycht na man se.

Then Mistress Musgrave came in, she could have taught all the rest, and when Dunbar saw her dance so neatly with such good carriage and countenance, then he wished for her sake that he was the greatest earl or duke in France. She is followed by Dame Dountebore—God knows what sour looks she gave—

---

[4] 32 ("Of a Danse in the Quenis Chalmer").

who made such rumblings with her hips when she was busily dancing that a blast of wind slipped from her and nobody could help laughing. After some five or six had come into the dance, the Queen's Dog began to stretch himself, burst out of his leash, and shaped up to the dance like a mastiff—some said he stank like a cur. This poem brings out Dunbar's intimacy with the Queen, and the nature of it, for this, like the other two poems mentioning Dog, is clearly meant to amuse the Queen with a write-up of an actual dance.

The picture of the lumbering old courtiers shuffling round, one with the Queen herself at only arm's length—and she would be a dancer—is finely contrasted with that of Dunbar in wild and gay mood leaping about in the "dirrye dantoun" until his slipper flies off. The reference to Musgrave is too light to be taken very seriously: she was the wife of Sir John Musgrave, and Dunbar probably would not have dared go any further than flattering banter—with the wish that he might be exalted enough to woo her. She was one of the Queen's principal attendants, and Dunbar would have every reason to keep in her good books without over-playing his hand. Unlike the other personages in the poem, all attested by historical documents, "Dame Dounteboir" seems to be a nickname: it was commonly applied to ladies' maids, and sometimes had a comic and lascivious *nuance*. The coarseness of what we might call "anal comedy" was traditionally accepted by the age, but the frequency of coarseness in the poems to the Queen makes one suspect that Margaret had a particular relish of it. Does this argue a vein of bitter disillusionment in her? She had reason enough, having been virtually traded to James in the first year of her teens; by the time of his death, when she was still only twenty-three, she had borne only one live child, or one, at least, who remained alive long enough to become James V: and she knew what it was to have an openly faithless husband. Dunbar himself, we know, had a streak of sexual disillusionment and represssion in him, and such men are apt to indulge in the sort of coarseness which degrades or at least deglamourises sexual love by associating it with other physical functions: but Dunbar must have known that the Queen had a taste for this or he would not have dared expose her to quite

so much of it. This is a very important point. Here we have
Dunbar in his happiest mood with a swift dancing measure
and a light gay theme. His association with the Queen seems
to have unbuttoned him and to have released his happier
creative energies, so that he bubbles and effervesces in verse
gaily and uninhibitedly, instead of brooding heavily over his
wrongs. He responds, like most poets, to the feminine influence.

"Madam, Your Men Said Thai wald Ryd"[5] is another
poem which bears out the uninhibited coarseness that Dunbar
allowed himself when addressing the Queen—if it be the
Queen, for there is no proof, but obvious circumstantial
evidence. This poem has given, and gives, great trouble of
interpretation and has never really been satisfactorily con-
strued. It opens:

> Madam, your men said thai wald ryd   1
> And latt this Fasterrennis evin ower slyd;
>   Bott than thair wyffis cam furth in flockis
> And baid tham betteis som abyd
>   Att haem and lib tham of the pockis.

The phrase "betteis som" has been variously read as "Betty's
summons"; as "Beatson", meaning a surgeon possibly in the
court employ;[6] and, since the Reidpeth MS. gives "son"
instead of "som" (as in the Maitland), as the "sound of Betty's
voice, i.e. the wife's";[7] and Mr M. P. McDiarmid, correctly
reading "son" as "at once" has offered "dogs at once stay
where they were". All these are unsatisfactory. No Beatson,
a surgeon, appears in the Exchequer Rolls from 1488 to 1522,
and the history of the Baty or Beatson (from Bartholomew)
clan of border rievers in the Solway area suggests that they
were most unlikely to provide the court with a surgeon, though
one was, appropriately, a falconer. I cannot trace Mr
McDiarmid's gloss of "betteis" as "dogs" (unless he is glossing
it "baty", a large dog); but he is right about one thing—
that "betteis" is not a possessive but a plural, the typical "-is"
Scots plural ending. But there is a word "bet", or "bete",
with various other spellings, which does fit the poem. In the

---

[5] 31 ("To the Quene").
[6] Baxter, *William Dunbar*, p. 64n.
[7] *The Poems of William Dunbar*, ed. Small, S.T.S., iii. p. 285-6.

plural, it means variously "remedies", "needful things", "strokes of punishment", "repairs", "mendings", etc. Now this is "Fasterennis evin", when all sins have to be shriven before the feast preceding the long fast of Lent—it is the end of Shrove-tide. What more proper to the poem, then, than this: "Madam, your men said they would ride out on foray and evade the duties of penance and shriving and feasting proper to Fastern's Eve, but their wives came out like flocks of sheep and ordered them to endure certain ("som") remedies, penances at home"—or "ordered them to endure at once ("son") remedies, penances at home"—"in order to cure themselves of the pox", which, like all illness in the Middle Ages, is regarded as punishment for sin. In other words, they are to be shriven and cured, not to ride out in evasion: "libbin" can mean either "cutting" or "curing by magic potions or charms", or, I suspect but cannot prove, "curing by religious confession and penance". The word "pockis" can mean sheep-rot, anthrax, a disease in which sheep develop a large pustule under the skin, treated by cutting; and also "syphilis". It can also mean "bags" or "pokes" in modern Scots. Dunbar is playing on all these meanings at once, but it is clear that the phrase was a cant one of the time for irregular sexual inter-course, "that perrellous play/That men callis libbin of the pockis". Was there a theory, magical and superstitious, but a primitive apprehension of the principle of inoculation, that the best cure for syphilis was to be found at the source—in intercourse? Anyway, clearly the phrase had some jocular and cant significance to Dunbar and his contemporaries which escapes us to-day, involving the ideas of sexual intercourse, cutting of sheep-rot pustules, curing of syphilis, and the like. There is a sexual innuendo in "pockis" as "bags", the scrotum, not unlike the innuendo on "purs" in "My panefull purs so prickillis me", where "purs" is at once money-bag and scrotum. That Dunbar does not entirely and simply mean syphilis by "pockis" is clear from his later reference to "the Spanye pockis", in which syphilis is specifically intended: according to R. S. Morton,[8] it was then thought that the great epidemic

<hr/>

[8] Cp. R. S. Morton, in *British Journal of Venereal Diseases*, 38 (No.4), pp. 175 ff. I am grateful to Mr A. J. Aitken for drawing my attention to this article.

of syphilis in the 1490's, which gave rise to the Act of 1497 by
James IV in which incurables were ordered to be sent to
Inchkeith, was caused by the Spanish sailors returning from
the New World. Morton says that this was a false theory,
but it did give rise to the name "Spanish pox" as a popular
term for syphilis.

Dunbar goes on to say that, as the Queen is not yet moving
court (probably a reference to the habit of the court moving
from castle to castle to eat up their rents in kind, moving on
when the stores were exhausted, or, more relevantly here,
when the stench of ordure from many retainers could no longer
be borne), her men now propose to have a feast of venery,
though they prove no cocks in the field: it would have been
better had they ridden off than stayed to let their wives "breid
the pockis". Some of these men, he goes on, were so randy
that they broke open doors and tore off locks to get at a wench
on a plea that they might "lib thame of the pockis". Some
who were randy as rams are now made tame as lambs and
settled down like any sorry ewes (note all this sheep imagery
in relation to "pockis" as sheep-rot), and have given up all
such sports as men call "libbin of the pockis". Some who
thought themselves strong as giants are now weak as willow
wands, with shins sharp as distaffs, able to span their own
waists, because of too often "libbin of the pockis". Dunbar
saw young whores near him leading young men to their
houses—such would be better lying in the stocks, for some
young men would not leave brothel-going till they got the
Spanish pox. He ends by exhorting all young men to stay
away from harlots, lest they repent (shrove theme) the en-
counter, and to beware of "that perrellous play/That men callis
libbin of the pockis".

The poem is not worth the energy spent on construing it,
being an inferior and distasteful thing, though morally serious
enough under the jocularity. Its value is more historical and
social than poetic.

The last poem directly concerning the Queen and
known to be by Dunbar is a very different one—"Blythe
Aberdeane".[9]

⁹ 64 ("To Aberdein").

This is Dunbar in his rare official garb as aureate court poet celebrating a state function, or event:

> Blyth Aberdeane, thow beriall of all tounis   I
>   The lamp of bewtie, bountie, and blythnes;
> Unto the heaven «ascendit» thy renoun is
>   Off vertew, wisdome, and of worthines;
>   He nottit is thy name of nobilnes,
>   Into the cuming of oure lustie Quein,
>   The wall of wealth, guid cheir, and mirrines:
>   Be blyth and blisfull, burgh of Aberdein.

He goes on to describe how first the burghers of the town met her, richly attired as became them, with four young men of renown in gowns of velvet to bear a pall of crimson above her head, as had been the custom, and great noise of artillery. Then she is met by a fair procession at the port, in caps of gold and silk, and she enters the streets to the sound of minstrelsy and salutations to the Virgin. Then they (the burghers, presumably) make the three wise men in the procession offer to the Christ-child gold, incense and myrrh, humbly treating Him as a king of greatest magnificence; then the angel with the sword drives Adam and Eve from Paradise for disobedience. Then the Bruce—one of the few references to Scottish history in Dunbar's work—is "gart" come riding by crowned as king, bold in battle, awesome, strong, large of stature, noble, and fierce, like the mighty champion he was. Then the noble Stewarts are "gart" spring up with new green branches to gladden the whole town. Twenty-four young maids follow, dressed in resplendent green, hair like threads of gold tressed under white caps finely embroidered, playing on timbrels and singing sweetly—this becoming cortege in seemly order meets the Queen, saluting her reverently. The streets were all hung with tapestry and a great crowd of people gathered about and played enjoyable pageants very well. The liegemen all bowed to their lady, who was escorted by a regal throng of great barons and beautiful women. The commons shouted their welcome to the Queen.

The Town Cross, he tells us, ran with wine joyfully at her coming:

> At hir cuming great was the mirth and joy,   57
>   For at thair croce aboundantlie rane wyne;
> Untill hir ludgeing the toun did hir convoy;
> Hir for to treit thai sett thair haill ingyne,
> Ane riche present thai did till hir propyne,
>   Ane costlie coup that large thing wald contene,
> Coverit and full of cunyeitt gold rycht fyne:
>   Be blyth and blisfull, burcht of Aberdein.

He ends by addressing the Queen: O mighty princess, pleasant and peerless, you have great cause to thank this noble town which did not spare their possessions, riches, substance, and person to do you honour, to welcome you in the best possible manner; they sought every way and means to please you— therefore, as you bear the crown long, so long be thankful to this "burcht of Aberdein".

A very different poem from the preceding ones, but very different also from the picture he paints of Edinburgh in his poem to the merchants of that city, and elsewhere. It is sad stuff to find Dunbar of the biting line, the corrosive image, descending to such inarticulate flabby maundering as "Ane costlie coup that large thing wald contene"—ane costlie line that large wind wald distene. And such graphic imagery as "cunyeitt gold rycht fyne" must have cost him effort and appeals to the Muse. This is cub-reporter stuff, for all its finery—"Our Special Correspondent writes . . ." The poem is conventional journeyman verse, of little value except as social history—Dunbar was a natural social historian in verse.

I have remarked elsewhere[10] on the vision of affluence given by the ostentation of having wine flow at the Town Cross, and on the very limited amount of wine usually so run. Yet (although Dunbar's handling of the long line is unsure and tends to be loose) the poem has colour, freshness, and, at its best, a certain majesty; and it does indeed bring over a picture of a more colourful, visually brighter age, with deft touches of custom and *genre*-painting. Readers who want to make out a case for attributing the anonymous poem on London to Dunbar may find some support here, in the Aberdeen one.

There are two poems addressed to Margaret which are

---

[10] Above, p. 16.

M

commonly attributed to Dunbar, although in fact they are anonymous in the manuscript. My rule has been throughout not to consider such poems as Dunbar's: but one of them, if not both, I feel strongly to be his. It is "Welcum of Scotland to be Quene",[11] a salute to the young Princess when she first came to Scotland:

> Now fayre, fayrest off everie fayre,   I
> Princes most plesant and preclare,
> The lustyest one alyve that byne,
> Welcum of Scotland to be Quene.

The three further staves rave on—she is a young tender plant of imperial blood, a flower of great beauty, a sweet desirable loveable spotless lady, a dear daughter of a most mighty king, etc.: welcome, O rose, both red and white, welcome, O flower of our delight, our secret rejoicing from the beams of the sun, "Welcum of Scotland to be Quene." The manuscript gives the notes of a musical setting but of one only of several parts, and that not the melody, it seems.[12] I know of no other direct evidence that Dunbar (if this be by Dunbar) wrote to tunes or was set to music: there is work here for musical scholars to devote time to: but feel convinced that many of his forms were drawn from songs originating in France. In the chapter on his metric I will return to this point.

"Gladethe Thoue Queyne of Scottis Regioun"[13] is almost certainly by the same hand, for it repeats whole phrases, or at least the same phrases appear in both, whichever came first—for example, "Welcum of Scotland to be Quene" has "younge tender plant of pulcritud", and "Gladethe Thoue Queyne" has "ying tender plaunt of plesand pulcritude", "descendyd of Imperyalle blude", "chosin of hye Imperiale blud" and many others. "Gladethe Thoue Queyne" opens:

> Gladethe thoue Queyne of Scottis regioun,   I
> Ying tendir plaunt of plesand pulcritude,
> Fresche flour of youthe, new germyng to burgeoun,
> Our perle of price, our princes fair and gud,

---

[11] 89 ("To the Princess Margaret").
[12] Mackay Mackenzie discusses it in his edition. p. 231.
[13] 89 (same title).

Our chairbunkle chosin of hye Imperiale blud,
    Our Rois Riale, most reverent under croune,
Joy be and grace onto thi Selcitud.
    Gladethe thoue Queyne of Scottis regioun.

The remaining three stanzas simply pile up the attributes, the last one mentioning Margaret by name—the first of course has a play on "perle", also Margaret. The use of aureate diction in this poem is strongly reminiscent of the final stanzas of "The Thrissill and the Rois", the same play being made with the flower imagery, royal blood, and so on. It is hard to believe that any other poet had quite that style and note of exaltation—there would surely be some idiosyncratic difference marking a different personality, even in such a conventional style. This makes me feel strongly that both these poems are by Dunbar, and that no other man could have written them. Dunbar had created such a style for himself, deliberately woven and embroidered, and no other man could have worn this mantle without revealing some trace of the different shape underneath. J. W. Baxter also attributes these poems to Dunbar, and he rejects many others which might have got past a less exacting critic.[14]

Such are the poems relating directly to the Queen—two or three "official" panegyrics, and some very earthy stuff indeed; if the earth be not defiled by such a comparison. There is one other poem, not directly addressed to the Queen, but to my mind almost certainly meant "to do hir gam"— to amuse her and her attendant lords and ladies. On the strength of the taste for strong sexual comedy revealed in these minor poems, and the atmosphere of gaiety, fun of a somewhat scurrilous nature, entertainment and amusement running through the poems addressed to the Queen, I feel convinced that this one was written also for her amusement. It happens to be Dunbar's longest and major work, "The Tretis of the Tua Mariit Wemen and the Wedo"; and it demands a chapter to itself. But before considering it there is one other poem must be looked at first, partly because it relates to the court directly, but chiefly because some of the technique of the

---

[14] J. W. Baxter, *William Dunbar*, Edinburgh 1950, p. 225.

"Tretis" cannot be understood before we have discussed its unique scurrility—"The Flyting of Dunbar and Kennedy". This strange, indeed unique poem, if it deserves the name of poem, develops the technique of extreme abuse which is used in some of the poems of court satire, and is an essential part of the "Tretis".

VIII

Flyting to Use Richt Gritly I Eschame

"THE Flyting of Dunbar and Kennedy"[1] has a very simple structure. It opens with Dunbar addressing his "second" in the coming duel, "Schir Johine the Ros", in three octaves, five-stress, rhyming *a b a b b c c b*. He tells Ross that Kennedy and his second, Quinting, have been miscalling him, as a challenge to a flyting, and goes on to say that he despises flyting as unworthy of a poet; but that if he must take action against Kennedy, he will shake the universe with his wrath:

> Bot wondir laith wer I to be ane baird;   17
>   Flyting to use richt gritly I eschame;
> For it is nowthir wynning nor rewaird,
>   Bot tinsale baith of honour and of fame,
>   Incres of sorrow, sklander, and evill name;
> Yit micht thay be sa bald in thar bakbytting
> To gar me ryme and rais the feynd with flytting,
>   And throw all cuntreis and kinrikis thame proclame.

Flyting neither wins nor gains reward, but is loss both of honour and of fame. Kennedy takes up the warning with a challenge of three similar stanzas:

> Dirtin Dunbar, quhome on blawis thow thy boist?   25
>   Pretendand the to wryte sic skaldit skrowis,
> Ramowd rebard, thow fall doun att the roist,
>   My laureat lettres at the and I lowis . . .

He goes on to denounce Dunbar and threaten to silence him for ever. It is clear that Kennedy is the one who is making the running and forcing the duel on Dunbar, who, in his own words, regards such use of poetic talent as an Irish (Gaelic) barbarity beneath his dignity. There follow twenty-five similar octaves from Dunbar against Kennedy, rhyming *a b a b b c c b*.

---

[1] 6 (same title).

The whole thing is a tour-de-force of the most outrageous abuse of each other, and I don't intend to dwell on details, but shall condense.

Dunbar opens out on Kennedy thus:

> Iersch brybour baird, vyle beggar with thy brattis   49
> Cuntbittin crawdoun Kennedy, coward of kynd,
> Evill farit and dryit, as Denseman on the rattis
> Like as the gleddis had on thy gule snowt dynd.

After more of the same vintage, he accuses Kennedy of having tried to "undo our Lordis cheif" in Paisley, and of being so cowardly that he waited until Dunbar had sailed for Europe before he dared stir up his malicious mind against him. Dunbar has now come home, after hard sea trials, to denounce him. He decries Kennedy's poetic ability (technically no whit below Dunbar's in this poem, but of a coarser grain and sensibility), which is limited to the Gaelic custom, he says, of flyting. Kennedy has little knowledge of true poetry and how to write it. Kennedy's poverty, state of health (he is said, for example, to be both syphilitic and gonorrhoeal), appearance, and skinny raw-boned personage are scorned. Even Quinting (or Quintane), Kennedy's second, despises him as a sponger and beggar. His character, misfortunes, his wolfish looks, his loathsome lodging-house (an ex-leper-house), his mistress, and their way of living together, are all denounced as criminal and depraved. His leprous appearance is described as frightening people like a dead thief in a halter. This kind of stuff is repeated *ad nauseam*, and his venereal disease and its treatment are described revoltingly, but vividly. Kennedy has been hunted in a borrowed beggar's gown through the streets by urchins. His table-cloth needs no spreading, for there is nothing to put on it, like that of a beardless rhymester. He has never bestridden a horse (chivalry reference, is low-born), but is a barefoot yokel who brings the Carrick clay to Edinburgh Cross, his shoes letting straw:

> Thow bringis the Carrik clay to Edinburgh cors   211
> Upoun thy botingis, hobland, hard as horne;
> Stra wispis hingis owt, quhair that the wattis ar worne.

If he comes near Edinburgh again the schools will be emptied
to hound him down the streets, the boys will chase him as
crows chase an owl, and women take in their washing at mere
sight of him, boys and dogs at his heels and fish-wives pelting
him with offal as he runs.   The last two stanzas pile up execra-
tions in triple and internal rhyme:

> Mauch muttoun, byt buttoun, peilit gluttoun, air to Hilhous;   241
>   Rank beggar, ostir dregar foule fleggar in the flet;
> Chittirlilling, ruch rilling, lik schilling in the milhous;
>   Baird rehatour, theif of natour, fals tratour, feyndis gett . . .

and so on, ending by threatening to kill him if he doesn't
surrender to Dunbar.

After this wallow in the pigstye of Dunbar's attack, we
take a header into the byre of Kennedy's retort.   He opens
with a string of abuse:

> Dathane devillis sone and dragon dispitous,   249
>   Abironis birth, and bred with Beliall;
> Wod werwolf, worme, and scorpion vennemous,
>   Lucifers laid, fowll feyndis face infernall;
> Sodomyt, syphareit fra sanctis celestiall . . .

threatening to silence Dunbar—no empty boast, it would
seem.   The name "Dunbar" is really "Dewlbeir", he says,
meaning born of a devil upon a she-bear.   Dunbar's ancestor
thus born was Corspatrick, the traitor who betrayed his
country (this part is true) to Edward I of England, and who
was therefore responsible for the appalling massacre of Berwick
by Edward, and for the cruel English occupation.   For this
reason, argues Kennedy, the whole house of Dunbar is held
(this also is true) in execration.   He says he will "put silence
to" Dunbar—a Gaelic idiom which occurs twice in Kennedy's
stanzas, and betrays the Gaelic cast of his mind—and puts a
curse on him.   Kennedy has a real stick to beat Dunbar with,
for to this day Corspatrick the traitor is execrated in Scotland,
and he makes the most of it, delving deep into history:

> Wallace gart cry ane counsale in to Perth   281
>   And callit Corspatrick tratour be his style;
> That dampnit dragone drew him in diserth
>   And said he kend bot Wallace king in Kyle:

Out of Dumbar that theif he maid exyle
Unto Edward and Inglis grund agane:
Tigris, serpentis, and taidis will remane
In Dumbar wallis, todis, wolffis and beistis vyle.

The "Dumbar" there of course is the castle, not the man, who
is named only "Corspatrick". Kennedy goes on to say that
Dunbar must acknowledge him king and cower before Quintane
offering submission to him—otherwise he will be burned alive.
In one of the few passages of genuine satire (as distinct from
abuse) in the poem, Kennedy says that whereas *he* repaired
to Mount Parnassus at a time when the fountain ran sweet and
clear, Dunbar had come in March (Corspatrick was Earl of
March) and drunk frog-spawn from a pool there. (The man
who was able to write this was a genuine poet of rare satiric
gifts—one wonders whether so much would be thought of
Dunbar if Kennedy's work had survived in comparable bulk.)
Kennedy draws the inference—this is why Dunbar writes
nonsense in gluey rhymes and diction (a reference to aureation?).

Gaelic, he goes on, is the true language of Scotsmen
("Scots" at this time meant Gaelic, in fact, in contrast to
"Inglis"), and he denounces Dunbar's attack on it as typical
of the traitorous house of Dunbar. He boasts of his lands and
possessions and jeers at Dunbar's empty purse, and he contrasts
the "Dewlbeir" family with the true "Dunbars" of Westfield.
Rejecting Dunbar's accusation that he tried to poison the King,
he claims to be a blood relation of James, whereas Dunbar's
forebears did homage to Edward (true, but so did the Bruce
family and many others exonerated later: did James perhaps
really hold this against Dunbar, and was this part of the reason
for his ill-treatment of him?). Dunbar has begged through the
land, he says, and been driven into exile in France, where he
ought to have remained as apprentice to the hangman. He
must pack up and go now, for he has no influence at court,
where no lord will employ him (again, this may be due to the
real hatred of the Corspatrick Dunbars in Scotland). At sea
in the *Katerina*, Dunbar made a foul mess of the ship with vomit
and diarrhoea, and had to be put ashore at the Bass Rock.
Dunbar ought to make his way to England and there earn his
living as a horse-marshal, which he should call himself at court

(horse-marshal, or veterinary surgeon—if there is truth in this assertion of Kennedy's that Dunbar called himself such at court, it might throw a glancing light on "Schir, Lat it Nevir in Toun be Tauld").

Kennedy then calls himself the "Rose of Rhetoric" (this rose by any other name would smell as foul), jibes at Dunbar's lack of benefice—who would give a benefice to such a beast? Kennedy, too, builds up into a crescendo of abuse, becoming more and more fantastic toward its foul end:

> Deulbere, thy spere of were but feir, thou yelde,   545
>   Hangit, mangit, eddir-stangit, strynde stultorum,
> To me, maist hie Kenydie, and flee the felde,
>   Pickit, wickit, convickit Lamp Lollardorum.
>   Defamyt, blamyt, schamyt, Primus Paganorum.
> Out, out, I schout, apon that snowt that snevillis.
> Tale tellare, rebellare, induellar wyth the devillis,
>   Spynk, sink with stynk ad Tertara Termagorum.

Thus ends the most repellent poem known to me in any language—a penance to read and write about, but essential to the understanding of Dunbar, and in particular his major work—"The Tretis".

The *genre* seems to be a descendant of the Greek "agon", is a relative of the Provençal *tenson*, though that was more of a debate, like Dunbar's *Merle and the Nychtingaill*, and Mackay Mackenzie says pieces of the type are known in Arabic, and, of course, in Celtic.[2] Dunbar clearly considers it to be a product of Gaelic tradition, as he knows it, and considers it beneath him, being fit only for a Gaelic bard who can't do anything better. In Bannatyne's manuscript,[3] we are invited at the end to judge "quha gat the war": on which matter I am in no doubt—both "gat the war": but as Kennedy clearly defeated Dunbar in terms of the contest, he probably gets the "warrer", being the more disgraced by the more disgraceful performance. He does, however, stick closer to the truth than Dunbar seems to do, and certainly takes the

---

[2] Mackay Mackenzie, intro., p. xxxii.
[3] The poem is found in Bannatyne's, Maitland's, Reidpeth's, and the Asloan MSS., and in the Chepman and M--llar prints (in which also the "Tretis" appears).

genre more seriously. The poem is a mine for social historians of the period and scholars of Dunbar, but here we are concerned with it only as poetry: not as evidence, but as value.

The question of the value of a poem depends on what that poem is meant to do, and what it does. What this poem does not, is satirise. The nature and purpose of satire is to expose and correct certain social and moral abuses of the author's age and society—vices which offend the satirist's vision of the good society and the good life. Its purpose is to reveal the contradictions which undermine and destroy society and life, re-establish a true sense of values, either negatively by denouncing the false, or positively by setting the true against the false, or a mixture of these approaches. This purpose is essentially creative and certainly curative, and its attack is on vices, not on persons. Flyting, on the contrary, seeks to vilify persons, is an exercise in personal vilification in which truth is demonstrably scorned (no persons could be such monsters as Kennedy and Dunbar make each other out to be—it is not humanly possible) and exaggeration reaches gargantuan proportions. The aim is purely destructive, no good is allowed the other person, no hint of possible redemption allowed to lighten the dark picture. In pursuit of this destructive aim, all human values, such as truth, pity, goodness, love, charity, and even mere justice, are sacrificed. Flyting is a kind of verbal all-in wrestling in which two literary brutes perform (and, like so many all-in wrestlers, often with their tongues in their cheeks) for the entertainment of a brutal and depraved audience. One person tries to annihilate the reputation of another, to destroy him socially for all time. This is clearly an unmitigated evil. It may be argued that the sheer extravagance of the form robs it of all reality, so that it has only a humorous effect: this no doubt is the excuse for indulgence in the *genre*. But true humour is laughter at ourselves, not at others' real or imaginary discomfort. Humour, in itself, is amoral: it may be either good or bad. The humour of a Roman audience watching Christians being devoured by lions is clearly a symptom of dehumanisation to something worse than beastly: humour at other people's expense is less evil only in degree: but the ability to smile at our own foibles and minor setbacks helps us to accept life and

to live better, thus doing ourselves and others good. The kind
of "humour" one finds in flyting is clearly at other people's
expense, and is a very ugly humour indeed.

Another case for the defence of flyting may be made out—
that, like Greek tragedy, it has a cathartic effect, isolating the
emotion of hate, building it up in the audience, and discharging
it so that the emotion is purified as a result and may thereafter
take its place in an integrated personality. This is the most
charitable view that one can take of the *genre*. Unfortunately,
the evidence points in the other direction. Hate grows by what
it feeds on, like most passions; and, unlike tragedy, flyting
does not have any climax which discharges the emotion—it
has merely a crescendo, as we have seen. Flyting was enjoyed
rather because it toughened and coarsened the sensibility, so
making it fitter for a tough and coarse life. It was cultivated
precisely because it encouraged brutality and cut-throat
competition in a society which valued these "qualities". The
social power-game is made easier if you can hate your com-
petitors—it thrives on hate. The opposite of hate, if only a
polar and not an absolute opposite, is love. Love and individual competitiveness are incompatible—you cannot sacrifice yourself to your neighbour and your neighbour to yourself
at the same time. That is why Yeshu of Nazareth developed
a religion of love (already implicit in Judaism and recapitulated
by and incarnated in him) against the power-mad acquisitive
society of Rome, and why this religion triumphed over Rome.
Flyting is akin to the brutality of the Roman arena, and played
to the same kind of depraved taste. In such contests the gladi-
ators both lose, and only the audience "win". Dunbar shows
his superior sensibility in scorning the *genre* altogether: but
the audience must have its fun; and if Dunbar had disdained
his competitor's challenge for fame and reward, he would have
lost face at court. Dunbar was the moral superior before the
flyting began at all. This "audience" was not, as might be
supposed, the dregs of humanity, the wretched masses hopelessly brutalised by poverty and despair—it was the court of
James IV, in Scotland's "Golden Age". In the ensuing reigns,
the reality of "flyting", as distinct from the literary form of it,
had to be put down by law—that crudest and most elementary

of human sanctions which it is rare to find in advance of human sensibility instead of lagging far behind.

The "Flyting" has many poetic merits and is a *tour-de-force* of language and versification, but it must be condemned as a whole, being to poetry much what slander is to life. Its values are execrable: poverty is derided, disease scorned, misfortune rejoiced in, and people blamed for things over which they have no control whatsoever, such as heredity. Behind it is the vile superstition that the unfortunate are being "punished" for their sins—altogether the thing is a poor testimonial to fifteen hundred years' worship of the God of Love, and of Forgiveness. One can almost reduce the "Flyting" to a rule, and that the rule of anti-Christ. You turn Christian values upside-down—hate instead of love, vengeance instead of forgiveness, meanness instead of charity, suspicion instead of faith, despair instead of hope, folly instead of prudence, injustice instead of justice. This is the world of the poem, and a vile world it is. For all its great technical skill—and for all its revelation of the high standard achieved technically, not only by Dunbar, but also by Kennedy—this is a thoroughly "bad" poem. Poetry is not merely verse, nor wealth of language, nor any other merely technical or clever thing: it is the spirit of life more abundant making these merely technical matters into a thing of life-giving virtue, breathing into us the spirit of life and of goodness, truth, and beauty— and the greatest poetry adds the more difficult and intangible quality of holiness. The "Flyting" is an anti-poem.

It can be said that the "Flyting" may be seen as "non-sense-verse"—but in fact it has none of the innocence of such. That it has great rhetorical force and "langage at large" I admit. That it is evidence of court amusement is true: but what amusement, and therefore what a court! Yet it is true that without a community taste for and appreciation of poetry, even such poetry, it could have not been at all. Lastly, and most importantly, the "Tretis" could not have been written without a flyting technique: and it is to the "Tretis" that we now turn.

IX

Quhilk Wald Ye Waill to Your Wif?

D UNBAR, the poet of courtly love, Dunbar the poet of women, Dunbar the satirist of social vice, Dunbar the castigator of the court of James IV, Dunbar the ribald entertainer doing the Queen's "gam," and Dunbar the flyter, all unite in the "Tretis of the Tua Mariit Wemen and the Wedo"[1] with yet another Dunbar—the poet of alliterative romance. The Queen's influence tended to liberate him, raise his spirits, bring him out, perhaps even inspire him: in this poem he throws away the French corset of rhymed metric and opens out into a maty, bustling, utterly native metre:

> Apon the Midsummer evin, mirriest of nichtis,   I
> I muvit furth allane, neir as midnicht wes past,
> Besyd ane gudlie grein garth, full of gay flouris,
> Hegeit, of ane huge hicht, with hawthorne treis
> Quhairon ane bird on ane bransche so birst out hir notis
> That never ane blythfullar bird wes on the beuche hard:
> Quhat throw the sugarat sound of hir sang glaid,
> And throw the savour sanative of the sueit flouris,
> I drew in derne to the dyk to dirkin eftir mirthis;
> The dew donkit the daill and dynnit the foulis.

The most notable feature of Dunbar's verse in general is its pace: this alliterative metre, the one native to Teutonic languages as distinct from Romance ones, allows him greater freedom of pace, the stress nature of Scots (and English) breaking free altogether of the syllabic nature of French verse, encouraging the vigorous use of native words and the tendency to alliteration. The regularity of the main stresses (four to a line, normally) and irregularity of the uncounted non-stress syllables bring out the true rhythm of Scots, and at last we are hearing the natural unforced voice of Dunbar in his most

---

[1] 47 (same title).

relaxed and least "put-on" manner. He is chatty, sociable, gossipy, engaging, and frank—a tale-teller who button-holes us with a confident bubbling gaiety, not holding us grimly like the Ancient Mariner, but fascinating us by his enthusiastic assurance that you will be as eager to hear as he is to tell this tale. Yet the apparatus of the poetry of *amour courtois* is there, and the diction close to that of "The Goldyn Targe", close to aureation—"savour sanative", for example—and the high-flown style of romance. It is, in fact, a fairly typical alliterative romance opening so far—the alliterative romances lingered longer in favour in Scotland than they did in England, and, as James Kinsley points out, the alliterative metre had come to be associated with sophisticated courtly poetry in the reign of James IV. [2] Yet the note of sly comedy is struck, too, in the phrase "to dirkin eftir mirthis"—we know already that this is not quite going to be a solemn allegory of the "Rose" type. He goes on to tell how he hears "under ane holyn hevinlie grein hewit" a high speech with haughty words, nearby, and pushes in to the hedge so hard that he is concealed by pleasant sheltering leaves: then he peeps through to see whether anybody will approach.

He sees three gay ladies sitting in a green arbour all decked with garlands of fine fresh flowers, their glorious golden tresses glittering like gold so that all the grass gleamed with bright colours. Their beautiful hair was combed and carefully shed above their shoulders and set with kerchiefs of a fine fabric. Their mantles were green like the grass of May, and fastened about their sides by their white fingers. Their meek faces were of wonderfully fine aspect, all full of flourishing beauty, like flowers in June, white and sweet as lilies. Nature surrounded them with all manner of rich verdure, full of fresh odours.

> Ane cumlie tabill coverit wes befoir tha cleir ladeis,   34
> With ryalle cowpis apon rawis of ryche wynis.

This reminds us of a very different poem (so far)—the one about the "twa cummeris" whom Lent made lean. Two of these fair beauties, he goes on, were married to "lordis" and the third was a widow secretly of loose conduct. As they

² *William Dunbar: Selected Poems*, ed. Kinsley, Oxford 1958, Intro.

chatted and gossiped, they drank more and more wine, so
that their tongues were loosened.

> Bewrie, said the wedo, ye woddit wemen ying,   41
> Quhat mirth ye fand in maryage, sen ye war menis wyffis;
> Reveill gif ye rewit that rakles conditioun?
> Or gif that ever ye luffit leyd upon lyf mair
> Nor thame that ye your fayth hes festnit for ever?
> Or gif ye think, had ye chois, that ye wald cheis better?
> Think ye nocht it ane blist band that bindis so fast,
>   That none undo it a deill may bot the deith ane . . .

Here, beginning at l. 41, the romance style is dropped—it is
not a tale of romance we are to hear, but a discussion of
marriage—that "rakles conditioun". Not only of marriage,
but of extra-marital relations, and whether the women could
choose better if they were allowed—women had no choice in
feudal marriage, at least conventionally. The note of *amour
courtois* and the high aureate style give way before the chilling
irony of the query—don't you think it a blessed bond that
binds so tightly? The question is rhetorical, the widow has
declared her cynical attitude there already. The tone now is
conversational, and we see a new virtue in—and reason for—
Dunbar's use of the alliterative line. Then comes the shattering
reply of the first wife, setting the whole tone of the discussion:

> Than spak ane lusty belyf with lustie efferris:
> It, that ye call the blist band that bindis so fast,
> Is bair of blis, and bailfull, and greit barrat wirkis.
> Ye speir, had I fre chois, gif I wald cheis better?
> Chenyeis ay ar to eschew; and changeis ar sueit:
> Sic cursit chance till eschew, had I my chois anis,
> Out of the chenyeis of ane churle I chaip suld for evir.

Marriage should be made only for a year's living together, for
longer is but folly, unless really wanted by the couple. It is
against the law of love, of mankind, of nature, to force together
hearts which conflict with each other. Birds have a better
law than men, taking mates for one year only, and changing
them every year (this bird tradition was common in medieval
literature, as in Chaucer's *Parlement of Foulis* and Holland's
Howlat—the latter being one of the last examples of it: the

genre probably stems from the School of Chartres). "Cryst gif sic ane consuetude war in this kin haldin", she goes on, for then women would for ever be free (here natural and moral law are invoked to uphold life against a social custom which thwarts and perverts life, as feudal marriage does—the play is all on the question of freedom of choice). Women would then take what lovers they wanted and desert all impotent ones (impotence is the key to her complaint: but it argues the strength of female sexual feelings).

The first wife goes on to indulge in a fantasy of "freedom": she would dress up and search for new lovers at fairs, plays, preachings, and pilgrimages (can the influence of the Wife of Bath be discerned here?): wherever there was a crowd of people, she would be there exhibiting her charms, noising her beauty abroad so that she might as a result be able to choose, and be chosen, as her whim suited (it never occurs to her that if she *had* the choice, she might feel differently: in Ibsen's *Lady from the Sea* this matter of freedom of choice for women is thrashed out, and Ellida, when allowed to choose between her husband and her lover, chooses her husband, but of her own free will).

She goes on to say that when she had chosen herself a lusty young paramour for a year and had had him for about a month, she would search about in church (this exposes her "religion"), market-place (where women had a modicum of freedom to look round), and the King's court (this shows her "breeding" and what it is worth), to spy out the likely gallants for her next year's choice. She would always go for bold, strong young fellows (this shows her materialism, and perhaps also her youth—it is not the spiritual power of the male she appreciates, but animal sexual vigour):

> A forky fure, ay furthwart, and forsy in draucht,   85
> Nother febill, nor fant, nor fulyeit in labour,
> But als fresche of his forme as flouris in May;
> For all the fruit suld I fang, thocht he the flour burgeoun.

This last line is nakedly sexual and lascivious. The fantasy of this passage stems from the frustrations of feudal marriage, which was an integral part of the power-game played by men, a contract between landlords involving trading of women as symbols of property: and a man of power in this sense was more likely to be old than young—hence the contrast between social power and physical. Women were treated as mere pawns in the game (the tragedy of Romeo and Juliet centres on this fact) and traded about shamelessly. Dante is torn between his sense of the justice of the love between Paolo and Francesca (another Romeo-and-Juliet pair of "star-crossed" lovers," even more horribly victimised by the feudal marriage system) and his moral or religious belief in the necessity of this marriage convention—the only one he knew.[3] He and Beatrice themselves were victims of it at one level, for she was already betrothed by her family to another man, and Dante to Gemma Donati. It would not have seemed possible to either to rebel against this: but this perhaps takes Dante's love of her at too material a level.

The first wife goes on to describe the husband she has obtained in the feudal lottery:

> I have ane wallidrag, ane worme, ane auld wobat carle, 89
> A waistit wolroun na worth bot wourdis to clatter;
> Ane bumbart, ane dron bee, ane bag full of flewme,
> Ane skabbit skarth, ane scorpioun, ane scutarde behind;
> To see him scart his awin skyn grit scunner I think.
> Quhen kissis me that carybald, than kyndillis all my sorow,
> As birs of ane brim bair his berd is als stif,
> Bot soft and soupill as the silk is his sary lume;
> He may weill to the syn assent, bot sakles is his deidis.

He may well desire the sin of copulation with her, but his performance is lamentable, indeed, innocent. The poem here modulates again, this time from satire on marriage to open flyting (scolding, extravagantly defaming) of the husband. This is the technique Dunbar uses in such poems as "Schir, Ye Have Mony Servitouris",[4] and the "Flyting of Dunbar and Kennedy" is the extreme example of it in Scottish literature. It is a technique of deliberate, violent abuse, a dehumanisation of the victim (and of the executioner, in my view) which is meant to make our blood curdle yet move us to laughter.

---

[3] *Inferno*, Canto V.   [4] 17 ("Remonstrance to the King").

N

Note how the lines fill up with powerful native words torn from
the soil like mandrakes, shrieking at the roots. The lines are
so full of "brs" and "grs" that they growl and snarl like
wild animals: in the first twenty-six lines of this passage only
four have no "rs" in them, and most of the other twenty-two
have more than one. She goes on with the catalogue of
"qualities": his two grim eyes are caked all round with matter
and gorged like two gutters stapped up with mud. When this
leering spectre takes hold of her she thinks the hideous Mahoun
(a medieval synonym for Satan) takes hold of her in his arms.
Signing herself with the cross does no good, for still he will
force himself upon her. When this old churl is shaven with
a sharp razor, he shoves his twisted mouth on her and parts
her lips and his hard hedgehog skin so roughs her cheeks that
her jaws glow like a flaming ember, she shrinks with the pain
but dare not shout. His love-leers depress her as if Beelzebub
winked at her, the bleary-eyed old scarecrow, and when the
weakling casts lustful glances on her, he fidgets like a diseased
horse excited by a mare.

> Quhen that the sound of his saw sinkis in my eris,   115
> Than ay renewis my noy, or he neir cumand;
> Quhen I heir nemmyt his name, than mak I nyne crocis,
> To keip me fra the cummerans of that carll mangit,
> That full of eldnyng is and anger and all evill thewis.

This is still the technique, not of satire, but of flyting; no
jot of alleviating goodness is allowed to temper the inhuman
diatribe—that would be as out of place in flyting as pathos in
Greek tragedy—no hint of love or affection allowed to lighten
the picture of dark lust. All motives must be entirely bad,
and the worst possible: for flyting demands not truth but the
extremity of hate. But the whole point is that Dunbar is
using flyting here as a double-edged sword that cuts the user
as much as or more than the victim. His real target is not
the husband but the wife. Those who use flyting—"Flyting
to use richt gritly I eschame"—are more harmed by it than
its intended victims.

She dare not, she goes on, look at her lover because of that
skinny gelded cat, he is so full of jealousy and false imaginings

(this is rich in feminine double-talk—the asumption of her
right to a lover, the indignation at his "false" imaginings
which we know to be only too accurate) and suspicions,
devising a thousand ways to catch her out by a trick. The mood
here moves from flyting rather to that of complaint as, with
self-pity, she says he is so worn with venery that he is no use
to her in bed, and that while he always suspects her (how rightly,
we know) of yearning for young lovers, yet he himself can do
nothing about her desires. The complaint mingles again with
flyting as she goes on:

> Ay quhen that caribald carll wald clyme on my wambe, 131
> Than am I dangerus and daine and dour of my will;
> Yit leit I never that larbar my leggis ga betueene
> To fyle my flesche, na fumyll me, without a fee gret;
> And thocht his pene purly payis me in bed,
> His purs pays richely in recompense efter.

Before she lets that forlorn cannibal climb on her body, she
makes him promise her a kerchief of the finest fabric, a gown
of embroidered cloth gaily trimmed with fur, a ring with a
regal stone or other rich gem in it, or she will end his stale ride
though he be mad-randy. His performance is so feeble that
she considers the endurance dearly bought with all the bribes
of John Blunt (a proverbially stupid character),[5] and she thus
sells him consolation—God defend her sisters from such a
Grandad.

After this charmer ends her dissertation, he says, they all
laugh in a hearty manner and pass round the cup full of rich
wine, joking long with riotous speech.

The widow then addresses the other beauty:

> Now, fair sister, fallis to yow but fenyeing to tell   151
> Sen man ferst with matrimony yow menskit in kirk,
> How haif ye farne be your faith? confese us the treuth:
> That band to blise, or to ban, quhilk yow best thinkis?

"To blise, or to ban"—the first wife has made it clear that
to her marriage is no bliss but a curse, making her sell her
body to a useless lover, forcing her into adultery, lies, cheatry

---

[5] *The Poems of William Dunbar*, ed. Small, S.T.S., III. 76, n. 142.

and general corruption—a mockery. Now the second wife, having joined in the laughter which is the worst feature of their depravity—it would shock the religious and idealistic in the audience, and is in itself a symptom of the disillusionment rife at this time—bears her witness in this trial of holy wedlock:

> To speik, quoth scho, I sall nought spar[6]; there is   116
>   no spy neir:
> I sall a ragment reveil fra rute of my hert,
> A roust that is sa rankild quhill risis my stomak;
> Now sall the byle all out brist, that beild has so lang;
> For it to beir one my brist wes berdin our hevy;
> I sall the venome devoid with a vent large,
> And me assuage of the swalme, that suellit wes gret.

There is to be no defence of marriage here, no debate of pros and cons—the evidence is to pile up against the accused. The little touch of comedy in "ther is no spy neir" is artless and naive, but effective, suddenly reminding us of the poet stuck in the hawthorn hedge, all ears.

Her husband, she goes on, was a whore-monger, and although a young man, already wasted and worn-out by his "work". Though he still looks virile, he is in fact impotent—again the insistence on the physical, the complaint against impotence—having been a rake so long that he has lost his natural vigour, his tool useless and limp in a swoon. Even after seven weeks' rest "it will nocht rap anys". He was played out on women before he chose her as his wife, and she has caught him in adultery many times since (the satire here is on the licence which the male traditionally allows himself, while demanding chastity of the female). Although he is so useless in bed, yet he swaggers and winks at females as if he were a better performer (there is more than a little of the burnt-out Don Juan about this character: Don Juan is a degeneration of the courtly lover, developed in Spain, and akin to that parody of the courtly lover, Don Quixote: he is the male type of these women, in depravity). She moves into flyting:

---

[6] "To speik and spar nocht" is a motto of certain families, and may be a clue to identity here.

He dois as dotit dog that damys on all bussis   186
And liftis his leg apone loft, thought he nought list pische:
He has a luke without lust and lif without curage;
He has a forme without force and fessoun but vertu,
And fair wordis but effect, all fruster of dedis;
He is for Ladyis in luf a right lusty schadow, . . .
He ralis, and makis repet with ryatous wordis
Ay rusing him of his radis and rageing in chalmer,
Bot God wait quhat I think qhuen he so thra spekis.

Directing her remarks to the first wife, she says that the woman who has an old man is not completely deceived, for he is no worse at Venus' work than he appears to be: whereas she thought she had got a jewel and it was only a piece of jet (Dunbar must bring out that the case of the second is worse than the first, for he is building a crescendo: "lilies that fester . . ."). He had the glitter of gold, but proved to be only of glass: and impotent men, she has found, have nothing in their hearts but jealousy and anger. Still addressing the first wife, she goes on:

Ye speik of berdis one bewch: of blise may thai sing,   205
That, one Sanct Valentynis day, ar vacand ilk yer . . .

If she had the happy privilege to separate when it suited her to change and choose again (the theme of "freedom of choice" again—the basic theme of the whole poem), then good-bye chastity: she would have a fresh companion, for it is folly to hold an impotent man in your arms. A deeper, sincerer, and more touching note comes into the complaint as she goes on to say that often at midnight lying awake she muses on such matters, grieving in her mind to the point of suicide, cursing her wicked family (here we have the feudal marriage-arrangement attacked directly) who threw her away on such a gutless coward, who soiled her peerless beauty, when there were so many brave knights in the kingdom. And her mind turns to fantasies of a worthy lover, and she sighs. But at this point her husband turns tenderly towards her "And with a yoldin yerd dois yolk me in armys", and asks her why she isn't asleep—she feels hot as if some fever were burning her: and she tells him to hold off, she has a sudden pain at her heart. She then pretends to swoon, the more to deceive him. When daylight comes, she casts a sour look at him, turning it to a look of tender love when he glances round; and inwardly cursing him in anger, she wears a fond smile (thus hypocrisy is added to the other ills of the "blissit band" of matrimony). She has thought of a particularly appropriate torment for him:

> I wald a tender peronall, that myght na put thole,   231
> That hatit men with hard geir for hurting of flesch,
> Had my gud man to hir gest; for I dar God suer
> Scho suld not stert for his straik a stray breid of erd.
> And syne, I wald that that ilk band, that ye so blist call,
> Had bund him so to that bryght, quhill his bak werkit.

And if the while she herself were brought to bed with a man who liked her, the girl would have no cause to laugh at her in her happiness.

When this sweetheart had ended her tale, the others laughed loudly and agreed with her. These gay women thoroughly enjoyed themselves among the green leaves drinking and chasing away care, quaffing the sweet wine, those milk-white swans— but all the more confidently their voices rose in complaint.

Dunbar has missed no part of the animality of the second wife. The element of sexual disgust, its association with excrement[7] in the "dog" reference (this is enhanced by the fact that if the dog were able to urinate on every bush, she would like it the better—she is a bitch, out of her own mouth) needs no insisting upon. Compare this with the poem about "libbin the pockis" addressed to the Queen: the disgust is relished. It is part of the essence of this poem that the women are allowed no rationalisation of their complaints into more socially acceptable dissatisfactions: nothing is allowed to come between us and the stark sexual truth. This is almost Freudian in its reductiveness. The alliteration here has a predominance of f, with s m w c close in attendance—more serpentine and soft than the angry gurliness of the first wife. The one euphemism she is allowed is deliberately ironical—"heart": it is not her "heart" she has a pain in. Women are said to give

---

[7] Cp. Yeats's "Crazy Jane and the Bishop": "Love has pitched his mansion in the place of excrement."

their "hearts" and "hands" to a lover—never what they do in fact give. Now comes the turn of the widow herself. Can she produce anything more vituperative than the two wives? Can worse have befallen her than marriage to an impotent dotard or marriage to an impotent rake?

She begins by invoking the Almighty to inspire her spirit and enliven her speech, granting her eloquent phrases, noble and of substance, so that her preaching may pierce their perverse hearts and make the two wives more submissive to men in manner and in demands. A Portia come to judgment? Dunbar has shown us two depraved women, and now through the widow decency and piety are to be restored, the social values upheld, the "blist band" of matrimony vindicated, and, with the help of God through His divine instrument the widow, these perverse creatures are to be brought back to the strait and narrow, led by the widow's great wisdom. This instrument of God and society begins:

> I schaw yow, sisteris in schrift, I wes a schrew evir,   251
> Bot I wes schene in my schrowd, and schew me innocent;
> And thought I dour wes, and dane, dispitous and bald,
> I wes dissymblit suttelly in a sanctis liknes:
> I semyt sober and sueit, and sempill without fraud,
> Bot I couth sexty dissaif that suttillar wer haldin.
> Unto my lesson ye lyth, and leir at me wit,
> Gif you nought list be forleit with losingeris untrew:
> Be constant in your governance, and counterfeit gud maneris,
> Thought ye be kene, inconstant, and cruell of mynd:
> Thought ye as tygris be terne, be tretable in luf,
> And be as turtoris in your talk, thought ye haif talis brukil,
> Be dragonis baith and dowis ay in double forme,
> And quhen it nedis yow, onone, note baith their strenthis;
> Be amyable with humble face, as angellis apperand,
> And with a terrebill tail be stangand as edderis;
> Be of your luke like innocentis, thoght ye haif evill myndis;
> Be courtly ay in clething and costly arrayit,
> That hurtis yow noght worth a hen; yowr husband pays for all.

The religion of the widow, in other words, is the discipline of dissembling, her "God" is the "god" of hypocrisy. Thus Dunbar adds at one stroke blasphemy, cunning, and hypocrisy to the sins of the two wives. The wives are too naive—

they must learn the essential lesson of married women: how to deceive with art. The answer to the problem of marriage is hypocrisy. There is no sin in sinning, but there is sin in being found out. Her creed might be reduced to the formula "Be respectable, and sin as you will": it is the the creed of the bourgeoisie to this day—not righteousness, but respectability, that most honoured of middle-class "virtues", taking precedence even over "genteelness". This is to be our good shepherdess to these wandering lambs—the final mounting crescendo in this tripartite sonata of female depravity. The wives, we see now, can be pitied as victims, to some extent, of a vicious marriage system which marries young girls to impotent dotards and (let us bear in mind the circumstances of the Queen's own marriage—is James perhaps struck at in the guise of the husband of the second wife?) a worn-out rake of apparently virile manhood—a handsome, but burnt-out Don Juan: but the widow is wilful of evil. She is a seasoned campaigner in what she has accepted as the amoral war of the sexes: in her we find a new meaning for the tag "All's fair in love and war". She is the supreme "realist" in the sense used by so many of our modern economists and politicians—amoral. It is a denial of the whole Christian witness, in favour of a vision of life which sees mankind as at the mercy of material forces over which it has no control, and morality as, therefore, a sentimental or idealistic irrelevance—a form of lunacy. [7a] We begin to see the "freedom of choice" in a new light, freedom to pursue individual gain at the expense of the good of the community—freedom from religion, freedom from morality, freedom from reality itself. We have already seen Dunbar rage against this bourgeois claim to "freedom" of the individual at the expense of the community—in "Quhy will Ye, Merchantis of Renoun",[8] for example:

> Singular proffeit so dois yow blind,   71
> The common proffeit gois behind. . . .

Both as churchman and as "aristocrat" (his claim to "noble" birth we have seen in "Schir, Yit Remembir as of Befoir")[9]

[7a] Cp. the rule of secrecy in *amour courtois.*
[8] 44 ("To the Merchantis of Edinburgh").   [9] 20 ("To the King").

he despises the "new" morality of the rising middle-classes, which is to him on both counts only the old immorality.

The widow goes on to say that she has had two husbands who held her dear, and though she despised them both, she never let them see it. The first was a hoary packman, a petty merchant, who coughed out phlegm, and she hated him like a dog, though she kept it private. She made a fool of him by kissing and petting, dressing his crooked back, combing his bald pate, making faces at him behind his back the while. She could lead him on to believing in her love with an easy conscience and merry mind: but behind his back she had a lover who could be secret, trustworthy, always preserving her honour (note the virtues here of Courtly Love) and woo her at appointed times and in safe places. When the old man angered her, she sought out the young for solace, and she was too intelligent (intelligence, too, is an amoral quality: the corollary to David Hume's dictum that "reason is . . . the slave of the passions" is that if the passions are evil, then reason will be evil, too) to waste time in grieving, but always let the sweet season the sour. She so led him on that soon he had assigned his chief mansion to her son, although the oaf had become impotent before the child was conceived (and therefore was not his own). Thus she behaved as a wise woman (here the satire is turned on what constitutes "wisdom") and not as a mad fool, won rather by guile than strength of hand.

The widow, therefore, is too far sunk in sin to be redeemable: the wives, we feel, are not so—there is still some hope for them. But the widow's deliberate perversion of her gifts to an immoral end is clearly beyond redemption, because she has made evil her god and Hell her Paradise. Dunbar's audience may not see her in this light: they may thoroughly approve of her ruthless self-seeking guile: but there is not much doubt about where Dunbar stands. His audience most likely stood somewhere between his view and the widow's, enjoying the cynical disillusionment, but not quite going so far as the widow— perhaps even gaining relief from the picture of someone further gone than themselves in depravity. What is clear is that he had an audience (he rarely wrote without one in mind) which would relish this poem—an audience chiefly of women.

After his death—we are not told whether she helped him on his way, but feel that she was quite capable of it—she married a real merchant, one with goods and possessions—she has apparently gone up in the world, for her first husband was only a "hogeart,"[10] a packman, a sort of door-to-door salesman, a dealer in small wares, a huckster. Yet she goes on to say that she and her new husband, a small, middle-aged man, were fellows neither in blood, friendship, liberality, nor outward appearance: the fool was always forgetting her superiority, being of low intelligence, but she so often reminded him of it that his heart was angry, and then she called him a pedlar. She loved to needle him about her being twice married, and having lost her innocence to her first husband, although she was precociously sexy according to the curate of her church. She soon gets the merchant under her thumb:

> I gert the buthman obey, ther was no bute ellis: 309
> He maid me rycht hie reverens, fra he my rycht knew:
> For, thocht I say it my self, the severance wes mekle
> Betuix his bastard blude and my birth noble.

This mere "page" never dared presume to any rights over her body, but took only what pity granted. She kept it always in his mind that she took him only out of pity, for mercy is a great virtue in women, and pity is never begotten except in a cultured heart: since he could not know these things himself, she very kindly taught him. He never once dared to ignore her summons but was so afraid of her displeasure that he ran at the first bidding. But woman's nature is perverse:

> Bot ay my will wes the war of womanly natur: 321
> The mair he loutit for my luf, the les of him I rakit;
> And eik, this is a ferly thing, or I him faith gaif
> I had sic favour to that freke, and feid syne for ever.

She liked him before marriage but hated him ever after. Once she had got complete power over him, she crowed like a

---

[10] *The Poems of William Dunbar*, ed. Small, S.T.S., III. p. 80 glosses it thus from O. Danish "hoger"; but there is a sense of "hog" in it, a pig, a boar, which may be all Dunbar means; and I incline to this view: the reader must make up his own mind, but the sense hardly bears out the S.T.S. meaning. Packmen don't have mansions. Mackay Mackenzie shirks this with the usual "obscure" gloss.

victorious cock over the coward (she has in fact usurped the male role by using class against him), but when she saw him so submissive she despised him and became so merciless to him that she decided to martyr him, spurring him like a beast to all menial tasks. She would have ridden him to Rome in a halter, but for the spoiling of her good name and other people's gossip (the respectability cult again). Yet she hid her hatred completely (God knows how in such circumstances—Dunbar stretches our credulity here) and never unstoppered her pent-up fury as long as she could get something more out of him. But once she had done him out of all his worldly goods, got his buildings, and high burgh lands for her own son:

> Than with a stew stert out the stoppall of my hals   339
> That he all stunyst throu the stound, as of a stele wappin.

After such long repression she was fierce as a dragon, eager for vengeance, having so long dissembled before she got the title-deeds of his property made over to her, she could no longer bear the bridle but threw up her head so that no bit might hold her mouth in (the horse imagery here, as of a spirited mare, is as appropriate as the cock imagery was perverse), and she makes the reins stretch and tear to pieces. She makes the womanish old man ("wif carll") do all women's work, leaving all manly things. Then she boasted to her neighbours (where now is the fear for her "good name," what others will say, her respectability?—Dunbar is inconsistent here, out of character) of how she had haltered that colt with a sharp bridle. The horse that once had thrown the baskets in the midden of chaff now draws the cart so courteously (in so "courtly" a manner) without plunging or shying or skipping from side to side. Thus he escapes neither harm nor scorn.

Thus Dunbar piles up the depravity of his widow with great ingenuity and subtle psychology. She is saved from complete monstrousness by that little give-away feminine naivety about hating him the more he gave in to her: this self-destructiveness reflects one of Dunbar's deepest insights into the nature of a shrew. This goes down to the primitive depths of the female fighting the male to prove his superiority, lest she father her young with a weakling. The instinct is

unconscious, and the widow is not looking for a sire for her
children, but the mechanism is the primitive one.

She goes on to say that as this man was no company for a
"gay lady", she put him to some more suitable employment.
He had been a very wealthy man before she defrauded him,
so she allows him to be her banker, looking after his own
money for her, freeing her from all business matters: this he
is pleased to do.   There seems to be another inconsistency
here, for she goes on to speak of his being still wealthy (the
meaning may be that she has acquired only his property, not
his wealth, his gold and jewels, nor his business, so that he is
still by no means a pauper,[11] although she has also just told
us that she has acquired all his legal property, reducing him
to a position as her servant).   He is on the one hand glad to
receive the office from her, and on the other, he continues to
seek her favour through many gifts:

> He grathit me in a gay silk and gudly arrayis,   365
> In gownis of engranyt claith and gret goldin chenyeis,
> In ringis ryally set with riche ruby stonis,
> Quhill hely raise my renoune amang the rude people.

If she had

> . . . severit that syre of substance in erd,   337
> And gottin his biggings to my barne and hie burrow landis,

so that he is dependent on her, how can he still heap clothes
and jewels upon her? "Substance in erd" may only mean
his lands, but it normally would carry the meaning, over and
above, of "all his worldly goods".   Which does Dunbar mean?
The context would seem to indicate the narrower meaning,
but is Dunbar not in fact trying to have his cake and eat it—
to defraud the husband and make him a servant of the wife,
banker of his own moneys, yet also to have him still lavishing
wealth on her? Is the poem running away with him here?
She goes on to say that she very craftily kept those courtly
clothes until his death, so that she could let her next lover
enjoy the finery at her husband's expense.   I suspect Dunbar
of letting his exuberance run away with his sense of reality—

---

[11] This is the only possible reading, if my following remarks seem unfair.

a common enough trait in him when the eldritch mood of extravaganza is on him. Here it jars, however, and is a flaw in the poem. She goes on to tell how she cuckolded him after she had thus exploited him, and snubbed him, slighting him as a servant. She imagined herself a popinjay, and him a plucked heron; she made him reinforce and fortify his own enemy, and strike himself down.

This element of inconsistency in the poem is a serious fault, and shows itself in several places. This man is both impotent, for instance, and a satyr, both a libertine (in imagination at least) and no good in bed. Up to now she has stressed the impotence—now she goes on to contradict herself by telling us of his libidinousness. This again is flyting technique—the only propriety is to pile up extravagant abuse of the victim, even if the vices are incompatible, such as being poor and rich at the same time, impotent and libidinous. The extremism and extravagance demand that yet another fraud is to be practised on this man and Dunbar doesn't scruple to give us it:

> Bot of ane bowrd in to bed I sall yow beir yit: 385
> Quhen that he ane haill year was hanyt, and him behufit rage
> And I wes laith to be loppin with sic a lob avoir,
> Als lang as he wes on loft I lukit on him never,
> Na leit never enter in my thoght that he my thing persit,
> Bot aye in mynd ane other man ymagynit that I haid;
> Or ellis had I never mery bene at that myrthles raid.

This free treatment of reality adds to the comic side of the poem, but at the expense of the satire. The influence of flyting reduces the poem from a higher to a lower kind—satire to farce.

As soon as she had castrated this oaf of goods and of nature, she goes on, she considered him to be beneath contempt, so help her God (how douccly the blasphemy slips in here). When he had spent all he had on her, she considered he had squandered his wits as well, and "I spittit quhen I saw That spendit evill spreit (note how she 'projects' her own evil on to him), spulyeit of all vertu" (the doubletake here again of manliness and goodness). The wives will understand how despicable and vile is a man who lacks all riches and manliness in venery: fine appearance is nothing if he fail at the critical moment (a hint here of a resolution of the impotence-libidinousness problem—the impotence is only at the climax. Did Dunbar know that a woman who fails to achieve her own climax is often as much to blame as the man? If so, he is adding to the viciousness of the widow here.) Again we have the insistence on female lust—the opposite of the ideal of the *dame* of *amour courtois*: from being a super-human ideal, woman here is degraded to the sub-human.

She tells how she dressed *her* children like sons of barons (at least one of her children was got illegitimately by cuckolding her first husband, we remember) and made nothing but fools of the spawn of his previous wife. She banished all his brothers and treated his friends as her enemies, extending her hatred to his whole kin—yet these wise men believe that all the evil in women is to be seen outwardly, in their behaviour.

Now that that bankrupt is dead and buried, all her grief is buried with him:

> Deid is now that dyvour and dollin in erd: 410
> With him deit all my dule and my drery thoghtis;
> Now done is my dolly nyght, my day is upsprungin,
> Adew dolour, adew—my daynte now begynis:
> Now am I a wedow, I wise and weill am at ese.

How powerful that word "dyvour" is—he is bankrupt of potency, bankrupt of goods, bankrupt of character, and bankrupt of esteem. Her "daynte" now begins—she will be looked-up-to now, respected, esteemed. The implication is that the marriage-bond is degrading and humiliates the woman by subduing her to the man—this is feudal marriage under attack, but by the widow, not by Dunbar. How conscious was Dunbar of the social implications of his poems? Much less so than we today are likely to assume. Society—feudal society—had the sanction of the Church behind it, and Dunbar was a churchman. Yet he knew the marriage problems well enough, and we have seen him already posit married love as the resolution of the courtly love versus feudal (loveless) marriage-of-utility conflict in "Sen that I am a Presoneir".[12]

[12] 54 ("Bewty and the Presoneir").

Dunbar's approach is essentially moral; his morality is catholic; and the social analysis incidental, only half-conscious —if that.

The widow pretends to be in mourning for her husband, keeping up appearances and winning repute, but her body and soul are gaily attired under her mourning weeds and crocodile tears. When she goes to Church in her widow's weeds she behaves like a fox in a lamb's fleece. She spreads out her elegant missal and draws her cloak over her white face so that she may spy without being seen. The climax of her hypocrisy is reached in the church itself where, in the very presence of God, she feigns grief and uses it as a mask behind which to seek opportunities for sinning: she has no scruple about this, for to her the Church is merely the secular feudal society at prayer; the male power-game in which women are pawns is played as much by priest as by landlord, and therefore she owes it no allegiance. The underlying reality of the widow's behaviour is that life is a war between men and women in which men have all the advantage and exploit it: therefore women are forced to fight back ruthlessly with any weapon that will work. "Morality" is a piece of male hypocrisy to be countered with a corresponding female hypocrisy; society is patriarchal, and everything in it is geared to masculine advantage. Women must fight an underground war behind a disguise, like spies in enemy territory, or more likely, native guerrillas in an occupied country, pretending allegiance to the conquering power, but never really compromising their true allegiance to their own side—and *their* side is God the Mother, not God the Father. Patriarchal religion is merely an extension of patriarchal society, one more piece of male chicanery, to be dealt with accordingly: the Church may be "Mother" Church, but she is ruled by "Father" priest, and that is enough to prove "her" in fact a "him".

At the social level, the widow is full of the kind of dualistic, schizophrenic attitude which was already claiming in Dunbar's time that the Church has no jurisdiction over economics, which should be "free" of all moral considerations: and the Church was soon to be reduced to a mere fragment of life, a part of society with its own limited sphere of activity, instead of being

the image of the whole within which all other things are mere
parts or members.[13]   The widow is a whited sepulchre, but
she merely reflects, in this, the society which produced her,
and that society was on the brink of becoming ours, in which
if God is worshipped at all by the ordinary middle-class people,
it is only on Sunday, while Mammon is worshipped the other
six days of the week.

Very often, she goes on, she glances up from her book of
devotion, to see which man has the biggest muscles or the
broadest shoulders, or is most powerfully shaped to furnish a
banquet in the chamber of love manfully, without vain boasting:

> And, as the new mone all pale, oppressit with change,   432
> Kythis quhilis her cleir face through cluddis of sable,
> So keik I through my clokis, and castis kynd lukis
> To knychtis and to clerkis and costly personis.

This is a very effective, indeed beautiful image, and, in the light
of the religious context, a very profound one: for the moon
is also Diana the pagan goddess of the hunt.   There is a faint
adumbration of this in Chaucer's *Troilus and Criseyde* (l. 175),
where he likens Criseyde in her widow's weeds to a bright star
under a black cloud: but if Dunbar borrowed here, he repaid
with interest, for his is vastly the better use.   This is one of
the finest similes I know of in any poetry.

The widow continues:

> Quhen frendis of my husbandis behaldis me one ïer,   436
> I haif a watter spunge for wa, within my wyde clokis,
> Than wring I it full wylely and wetis my chekis,
> With that watteris myn ene and welteris doun teris.

Then they all pity her as an unhappy, loyal creature—how
sad such a pearl (a synonym for "Margaret"; it is well for
the Queen's reputation that this poem was already in print
five years before James's death at Flodden) of virtue should
suffer such pain.   She crosses herself like a saint and seems (to
herself as well as to others) to be an angel.   She pretends to be
offended by indecent talk, sighs as if with a sore heart, but

---

[13] I am indebted here and throughout to *Religion and the Rise of Capitalism*,
R. H. Tawney, 1937, p. 273, e.g.

without any real pain, and has sad manners to match her sad
clothes, for safety.   Be sure all women, she says, hide themselves
from sight to deceive honorable men, and grieve for no mis-
conduct so long as it is secret (the hypocrisy of "respectability" again).   She further expounds her philosophy:

> Wise wemen has wayis and wonderfull gydingis   451
> With gret engyne to bejaip their jolyus husbandis;
> And quyetly, with sic craft, convoyis our materis
> That, under Christ, no creature kennis of our doingis.

But people without knowledge may miscook a meal, and have
no defences to cover their own natural feelings, as young girls
hold worthless men in esteem, and make fools of themselves
before the whole country.   Faith, she says, has a fair name,
but falsehood gets on better—here is her essential utilitarianism—and of course "getting on" matters more than being
good.   How well we know the argument!   She despises women
who cannot feign to save their own respectability: she herself
is wise in such work (again her "wisdom"—Christ to her
would be a fool) and has been all her life.   Although she may
lack the brains for business, yet she has no lack of wiles in
love—like any "noble" woman: mature women who behave
like silly girls should be ashamed of themselves.

To aid her in her intrigues she keeps a very circumspect
servant who supports her in need when she gives the signal
(again we are reminded of Don Giovanni with his Leporello—
she is the female counterpart).   Although he is of humble
appearance, yet he has a safe tongue, and many men of better
appearance do worse service.   Thus, although she is under a
cloak of mourning all day, yet she has solace at night under
her night-dress till sunrise, and is still held to be a pious woman
by everybody in the country (this is her great triumph in her
own eyes—that she can plumb the depths of sin and yet be
held a pillar of virtue).   When there are lots of people about,
she shows charity to the poor, but only to impress people and
attract lovers.   This is her image of the successful woman in
an over-masculinised feudal society in which she is treated as
an inferior being: the supreme hypocrisy.   Her reference to
how she gives charity, be it noted, is a direct refutation of

o

Christ's injunction on this matter: like the hypocrite that she is, she gives only to be seen of all, not in secret so that her Father in Heaven may so reward her. She has her reward, and it is the only one she wants. Dunbar here, as always, is steeped in the Catholic tradition.

But the best joke of all, she says, is when her house is crowded out with barons and knights and bachelors:

> Bot yit me think the best bourd, quhen baronis and　　476
> 　kynchtis
> And othir bachilleris, blith blumyng in youth,
> And all my lufferis lele, my lugeing persewis,
> And fyllis me wyne wantonly with weilfair and joy:
> Sum rownis and sum ralyeis, and sum redis ballatis;
> Sum raiffis furght rudly with riatus speche;
> Sum plenis, and sum prayis, sum prasis mi bewte,
> Sum kissis me, sum clappis me, sum kyndnes me proferis;
> Sum kerffis to me curtasli, sum me the cop giffis;
> Sum stalwardly steppis ben, with a stout curage,
> And a stif standand thing staiffis in my neiff.

Now the poem crescendos to its detumescence in an orgy of female lust—not simply of sex, but of power over men—and wild fantasy. Again we have the wild inconsistency, for we simply cannot credit that this is compatible with an outwardly successful show of piety—but we must simply suspend our disbelief, for this is as wild as a dance of witches.

Continuing the catalogue, she says many glance longingly at her, sitting too far away because of the density of the crowd. But she, with her vocational generosity, comforts them all— here is the peak of her fantasy, seeing herself as a sort of great whore of Babylon, all things to all men, an omnipotent goddess with a world of males worshipping at her feet. She has become the Great Mother, the goddess of a fertility cult, the earth itself bringing forth its fruits to feed the hungry multitudes: and her "party" in her own house is a great harvest-festival, a wine-feast, in which her worshippers revel and enjoy her mighty fertility. Here Dunbar strikes through fifteen hundred years of Christianity in Europe to the old pagan cults, dives through history and time and comes up with an eternal image

out of the depths of ancient experience.   He has found his
Woman, defined her at last, solved the mystery of the sex—
and he shudders at the discovery, even as he joins in the great
dance of fertility, his monastic soul repelled even as the poetic
sensibility rejoices.   The Widow goes on:

> For he that sittis me nixt, I nip on his finger;   490
> I serf him on the tothir syde on the samin fasson;
> And he that behind me sittis, I hard on him lene;
> And him befor, with my fut fast on his I stramp;
> And to the bernis far but sueit blenkis I cast:
> To every man in speciall speke I sum wordis
> So wisly and so womanly, quhill warmys ther hertis.

Thus she has something for everybody "in speciall", and the
men, miraculously, appear to be satisfied with the morsels
they get—none gets her entirely, yet all are satisfied.   This is
the fantasy of female power, conflicting not only with the
possessiveness of the male, but with the realities of sexuality.
Not only that, but she transcends all limitations of social rank—
one of the "lower" classes in a patriarchal society has always
been women, and in triumphing over her own class-oppression,
she destroys "class" altogether and accepts all mankind as
her lover:

> Thar is no liffand leid so law of degree   497
> That sall me luf unluffit, I am so loik hertit.

And if his desire for her white body is so great that he would
be lost if he could not sleep with her, his life shall be in no
danger: she is so charitable in mind that her blessed soul shall
be saved when the Lord judges all—she is a saint of love, and
this is the legend of her life, and though it be no Church Latin,
the young wives should follow her example (Mary Magdalene
was forgiven for having loved much—she parodies the Christian
story and gives "caritas" a purely physical connotation).

The widow ends her speech and the others laugh uproari-
ously and vow to follow her teaching, since she is so "wise"—
and they go on drinking and gossiping.   The poem proper
ends here, at l. 510: but Dunbar adds a twenty-line coda
returning us to the original scene and style.   They pass the

night away thus, and the sky breaks in true aureate
style:

> The morow myld wes and meik, the mavis did sing,   513
> And all remuffit the myst, and the meid smellit;
> Silver schouris doune schuke as the schene cristall
> And berdis schoutit in schaw with thair schill notis;
> The goldin glitter and gleme so gladit ther hertis,
> Thai maid a glorius gle amang the grene bewis.

The soft soughing of the wind in the vale and the sound of
the brooks, the pleasant tang of the grass and birds singing,
might bring solace to any creature of Adam's kin and relight
the fires of youth in him though they were slaked and cold.
Then these royal roses (the Queen herself is the royal rose in
the "Thrissill and the Rois" we remember) in all their finery
got up from their seats and went home through the blossoming
undergrowth—and Dunbar himself slips quietly away to report
their "pastance most mery" with his pen. He addresses his
listeners:

> Ye auditoris most honorable that eris has gevin   514
> Oneto this uncouth aventur, quhilk airly me happinit;
> Of thir wantoun wiffis that I haif written heir,
> Quhilk wald ye waill to your wif, gif ye suld wed one?

This is the supreme stroke of his "sleekit wut", that most
notable of his psychological qualities. Dunbar is outwardly
joking, but it is a grim joke, and inwardly he is in earnest.
There is real bitterness and venom in the remark—how
personal is it? Again we come across the note of sexual disillusionment and unhappiness in him—something not entirely
to be attributed to his clerical vows, though the repressive force
of these obviously must reinforce the disillusionment. It is
idle to speculate on possible sexual misadventures: but the
internal evidence of the poems is enough to point to a personal
rancour, a feeling of deprivation, of lost heritage. More than
that one cannot say. The poem was written by a bachelor
committed to vows of chastity; and, while there is an objective
morality, there is a deeply neurotic undertone to it. The final
question turns the satire back to the audience—ostensibly to
men but perhaps also to women (which would you like to

have, as wife?). One suspects that the question has a good
deal to do with Dunbar's own trouble—which one would
Dunbar wale to his wife, gif he suld wed one?

The audience have been looking on, enjoying the spectacle
of the satire on the three women—on "others": now suddenly
the satire is turned back on them and they are implicated in
it. One can imagine that if there were husbands and wives
together in the audience, they might well be made uncomfortable by the sudden switching of the satire from fiction to reality,
from the women to themselves. There is even a faint echo of
Christ's words to the "audience" who were about to stone
the woman taken in adultery: let him who is without sin among
you cast the first stone at her. There is, in this last line, the
same turning of guilt from the condemned to the judges, the
involving of all in the same guilt. In any case, he has here
led the audience into the trap, and now he springs it—the
jocular mask is still in place, but the grim underlying seriousness strikes home. The final twist is almost Swiftian in its
inclusiveness: we are all guilty; and, if we laugh, it is ourselves we laugh at—Hell is for us as well as other people; and
if we judge, we will be judged.

This poem is the polar opposite of "The Goldyn Targe",
but it seems to bear an almost causal relationship to it, as a
sort of satirical sequel. It is as if it grew out of the "Targe"—
not deliberately (as if Dunbar said "having rejected the courtly
love ideal of woman, I will now show what she is really like")
but inevitably, in that, in terms of poetic development, when
Dunbar rejected the outworn tradition of the "Rose", he was
almost compelled along a road which led to the opposite—
the "Tretis". This is not merely a swing from romanticism
to realism—but rather from dream to nightmare. Realism
is by definition a balanced, moderate approach to things as
they really are—a complex blend of qualities both negative
and positive, good and bad: this is extravagant exaggeration
on the negative side. These women are, in their way, as hard
to believe in as the Virgin Birth[14] is, in its way—they are
outwith the human, the one subhuman, the other superhuman,
but both inhuman. Yet at the end of the "Targe" it is

[14] Cp. 82 ("Ane Ballat of Our Lady").

reality that Dunbar seems to desire—the restoration of reason
and reality—and his last stanza before the coda is indeed full
of the mild sweetness of a real summer day. A poetry of
concrete realism replaces that of the abstract allegory. But
one extreme here has led to the other—the way to reality from
one excess is via another, opposite excess. Dunbar was himself an extremist, like most good poets (perfection is itself an
extreme): but one feels that it is not merely a temperamental
force which impels him—it is an external force, something in
the nature of poetry and life, something almost dialectic. If
love as a great cultural force is the thesis of Courtly Love, the
antithesis is lust as a destructive form of decay. The reality
is somewhere else, a resolution of these into something else—
Dunbar hints at it in "Sen that I am a Presoneir"[15]—namely
married love. One must not, of course, force this too far—it
is too tidy for the complex variety of Dunbar: but it does have
a limited validity.

The two poems open in much the same way, but with two
significant changes: the "Targe" is in the French stanza, the
"Tretis" in the native alliterative metre: and, whereas in the
"Targe" the poet is merely innocently meandering and enjoying the scenery, in the "Tretis" he is a Peeping-Tom out "to
dirkin efter mirthis". The "Tretis" in fact is something of
a burlesque of the "Targe" type of poetry—ultimately, of
the *Roman de la rose*: and like most burlesque, its characters
are nearer caricature than truth, although the depth of Dunbar's
women, their three-dimensional quality, manifests an art far
beyond mere caricature.

There is an element of masochism in the "Tretis"—the
hyper-sensitive Dunbar is torturing his own sensibility by piling
up the evidence, delving deeper and deeper into the depravity
of his women, thrawnly hurting himself unnecessarily. But is
this a personal matter, or does the poetry demand it? Probably
something of both, but with the weight on the latter cause—
the poetry demands it. His real purpose is to break with the
romance, to destroy it utterly, so that something else can take
its place. In this sense, the "Tretis" is a work of literary
destruction as well as of creation—indeed rather than, for

[15] 54 ("Bewty and the Presoneir").

after this poem the same job will not need doing again in
Scots. The old decaying building has been pulled down, the
ground levelled for a new one. Dunbar was the most French
of Scots poets, in that he was most influenced by French lyric
forms and the aureate style: the "Tretis" is a rebellion against
this influence, asserting more native traditions—even flyting
can be so regarded—against the over-sophistication of the
Continental influence. Scottish poetry henceforth swung
away from romance; and although Lyndsay, the next major
poet[16] after Dunbar (Douglas was a near-contemporary of
Dunbar, dead by 1522), wrote one very fine poem of the romance type (but heroic romance, not allegoric) in "Squyer
Meldrum", the bulk of his work was satiric and realistic.
Montgomerie's work in allegoric form is something of a
throwback, but is in any case different in purpose: and his
was the end of it.

Dunbar never speaks of his deepest sufferings—his sufferings
as an artist whose talent makes him responsible to poetry,
both for its past and its future, between which he is the bridge.
This is part of his conventionality: he cannot but have been
conscious of it, but he probably never thought of it as poetic
material: there was no precedent. It is, therefore, his sufferings
as a man which come through the poems; and this is as it
ought to be, for poetry is for other people, and other people
do not have, and cannot share, the sufferings of a poet, as
such: but the common humanity is sharable. The "Tretis"
is full of a sense of suffering. The women are flayed alive,
vivisected, their insides revealed to us as by a scalpel; it is an
anatomy lesson, not a strip-tease. There is a vein of unpleasant-
ness, nastiness, even of morbid curiosity running through the
poem, an obsessive licking over obscure wounds. To talk
about it closely is to turn to Scots—there is a thrawnness in
it, a revelling in pain, hurting the audience and hurting himself,
piling up the agony. He is not detached and objective, but
is himself involved, hurt and unforgiving, and he gives us the
shudders, gars us grue. His wit is sleekit, cunning, and complex, but subversive and of low motivation—the wit of Iago
or Thersites. He may laugh, as well as grin and sneer: but

16 And it is high time that this was again recognised.

he rarely smiles. His humour is a hurt, slightly mad humour—
wild at times, at times gruesome, dark, and unpleasant or
sweetly pathetic—never the serene humour of a Henrysoun
or a Chaucer. Kinsley has rightly compared him to Dryden,
but in this respect his temper is nearer that of Pope, who was
able to speak of "this long disease, my life" ("Letter to
Arbuthnot"). Certainly he has none of the large genial humour
of his great successor, Burns. Dunbar was a wounded man,
and this poem among others reflects his pain—too much so
for unreserved enjoyment. We suffer with him, and he does
little to relieve his own pain or ours, but, on the contrary,
rubs it in. But even when we admit all this personal element
in the poem, the fact remains that it is predominantly a
burlesque of the "rose" tradition, as l. 523 specifically reveals
—"Than rais thir ryall roisis in ther riche wedis". The man
may suffer, but the artist creates beyond the merely personal,
rescuing poetry from the decadence into which it had fallen—
and with it, of course, the sensibility which it nourishes. He
is not alone in this, but his is a major contribution. The position
of the "Tretis" in Scottish literature is not unlike that of *The
House with the Green Shutters*: George Douglas Brown went to
the opposite extreme from the Kailyard School, and the
"Rose" tradition was the Kailyaird of Dunbar's time. The
"Tretis" is not "realism", but rather the first work of what
Douglas Young has called the "Stinkan-fush School". It
smells, all right, and the taste it leaves in the mouth is gey
harsk.

     The poem satirises women, flytes at them, complains
against them, sneers and jeers at them, makes a rather ignoble
use of the golden targe of reason against them—but the real
subject of the poem is not merely women at all. The real
subject is marriage: and that means marriage as known to
Dunbar, as instituted in feudal society—one, that is, in which
land is the main currency. The poem is a satire on marriage,[17]
among other things, for it is out of the ills of feudal marriage
that Courtly Love emerged as an adulterous cult—love sought
outside marriage because it is impossible (and even immoral

---

[17] This is not to argue that Dunbar was socially conscious, in our sense: but
the evidence is in the poem.

and anti-social) within. The poem therefore is not only about women, but about men also, for, in a patriarchal society, women, socially speaking, are what men make them. The men in the poem are little less important than the women—indeed, they are the instigators of the action: they are causal. The marriage to the impotent old man makes the first wife what she is (Dunbar here is a determinist and a behaviourist—this is the law of nature, from which the Christian is saved only by grace) or has become. The degenerate rake who marries the second wife, the two husbands of the widow, and—most importantly—the family influence which contrived such marriages for them, all make the women what they have become. The guilt of the Church itself in solemnising such monstrous mismatches is hinted at in the widow's reference to the priest—though it is the secular side of marriage, the social, which is really under the hammer of Dunbar's scorn. These forces dam up the life in the women, thwart their natures, and cause the flood of their proper energies to take devious and twisted courses past the obstacles in their way. It is significant that the best state of womanhood, in terms of the poem, is widowhood: the death of the husband removes the obstacle altogether but not her status. Until very recent times—and even today over most of the world—freedom, like everything else of value in a patriarchal society, has been the prerogative only of the ruling male class. Woman is a piece of property, she must "belong" to some male or other. When she is a girl unmarried, she belongs to her father or father-substitute: when she is married, she belongs to her husband (and whatever property she brings with her): and it is only in widowhood that she has some sort of freedom as herself, in her own right—though even that is derived from her status as the wife of her late husband. Even then, she might "belong" to her grown-up son(s) or other relatives: but this is as near as she gets to freedom. The orgy described by the widow is sheer fantasy—but it is the compensatory fantasy of revelling in an impossible freedom indulged in by one who knows only too well an all too possible imprisonment in the marriage-bond as the body-slave of a man. The whole poem turns on the theme of freedom of choice: the women have less than their appropriate degree

of freedom—as much as is compatible with the nature of
reality—and so they demand more than is possible in reality.
Were they given enough, they would find it as good as a feast—
the answer to the problem, therefore, is implicit in the nature
of it, namely equality of the sexes in a free marriage system
allowing both sexes as much freedom as is compatible with the
nature of reality, and no more. The chief causes of corruption
in the poem are the evils of families marrying off their young
women like stud cattle to the highest bidder; of men acquiring
wives they can't satisfy, and/or don't really want, for reasons
other than the natural and biological ones of love and procreation—such as acquisition of wealth; and of husbands,
once married, not knowing how to treat their wives like equal
human beings. Dunbar is saying, in effect, not that this is
the wicked truth about women for all time, nor yet this is how
immoral life is, but this is what women are apt to become
under the contemporary marriage system: therefore what man
will rush into marriage, and with which of these types?

It is here that Dunbar reveals his true quality. He has the
eye of a great writer for the things in his time that make for
sickness and health of people in society, of culture, of civilisation.
He sees what things are moribund, vicious, counter to life—
and this implies a profound, high, and broad insight into life
sub specie aeternitatis—such as the insight with which Dunbar,
for instance, was provided by the Christian tradition, with its
incomparable vision of human life in the heights, in the depths,
and at the plain everyday level, in any time, for all time, and
beyond time. The whole of his work, the vast bulk of it anyway,
is an exposure of these contradictions in society, the lethal
customs of vested interests which promote death instead of
life, thus making a mockery of the very function of society—
to promote for its members life more abundant. Dunbar sees
with the eyes of fifteen centuries of Christian thought and
feeling, not with the eyes of a mere "person". And despite
the corruptions of Christianity in Church and State, the authority of that vision in its purity lies behind the best of his work
and the most trenchant of his social criticism. The real lesson
of the "Tretis" is that, just as the man who puts away his wife
causes her to commit adultery, so the man who takes a woman

in the way of feudal marriage causes her to sin in some such
way as these women, and is guiltier of the resulting moral and
social corruption than the women themselves—for he is a male
in a male society.   Dunbar here, like most major poets, is at
once the victim and the doctor of the diseases of his time—and
perhaps, occasionally, of all time.   Even in seeing the morbidity
of romanticism, he is infected by it;   in denouncing the evil of
flyting, he succumbs to it;   in denouncing James IV's values,
he craves his favour;   in exposing the vices of the benefice-
racket in the Church, he himself seeks to benefit by it;   in satirising the vices of the court, he pursues his own advancement
in it;   in excoriating the Edinburgh bourgeoisie, he continues
to live in the town, seeking to improve them, and it.   It is
this deep sense of reality, of social and human sickness and
health, this penetrating socio-psychological intelligence, which
is at the core of his work—he is a great "critic of life", a re-
establisher of the rock of reality under the tide of social change
and viciousness—a prophet and poet.

The Arnoldian phrase is very apt here, for Dunbar is the
most critical of Scottish poets, at least up to his own time, and
probably of any time up to date.   Less serene, less universally-
minded, than Henrysoun, certainly of lesser mental stature,
he is more acutely involved in his time.   This is a strength at
one level—the level of critic of life immediately impinging on
his own life: but it is a weakness at another.   He lacks the
Olympian humour of Henrysoun, who looks down benignly,
but critically, too, at the little creatures of the human fable,
sending down his lay sermons and loving parables as guides
and correctives.   He lacks also the creative imagination which
can project itself outside its own time into other ages and other
places: he could not have written "The Testament of Cresseid",
nor "Orpheus and Eurydice" nor the "Fables", any more
than Henrysoun could have written the poem just considered
above.   He was a lyric poet, formally, short-winded, a hundred-
yards man, whereas Henrysoun was a narrative-dramatic
poet (the greatest kind of poet), able to sustain high and long
flights—a miler, if not a marathon-epic-runner.   But Dunbar
has more bite, more immediacy; and it is this bite, this critical
involvement, this passionate commitment, with its exasperated

sensibility, its outraged intelligence, which Dunbar brings, more than anything else, to Scottish poetry, and which has so much to say to us today when the legacy of Dunbar is so much needed if our society is to be saved at all from itself.

This legacy was taken up by his successor, David Lyndsay, the most popular of Scots poets before Burns. It was Dunbar's unique genius to be intolerant of the intolerable in an age which had too long been too tolerant of what ought not to be tolerated. This inspired irritability is the unique note of Dunbar, the note of protest, which, with more objective direction and intellectual reinforcement, was to swell into the Reformation: and in literature led to Lyndsay's great work *Ane Satyre of the Thrie Estaitis*. It is the chief source of his remarkable originality within a highly formal tradition.

Dunbar may be seen most truly as a poet of revolution before the time for revolution was ripe—before personal protest had broadened into a mighty current of social ideas and action. His work reflects various elements of a society in turmoil, in a state of revolutionary change; and this factor, as much as any personal or temperamental one, accounts for the element of innovation and originality in his work: the preference for short poems rather than long; the ferocity and personality of his satire and complaint; the tormented sensibility; the conflicting loyalties which seem to pull his personality in different directions, straining the powerful integrity underneath the surface turmoil; the bitterness; the frustration; the near-despair; the sense of insecurity, spiritual as well as material; the note of private, ingrown pain, instead of public and social (as in Henrysoun before him and Lyndsay after); the savage sub-realism, cynically contrasting with romance. The period of revolution came with and after Lyndsay, who inherited and continued the social-critical vein which is the core of Dunbar's best work (a few religious poems apart). This revolution ended in the triumph of the lairds, masked by a soon-to-be gelded religious reformation.

This, of course, was not merely a Scottish phenomenon; and, like most great Scots poets, Dunbar has his place, not merely in a national, but it an international, European context: the uniquely Scottish contribution is perhaps the energy

of the protest,[18] the fierce intensity of passion, the earthy
intolerance of high-flown nonsense, the strength of intellectual
assault. Art values were moving increasingly in the direction
of realism, as the middle-class elements took over more and
more from the barons of land. This change was already there
in the work of Chaucer, of Dante before him, of Boccaccio,
of Jean de Meun, in Dunbar's elder brother in the Muse,
Villon, and the whole revolution culminated in the great work
of Cervantes—*Don Quixote.* In that work the realist tradition
of the *fabliau* blew away the last rags of romanticism in a
gale of laughter, and feudal supremacy (over the mind at
least, for it still lingers on in various slum countries in capitalist
Europe) with it. It is the triumph of bourgeois "common
sense" over the noble idealism of the chivalric code, with the
Don as a burlesque of the *ami* of romance, Dulcinea as the
dame, and Sancho as the touchstone of reality, the peasant-
bourgeois realist and factotum (Figaro is another such figure
in a later age) who has too much necessary work to do to be
taken in by fantasies of romantic grandeur: and who has,
typically, too much sense of the value of the new dominant
currency—money.

Thus far we have seen Dunbar, as it were, in search of
reality.[19] Reason prevents him mistaking romance for it: the
turning away from that fashion leads him into satire, cynicism,
and an extreme as far below reality as idealism is above it.
Where, then, is reality itself to be found? Where is the mean
between these two extremes? The way leads in two directions
—the one to comedy instead of satire: the other to religion
and the Christian love, which is not merely Eros, but also and
chiefly Philia, Caritas, and Agape.

[18] Under the cynical comedy of the surface.
[19] This is my reading: other views are possible.

X

Bonum Vinum ad Bibendum

JAMES IV's court and its doings are Dunbar's main "matter," and the court, or part of it, was his main audience. His treatment of it is mainly satirical, with humorous interludes here and there: but even the humour tends to be a pretty grim one. This is especially true when the subject is of a sexual nature. An exception, perhaps, in which the comic element is more genuinely funny than grim, is "In Secreit Place this Hyndir Nicht",[1] considered in Chapter IV among the poems of women, but which might have been treated here, had I not felt it had more force close to " The Goldyn Targe".

Another poem of humorous treatment of a sexual theme is "This Hinder Nicht in Dumfermeling".[2] It is a parody of the type of Aesop's fables—in this case of a fox and a lamb:

> This hindir nycht in Dumfermeling   I
> To me wes tawld ane windir thing;
>   That lait ane tod wes with ane lame,
>   And with hir playit, and maid gud game,
>   Syne till his breist did hir embrace,
>   And wald haif riddin hir lyk ane rame:
>   And that me thocht ane ferly cace.

He put his arms round her fine sweet body and clasped her round the neck with his forefeet, then shook his tail with whines and cries, playing with her like a fox-cub—then laid her on the ground, asking for grace of her, while she cried "Lady, help!" The sustained play here is reminiscent of "Schir, Lat it nevir in Toun be Tald";[3] and Dunbar goes on to give, in the guise of a fox, a remarkable description of James IV:

[1] 28 (same title).
[2] 27 ("The Wowing of the King quhen He wes in Dumfermeling").
[3] 22 ("The Petition of the Gray Horse, Auld Dunbar").

The tod wes nowdir lene nor skowry,   15
He was ane lusty reid haird lowry,
  Ane lang taild beist and grit with all;
  The silly lame wes all to small
    To sic ane tribbill to hald ane bace:
  Scho fled him nocht; fair mot hir fall!
    And that me thocht ane ferly cace.

The fox was red, the lamb was white—a luscious morsel; and
since this lamb was young and tender he ran at her as in a
race—he had no love of old ewes, tough and skinny—and she
made no attempt to defend herself. He gripped her round
the waist and handled her as it pleased him; and she, who had
never trespassed, took courage from being so strongly handled,
and let him kiss her pretty face, in no way frightened by the
fox's grinning gums. He held her to him by the neck and coaxed
her with loving words—utterly false—and said he would not
touch her pin-cushion. The guileless creature believed him—
the lamb believed the fox, which seems to Dunbar a supernatural matter.

I will no lesingis put in vers,   42
Lyk as thir jangleris dois rehers,
  Bot be quhat maner thay war mard,
  Quhen licht wes owt and durris wes bard;
    I wait nocht gif he gaif hir grace,
  Bot all the hollis wes stoppit hard:
    And that me thocht ane ferly cace.

Unfortunately for this pair of unnatural lovers, when "men"
(one of the few lapses from the animal convention) float far
in joy like this, grief comes upon them before they are aware
of it; and, while they are snugly conferring together, the wolf
besieges the house to hunt the fox, and the lamb squeaks like
a mouse. The wolf bays so hideously that the fox creeps into
the lamb's skin as far as he is able—the attendant ewes keep
silent—and hides himself. The wolf is taken in by the silence,
thinks everybody asleep and goes off to his lair:

And this report I with my pen   69
  How at Dumfermling fell the cace.

The humour is obvious enough, but, typically, it still has an edge to it—more wit than humour, more irony than pathos or tenderness. Dunbar is tender and genuinely humorous, in the "kindly" sense, only when, as in "Schir, Lat it Nevir in Toun be Tald", he himself is the object of his own tender concern—which is to say that he is no humorist at all. His tenderest emotion is self-pity. This poem has "fun" in it rather than true humour—fun of a rather crude sort. The evidence of the poem suggests that James here is seducing a young girl under the eyes of her chaperones, and the "wolf" is her father: the word "lamb" itself suggests this, the contrast with old "ewes" is made, the girl's innocence, guilelessness, and lack of "trespass" insisted on, her gullibility, lack of experience, and confused acceptance. The poem weaves together strands of various traditions—the fable, the *fabliau*, and even a burlesque of courtly love. This latter would demand that the "wolf" would be a husband, and the "lady" his wife—but Dunbar is clearly writing about a real event, merely borrowing the traditional apparatus, as usual, for his own very different purpose. The internal circumstances point to the seduction of a virgin whose father comes on the scene—would a husband have his "lair" in some other part of the steading? The reference to skinny tough ewes is a plain enough declaration that when James went on one of his sexual forays, it was not married women but young girls he was after: Margaret Drummond, only one of his mistresses, was unmarried, as was Mariot Boyd,[4] who bore him a son three years before the Drummond affair began.

What was going on here, most likely, was the sowing of another Stewart bastard in the virgin womb of a girl whose life thereafter would be that much the worse for the attentions of her King; and the "wolf", whether father or husband, would be quite powerless against the King's strong-arm men. Legend has long asserted that the early Stewarts—and indeed up to and including James V—often went in disguise, with but few companions, on ploys of one sort or another among the people: this poem would seem to bear out the legend, for if the "wolf" had known who the "fox" was, by the presence of liveried

[4] R. L. Mackie, *King James IV of Scotland*, p. 81.

retainers, say, outside the house, he would not have dared "yowl". It is typical of Dunbar's callousness towards other people that he, who could be so tender about the "gray horse", shows no sign of pity for the men whose daughter or wife was being misused by his royal master. Had this been any relative of Dunbar's, the chariots of wrath would have streamed the firmament, the howls of agony, accusation, execration, abomination, damnation (and pleas for kingly compensation) would have made Rigoletto's aria denouncing the "Cortigiani, vil razza dannata", sound like saintly forgiveness.[5]

The poem, however, is excellently handled: and the sustained play of the fox-lamb metaphor is scarcely less triumphant than the similar paralleling in "Schir, Lat it Nevir in Toun be Tald". The poem thus has much more weight than his other essay in sexual comedy, "In Secreit Place this Hyndir Nicht"; successful essay, that is, for the poem to the Queen on "libbin of the pockis" scarcely qualifies as "comedy". The note of sly urbanity in the refrain (the word "ferly" has much the same *nuance* as the word "surprising" in the famous political wisecrack about some flagrant piece of nepotism: "It is the most surprising political appointment since Caligula made his horse a consul") is witty, cynical, poised, ultra-sophisticated with the *blasé* manner of the court. The poem is clearly meant for James's own ears, and this tells us a great deal about him and his taste. "Ferly" has a wide range of associations, all of which enrich the use here: wonderful supernatural, remarkable, unusual, astonishing, marvellous, miraculous, etc. The mock-seriousness of Dunbar's iteration of it is bubbling with dead-pan amusement. The remark about the fox being "Ane lang taild beist and grit with all", has of course a sexual connotation. Dunbar revels in the deliberate and effective ambiguities to be wrung out of his convention:

> The silly lame wes all to small   18
>   To sic ane tribbill to hald ane bace

---

[5] Adultery was commonplace in Dunbar's society, but so was much else which he manifestly girded at.

P

—another argument, surely, for her youth and virginity. This pun is unique in Scots poetry, and the ease with which it flows into the poem argues a considerable and habitual acquaintance with music: this would be as much courtly as ecclesiastic. One would like to know whether he himself had any part in singing his own poems at court, and if so, which ones: but here we have as yet no evidence.

The poem on the court jester, "Now Lythis off ane Gentill Knycht",[6] has something of the technique of the abusive poem on "The Fenyeit Freir of Tungland",[7] but it is good-natured and essentially comic, not satiric. It is also a burlesque on the tradition of the romantic knight, which suggests that the guying of the chivalric code was now favourite entertainment at court (Chaucer's tale of "Sir Thopas" had been howled down by the pilgrims, we remember) and probably good material for jesters—Norny would be in on the joke:

> Now lythis off ane gentill knycht, I
> Schir Thomas Norny, wys and wycht,
>   And full off chevelry;
> Quhais father was ane giand keyne,
> His mother was ane Farie Queyne,
>   Gottin be sossery.

No finer knight mounted a horse, strode on foot, bore sword or buckler better, nor came more fearlessly to this court, having done many valiant deeds in Ross and Moray. He had chased many caterans and annoyed many a Highland ghost among those sad glens (the traditional view of the Highlands before Walter Scott romanticised them), driving twenty score of the Clan Chattan before him like oxen—but no man knows of this deed. He won the prize and the garland at feasts and marriages in the provinces, none danced so well, and though he had been in a hundred wrestling matches, he had never yet been defeated: and only he knows whether these are lies. Neither wild Robin under the boughs, nor Roger of Clekniskleuch was ever as brave a warrior: nor were Guy of Guisborne, nor Alan Bell, nor the son of Simon of Whinsfell, ever so skilled at shooting. Wherever he went, this adventurous knight

---

[6] 35 ("Of Sir Thomas Norny").   [7] 38 (same title).

always won the prize at jousting and tournament, and Sir
Bevis of Southampton was never so famous—curse him if I lie.

> Therefoir Quenetyne was bot a lurdane   36
> That callit him ane plum full Jurdane,
>   This wyse and worthie knycht;
> He callit him fowlar than a full,
> He said he was ane licherus bull,
>   That croynd baith day and nycht.

Quintane, indeed, would have made him Curry's stooge—
God forbid his honour should ever be so slighted: he never
in his life soiled a saddle, whereas Curry has soiled two.
Dunbar calls him Lord of All Fools at every Easter and
Christmas, and very properly, for he wants nothing of a knight
of high fame except bells.

The poem is well written in a sort of mythopoeic way,
but the joke is rather private. The comparison with Robin
Hood, Guy of Guisborne (slain by Robin Hood), and the
other archer-heroes mentioned, not only reflects the reading of
the day, but the mythic or legendary romance which the
imagination made use of these figures. The poem suffers from
lack of universality—the fate attendant on poems too bound
by time and passing fashions. We not only don't know Norny,
but the trade of court jester is long obsolete—and these are
basic to the poem. The type of joke is common enough
universally among schoolboys, but that helps us little. One
needs to make an imaginative translation into some equivalent
of a jester in our time, to get it quite: such as Charlie Chaplin
—"There was a famous knight called Sir Charlie who every
morning put on his riding Boots, roped up his famous steed,
Bags, put on his trusty helmet, Bowler, and took up his trusty
lance called Cane, and rode forth to battle with the giant
race of Cops, etc. Norny would be as well known to Dunbar's
audience as Chaplin is to us, and they would grasp every *nuance*
and innuendo; we do not. The piece has skill, but never
enough to make up for lack of imaginative weight; and though
it is of interest as a *genre* piece reflecting the customs of the
court and age, it has but limited merit as a poem. Yet the
humour is real, unforced, and not flawed by malice.

"We that are Heir in Hevins Glory"[8] is a comic poem in parody of the religious service for the dead, beginning "Dirige, Domine . . ." It is addressed to the King, who this time is not "wowing" in Dunfermline, but doing penance,[9] or at least in retreat, in the Franciscan monastery at Stirling. Dunbar tweaks James about his would-be piety:

> We that ar heir in hevins glory,   I
> To yow that ar in purgatory,
> Commendis us on our hairtly wyis;
> I mene we folk in parradys
> In Edinburgh with all mirrines,
> To yow of Strivilling in distres,
> Quhair nowdir plesance nor delyt is,
> For pety this epistell wrytis.

O you hermits and anchorites who do penance at table, he goes on, eating no real food nor drinking heartening wines, nor any ale but the weakest possible, half-starved, solitary, seeing nothing but stocks and stones—we begin our wail of sorrow, a devout and humble dirge to help you through Purgatory and back to the bliss of Edinburgh, beseeching the Lord of bliss to deliver you here from your tribulations to be merry among us. And the dirge begins thus:

> *Lectio prima*
> The Fader, the Sone, and haly Gaist,   29
> The mirthfull Mary virgene chaist,
> Of angellis all the ordour nyne,
> And all the hevinly court devyne,
> Sone bring yow fra the pyne and wo
> Of Strivilling, every court manis fo,
> Again to Edinburghis joy and blis

for here in Edinburgh honour, wealth, welfare, sport, pleasure (he knows James's real temperament) reign—and also honesty. "Say ye amen for charitie". The response follows:

[8] 30 ("The Dregy of Dunbar").
[9] James's guilt-feelings about his father's murder are well-attested: he is said to have worn an iron belt which he made heavier every year. This may have been the cause of these retreats: but they may also have been normal religious practice.

Responsio, Tu autem Domine

Tak consolatioun   39
In your pane
In tribulatioun
Tak consolatioun:
Out of vexatioun
Cum hame agane
Tak consolatioun
In your pane.

This surely is a very original use of the triolet form. The
Lord is invoked:

Jube Domine benedicere
Oute of distres   43
Of Strivilling toun,
To Edinburch blis,
God mak yow boun.

The *lectio secunda* is a parody of another part of the service
calling upon all the patriarchs, prophets, apostles, confessors,
virgins, and martyrs, all the heavenly court to deliver the King
out of his deadly agony to the Edinburgh life of dining off
swan, crane, partridge, plover, every fish that swims, new
Rhine wines, French clarets, etc.—all catalogued to make
James's mouth water—and the *responsorium* which follows is
another triolet invoking God and St Giles to escort the King
home to abundance and joy, with the *Jube* echoing "May he
soon live again in Edinburgh". The *lectio tertia* invokes the
saints to much the same effect, but making the unusual point
that the pains of Stirling will enhance the appreciation of
Edinburgh—as if this were the motive for going. The *responsorium* is a plea to come home and never again live in Stirling—
also a triolet. The poem ends in Latin, parodying the Lord's
Prayer:

Et ne nos inducas in temptatione de Strivilling
Sed libera nos a malo illius.

Grant them rest in Edinburgh, Lord, and let its light itself
shine upon them! So the thing goes on for another ten lines,
playing on the Stirling-Edinburgh theme. It is genuine

comedy, and a very skilful parody indeed, with its inversion of the Church's values—sensuality is life, and spirituality is death. This Paradise is more like the Mahommedan one than the Christian, and it is clear that both James and Dunbar himself have more leaning towards a sensual hereafter than a "spiritual" one. There may be, for all its sly joking, a quite serious purpose behind it: that of trying to alleviate a depression in James, to tease him out of it.

This is one of Dunbar's most original poems, quite startlingly irreverent in places (this is not original, of course, but traditional), and very skilfully done. The final lines in Latin are drawn line by line from the appropriate portion of the service, but for

> *A porta inferi erue,*
> *Domine, animas eorum . . .*

we have:

> *A porta tristitie de Strivilling,*   101
> *Erue, Domine, animas et corpora eorum*

and *et corpora* gives these lines a comic twist which suits Dunbar's purpose. This kind of thing is still popular with Scottish students, and is a medieval tradition: but this is one of the few examples in Scottish poetry. The description of the foods eaten at Holyrood is an interesting sidelight on the court. Religion and comedy mingle here, the solemnity of the one setting off the frivolity of the other—and *vice versa*: the two apparently irreconcilable elements are often quite close to each other in Dunbar's work. This is not surprising, for both are related to a fundamental happiness of spirit, and to a balanced vision of reality, a good-humoured acceptance of life. Even the mystic, following the terrible path that leads to the dark night of the soul, emerges with a beatific vision of inexpressible joy in being.

In "I, Maister Andro Kennedy"[10] Dunbar carries the irreverent parodying of religion to an extreme, and the use of Latin here (the Church language) takes up half the space of the poem, every alternate line being in that language. This

[10] 40 ("The Testament of Mr. Andro Kennedy").

was a favourite comic mode at the time, and for long after, and probably owes much to the Goliards.   It is not the King, nor a court jester who is the butt of the joke this time, but an unknown person, not to be confused with the poet Walter Kennedy.   Payments are recorded to one such in the Treasurer's Accounts of 1502-3, and Mackenzie thinks this may be the same man.[11]

> I, Maister Andro Kennedy,   1
>   *Curro quando sum vocatus,*
> Gottin with sum incuby
>   Or with sum freir *infatuatus*—
> In faith I can noght tell redly
>   *Unde aut ubi fui natus,*
> Bot in treuth I trow trewly
>   *Quod sum dyabolus incarnatus.*

Nothing is more sure than death, we must all die when we come to the end, we don't know in what manner any more than Blind Allan knows of the moon.   I suffer in my breast, I cannot sleep a wink tonight—weakness is permissible in the body, but would my mouth were wet with drink (this sets the most solemn religious occasion—impending death, when the sinner makes his peace with God and the world, and composes himself for the great pilgrimage ahead).   Mr Kennedy, in this solemn hour, is to make his will and prepare for the life to come.   He goes on:

> *Nunc condo testamentum meum*   17
>   I leiff my saul for evermore
> *Per omnipotentem Deum,*
>   Into my lordis wyne cellare;
> *Semper ibi ad remanendum,*
>   Quhill domisday without dissever,
> *Bonum vinum ad bibendum,*
>   With sueit Cuthbert that luffit me nevir.

This Cuthbert is himself sweet and loving, often cursing Kennedy under his breath (give me mead to drink): but he is forgiven his hate, because it is better to drink both early and late, naked in your shirt, in the cellar than to lie in a noble

---

[11] Mackay Mackenzie, p. 213.

bed of state. With a barrel bung always at my breast, Kennedy
goes on, I would demand no more of the world's goods. I
leave my besotted body to the town of Ayr, that I may be
buried thus in a midden of malt-husks where every day drink
and malt would be cast on my face. My heart, ever constant
and true, I leave to my friend Iacobe ("James", whoever he
may be: probably the King)—for though I should bind it
with a willow, it would deny the true God; but if I promised
to empty a tankard, that poet I always honoured. Dunbar
would seem here to be harping on his old theme of the king's
broken promises—Kennedy's heart will fit the king, being also
perverse and unreliable.

> Syne leif I the best aucht I bocht,   49
>   *Quod est Latinum propter caupe,*
> To hede of kyn, but I wait nought
>   *Quis est ille,* than I schrew my scawpe;
> I callit my Lord my heid, but hiddill,
>   *Sed nulli alii hoc dixerunt,*
> We weir als sib as seve and riddill,
>   *In una silva que creverunt.*

This stanza is rather troublesome to construe, the main
difficulty being over l. 50, which refers to an obsolete Scots
law. Gregor notes it as a custom in Galloway and Carrick
(*Walter* Kennedy's home) for liegemen to give a present of a
valuable, or best possession, to the head of the clan or family,
or other man in authority over them.[12] He says "James IV
in his second Parliament passed two laws (cc. 18, 19) abolishing
the custom, the one relating to Galloway (18) and the other
to Carrick (19)".[13] Dunbar's text can perhaps best be para-
phrased: "Next, in accordance with the custom of caupe (or,
which is Latin, *propter caupe*), I bequeath the best piece of
property I ever bought to the head of my kin—but who that
is, I don't know", a dig at the Kennedy clan, and at the Gaels
in general, "and then I scratch my head". Andro calls his
"Lord" (James the king, presumably) his head of kin, but
none of his kinsmen call him so[14]—another dig at the rebellious

---

[12] *The Poems of William Dunbar,* ed. Small, S.T.S., III. 210-1.   [13] *Ibid.*
[14] Or "Andro calls Lord Kennedy head of his clan, but his kinsmen don't all
agree with him"?

Gaels. He and his "heid" of kin were as closely related as a sieve and a riddle cut from trees in the same forest.

All his consolations were but lies, one and all, and he leaves all frauds and fallacies to the Master of St Anthony's, William Gray (his own dear relative, as he believes), without payment —he never tells lies but when the holly is green. He leaves his hypocrisy and insincere complaints to false friars, for it is the will of God to give alms to the poor—the friars falsely claim to sing for men's souls, but they do it for money, and may God give them a bad end for their crooked dealings. He leaves his unbridled folly to Jock the Fool, as a legacy, being a greater fool than he is: for Jock only pretends to the King to be a fool, in fact having much corn and cattle, gold and money. And to John Clerk he leaves as intimate legacy the ill-will of God and himself, because he is the cause of his death—were I a dog or a pig, he says, many would marvel over me, but I should make that dull oaf squeal with biting composition without end. My Lord (the King?) shall have all the rest of my goods to dispose, with guardianship of the children Ade, Kitty, and all the rest of them (as "Maister", i.e., Master of Arts, Kennedy would be a cleric and probably have taken the vow of celibacy), I will rave no longer but make arrangements for my tomb in the new manner, not the old-fashioned (Christian) one. The new manner is thus:

> *In die mee sepulture*   97
>   I will nane haif bot our owne gyng,
> *Et duos ruticos de rure*
>   Berand a barell on a styng;
> Drynkand and playand cop out, evin,
>   *Sicut egomet solebam;*
> Singand and gretand with hie stevin,
>   *Potum meum cum fletu miscebam.*
>
> I will na preistis for me sing
>   *Dies illa, Dies ire;*
> Na yit na bellis for me ring,
>   *Sicut semper solet fieri;*
> Bot a bag pipe to play a spryng,
>   *Et unum* ail wosp ante me;

In staid of baneris for to bring
  Quatuor lagenas cervisie,
Within the graif to set sic thing,
  In modum crucis juxta me,
To fle the fendis, than hardely sing
  De terra plasmasti me.

The style of the poem has been called "macaronic", a mixed mess of languages. Laing objects to this, claiming that the mixture as used by Dunbar, Skelton, and others is not strictly macaronic at all, as that term really applies only to using native words with Latin endings—a mixture of inflexion and non-inflected words.[15] Laing may be strictly correct, but it seems to me a rather pedantic point. Gregor rightly upholds the name, and gives instances of the type of poetry, sometimes in three languages, Bacchic parodies of Latin hymns from different countries.[16] The fashion has almost a folk-song ubiquity, and reflects, not merely the lighter side of Goliardic student life, but also the deflation of the dominant Latin by the rising vernaculars and the popular (and necessary, as a safety-valve) religious irreverence. The "new" burial manner is a harking back to the cult of Dionysos—but reducing it to the level of the comic. Here again religion and comedy march side by side in the one poem. The testament form, of course, reminds us of the great examples of this ironic poetry in the two major works of Villon, Dunbar's French predecessor and nearest poetic kinsman. Dunbar again is writing in the centre of a wide European tradition, not merely an English one. It is necessary to stress and perhaps over-stress this point here, because the isolation of England from the Continent from at least the time of Henry VIII, and probably beginning as far back as the French wars of Edward III and his successors, has led in England (but not in Scotland) to an insular anglicising tendency which has played down the Continental influence and exaggerated the English. Chaucer, for example, is usually credited with all the qualities of European poetry as if he had invented them.

[15] *Poems of William Dunbar*, ed. Laing, Edinburgh 1834, II. 918.
[16] *The Poems of William Dunbar*, ed. Small, S.T.S., III. 100.

Although England was going through a period of nationalism, of parochialism almost, resisting the Continental influence, Scotland was still, until 1560, a European country living
in the centre of the broad European tradition. Chaucer was
a great poet in this European tradition, but only one of them,
and he owed almost all he had, apart from his talent, to that
tradition. It is significant that when the Continental influence
waned in England, she produced after Chaucer nothing better
than that overrated eccentric, Skelton, whereas Scotland
produced poetry in the central tradition. In the poetry of the
Middle Ages Europe pre-eminently meant France, as we now
call it; and when English poetry emerged from the doldrums
which it had entered as European (French) influence had
waned, it was under the impact of another wave of influence
from the Continent—the Italian, without which Shakespeare
could never have been. Chaucer was the great clearing-house
through which as much as possible of the great European
tradition was made available in English. He often vastly
improved the material (as Shakespeare was to do) by his own
genius, but he was still essentially indebted to it; a great
reformer of English, and transmitter of European culture to
England. He inspired the Scots Makars more by his example
in this regard than by any originality as the so-called father
of English poetry. Chaucer and the Scots were both sired by
French fathers; and, but for the English habit of claiming to
be creditors, in literature, where they are more properly
described as debtors, it would scarcely be necessary to assert
this.

The spirit informing this poem is that of the Goliardic
tradition of Renaissance Europe, which knew no national
boundaries. It is yet another variation on the theme of "Mihi
est propositum in taberna mori", but given a new turn by its
application to a real person—which strengthens the attribution
to Dunbar. The opening stanzas of the poem are Rabelaisian
—the monstrous birth, the Gargantuan thirst, the irreverence
and exaggeration, the large wildness of the humour. It is a
devilish poem, with the merry devilishness which was still
abroad in Scottish poetry in the eighteenth-century revival—
Burns's "Deil" is a good chap to spend a night's drinking

with—and in the twentieth century still lives on in Hugh MacDiarmid's *A Drunk Man Looks at the Thistle*, and in the work of Sydney Goodsir Smith. In our own time, however, this tradition has lost its significance and *raison d'être*: it was the necessary product of an age of piety, without which the irreverence and audacity have no meaning: it was the pressure of deep water against the wall of a dam, but now is more like straining at an open door.

The fear of death, the awesomeness of death—the *Timor mortis conturbat me* of "I that in Heill wes and Gladnes"—was the attitude of piety: this poem is a rueful shrug at death, asserting the philosophy of the "sensual man in the street", the "ordinary" man—let us eat, drink, and be merry, for tomorrow we die. The fear of death is apt to lead to a fear of life, and this attitude—it has a Stoical as well as an Epicurean side—is apt to lead also to an acceptance of life through acceptance of death—but only at the price of a certain lowering of values, of spiritual seriousness and responsibility. One of the defences against an insoluble problem or hard fate is the attitude of "couldn't care less"—and this entails a lowering of standards. The caring is drowned in the wine, which has, among other things, an anaesthetic value, a dulling of pain as well as of wit. The hearty attitude masks an inward uncertainty. The rueful shrug is a recognition that one can't really do anything else—as in Villon's little poem written when he had been condemned to death, as a citizen of France,[17] while his non-French companions were reprieved:

> Je suys Francois, dont il me poise,
> Née de Paris, emprès Ponthoise;
> Et de la corde d'une toise,
> Scaura mon col que mon cul poise.

This is not so much heroic resignation as passive acceptance of what can't be helped—otherwise, one might break down. Although there is a genuine heroism in the fearlessness with which Villon confronts a vision of himself hanged on the gibbet in the third stanza of the ballade "Frères humaines qui après

---

[17] Therefore coming under French Law.

nous vivez"—it coincides, not with the wine-bibbing devil-
may-careness, but with a quiet and gentle, deeply moving
piety: "Mais priez Dieu que tous nous veuille absoudre".
The defiant alcoholism—if one may call it that—of the imaginary
burial service with wine-barrels parodying the shape of the
Cross is merely the other side of the "timor mortis"—both
are unhealthy and inadequate attitudes to the fact of death,
the ephemeralness of personality, of the individual. This, of
course, is not the voice of Dunbar, merely, but of an age, a
society.

The mixing of the Latin with the vernacular in one poem
is not only a symptom of the rising revolt against the domination
of the *lingua franca*. It is also a sign of rising nationalism
against the supra-national feudal state of "Christendom".
The status of a vernacular and the status of a nation are bound
together indissolubly: one of the first aims of imperialism is
to destroy the status of the local tongues, degrading them to
inferior and even vulgar dialects. In this regard, it is Roman
imperialism which is so belatedly under attack, having maintained its cultural dominance, through the Church, so long
after it had ceased to have any political power—yet the sack of
Constantinople in 1453, only a few years before the birth of
Dunbar, is widely accepted as the date of the final liquidation
of the Empire. Latin was the language of the conqueror, as
English became throughout the British Empire. "Christendom" was almost synonymous with what had been the Roman
Empire. The humorous use of the pompous and solemn
tongue of the conqueror, by off-setting it with vernacular lines,
was a way of deflating the Latin, cutting it down to size,
putting it on a level of mere equality with the despised vernaculars, of asserting the equal worth of the local with the central.
There is also a class element in this, for the vernacular is the
speech of the uneducated, the Latin *lingua franca* a possession
of the educated classes. This type of poetry[18] is essentially a
poetry of learning, for the "vulgar" would not be able to
appreciate the joke: yet it is of the educated classes in revolt
against authority—ultimately, therefore, allied with the rising

[18] This may be rather heavy treatment of a light poem: but a poem is as big
as the associations it stimulates.

bourgeoisie—and of national and cultural individualism as the corollary to the economic individualism rebelling against all restraint by the religious community. The clergy are a highly privileged class—they were the real aristocracy of the Middle Ages, the aristocracy of mind and spirit, not of mere ham-fisted baronial power—but most of them are comparatively poor, and the student element certainly so. Their material position was, therefore, as a class, rather below the baronial than equal with it: and their very work kept the majority of them in close contact with the producing classes.

The poem is a unique one in Scots, and of major importance in the canon of Dunbar's poems. "Harry, Harry Hobbil-schowe"[19] would belong to this group: but we have no authority to call it Dunbar's—it is by one of the tribe of Anon.

[19] 86 ("The Manere of the Crying of ane Playe").

XI

Mahoun Gart Cry Ane Dance

Off Februar the fyiftene nycht,   I
Full lang befoir the dayis lycht,
   I lay in till a trance;
And then I saw baith hevin and hell:
Me thocht, amangis the feyndis fell,
   Mahoun gart cry ane dance
Off schrewis that wer nevir schrevin,
Aganis the feist of Fasternis evin
   To mak their observance;
He bad gallandis ga graith a gyis,
And kast up gamountis in the skyis,
   That last came out of France.[1]

THUS opens Dunbar's account of the dance of the seven
deadly sins. This is one of the few poems of Dunbar's
which dates itself.[2] Fastern's Eve is the eve of Lent, and
this fell on 15 February only twice in Dunbar's known lifetime:
in 1496 and 1507 (1518 also, but this is really outside the
records relating to Dunbar). It is Dunbar's favourite situation
—the dream of trance leading to a vision which liberates his
imagination from the day-to-day world. The last line of the
stanza is a pointer to where Dunbar gets the bulk of his lyric
and dance forms—"out of France". Mahoun, or Mahomet
(i.e. the Devil), goes on:

"Lat se," quod he, "now quha begynnis". . .   13

and the Seven Deadly Sins began to leap about at once. Pride
was first of all in the dance, with hair combed back and bonnet
cocked on one side, as if he were about to be the ruination of
homes, his robe hanging round him in folds like the spokes of
a wheel, down to his heels. Many proud deceivers danced

---

[1] 57 ("The Dance of the Sevin Deidly Synnis").
[2] Cp. *The Poems of William Dunbar*, ed. Small, S.T.S., III. 192.

with him, through scalding fire, grimacing with hideous
groans. Contemptuous rogues came in various disguises and
haughty manner, but Mahomet never laughed at that, till
priests with bare shaved necks came in, then all the fiends
mocked and laughed, Black Belly and Bawsy Brown.

> Than Yre come in with sturt and stryfe;   31
> His hand wes ay upoun his knyfe,
>   He brandeist lyk a beir:
> Bostaris, braggaris, and barganeris,
> Eftir him passit in to pairis,
>   All bodin in feir of weir;

They were dressed in jacks, knapsacks, and steel bonnets. Their
legs were armed in chain-mail to the heel, and their behaviour
was truculent. Some struck at others with swords, some
stabbed with daggers right up to the hilt. After Pride and
Anger, next in the dance came Envy, filled full of enmity and
crime, hidden malice and spite—this traitor trembled with
secret hate. He was followed by a train of dissemblers feigning
purity, of flatterers and defamers who delight in telling lies
in secret places (here is this image again of the "rouners in
corners" who seem to have bothered Dunbar at court), and
whisperers of false tales:

> Allace, that courtis of noble kingis   53
>   Of thame can nevir be quyte.

After Pride, Anger, and Envy, came Avarice (Covetyce), root
of all evil and ground of all vice, who could never be content.
In the train of that sorcerer were cowards, outcasts, usurers,
misers, hoarders, and collectors, vomiting hot molten gold on
each other, burning like lightning, in cart-loads: and whenever
they emptied themselves of the gold vomit, fiends filled them
up to the neck with all manner of stamped gold once more
(again we notice that Dunbar takes a much harsher view of
the Avaricious than Dante does in *Inferno*, Canto VII).

Sloth came like a sow out of a midden, after Pride, Anger,
Envy, and Avarice, as if he was coming only at the second
bidding, with sleepy excuses. He drew them along on a chain,
and Belial lashed them continually on the loins with a bridle

rein—a touch of the fire made them quicker of foot in the dance. Then Lechery, that loathsome corpse, followed the others, roaring like a rutting stallion, and led by Idleness. He is followed by a train of stinking corpses that had died in sin, weird of countenance in the dance, burning red like hot tongs. Each led the other by the penis:

> All led thay uthir by the tersis,   88
> Suppois thay fycket[3] with thair ersis,
>   It mycht be na remeid.

Last of all the seven comes Gluttony, the foul monster with insatiable and greedy belly, shaping up to the dance, and followed by many foul drunkards with can and flagon, cup and quart taken in surfeit and excess, and many huge-bellied sluggards with unmanageable bellies waddled forth in greasy fat that kept getting bigger and bigger. Drink, always they cried, with many a gaping mouth—so the fiends gave them hot lead to lick, no lesser allowance.

No minstrels played to these dancers, be sure, for gleemen were kept out by day and night, except for one who had slain a man and thus won into his heritage and entered by right of law.

Then Mahomet called for a Highland pageant, and a fiend ran to bring MacFadyan from a corner in the far north. By the time that he had shouted the coronach (lament), he was so hemmed in by Gaels that they took up much room in Hell. It ends:

> Thae tarmegantis with tag and tatter,   115
> Full lowd in Ersche begowth to clatter,
>   And rowp lyk revin and ruke:
> The Devill sa devit wes with thair yell
> That in the depest pot of hell
>   He smorit thame with smuke.

This last stanza is really a second poem **in** its own right, in a sense—it has no obvious connexion with the Deidly Synnis as such, but follows on with a "then"—after the dance of the sins, in other words, something worse followed; a pageant

---

[3] This is Bannatyne's reading: Maitland has "fyllit."

Q

of Highlanders—just as the Highland pageant is followed by
"Nixt that a Turnament wes Tryid".   In my reading, therefore, there are four poems, not three in the series—namely the
"Dance", "The Heleand Padyane", "The Turnament", and
"Amendis".   The first three are all part of the one vision of
Hell, while Dunbar is in the same trance; and the fourth is a
sequel.   There are three sections of one narrative, followed by
a sequel.   This is rather an important point, for all the editions
to date have quite wrongly, in my view, printed the "Padyane"
as if it were part of the "Dance"—no doubt justifiably from
the manuscripts: but if that were to be the standard, then the
editions have already taken far greater liberties with their
originals.   Dunbar seems to me to make it quite clear that
they are separate.   First, in the "Dance":

> Mahoun gart cry ane dance . . .   6

Secondly:

> Than cryd Mahoun for a Heleand padyane . . .   109

Thirdly:

> Nixt that a turnament wes tryid,   1
> That Lang befoir in hell wes cryid,
> In presens of Mahoun.

Mahoun is master of ceremonies, "crying" up one entertainment after another, beginning with the grim dance, then
moving into wilder and wilder comedy, like a dance mounting
to a climax, a sort of hellish orgy, moving from the dance to
the "padyane", and on to the riot of the turnament.   The
structure seems quite obvious, and there is no excuse at all
for printing the "Padyane" as if it were a final stanza of the
"Dance".   Why this has not been remarked before is one of
those mysteries of scholarship.   Perhaps scholars read only
texts, and not poems as such.

   The Dance of the Seven Deadly Sins, of course, is a common
feature of medieval life and literature, popular throughout
Christendom—the *"danse macabre"*.[4]   It belongs in one sense

---

[4] Cp., for example, *The Parson's Tale*, *Piers Plowman* (Pass V), Lydgate's *Dance of Death*.

among the humorous poems, but it differs from them in one
essential and cardinal respect—it is the humour that laughs
because it is afraid. The dread of death, of sin, of punishment
in Hell eternally is very real—the laughter is a nervous one to
relieve the tension of fear. The fear itself is a concomitant of
faith in the Church's teaching, and therefore the poem is
essentially a religious one, the humour masking a deep belief
in the horrors defensively laughed or smiled at: whereas the
companion pieces are pure fun, or fun mixed with satire. This
is a sort of comic *Inferno*, introduced by Dunbar's favourite
dream-device. Although this use of it may have been purely
conventional, he is always mixing convention with fresh real
experience; and one cannot help wondering whether he so
often availed himself of the dream-device because it was only
at bedtime that he ever got freedom to exercise his imagination
untrammelled, or because the relaxed state between waking
and sleeping is, of all states of consciousness, the most conducive
to the poetic trance, the rapt state of being bemused, possessed
by the Muse. Lent, of course, is the time of year before which
sin traditionally was (and, amongst the faithful, still is) held to
be at its height, and when the seven deadly sins have their final
fling before the shriving of the long fast. Dunbar's catalogue
is a mounting one, ending in the dance of Gluttony—the one
most affected by fasting, in the traditional manner: his private
view being, as his poems evidence, that in his experience of
the court and country of James IV, the sin of avarice is the
worst and most prevalent. The purpose of the poem is at
once to give the sins of his audience their last fling, in the form
of imaginative art, and at the same time to frighten them into
a mood suitable for the forthcoming fast: his great powers of
sensual imagination are used to conjure up a picture more
gruesome than comic, more grim than funny. The seven sins
are in fact deadly, and Dunbar never loses sight of that. We
of a later age are perhaps less likely to see the seriousness of
purpose behind the poem: we tend unconsciously to see it
through such later poetry as "Tam o' Shanter", with its
comic dance of witches conducted by the Deil in Kirk Allowa'
—and this is fatal to a real appreciation of the poem. In this
poem Dunbar's art is an art closer to caricature than to

comedy—and horrendous caricature at that. The type of thing is still to be seen—I remember a truly hair-raising caricature of Stalin in a Catholic paper in Sicily, which I saw there in 1951; it was crude and melodramatic, but for the unsophisticated people at whom it was aimed it must have been very effective indeed. There are some fine touches of realism in the characterisation, too—Anger, for instance, whose "hand wes ay upoun his knyfe", and Sloth coming "lyk a sow out of a midding". It is typical of Dunbar's art, an art essentially of making the old new, changing the living water of age-old and universal material into the wine of contemporary Scottish idiom, that he should personalise the archetypes of sin.

"Nixt that", he tells us, "a turnament wes tryid";[5] and it opens with a tailor and shoemaker before Mahomet in Hell. The tailor was escorted into the field, bearing spear and targe, by many rascals of seam-biters and flea-killers and thieves of clothing—a disgraceful bodyguard.

> His baner born wes him befoir,   13
> Quhairin wes clowttis ane hundredth scoir,
>   Ilk ane of divers hew;
> And all stowin out of sindry webbis,
> For, quhill the greit sie flowis and ebbis,
>   Telyouris will nevir be trew.

As soon as the Tailor saw the barrace his courage deserted him —if he ever had any—and he changed colour out of fear. Mahomet came forward and knighted him, and his heart grew light at such an honour. He promised Mahomet to strike down the shoemaker, but when they were confronted, he himself was struck dumb with fear:

> Off all sic wirdis he was full dum,   32
>   So soir he wes agast;
> In harte he tuke yit sic ane scunner
> Ane rak of fartis, lyk ony thunner,
>   Went fra him, blast for blast.

The Shoemaker was escorted on to the field by a stout man of defence from the west, with no proper squire, but with many

[5] 58 ("The Sowtar and the Tailyowres War").

lousy rogues about him.   His banner was of tanned leather,
whereon St Crispin glided before that ribald crowd.   He was
very shoemakerlike in manner, for oil kept on bursting out
from between the plates of his armour.   He was so terrified at
sight of the Tailor that he could scarcely sit upright, and there
was such a commotion in his breast that his stomach revolted
at his dear-bought dinner.

> To comfort him or he raid forder,   55
> The Devill off knychtheid gaif him order,
>   For sair syne he did spitt,
> And he about the Devillis nek,
> Did spew agane ane quart of blek,
>   Thus knychtly he him quitt.

The Fiend called "Fie", forty times, and the Shoemaker sought
the field readily enough.   The two jousters, still quaking, ride
against each other with spears, and

> The tailyeour that wes nocht weill sittin,   70
> He left his sadill all beschittin,
>   And to the ground he socht.

His harness broke and made a shattering noise, so frightening
the Shoemaker's horse that it ran to the Devil, who was standing
well to one side lest he be spewed on again:

> He thocht he wald agane Debait him,   82
> He turnd his ers and all bedret him,
>   Evin quyte from nek till neill.

So powerful was the force with which Mahomet let fly that
both horse and rider were struck to the ground.

> "Now haif I quitt the," quod Mahoun.   88

Both these new-made knights lay fainting, and forswore all
arms, and the Devil deprived them of knighthood, making
them both servants for ever, which rank they much preferred,
and drove them to a dungeon.   Dunbar ends:

> I had mair of thair werkis written,   97
> Had nocht the sowtar bene beschittin
>   With Belliallis ers unblest;
> Bot that sa gud ane bourd me thocht,

> Sic solace to my hairt it rocht,
> For lawchtir neir I brist;
> Qhairthrow I walknit of my trance.
> To put this in rememberence
> Mycht no man me resist,
> For this said jousting it befell
> Befoir Mahoun, the air of hell:
> Now trow this gif ye list.

Here we have yet another dream-waking ending—this time
by his own uncontrollable laughter. The "trance" is the one
mentioned at the beginning of "Off Februar the Fyifteen
Nycht". That tailors and shoemakers, of all trades, should
be chosen for ridicule must be attributed to custom. In
"Renunce thy God"[6] Dunbar satirises all trades, but tailors
and cobblers seem to have had a particular popularity as butts.
The object of Dunbar's laughter, however, is not merely the
two tradesmen, but the code of chivalry and the custom of
jousting. Not merely are the petty bourgeois tradesmen being
laughed at under the guise of knights, but knights are being
laughed at under the guise of tradesmen: this is a foreshadowing
of Don Quixote. Dunbar's main attack on and scorn of the
trades and other bourgeois occupations—it is always master-
tradesmen he has in mind, self-employed—is that they have
no honour—the great and real virtue of the chivalric code.
But in this poem, while the lack of chivalrous qualities in the
tradesmen is the obvious target, yet the custom of jousting is
itself, inevitably, called in question, and the two ways of life
contrasted and compared. If the tradesmen lack the courage
and daring of knights, yet they have better things to do than
waste their time and blood in useless activities like jousting.
It is not merely that in this poem two tradesmen confront each
other; the reality is that two worlds, two classes, two codes of
value confront each other, and the despised " lower " one is
destined to oust the other from social domination, for ever,
and for better.

Whatever exaggerated profits they may pile up for private
individuals, the present-day heirs of these two jousters, the large
tailoring and shoemaking houses are notably less harmful and

[6] 42 ("The Devillis Inquest").

of more real value to the community than medieval landlords were. This clash of the two classes is implicit in the fact that tailors and cobblers are depicted as figures of low comedy merely as such—a class judgment. They score off each other in the poem, and Dunbar scores off both: and possibly all three sides, and others, enjoy—certainly are intended to enjoy —the fun. The poem is fast in pace and unflagging—again the short-lined dancing stanza brings out the best in Dunbar, the metre well-controlled, the earthy Rabelaisian humour well-sustained and gleefully executed, the slapstick with great power, zest, and drive behind it. The poem is set in "Hell", but once again "Hell" is remarkably like the ordinary human world: "Hell" is society.

Dunbar in this poem, it seems, has too irreverently used the holy orders of tailors and cobblers, and in "Betuix Twell Houris and Ellevin"[7] he speaks of his correction from on high:

> Betuix twell houris and ellevin, I
> I dremd ane angell cam fra Hevin
> With plesand stevin sayand on hie,
> Telyouris and Sowtaris, blist be ye.

> In Hevin hie ordand is your place,
> Aboif all sanctis in grit solace,
> Nixt God grittest in dignitie:
> Telyouris and Sowtaris, blist be ye.

The reason for this high rank of these tradesmen is well known to them—by great skill and craft they mend those people whom God made a bad job of: cobblers mending the faults of misshapen feet by their shoes, hiding corns, knotty toes, chilblains, and so on—and for this their souls will go to Heaven: and tailors mending ill-shaped men with well-shaped clothes, hiding broken backs, making the crooked straight, disguising limps. Such miracle-workers will clearly be saints in Heaven, though they be rogues in this country.

Here the typically "sleekit wit" of Dunbar makes a cruelly telling point about reality and appearance. Those whom God made ill can be faked up by skilful art to look much

---

[7] 59 ("The Amendis to the Telyouris and Sowtars for the Turnament Maid on Thame").

better than they really are—the narrow shoulders padded out, the long back broadened, the short back lengthened, the lumpish figure streamlined, the square foot made elegant— and what can be done with women, of course, ranges from footbinding and wasp-waisting to the current regular heightening and lowering of waists, hiding or revealing breasts, etc., etc.   But of course clothes are mere symbols of personality, and Dunbar has his eye on the tailored persons, even the tailored soul: on spiritual dissembling, in fact, assuming a virtue not really possessed.   Dissimulation is attacked as a favourite vice of his time (as of all times, I suppose) in the satires and complaints, and he returns to it here.   The irony of the reference to God is telling: God is supposed to approve of dissembling—God, in fact, is tailored to suit men's needs,[8] and thus he is depicted as having a high regard for those who help dissemblers—God, in the poem, is seen ironically in the image of the tailors and cobblers.

This group of four-in-one poems, this religious extravaganza, forms a natural bridge to the gloomier poems of meditation, death, despair, world-weariness, and depression.

[8] Cp. Robert Fergusson's "Braid Claith " as a more conscious and serious development of this theme.

XII

Timor Mortis Conturbat Me

THESE poems are much more various, occasional, and personal than the groups hitherto considered here: they are often short pieces almost thrown away, certainly many of them among the most personal, unselfconscious, unaudience-conscious that have come down to us from Dunbar. They are mostly moralistic lyrics, poems of mood, fleeting, changing, variable, and the link between them is a very loose one: yet some loose interconnection they do have. The first of these is short enough to be quoted whole:

> Quhat is this lyfe bot ane straucht way to deid,   1
>   Quhilk hes a tyme to pas, and nane to duell;
> A slyding quheill us lent to seik remeid;
>   A fre chois gevin to Paradice or Hell;
>   A pray to deid, quhome vane is to repell;
> A schoirt torment for infineit glaidnes,
> Als schort ane joy for lestand hevynes.[1]

This strikes the note of sombre brooding on death which we will hear again and again in these poems—life is fleeting, a time to pass, but not to stay. Death is the great mystery, the ultimate end of life, and no man is spared for his gifts, his rank, his wealth, or for anything else. The dance of sin leads on to the dance of death, which is the ultimate evil: a man may be saved from sin as long as he has the power to repent, but from death there can be no reprieve. This life is but "ane straucht way to deid", and no virtue can save us from that inexorable sentence.

This is the ultimate problem of human fate which the religious have answered with a belief in a metaphysical life after death, a life much better than this, and having the quality

---

[1] 76 ("Of Lyfe").

most completely lacking in this—eternal being. Thus Dunbar speaks in "O Wreche, be War":[2]

> O wreche, be war! this warld will wend the fro,   I
>   Quhilk hes begylit mony greit estait;
> Turne to thy freynd, belief nocht in they fo,
>   Sen thou mon go, be grathing to thy gait;
>   Remeid in tyme and rew nocht all to lait;
> Provyd thy place, for thow away man pas
>   Out of this vaill of trubbill and dissait:
> *Vanitas Vanitatum, et omnia Vanitas.*

In this pilgrimage one should walk forward while there is daylight, leaving the desert, drawing toward home, hurrying, for the night is in diligent pursuit. Bend all sail to win the port of grace, lest death overtake you in sin. Nothing remains stable in this world—false and flitting; now day-bright, and then night-black; now ebb, then flood; now friend, then foe; now glad, then sad; now hale, now sick; now wealthy, then ashes— so goes this transitory world: *Vanitas vanitatum, et omnia vanitas.*

The Biblical clichés pile up in this poem, but the impulse and drive of the lines are sufficient earnest of its deep-felt sincerity: cliché, the death of literature, is the life of religion— what are dogmas, after all, but clichés of the spirit? The new in religion is heresy: in literature it is a first principle. It is this fact which makes so much religious literature so dull, repetitive, monotonous: and Dunbar does not escape the vice attendant on such virtue. The biggest problem in creative writing of any sort is the tracing accurately of the line between that which is not merely old but eternal and undepartable-from, and that which must be new or cannot but be bad. There is no easy rule—each work faces it anew, like a recurring sphinx—and failure to solve it means the death of the work. Dunbar is constantly facing and solving this problem—making something new out of traditional material. In this poem, too, he succeeds, but there are dangerous rocks showing above the water-line here and there. For the traditionalist—and all medieval poets are traditionalists, with the possible exception of the great experimenting troubadours—it is true that "there

[2] 75 ("Of the Warldis Vanitie").

is nothing new under the sun": but everything under the sun must *seem* to be new, must be seen anew, in the work.

"I Seik about this Warld Unstabille"[3] continues the mood of dissatisfaction with the world:

> I seik about this warld unstabille   I
> To find ane sentence convenabille,
>   Bot I can nocht in all my wit
>   Sa trew ane sentence fynd off it,
> As say it is dessaveabille.

Yesterday the season came in soft and fair as a peacock's feather—today it stings like an adder; yesterday the flowers sprang up beautifully and birds sang—today the flowers are killed by rain and the birds languish in cold bowers. Thus winter follows summer, distress comfort, sorrow joy—"So is this warld and ay hes bein". The note of depression here, as elsewhere in these poems, is appropriately expressed in terms of the Scottish weather, of which it has been said that one might experience all four seasons in one day: "changeable as the weather" is proverbial. The trouble with this kind of poem is that neither logic nor reality is in any way affected if one reverses the order of the sequences: spring follows winter, sunshine follows rain, joy follows sorrow—the poem chooses the pessimistic one only because it suits his mood, not because it proves anything. Dunbar had much to complain of, but his complaints against rightable wrongs have more verve, more poetic tension, more humanity and hope in them than these rather fatalistic complaints against what cannot be changed, being eternal conditions of human life. But the mood is well-sustained, the poem finely wrought.

> Off lentern in the first mornyng,   I
> Airly as did the day up spring,
> Thus sang ane bird with voce upplane,
> "All erdly joy returnis in pane."

Thus opens another poem[4] which is usually given the title of the refrain. O man, the bird goes on, remember that you must die, that you are nothing but ashes and will return to

---

[3] 66 ("Of the Changes of Lyfe").
[4] 71 ("All Erdly Joy Returns in Pane").

ashes; that age follows youth, death follows life with gaping
mouth devouring fruit and burgeoning grain; that wealth,
worldly glory, fine clothes are but thorns covered with flowers
—a trap on your way.

> "Come nevir yit May so fresche and grene,   17
> Bot Januar come als wod and kene;
> Wes nevir sic drowth bot anis come rane:
> All erdly joy returnis in pane."

Trouble succeeds the world's pleasure as his heir, and always
will; health turns into sickness, merriment into depression,
town into desert, meadow into forest; liberality becomes
miserliness, truth falsehood, virtue vice, honour becomes
avarice (the feudal virtue gives way to the capitalist vice, as
he sees it), and conscience is slain by envy. The moral to all
this:

> "Sen erdly joy abydis nevir,   37
> Wirk for the joy that lestis evir;
> For uder joy is all bot vane:
> All erdly joy returnis in pane."

Reality, when found, is a desolation; painful, joyless, depress-
ing, deceitful, unbearable—so one looks to another, immaterial
world for the satisfaction of human needs and desires. The
stanza here is elegiac, and the elegy is for human mortality—
that most unbearable of realities. For Dunbar, too, "man
cannot stand too much reality". The high-flown romanticism
of the allegory of Courtly Love, the sub-realism of the "Tretis",
the comedy of the drunken defiance of death and the hereafter,
are all ways of escape from the unbearably bleak vision of
reality itself—that we all must die, golden lads and girls as
much as chimney-sweepers. The idea of change running
throughout the poem is reminiscent of Fortune's wheel, but,
like the cycle of the seasons, this has its ups as well as its downs
—Dunbar is more interested in the downs. Yet this is only
one side of reality, the dark side, the "dragon blak" which
threatens to devour us with morbid depression. The last
stanza here is very weak—as so often in Dunbar. This is not
true religion, but religious escapism, sentimental, weak: this
joy, too, we might point out to him—or to the bird—is also

self-deception, being a self-saving view of religion: which
is to say, an irreligious view.

The theme of "ashes to ashes" is taken up again more
fully in "*Memento, homo, quod cinis es*":[5]

> Memento homo, quod cinis es.
> Think, man, thow art bot erd and as.
> Lang heir to duell no thing thow pres,
>   For as thow come so shall thow pas;
>   Lyk as ane schaddow in ane glas
>   Hyne glydis all thy tyme that heir is.
>   Think, thocht thy bodye ware of bras,
>   *Quod tu in cinerem reverteris.*

Hector and Hercules, Achilles and Samson, Alexander, David
and Absalom have all played their parts here and are gone by
the will of God—there is no exception of persons: all return
to ashes. Though one may now be most fortunate and handsome, in less than a year one may be an ugly repulsive corpse.
And since you know that your life is in hazard at all hours,
think, *Quod tu in cinerem reverteris.* Your full handsomeness of
youth will fade like summer flowers. The dragon Death, who
devours all, will swallow you up—no castle nor tower can
protect you or your companions from him. Though you may
be possessed of all this world, after death you will own nothing
but your good deeds—therefore, confess with humble heart
and sober tears . . .

> Thocht thow be taklit nevir so sure,   17
>   Thow sall in deathis port arryve,
> Quhair nocht for tempest may indure,
>   Bot ferslye all to spair is dryve.
>   Thy ransonner with woundis fyve
>   Mak thy plicht anker and thy steiris
>   To hald thy saule with him on lyve,
>   *Cum tu in cinerem reverteris.*

This last stanza has a genuine religious note, though it still has
rather a weak impulse behind it—too conventional, not passionate enough, not deeply enough felt.

This is partly due to the fact that the poem is a conventional

---

[5] 76 ("Of Manis Mortalitie").

performance for Ash Wednesday, aimed at an audience, rather than a personal meditation. The tone is homiletic, owing more to the sermon literature than to original genius,[6] and the second stanza is a typical *"ubi sunt"* passage. In the first stanza the remarkable image of life as a reflexion gliding across a mirror is as likely to have been drawn from the sermon literature[7] as created white-hot in the imagination—there is little white-hot in this poem. Dunbar got a remarkable range of poems out of the theme of Lent: compare this with "Madam, Your Men Said thai wald Ryd",[8] for instance, with "This Lang Lentern Makis me Lene",[9] and with "Off Februar the Fyiftene Nicht".[10] This one is very dependent on its religious setting, for if it were taken as a general moralising, it would be a very unhealthy one indeed, more likely to lead to neurosis than better living. The image of the corpse, for instance, has the same kind of sick morbidity one finds in Baudelaire, the great poet of spiritual defeat by the "dragon blak". But the religious function of the poem is seasonal—it is the time of year to remember these things, and, by so doing, to purge the spirit of precisely this sick morbidity: it is the same principle as inoculation against physical disease, and as such is sound psychological medicine—like so much else in true religious practice.

The influence of the weather on some of these poems has been remarked, and the seasonal nature of their preoccupations. In "In to thir Dirk and Drublie Dayis"[11] this becomes paramount, with the underlying theme of the winter of the spirit, of old age and death.

> In to thir dirk and drublie dayis   1
> Quhone sabill all the hevin arrayis
>   With mystie vapouris, cluddis, and skyis,
>   Nature all curage me denyis
> Off sangis, ballatis, and of playis.

---

[6] I am indebted here in general to G. R. Owst, *Literature and the Pulpit in Mediaeval England*.

[7] On religious poetry, cp. Carleton Brown, Religious *Lyrics of the Fourteenth Century*, nos. 79 (l. 26), 101 (l. 59) and 121 (l. 90).

[8] 31 ("To the Quene").   [9] 46 ("The Twa Cummeris").

[10] 57 ("The Dance of the Seven Deidly Synnis").

[11] 10 ("Meditatioun in Wyntir").

When the night lengthens with wind, rain, and hail, his sad spirit hides from the menacing din, his heart faints with loneliness, for want of summer with his flowers. He wakes, tossing and turning, unable to sleep, and vexed by heavy imaginings, examining his experience of the world—and the more he seeks comfort, the more he is agitated by doubt. Despair counsels him to provide for himself before it is too late, getting himself a living—otherwise he will continue to live in this court with great trouble and mischief. Patience retorts that he should not be afraid but hold Truth and Hope firmly with him, letting Fortune work out her anger—for no reason will placate her before her glass has run out. And Prudence adds—why cling to that which must away? Or crave that you may have more time when in fact you are moving nearer every day to the pilgrimage to the other world?

> And than sayis Age, My freind, cum neir   31
> And be not strange, I the requeir:
>   Cum, brodir, by the hand me tak,
>   Remember thow hes compt to mak
> Off all thi tyme thow spendit heir.

Then Death throws his gates wide open saying, these shall await you open, and if you were never so huge, under this lintel you will stoop, there is no other way. All day he droops because of this—no gold in chest, no wine in cup, no lady's beauty, nor bliss of love prevents his remembering this, no matter how well he may dine or sup. But there is for him in the end:

> Yit, quhone the nycht begynnis to schort,   46
> It dois my spreit sum pairt confort,
>   Off thocht oppressit with the schowris.
>   Cum, lustie symmer with thi flowris
> That I may leif in sum disport.

There is some ambiguity in ll. 4-5. Does he mean that nature denies him all enjoyment of songs, ballads, and plays—or that she denies him the heart to make these things? My own view is that it is the latter he means; for, whereas it is likely that depression would prevent his "making", it might have the opposite effect of driving him to seek solace in merely receiving these things. But the point is worth noting, for the latter meaning is too easily assumed. Accepting it, though, the query follows—if Dunbar made plays,[12] where are they? *Mais ou sont les pièces de Dunbar?* Gone, with the bulk of lost Scottish literature. There is "Harry Harry Hobbilschowe", mentioned at the end of the last chapter, the anonymous piece attributed, with good reason, to Dunbar. This may have been part of an interlude in a much larger drama. We have the example of Lyndsay with his great *Satyre of the Thrie Estaitis* to suggest that making plays was expected of court poets: and Lyndsay, who succeeds and fulfils Dunbar as a satirist, must have had models for his own great work: so fully achieved a work cannot be any more *sui generis* than *Hamlet* is, and the models must have been closer to Lyndsay's idiom than Bale's *King Johan*, the one which is usually cited. We have proof enough of the lost literature in "I that in Heill wes and Gladnes", next to be considered, with its catalogue of poets whose work is almost entirely lost to us: and we have seen the skill of Kennedy in the "Flyting" to be little less than that of Dunbar himself. It is possible that we have only a fragment of even Dunbar's work, and that more than plays have been lost.

The intrusion of the allegorical personifications of Despair, Patience, Prudence, Age and Death reminds us that Dunbar mixes the categories as he pleases—and they are not altogether out of place, though a little bit disturbing, in this superb meditation. The old note of his position at court is heard once again, and the insecurity and fear he expresses is not entirely of death or other spiritual matters.   Yet it is ultimately of age and death that he is afraid, and the second last stanza is the most excellent elegiac stanza on aged loneliness known to me in either Scots or English. One should contrast this poem with the serenity of Henrysoun in his "Prais of Aige":

The moir of aige, the nerar hevynis blis.

Nothing could better stress the difference between the two poets, and of the two eras they express. Dunbar's *Angst* is as

---

[12] "Plays," of course, might simply mean "pageants", such as "Off Februar the fyiftene nicht" *et seq.*

sincere as Henrysoun's serenity, his melancholy as profound as Henrysoun's humour. There are many strands of Dunbar's poetry woven into this one poem, strands of traditions he has used, from the hint of the garden of the "Rose" in the summer references, to the satirical echo of the reference to the court. His material poverty and complaint is quite swamped by a deeper, more incurable ill—the lament for lost youth, and the nearness of death. The pathos evoked by this poem is real and full, not the reserved one struck by self-pity—there is no audience for this poem—he speaks out of a deep compulsion, and we merely overhear him. The chief note is loneliness, the loneliness of old age facing death, deserted, comfortless, a social outcast, or at least socially neglected, fearful, menaced by poverty and hardship, attacked by anxieties too severe to be borne—the fate of so many old-age pensioners in our own time. The poet has even lost his courage to dream creatively, to sing up out of the gathering darkness, like Yeats's swan adrift on its darkening flood. He has already begun to die, is dying daily by inches, a soul "tied to a dying animal", in Yeats's phrase. The speech Age makes in ll. 31-5 is very powerful in its blending of the sinister and the friendly—a master-stroke.

The kind of fear of death in this poem is not so morbid as that given below in "I that in Heill wes and Gladnes":[13] it has great dignity and a deep love of and reverence for life, though nostalgically expressed. He is reluctant to give in to the unconquerable enemy. He enriches life in the very act of making clear to us what old age has in store. This is one of Dunbar's finest poems, and one of the finest ever written.

> I that in heill wes and gladnes   1
> Am trublit now with gret seiknes
> And feblit with infermitie;
> *Timor mortis conturbat me.*
>
> Our plesance heir is all vane glory,
> This fals warld is bot transitory,
> The flesche is brukle, the Fend is sle;
> *Timor mortis conturbat me.*

---

[13] 7 ("Lament quhen He was Seik").

R

> The stait of man dois change and vary,
> Now sound, now seik, now blith, now sary,
> Now dansand mery, now like to dee;
> *Timor mortis conturbat me.*
>
> No stait in erd here standis sickir;
> As with the wind wavis the wickir,
> Wavis this warldis vanite;
> *Timor mortis conturbat me.*

Thus opens Dunbar's most famous poem. That fourth stanza is not only one of the greatest elegiac stanzas ever written, but one of the greatest stanzas of any sort: the counterpoint from "wickir" at the end of l. 2 to "Wavis" at the beginning of l. 3 is the most telling reversal of rhythm I can think of. Here, surely, Dunbar transcends his limitation as a poet of major, but not maximal talent, and joins the ranks of the maximal. Sophocles, Shakespeare—Dante himself—would not be disgraced by such a stanza. This is great classical art, an art of bare statement, stark as Greek tragedy, bleak as the prospect of death itself, the hard granite face of destiny, unsmiling, unflinching, unmoving. On to death go all estates, princes, prelates, men of power, both rich and poor of all degree— Death takes knights in the field, babes at the breast, champions in strife, captains in towers, ladies in boudoirs, strong lords, intellectuals, magicians, astrologers, rhetoricians, logicians, theologians—none are spared for their qualities, none can outwit him. The most skilful doctors of medicine, surgeons, physicians cannot preserve themselves from the last illness. Poets, too:

> I see that makaris amang the laif   45
> Playis heir ther pageant, syne gois to graif;
> Sparit is nocht ther faculte;
> *Timor mortis conturbat me.*
>
> He has done petuously devour
> The noble Chaucer, of makaris flour,
> The Monk of Bery, and Gower, all thre;
> *Timor mortis conturbat me.*

The good Sir Hew of Eglintoun, Heriot, and Wyntoun[14] have

---

[14] Author of the *Originale Cronykill*.

all been taken from this country, and that fell scorpion has stung Maister Johne Clerk and James Afflek who made ballads and tragedies (tragedies might be drama or narrative: but if drama what a loss is recorded here!): Holland,[15] and Barbour,[16] have been taken, and Sir Mungo Lockart of the Lea, Clerk of Tranent[17] who made the *Anteris of Gawane* (the Gawane poems that have come down are anonymous), and Sir Gilbert Hay. Blind Hary[18] and Sandy Traill and Patrick Johnestoun[19] have been slain by his shower of mortal hail. Merseir,[20] too, he has taken, Merseir who wrote of love so lively in brief poems of high art, and Roull of Aberdeen and his namesake of Corstorphine, two gentler men were never seen.[21]

> In Dumfermelyne he hes done roune 81
> With Maister Robert Henrisoun;
> Schir Johne the Ros enbrast hes he;
> *Timor mortis conturbat me.*

Schir Johne the Ros is probably the man referred to in the "Flyting" as Dunbar's "second", or squire. And now, he goes on, Death has taken last of all good gentle-born Stobo[22] and Quintyne Schaw.[23] Good Master Walter Kennedy[24] now lies at point of death, which is a great pity. There is only one makar left who has as yet escaped the common fate— the one now writing:

> Sen he hes all my brether tane, 92
> He will nocht lat me lif alane,
> On forse I man his neist pray be;
> *Timor mortis conturbat me.*

---

[15] Author of the long alliterative peom *The Howlat*. [16] Author of *The Brus*.

[17] Author of a lyric or two preserved in Bannatyne's and Maitland's MSS.

[18] Author of *The Wallas*.

[19] Bannatyne's MS. includes one poem by a "Patrik Johnstoun."

[20] Author of three poems in Bannatyne's MS. and one in Maitland's.

[21] Bannatyne's MS. includes a poem entitled "The Cursing of Sir Johine Rowlis Upoun the steilaris of his fowlis".

[22] Mentioned in the "Flyting", but nothing that has come down to us is known to be his.

[23] Also mentioned in the "Flyting"; author of one poem in Maitland's MS.

[24] Of the "Flyting". This would seem to corroborate the belief that the "Flyting" was a friendly one intended as a joke: but there is, to my ear, a false note in "Gret reuth it war that so suld be".

There is only one thing to do about this grim prospect, and the poem ends:

> Sen for the deid remeid is none,   96
> Best is that we for deid dispone,
> Eftir our deid that lif may we;
> *Timor mortis conturbat me.*

That internal rhyme in l. 97 at once tolls like a death-knell and marches like a dead march, heavily, with a slow thump. But l. 99 is again rather weak and conventional—did he really believe faithfully in the after-life, or does the pious conventionality conceal both a wish and a doubt? In any case, the effect is weakening, being at best inadequate.

The refrain is from the Office for the Dead, and was used by Lydgate (a stronger influence on Dunbar than Chaucer[25]) in the poem beginning "So as I lay this othir nycht". The tradition behind it is the *danse macabre*—not sin this time, but death itself. Henrysoun has a macabre poem called "The Thre Deid Pollis", and there is a *danse macabre* frieze in the fifteenth-century Roslin Chapel, near Edinburgh—the whole century seems to have been possessed of the *timor mortis* rather more than most. But the nearest kin, as usual, is Villon in his *Grant Testament*, and particularly in the two ballads of the ladies and lords of former times. Gregor traces parallels also with Richard Rolle's "Pricke of Conscience", Barbour's *Bruce*, Lyndsay's "The Deploratioun" (a later poem of course), and the *Chanson de Roland*.

It is odd that little attention has been paid to the chief key to the poem—the fact that Dunbar wrote it " Quhen he wes seik". It is not his normal vision of life that we are getting, but the vision of a man whose vitality has been lowered, who is "feblit with infermite". In ll. 1-3 he tells us that he is used to being healthy and cheerful (an extraverted personality, to use the current term), but illness has now brought him low. There is of course the hint of old age in "infermite", of the infirmity being that of age, and therefore part of a permanent change, not the temporary one of illness; and the theme of

---

[25] Cp. P. H. Nicols, "William Dunbar as a Scottish Lydgatian," in *PMLA*, XLVI (1931).

age indeed is there throughout the poem, especially in the closing stanzas: but it is an actual sickness which has precipitated the depression, and which leads on to his perception of the transience of things, and gives rise to this particular "timor mortis". As usual, it is some specific private experience which starts him off on the use of the traditional material. The poem is a lyric, in fact, a poem of mood, [26] not a balanced and considered vision of life. There is no necessary reason why, once he has recovered from the illness, he should not again be the liveliest spark at another dance in the Queen's chamber. It is of some importance to note that he sees himself as being normally healthy and happy—depression is a quite common ill attendant upon extraverts: Robert Burns was another so plagued. Dunbar is essentially a man of the world—there is nothing mystical in his nature: compare his lament for the deaths of the Makars with Vaughan's:

> They are all gone into the world of light,
> And I alone left ling'ring here . . .

This is the opposite attitude to that of Dunbar, and it is this essential worldliness which makes the ending so weak and dubious, and makes us often suspicious of his pious conventionalities: his doubt we know too well as a thing of utter and deep-felt sincerity, but his faith, so far, has been more of the head than of the heart. But the two moods of Dunbar are the mood of gaiety and sensual delight, and the opposite mood of gloomy forebodings: the whole variety of Dunbar's wide range of sensibility is held between these polar moods. "Schir Jhon Sinclair Begowthe to Dance" [27] is an example of the normal mood: this particular poem, "quhen he wes seik", is *the* example of the opposite. We misread it if we do not keep in mind the fact that it is a "sick" poem. This is not a true religious poem—the Vaughan one is nearer being that: the mark of true religion is not fear of death but faith in life, the heroic courage—"faith"—enjoined on his followers by Yeshu of Nazareth to lose your life in order to save it. This

---

[26] And, of course, as a poem of the mood of universal lament, of "Ubi sunt?", it is a masterpiece.

[27] 32 ("Of a Dance in the Quenis Chalmer").

alone has the heroic power to achieve God's kingdom on earth.

Again, one must bear in mind that each part of Church teaching is designed to deal with specific problems, each part of ritual is a therapeutic measure whose meaning can only be seen in relation to the whole: diseases must be brought out before they can be cured—and the fear of physical death is a destructive disease which can be cured, according to the Church, by faith in the central Christian mystery, not the immortality of the soul, but the resurrection of the body. The place of the *timor mortis* in ritual is that the confessing and facing of it leads to the saving grace of faith in the resurrection of the body on the Day of Judgment. No confession of *timor mortis*, no salvation through faith in resurrection. In the last stanza, "Eftir our deid that lif may we", Dunbar does hint at the hope, though it is a rather pallid statement of it: but the point is that, the disease having been exposed, the medicine begins to work.

In his sickness he sees life as all vain glory, illusion, helplessness; change, which is in fact the joyous essence of life, is seen as an unbearable condition—he longs for the static changelessness of death, and it is the *longing* that he fears. This is the suicidal state—life is too painful therefore death is to be preferred: yet it is not death that is longed for, but a posited better life—the life after death. There is a profound sense in which it is true that an organism dies because it wants to die: but this longing for death presents itself to human consciousness as a longing for a better life; and religion meets the need by positing precisely that, beyond the grave. Yet the prayer recommended by the founder of Christianity was not "Grant us life eternal after death", but "Thy kingdom come, Thy will be done on earth, as it is in heaven". To that is added the defence against anxiety—"Do not want more than enough for the day"—and the necessity of forgiving offence, in a good community. That is the core of the teaching. Much of Dunbar's anxiety comes from wanting more than enough for the day—he wanted security and plenty, and, not getting them, was a prey to *Angst*. It is typical of his self-centredness that the climax of this great roll-call of the dead should be the fact

that he himself is going to die, should be the most momentous
and impressive fact of the momentous and impressive catalogue.
This is not merely personal, but traditional, in terms of the
religious ritual which gives him his refrain—the agitation by
fear of personal death, the recognition of which may lead to
salvation. But there is a danger here, because for those—the
majority today—for whom the faith in resurrection offered by
traditional Christianity is untenable, the poem may encourage
a fear which, not meeting its intended medicine, becomes
merely neurotic and morbid.

It is therefore necessary to stress that we should always
see this poem in its context—a context of the medieval Catholic
mind and of Dunbar's personal participation in that mind, and
contribution to it, in his poetry. One should read it also with
the spiritual defeat of Baudelaire in mind.[28] One's approach
to it should have an element of the clinical in it, remembering
that he wrote it "quhen he wes seik". Then, like Aeneas
armed with the golden bough, we may let the great army of
the dead roll over us, and survive. Let the dead bury their
dead. If the Christian witness stresses one truth more than
another, it is that the fear of death should never prevent anyone from living the good life, doing the will of God, bringing
the kingdom of God on earth—a heroic task. There are two
questions a human being need never ask, since they are
completely unreal—how to get by without guilt, and how to
live for ever: both are impossible.

This poem is the climax of this group, but there are others in
meditative or moralistic vein best considered here. In marked
contrast to the foregoing poem is the "Full oft I Mus":[29]

> Full oft I mus and hes in thocht   I
> How this fals warld is ay on flocht
>   Quhair no thing ferme is nor degest;
> And quhen I haif my mynd all socht,
>   For to be blyth me think is best.

The false world always flits and changes, Fortune (who
traditionally has power over all beneath the moon in the

---

[28] It is interesting to compare Baudelaire's treatment by General Aupick with
that of Dunbar by James IV.   [29] 69 ("Best to be Blyth").

medieval cosmology) turns her wheel so fast, never still, that none should fret at its variability—it is best to be cheerful. If man would consider well in mind, before Fortune turns her wheel on him, that earthly glory cannot last, his fall would be less painful. To struggle with and worry about this world brings misery even to those of lordly rank; what use is wealth and property without happiness? Ownership of the whole world would be mere poverty without happiness. Who should be depressed, or die, for want of that which is but tinsel, vanity, since life here is but the twinkling of an eye to life eternal. If Dunbar himself had indulged in depression because of the world's cruelty, or been driven from his enjoyment, he would have been dead long ago.

> How evir this warld do change and vary   36
> Lat us in hairt nevir moir be sary,
>   Bot evir be reddy and addrest
> To pas out of this fraudfull fary;
>   For to be blyth me think it best.

This poem bears out what has been said about the first stanza of the last: Dunbar sees himself as normally gay, enjoying life, despite its cruelty to him and his many complaints about his abuse, and the mood of "I that in Heill wes and Glaidnes" is induced by sickness. It is well that he told us, for the weight of the poetic evidence would go against him: but this, of course, is due to the fact that a man is more apt to write about his frustrations, precisely because he can do nothing but write of them, than about his happy satisfactions which are sufficiently fulfilled in action. A writer is a man who has "something he is compelled to say", and that something is often critical of life or society. It is interesting that this optimistic poem is one of his duller ones—it is conventional, trite, of low tension, lacking in verve and that passionate intensity which makes the best of his work vibrate with energy. Yet we are not to think it an insincere poem—it is quite sincere: but it is also unremarkable.[30]
   In similar vein is "He hes anewch that is Content".[31]

---

[30] I may be unfair to this poem: the refrain contrasts with Timor mortis, and may be seen as courageous and noble.   [31] 70 ("Of Content").

Quho thinkis that he has sufficence,   1
Off gudis hes no indigence;
   Thocht he have nowder land nor rent,
Grit mycht, nor hie magnificence,
   He hes anewch that is content.

Those who, like the avaricious, have all the wealth of India,
are not satisfied in mind, are destroyed by poverty—therefore
seek not multifarious pleasures, but thank God for what comes
your way and enjoy it.   Despise the false world of honeyed
throat and heart of gall, for who most serves it shall have most
cause for repentance—the sauce of its abundance is sour.
Those with power should be cultured and liberal; those in
poverty should willingly accept it—thus they become rich
again.   Let us, the brotherhood of want, not be stamped by
languor—if we climb not, we fall not.

      For quho in warld moist covatus is   31
      In world is purast man, I wis,
         And moist neidy of his intent;
      For of all gudis no thing is his
         That of no thing can be content.

A remarkable poem to come from this most discontented of
poets: but again, he is doing a piece of conventional moralising
—Heaven for other people—and not unburdening himself.
Yet even at that, his discontent is always with his poverty,
not his lack of wealth—we may take it that he means what he
says, when in "This Waverand Warldis Wretchedness",[32]
he declares:

      Greit abbais grayth I nill to gather,   85
      Bot ane kirk scant coverit with hadder . . .

His desire is to have a door from which to keep the wolf; and
he would no doubt defend himself from the charge of hypocrisy
by saying that to be content with enough, one must have
enough.
    He might further say that a moral "truth", if such it be,

[32] 13 ("Of the Warldis Instabilitie").

is still true whether the poet expressing it is himself able to live by it or not—a poet is a makar, not a philosopher, and belief has nothing to do with it. A poet who is also a devout Christian might perfectly well make a good poem expressing the creed of Islam, of Buddha, of Mithra, or even of Satan himself: though most poets "make" out of their own beliefs because they can make best out of what they know best and feel most passionately. Some few are poets only because they have a "message" which inspires them to heights of utterance they could otherwise never achieve: Blake was one such: but Shakespeare could sing with any man's voice, and create the most wonderful poetry out of all sorts of beliefs, disbeliefs, and non-beliefs. But Dunbar wrote best when he was most roused; and compared with his best, this is a slack and pedestrian performance. As with all moralisers, we would find his precepts easier to follow if he gave us also an example—but that is to ask a teacher to be a saint, and Dunbar was neither—he was only a poet: and as a poet, if he was not an out-and-out materialist, he was at least an in-and-out one. He was not the man to defy the world and seek the strait gate as "This Nycht befoir the Dawing Cleir"[33] shows.

Another poem in this rather forced mood of being happy with what you've got is "Without Glaidnes Availis no Tressour":[34]

> Be mirry, man! and tak nocht far in mynd   1
>   The wavering of this wrechit warld of sorrow;
> To God be humill, and to thy freynd be kynd,
>   And with thy nychtbouris glaidly len and borrow;
>   His chance to nycht it may be thyne to morrow.
>   Be blyth in hairt for ony aventure,
>   For oft with wysmen hes been said a forrow,
>   Without glaidness availis no tressour.

Enjoy whatever God sends, for worldly goods avail nothing without well-being. No goods are yours except what you can spend—anything left over is only trouble. Seek comfort in depression, life won't last long in pain, set sail for comfort—

[33] 4 ("How Dumbar wes Desyrd to be ane Freir").
[34] 73 ("No Tressour Availis without Glaidness").

without gladness no treasure avails. Be charitable, flee trouble, keep good company, be humble, for worldly honour lasts no longer than a cry, be rich in patience if poor in possessions, don't be depressed—he lives mightily that lives merrily. You see these wretches who grab for money all their lives, filling their purses and emptying their souls—what have they but the bother of looking after all their riches until others, with more grace, come to spend it without having worked for it: spend with pleasure. If you alone possessed all the wealth that man can have, nothing would fall to you but your food and drink and clothes, and a sight of the rest.

> Ane raknyng rycht cumis of ane ragment small;   37
>   Be just and joyous do to non injure,
> And trewth sall mak the strang as ony wall:
>   Without glaidnes availis no tresure.

"Eat, drink, and be merry"—does he mean it? Is this the answer to the *timor mortis*? It is perhaps a possible answer—he may be looking at it as a possibility, trying it out, "experimenting", as we would say. More likely he is simply writing a poem in the tradition of mild hedonism: but Dunbar rarely touches a traditional subject without having some personal reason for doing so. The poems in this vein, therefore, are not mere exercises, nor are they sermons in verse for the edification of other people. They have some more or less close relevance to his own life and experience and spiritual needs. They are in fact set against the mood of *timor mortis* which underlies them as a negative undertone, an enemy to be opposed by a deliberate boosting of morale, a "looking on the bright side". But they are shallow and mediocre—spiritually inadequate. One prefers the stoic approach which involves the long look at the worst evidenced in "I that in Heill wes and Glaidnes". The black dragon will not be conquered by a reduction of standards, a mere cheer-up attitude. The dragon of the fear of death will not be put off with a bun, like a bear at the zoo—it is not behind bars. At best this is only a half-way house toward its exorcism.

    This poem stresses the value of spending rather than saving—enough to make us wonder whether it has much personal relevance at all—and in "Thyne Awin Gude"[35] this becomes his main theme:

> Man, sen thy lyfe is ay in weir,   I
> And deid is evir drawand neir,
> The tyme unsicker and the place;
> Thyne awin gude spend quhill thow hes space.

Use what is your own yourself, and refuse what isn't; for somebody else will gain from it. You may be wealthy today and have to leave it tomorrow for somebody else's benefit— while you have time see to it that no man can hunt or slay another for your goods. Some spend their lives in miserable accumulation of goods, never happy at Easter or at Christmas, and somebody else comes along, glad of the first's misfortune, never having prayed for him, and seizes it all gladly. Some gather great wealth and are mean about it, and are followed by heirs who put no value on such thrift. All you spend here is your own, and not even all that you have can be spent by you, but by somebody else who is given grace to do so—trust nobody to do for you what you won't do for yourself. And he ends:

> Luke how the bairne dois to the muder,   37
> And tak example be nane udder,
> That it nocht eftir be thy cace;
> Thyne awin gude spend quhill thow hes space.

I hold this to be the worst poem Dunbar wrote—at least of those that have come down to us. The theme of spending rather than hoarding, of casting one's bread on the waters, is unexceptionable, and is part of his attack on the increasing avarice he sees around him—but that should be a generous spending, administration of love, giving back gladly what is given. But this poem is mean and vile, its theme being not to spend in order to enjoy life, but in order to prevent your heirs getting what you have not been able to spend.[36] From this poem one might deduce that Dunbar had never been a father— the impulse to leave one's children better off, whether materially or spiritually or both, is one of the deepest in human nature—

---

[35] 72 ("Advice to Spend Anis Awin Gude").
[36] See ll. 9-16, e.g. and 21-28.

and not even confined to patriarchy. Dunbar reveals here
the poverty of instinct we have noticed elsewhere, as in his
relations with women—he was repressed, defeated in his
biological being. Much of his misery stems from that. He
was an intellectual, in the bad sense—one whose intellect was
developed at the expense of his deeper nature, indeed was
partly the product of a dried-up emotional life. This is the
worst side of Dunbar, this meanness of soul, this poverty of
spirit, perversion of vital impulses. It is for this we feel he is
a lesser man than the noble Henrysoun or Villon—Villon
whose essential innocent nobility and generosity shine like a
halo through the misery of his appalling life. Villon is truly
and really noble at the core: Dunbar's nobility is flawed: it
is more of rank than of nature. There is a wound in Dunbar,
a wound at the core of his manhood, his procreative vitality,
which keeps tainting the wine with gall. If, as Edmund Wilson
has said in *The Wound and the Bow*, the poet, like Philoctetes, is
isolated by his companions because of the stench from his
wound, and creates out of pain, yet that pain flaws the work:
the greatest are not so. A Pope, yes, perhaps—but never a
Shakespeare. Did Dunbar's reputed dwarfishness have anything to do with this streak in him? Or are other factors
sufficient to account for it—for instance, his celibacy? This
poem cannot be accounted for as appropriate to a seasonal
religious ritual: it is more personal than any of these others,
and reveals a want in him. The final stanza (unless I misread
it) is the most repellent of all—be careful lest your heirs treat
you with the same ruthless selfcentredness as a baby its mother.
By this one short stave he dishonours motherhood, fatherhood,
infancy, and human life. The mother's selfless giving of herself
to the infant is an instance of the highest love—Agape, the
love which is self-sacrifice, the ultimate meaning of Christian
love. The other forms of love, Eros, Philia, and Caritas, imply
reciprocity, exchange: only Agape is pure giving without hope
of return, and without stint. This is the highest value known
to mankind, and here Dunbar turns the value upside down.
If it were ironical, satiric, one could understand—but there is
no evidence that it is so. The sentiment here strikes at the
deepest human reality—the working for progress, the attempt

to leave the world a better place than you found it, to hand on to your own children the heritage you received plus whatever you have managed to add to it, the sacrifice of self for others, of the present for the future. It is the voice of Satan speaks in this poem, disguised as that of Dunbar. In the Maitland Manuscript, it is anonymous; and, but for the fact that in the Bannatyne Manuscript it is ascribed to Dunbar, I would reject it as apocryphal. In any case, it is a thoroughly bad poem, obscure, vague, slack of utterance, muddy of texture, and vile of sentiment. The best that can be said is that it is meant simply as an attack on avarice which misfires because it goes beyond that.

This really ends this group of similar poems, but there are one or two others in moralistic vein, mostly concerned with death and the vanity of the world, which are best considered here. The two poems on Lord Bernard Stewart—the one welcoming him in laureate verse as a conquering hero, the other lamenting his early death—are almost examples, drawn from life, of the theme of *vanitas vanitatum*. The first of these is the "Ballade",[37] which opens:

> Renownit, ryall, right reverend and serene   1
>   Lord, hie tryumphing in wirschip and valoure,
> Fro kyngis downe, most Cristin knight and kene,
>   Most wyse, most valyeand, moste laureat hie victour,
> Onto the sterris upheyt is thyne honour;
>   In Scotland welcum be thyne excellence
> To king, queyne, lord, clerk, knight and servatour,
>   With glorie and honour, lawde and reverence.

The high rhetoric is sustained for ninety-six lines, ending with an acrostic on the letters of his name, *B A R N A R D V S*, a pæan of courtly welcome comparing Stewart to the great heroes of the past and gods like Mars. Here is human pomp and power at its highest. The second, the "Elegy",[38] opens:

> Illuster Lodovick, of France most Cristin king,   1
>   Thow may complain with sighis lamentable
> The death of Bernard Stewart, nobill and ding,
>   In deid of armis most anterous and abill,

---

[37] 61 ("The Ballade of Lord Bernard Stewart, Lord of Aubigny").
[38] 62 ("Elegy on the Death of Lord Bernard Stewart, Lord of Aubigny").

> Most mychti, wyse, worthie, and confortable,
> Thy men of weir to governe and to gy:
> For him, allace, now may thow weir the sabill,
> Sen he is gone, the flour of chevelrie.

One day the "flour of chevelrie", the next, reduced to that equality of dust with all other men:

> He sparis na lord for his piscence . . .   33
> His awfull strak may no man fle.
> *Timor mortis conturbat me.*

The first poem is like a trumpet voluntary, and was probably recited between actual trumpet voluntaries when Stewart, Lord D'Aubigny, came to court on 9 May 1508. The use of the run-on device from the end of l. 1 to the beginning of l. 2— "Renownit, ryall, right reverend and serene/Lord"—is the earliest example of this I can think of in Scottish poetry. It is, in its way, as powerful as the opening of Hopkins's poem on the wreck of the *Deutschland*—"Thou mastering me/God." This is the great bardic voice of poetry, and Dunbar uses it like a tannoy: but a month later Stewart has died, and the same stanza serves for his elegy, but in the minor key. Dunbar's range of volume is as large as his range of pitch—from the *pianissimo* of "Sweet rois of vertew and of gentilnes" to the *fortissimo* of "Don is a battell on the dragon blak." The high rhetoric of the welcome to Stewart is a forerunner of the great Resurrection ode. But the interest of these poems is more technical than poetic—it is interesting to compare the pathos and deeply-felt grief of Wallace's "Lament for the Graham" in Blind Hary's *Wallas* (x. 563-82) with the formal *tour-de-force* of Dunbar's "Elegy on Lord Bernard Stewart".

If the court had its hero in Stewart, it had its anti-hero in Donald Owre. He was a grandson of the Lord of the Isles— the last of the ilk, dubbed illegitimate by the government, imprisoned while still a boy, escaped in 1501, and led an insurrection against James's severity to the clans in 1503. Defeated, he was again imprisoned in 1507, still a very young man. It was about this time that Dunbar wrote "In Vice most Vicius".[39] James did not take the advice to hang him,

---

[39] 36 ("Epetaphe for Donald Owre").

and Donald was kept in prison for forty years, when he headed another rising. Mackay Mackenzie's note on the poem is worth quoting:

> But the whole tone of the poem is unnecessarily malignant to-wards one who had known no personal freedom save for the few years he was "out" against the government. He was partly the victim, partly the instrument of higher powers (cf. Gregory, *History of the Western Highlands and Islands*, pp. 98-103.).

One remembers, too, that Scotland was the first united kingdom of any Celtic nation, and had been filched from the Gaels by Saxon and Norman influences after the coming of Margaret of England in marriage to Malcolm Canmore—a "sair sanct" for Scotland. To the Gaels, the Stewarts were simply a bunch of Anglo-Norman upstarts who had usurped the crown. Dunbar's poem opens:

> In vice most vicius he excellis,   I
> That with the vice of tressone mellis;
>   Thocht he remissioun
>   Haif for prodissioun,
>   Schame and suspissioun
>   Ay with him dwellis.

Dunbar, as the descendant of the traitor Corspatrick, has some authority indeed to speak of treason: his family was rooted in it. A traitor, he goes on, is ever loathsome as an owl, so vile and filthy is his fault, and horrible to nature as a fiend under a cowl in a monastery-hall. Whoever is a traitor or a thief does mischief to himself—it boomerangs on him, and his fraudful wiles lead him astray. This is now proved in the Isles. The very treacherous traitor Donald Owre had more falsehood than four others around the Isles and seas; he will yet glower from the gallows-tree. Falsehood has no feet nor means of defence by power, practice, or influence; though it be smothered by guile from the light, God reveals justice with severe vengeance. Every thief and traitor has kinship with the false and dissembling fox, which has by nature a desire to work more spitefully after a respite. If he were captured a thousand times and pardoned as often, he will take to hunting hens again as soon as he is back in the fields.

> The murtherer ay murther mais, 43
> And evir quhill he be slane he slais;
>   Wyvis thus makis mokkis
>   Spynnand on rokkis;
>   "Ay rynnis the fox
>   Quhill he fute hais."

Dunbar's nature-analogy works against his own case: the fox has as much right to the hens as man has, by nature, and as much right to be true to its nature as any other creature: and the Gaels have as much right to Scotland as any thieving Anglo-Norman barons organised as a "government"—the gang that grabs the power to make the laws fit its own desires.

The Gael-Lowlander situation was not unlike that of the black-white set-up in South Africa today. Scotland needed unity, and it is to James's credit that he sought it in more intelligent ways than Dunbar would have had him do. The word "treason" needs defining. Edward I thought Wallace a traitor—i.e., to him. Wallace saw Edward and his ilk as enemies of Scotland.[40] In 1707 makers of the Treaty of Union seemed to the Scottish people to be traitors: but today Scottish Republican Army men are considered by law to be traitors to the Union government. And to complicate matters, the Nuremberg trials condemned and executed men for *not* being traitors to Hitler Germany. "Treason", in other words, means pretty well anything that people want it to mean. To Scottish Home-Rulers today, Scotland is run by quislings and traitors under the English central government—the same view as the Irish nationalists took of the pre-1922 situation. A Marxist, today, moreover, conceives of treason and loyalty in terms only of class—if a man is loyal to his class, which is universal, he cannot be a traitor to his country: the "traitors" of the recent trials for betrayal of secrets to Russia, for example, do not regard themselves as such. No man would be a "traitor" if he believed that that was what he was being, not even the crook who is only in the game for money—for he believes that he has no loyalty except to himself, and the only treason

---

[40] Cp. *Manchester Guardian*, 16 Oct. 1946: "Could any *Englishman* [my italics] doubt that justice was done, if brutally, when Wallace was executed?" Or any German doubt that justice was done when Edith Cavell was executed?

S

he could commit would be against himself. Dunbar's own
ancestor, Corspatrick, one of the worst traitors in Scottish
history, did not see himself in that light. Dunbar too easily
assumes that he knows what treason is, and reveals that he
doesn't. More thought would have produced a very different
poem—but, of course, he is merely playing to an audience, as
usual, and no doubt hoping to advance his own cause at court
by howling for the blood of a clansman: there was more than
a little of the despicable in Dunbar's character. His self-
righteousness comes ill from a man who spent so much of his
life and talent begging for the right to sorn off the peasantry
in a "benefice".

Technically, the poem is very good, as usual, the form
another example of his happiness in a tight, short, dancing
measure. This form was taken up again by Maitland of
Lethington, who produced a better poem, in my view,
"Aganis the Thievis of Liddisdale": though again, one cannot
help remarking that the Liddesdale thieves he rails against are
only the peasantry forced to petty thieving outside the law by
the large-scale operators inside it.

A curious poem in moralistic vein is "To Speik of Science,
Craft, or Sapience".[41] This reads rather like an after-dinner
speech of didactic purpose—in this case a lecture to Oxford
dons on the importance of uniting theory and practice. No
date can be assigned the visit, but Small suggests 1501 as
probable on the ground that Dunbar was in England at that
time. The poem opens:

> To speik of science, craft or sapience,   1
>   Off vertew, morall cunnyng, or doctrene;
> Off jure, of wisdome, or intelligence;
>   Off everie study, lair, or disciplene;
>   All is bot tynt or reddie for to tyne,
>   Nocht using it as it sould usit be,
>   The craift exerceing, considdering not the fyne:
>   A paralous seiknes is vane prosperite.

The careful exposition of logical argument, the eloquence of
adorned rhetoric, the philosophical natural science, the obscure

----

[41] 53 ("Dunbar at Oxinfurde").

aspect of astronomy, the sermons of theologians, the imaginary
tales of poetry—all die in the self without good living, like
May flowers in dry September: vain progress is a debatable
life.   Therefore, you learned men and most constant, full of
knowledge and science, should be mirrors in your conduct,
lamps shining in the darkness—otherwise your long labours
at study are wasted.   If your deeds are contrary to your
sayings, your own conscience will be your greatest accuser.
This is not—like D. H. Lawrence's views on Cambridge, for
example—an attack on academics by a creative artist: it is
merely a set of platitudes common among the learned of his
time, made by one of themselves in the sure knowledge that
approving lip-service, if nothing else, would be paid to his
sentiments by his audience.   The same kind of thing can be
heard at learned gatherings today, meaning as little.   The
poem is as unexceptionable as its sentiments, and as undistinguished.

The last, and one of the most important and certainly
unique of these sombre moralising poems is "Thow that in
Hevin, for our Salvatioun".[42]   It deals with the plight of
Scotland after Flodden, and is the best possible evidence
against those learned gentlemen who seek to play down the
importance of that catastrophe in Scottish history—an eye-
witness report, a cry from Hell.   This was written at least four
years after Flodden, when the Regent, the Duke of Albany,
deserted Scotland in 1517 for France, where he remained for
four years.   Dunbar opens:

> Thow that in hevin, for our salvatioun,   I
>   Maid justice, mercie, and petie to aggre;
> And Gabriell send with the salutatioun
>   On to the mayd of maist humilitie
>   And maid thy sone to tak humanite
>   For our demeritis to be of Marie borne;
>   Have of us pietie and our protectour be!
>   For but they help this kynrik is forlorne.

O high eternal Father of wisdom, who out of your virtue chase
every folly, give us a spark of Your high excellent prudence—

[42] 65 ("Quhen the Governour Past in France").

we who have neither intelligence nor reason (this from Dunbar!), in whose hearts prudence has no place, example, nor previous experience, send a drop of Your grace to us sinners, for without Your help this kingdom is utterly lost.   We are so beastly, stupid and ignorant, that our crudity will not easily be corrected, but You, who are militant with mercy, stop avenging Yourself on us because we are subjected to sin, and make Your justice be balanced by pity, for peace has utterly run wild from us and we are so much diseased by folly that without Your help this kingdom is utterly lost.   You who ransomed and redeemed us on the Cross, have pity on our sins judged before Your sight— forgive our trespasses which are so many that a summary of them cannot be prepared for a court of justice, as we cannot endure it.   Help this poor kingdom, which is divided in all parts, send succour to us, You who wore the crown of thorn, that by the gift of grace the country may be guided.

> Lord! hald thy hand that strikken hes so soir;   33
>   Have of us pietie aftir our punytioun;
> And gif us grace the to greif no moir,
>   And gar us mend with pennance and contritioun;
>   And to thy vengeance mak non additioun,
>   As thow that of michtis may to morne;
>   Fra cair to confort thow mak restitutioun,
>   For but they help this kynrik is forlorne.

Flodden was the almost inevitable outcome of James IV's irresponsible career; and the sins of the monarch are visited upon the subjects.   There is no need to stress the despair out of which the poem is written—it cries out.   Dunbar, of course, sees it all in Biblical terms, as if God were responsible for the follies of men, and as if the God of love were in fact a God of vengeance: but there is not a vestige of personal self-pity in the poem—he has at last "lost" his life in that of his people, and passionate sincerity and real care for the people make it one of the most remarkable utterances in Scottish poetry.   It is also one of Dunbar's most genuinely and deeply-felt religious poems, no longer a faith of the head speaking, but the passionate faith of the heart, unquestioning, undoubting, strong, sure, and utter.   It is a poem of grief, lamentation, humility, anxiety, despair, contrition, heavy with feelings of guilt—and Dunbar's satires on the court, the bulk of his work, proved that he was one of the least guilty of the catastrophe—and self-reproach: a veritable *De Profundis*. That it reveals a tragic misconception of the nature of reality—of God—in no way invalidates the powerful religious faith it springs from. Had Dunbar found this passionate faith before 1513? Or did he discover it only when a greater tribulation than his own petty troubles suddenly called forth the best in him, leading to his salvation? Whatever may be the answer, this poem is truly religious, and leads over into the religious poems proper, in the next chapter.

There is a similar poem on the same subject of Albany, beginning "We lordis hes chosin a chiftane mervellus",[43] but it is anonymous, though often attributed, with some reason, to Dunbar: but "We lordis" alone suggests another hand. The poem is more satirical and secular, with its refrain "In lak of justice this realme is schent, allace". It is a powerful work in its own right, but, I suspect, by another hand.

[43] 92 ("To the Governour in France").

XIII

Don is a Battell on the Dragon Blak

DUNBAR was brought up to regard himself as destined to
become a bishop—so he tells us in "Schir, yit Remembir
as of Befoir":[1]

> I wes in youthe, on nureice kne,   61
> Cald dandillie, bischop, dandillie,
>   And quhone that age now dois me greif,
> A sempill vicar I can nocht be:
>   Exces of thocht dois me mischief.

He was destined for the Church,[2] and his education up to the
rank of M.A. argues that this design was carried out successfully thus far: and the word "bischop" above implies that
it was the administrative, practical, comparatively worldly and
lucrative side of the Church, and not the contemplative
mystical side, which was intended. Yet he became, in fact, a
court hanger-on whose scribbling of verses was slighted by the
King, and he seems to have spent some time as a mendicant
friar or novice, wandering about from place to place. What
happened between his university career, which must, at that
time, have lasted seven years for the M.A. degree, and his
becoming the disgruntled and abused courtier? This is a
mystery which cannot be cleared up without further knowledge
coming to light. But something untoward must have happened
to deflect him from the aim of higher Church preferment—
people did not need to spend seven years at university and
take the M.A. in order to become mendicant novices. There
must have been considerable influence behind him up to the
taking of his degree: what happened to it after that, that he
should have to seek it at court? That he was seeking preferment at court is obvious—but why was it necessary? Much

---

[1] 20 ("To the King").

[2] This seems to be implied in l. 2; and the following lines bear it out—he is
disappointed.

humbler influences, those presumably which helped him through
his early studies, would have sufficed to see him started on a
career in the Church. Was it that he lacked vocation, and
took time off to try to find it? Had his guardians died? Did
he kick over the traces at first, repent, try to make a come-
back via the court? How did he get into court at all, if he
was only a mendicant friar?

These and many other questions of his strange position
must arise in the mind of any close reader—he seems neither
to have been courtier-proper nor cleric-proper, neither a real
churchman nor a real courtier—then what was he? The only
thing we know beyond all doubt is that he was a poet of genius.
Did his obvious vocation for poetry stand in the way of his
having any other? He himself clearly thought that a "benefice" would be good for his poetry, and he did not seem to
regard that as a conflicting "vocation" so much as a source
of bread and butter.

One must resist an attempt to answer these questions without further knowledge than is at present possible—and they
don't matter to the poems very much. But the best authority
on Dunbar—indeed, the only one—is Dunbar himself. Does
he give us any clue? There is only one poem which deals
with the problem of his vocation, "This Nycht, befoir the
Dawing Cleir",[3] which begins:

> This nycht, befoir the dawing cleir   1
> Me thocht Sanct Francis did to me appeir,
>   With ane religious abbeit in his hand,
>   And said, "In this go cleith the my servand;
> Reffus the warld, for thow mon be a freir."

Dunbar started both at him and his habit, like a man who
has been frightened by a ghost, and it seemed to him that the
apparition laid the habit on top of him; but he quickly leapt
on to the floor to get away from it. The apparition said:
"Why do you start at this holy dress? Clothe yourself in it,
for you have most need to wear it, you who have long taught
the laws of Venus—you shall now be a friar and preach in
this habit, without fear or delay. My brethren have often

---

[3] 4 ("How Dumbar wes Desyrd to be ane Freir").

appealed to you by letters, sermons and exemplary stories, to take the habit, but you have put them off with excuses of not being ready yet; stop this at once and take it without any more excuses and procrastination". Dunbar answered: "Praise be to you, St Francis, and thanks for your good-will to me, you who are so generous with your clothes (an innuendo referring to the legend that Francis stripped himself naked to give back his clothes in public to his father, thereafter embracing poverty), but really it never occurred to me to wear them— don't be hurt, sweet confessor:

> "In haly legendis haif I hard, allevin,   26
> Ma sanctis[4] of bischoppis nor freiris, be sic sevin;
> Off full few freiris that hes bene sanctis I reid;
> Quhairfoir ga bring to me ane bischoppis weid,
> Gife evir thow wald my sawle gaid unto Hevin . . ."

"If ever it had been my fortune to be a friar, that time has long past, for in every town and place in all England from Berwick to Calais I have made merry in your habit. In the habit of a friar I have flattered often, preached in the pulpit in Darlington and Canterbury, and crossed the Channel from Dover and taught the people in Picardy. As long as I assumed the guise of friar I was full of guile and cunning, as God knows, and every falsehood and flattery of all men, which no holy water could chase away: I was always ready to beguile everybody". At this the apparition goes through a strange transformation:

> This freir that did Sanct Francis thair appeir,   46
> Ane fiend he wes in liknes of ane freir;
> He vaneist away with stynk and fyrie smowk;
> With him me thocht all the hous end he towk,
> And I awoik as wy that wes in weir.

At first sight this would seem to be yet another poem in the tradition of satirising friars, and certainly it has both satiric and comic content. But Dunbar rarely uses traditional material without having some personal use to make of it, changing it in the process. This poem is saying something

---

[4] I.e. "more saints."

more serious than appears. The opening is his favourite
dream situation, but it has an almost hallucinatory force: his
jumping out of bed, the panic he was in, are typical nightmare
elements, and too striking and original to be mere poetic
exercise. He is writing about a real dream which he actually
had, and reproduces much of the dream in his poem. Most
interesting is the accusation of Francis that Dunbar has been
teaching the "Venus lawis" for a long time: surely this is a
reference to the rules of Courtly Love, and to the poetry of
Courtly Love? In any case, this is personal material, not
conventional. The meaning, I take it, is that Dunbar is to
give up poetry (associated with Courtly Love) and become a
friar. St Francis further accuses him of putting off written
requests by Franciscan friars to become one of them—suggesting
that he has been too long a Franciscan novice: clearly personal
material again. Dunbar's reply is at once comic, with its sly
dig at Francis's generosity at giving his clothes away, and the
reference to more saints coming from the ranks of the bishops
than from the monasteries: but the injunction "ga bring to
me ane bischopis weid," while comic in situation, is perfectly
serious in motive—this is indeed what Dunbar wants, or thinks
he wants. Again, the stanza telling that he himself has wandered
throughout England and the north of France as a novice is
unquestionably personal material; and in the "Flyting", l. 425,
Kennedy refers to his begging "Fra Etrike Forest furthward
to Dumfrese". The traditional anti-friar material alleging
that he had been corrupt while in friar's guise is probably also
to be taken quite seriously. The point here, I think, is that
St Francis had married "Lady Poverty" as an exalted value,
but that in practice poverty had tended to corrupt his followers:
an empty stomach has no conscience. This criticism is no
mere comic satire: it is heart-felt and makes it clear that
Dunbar hated the life he had led with a real personal hatred.
This builds up, in the dream disguise, to a hatred of St Francis
himself, who turns into a fiend at the end: and (though he has
his typical wakening device) this again strikes a note of truth
in the remark that he woke as a man vexed with doubt. His
point, of course, is that it was not St Francis at all, but a fiend
disguised as him; but the psychology is too obvious—Dunbar's

hatred is making the whole Franciscan order seem evil, by projection.

This poem clearly involves the question of vocation. That Dunbar was expected to be "called" to the Franciscan order is as clear as that he himself has more worldly ambitions. The appearance of Francis himself is, in fact, a real "call"— Dunbar is in fact receiving his religious vocation in a dream-vision from one of the great saints in person: to a devout Catholic there could be no other interpretation, though there would be a cautious watching-out for further evidence that this was indeed the will of God. Dunbar's response is one of horrified terror, a refusal and rejection which go on to a defensive vilification of the saint himself, and his order: this is a denial of the Spirit, the sin against the Holy Ghost. How seriously are we to take it? Quite seriously, I think, with the reservation that a man in the state of mind Dunbar was in with regard to the order he was called to was scarcely ready for his vocation. But his case was no worse than that of Saul of Tarsus on the road to Damascus. It is perfectly understandable that a true vocation, coming with compulsive force from outside the personality and its egotistic pre-occupations, should terrify the recipient. The most exalted vocations have been so received. Moses questioned his own ability, sought some assurance of authority, and received only the awesome command: "Say that *I am* hath sent you". Mahomet (who, like Moses, was said to have stammered) was so terrified when the angel appeared to him that he hid his head in his burnous, and in his wife's bosom, for days—but every time he dared look out, there was the angel uttering the terrible command: " Go and preach the true God". It was agony for the prophet (Koran, the "Chapter of the Covered") to face the ordeal of preaching. English students will recall also the story of Caedmon. It is typical that these vocational crises involve a personal revolution of so marked a character that they involve almost a reversal of roles, a turning inside-out of the personality: the Hebro-Egyptian prince becomes the leader of the Exodus; Saul the persecutor of Christians becomes the great saint of the founding of the Church; the shy, stammering, scholarly Mahomet becomes the fiery prophet of the Sword and Koran, and the

tongue-tied Caedmon becomes the poet and singer. Thus,
Dunbar, full of worldly ambition for material success, is forced,
apparently, by circumstances along the road to becoming a
Franciscan friar vowed to a lifelong marriage with " Lady
Poverty". Moreover, this sort of call tends to come to its
recipients when youth is already giving way to middle age, or
even later—as in all the above examples. Dunbar himself
says:

> Gif evir my fortoun wes to be a freir   31
> The date thairof is past full mony a yeir . . .

which indicates that, having taken his degree, wandered for
some time as a novice (presumably) many years ago, he is now
no longer a young man: he is one old enough to be a bishop.
The case of Jeanne d'Arc is the only one that occurs to me of
an important vocation—and in her case not strictly a religious
one—coming to a very young person: but of course there must
be many others: I merely stress a tendency.

There is one element in Dunbar's reaction which is notably
different from the fears of the above examples: theirs are fears
of inadequacy, inability, unworthiness—his merely of distaste,
and superior distaste at that.[5] He has better ideas for himself
than to become a little brother. But the force of this dream
suggests that there must have been considerable conflict in
him between his practical and his contemplative sides. The
dream is full of such conflict, and indeed it could not have
been without it: but there is no question that his conscious
ego rejects utterly the promptings of his contemplative side,
symbolised as St Francis. The active cause of it was probably
grounded in a reality situation—the written appeals from the
friars, referred to in ll. 16-20. Dunbar's excuses are specious—
he wants to be a bishop, because thus he would have wealth
and power, not because he has the faintest interest in becoming
a saint. The really important thing to grasp is that this
"call" has sufficient force behind it to cause a strenuous and
frightened refusal, and that this refusal would involve him in
mortal sin—in a spiritual failure and defeat which would

[5] The friars were a conventional medieval butt: yet Dunbar, as usual, is not
merely conventional here—here is real, strong, personal distaste.

haunt him with guilt and leave him no peace of mind for the rest of his life: his life would be a near "posthumous" one, if the vocation was genuine. Was this a contributory cause of that note of *malaise* we have remarked before in his poems? I suspect that it was, and a very strong one. His religious training and education prepared him for a vocation, which he had always assumed would be of the sort that he envisaged for himself. But something went wrong there: when his vocation came, it was one which conflicted with will and pre-conceived ideas, so he rejected it; the guilt of this would be immense.

The key to the whole problem, however, is perhaps contained in the line spoken by St Francis in l. 13: "Thow, that hes lang done Venus lawis teiche . . ." This means, I take it, that he has long been a poet, and that being a poet was almost synonymous with being a love-poet, in the tradition of Courtly Love. Dunbar was not cut out to be either friar or bishop: he already had his own vocation, although not recognised as such by Church or State. Poetry has been an unofficial and persecuted profession (though, of course, paid much lip-service by its worst enemies) in these islands since at least Edward I's massacre of the Welsh bards, which called forth the poem by Thomas Gray. This may be the reason why Dunbar's early promise as a cleric—the achievement of his M.A. at St Andrews—did not lead, evidently, to the kind of preferment he might have, and had, expected. It might also account for his desire for a benefice, whether a bishopric or a kirk "scant coverit with hadder"—these were more in the nature of bread-and-butter jobs (if "jobs" at all, in many cases) than vocations, whereas the monastic life would be very hard to bear without some inclination toward it, if not a genuine vocation. Dunbar was a poet born; and that meant, in the words of the poet George Barker, born with:

> The unconditional liberty
> To do a job for which I starved.[6]

Dunbar accepts reality much as it was, and it never occurs to him to mention his real vocation: only in "Schir, Ye Have

[6] *The True Confession of George Barker*, London 1950.

Mony Servintouris", [7] does his suppressed consciousness of his
own real worth break out into open assertion—and a very
accurate assessment it is, though a little below the mark.

One remarks, in passing, that the poem bears satiric
evidence of how much the Franciscan order had degenerated
from the greatness of its saintly founder. It is of prime importance in Dunbar studies, although its precise nature has
not, I think, been remarked before.

The above poem seemed to indicate that Dunbar preferred
to teach the "Venus Lawis"[8] than to seek a diviner love:
but in "Now Culit is Dame Venus Brand"[9] he reverses his
position:

> Now culit is Dame Venus brand;   1
> Trew luvis fyre is ay kindilland,
> And I begyn to understand.
>> In feynit luve quhat foly bene:
>> Now cumis aige quhair yewth hes bene,
>> And trew luve rysis fro the splene.

Until the fire of Venus is dead and cold, the fire of true love
never burns bravely; but as one love grows cold, the other
becomes more fierce—now that age comes where youth has
been, true love rises from the spleen/heart. No man has the
courage to write of the pleasure of perfect love, if he has delighted in illusory love—their nature is so irreconcilable; but it is
well for any man who can get his heart to consent to true love,
bear its imprint, and still struggle on. He himself has experience, having once lived in the court of love (a very important
biographical remark); but for one joy he might speak of, he
could speak of fifteen pains. Whereas he used to be in dread,
now he can go forward comfortably, and whereas he had unhappiness to drink (features, these, of Courtly Love), now he
hopes for reward and thanks. Love used to make him miserable, but now it brings him ease; and where he had danger
and illness, now his breast is full of consolation. Where he
was wounded by jealousy (all this also belongs to the convention
of Courtly Love) and wished there were no lovers but himself,

---

[7] 17 ("Remonstrance to the King").
[8] As in 68 ("Gude Counsale"), for example.
[9] 52 ("Of Luve Erdly and Divine").

now he wishes all men loved where he loves, for sure. Whereas before he dared not disclose his love for shame, nor reveal her name (Courtly-Love rules), now he thinks it honour and good repute that all the world should see it. He did not confide in any man (the rules of *amour courtois* allowed only one confidant, the "friend") being too afraid of harming her (in other words she was married, as the code demands)—but now he wouldn't give a bean for the beauty of her eyes, having a love fairer of face, who cannot be put in danger, who will always give him reward and grace and mercy when he pleads (he is referring to Christ—a somewhat ambiguous passage). He neither does nor says anything unrequited, spends no thought of love in vain, and no gossip may prevent his loving.

> Ane lufe so fare, so gud, so sueit,   73
> So riche, so rewfull and discreit,
> And for the kynd of man so meit
>   Never moir salbe nor yit hes bene:
>   Now cumis aige quhair yewth hes bene,
>   And trew love rysis fro the splene.

No love is so true as He who died for true love of us; He should be loved in return, it seems to him, since He so desires our love.

> Is non but grace of God, I wis,   85
> That can in yewth considdir this;
> This fals dissavand warldis blis
>   So gydis man in flouris grene:
>   Now cumis aige quhair yewth hes bene,
>   And trew love rysis fro the splene.

The form of the poem is the same as that of "Schir, Lat it Nevir in Toun be Tald"; and both poems seem to belong to Dunbar's old age. The poem is a contrasting of Courtly Love and the religious love of Christ. The rebellion of the young man's reason in "The Goldyn Targe" against the irrational enslavement by the tradition of Courtly Love here finds its journey's end in the love which passeth all understanding. The resolution for him is not ultimately in married love, grounded in Philia, but in that Agape which is the polar opposite of Eros: it is, as he says himself, an old man's solution, and therefore one which is biologically determined, as much as

spiritually or intellectually. "Those who restrain Desire",
says Blake, "do so because theirs is weak enough to be restrain-
ed". He goes on to say that Reason is the restrainer, and its
government leads to a mere shadow of Desire—the history of
which is written, he says, in *Paradise Lost*, "and the Governor
or Reason is call'd Messiah".[10] Thus the Reason which
defends Dunbar in youth from the carnal desires of Courtly
Love becomes, in old age, Christ, the Messiah. The story
underlying the spiritual struggles everywhere manifest in
Dunbar's poetry is the story of his tormented love—the pilgrimage of the man who was accustomed to teach the "Venus
Lawis" from the "feynit luve" (see "My Hartis Tresure")[11]
which is erotic, to the "trew luve" which is Agape: the
pilgrimage of a lifetime. It is, after all, a natural cycle from
youth to age—but in Dunbar's case the central, middle experience is entirely lacking: the experience of married love and
children. This was his real tragedy, and did him more harm
than any lack of benefice. One cannot help remarking once
more on the most striking truth of the Catholic Middle Ages—
that by far the best men of the time, the cream of Europe, were
forbidden by their religious vows from passing on their sheer
human quality as a biological heritage to their own children.
The loss to civilisation is incalculable, and only offset by the
fortunate "weakness" of the flesh. (One day some learned
gentleman should put us in his debt by trying to assess how
much we owe to the fortunate prevalence of the sin of Lust.)
Dunbar knows only the contrasting loves of Eros and Agape—
"Thair kyndnes is so contrair clene". The celibacy of the
priesthood amounts to a mental castration—the figure of
Abelard takes on a symbolic significance here—depriving
priests of their own physical children. This may be no loss
to the individual, if his vocation is real enough—Robert
Henrysoun was, presumably, subject to the same restriction
as Dunbar, but shows none of Dunbar's resulting spiritual
wound—but the loss to humanity is immense. Tradition
asserts that Yeshu of Nazareth never married: married love
is essentially reciprocal, Philia, whereas Agape gives all but

[10] *The Marriage of Heaven and Hell.*
[11] 50 ("Quhone He list to Feyne").

takes nothing—it is, in its way, as much a one-way street as selfish lust, its opposite. But the Love attributed to Christ— the supreme self-sacrifice of the Cross—is Agape, and it is that which the Christian tends to take as example.

Technically, the triplets of the verses lend themselves to close meditative reasoning, as well as symbolising "tri-unity" —very much to Dunbar's purpose here. The use of the word "bene" twice in ll. 4-5, and again in ll. 71-2, is a technical fault. It is surprising that Dunbar passed it. This is a small blemish on a poem which, though rarely remarked on, is one of Dunbar's most important poems—traditional, as usual, but deeply personal, too.

A similar poem is "The Merle and the Nychtingaill".[12] Here the theme of "erdly luve" versus "trew luve" is treated in the debate form, the blackbird taking the first position and the nightingale the second, each taking stanza about:

> In may as that Aurora did upspring   I
>   With cristall ene chasing the cluddis sable,
> I hard a merle with mirry notis sing
>   A sang of lufe, with voce rycht confortable,
>   Agane the orient bemis amiable,
>   Upone a blisfull brenche of lawry grene;
>   This wes hir sentens sueit and delectable—
>   A lusty lyfe in luves service bene.
>
> Undir this brench ran doun a revir bricht,
>   Of balmy liquor, crystallyne of hew,
> Agane the hevinly aisur skyis licht,
>   Quhair did, upone the tother syd, persew
>   A nychtingaill, with suggurit notis new,
>   Quhois angell fedderis as the pacok schone;
>   This wes hir song, and of a sentens trew—
>   All luve is lost bot upone God allone.

The blackbird sings merrily on, waking the May lovers, directing their attention to the natural beauties, and repeating her refrain—"A lusty lyfe . . ." But the nightingale sings sweeter, her sound mingling with the running of the river, telling the foolish blackbird to be quiet, for "All luve is lost

---

[12] 63 (same title).

bot upone God allone." The blackbird asserts youth against
the hypocritical preaching of the nightingale, saying: "Of
yung sanctis growis auld feyndis but faill". The nightingale
replies that youth and age are the same in this matter—Christ's
love is the true one for all mankind. Why should God make
women so beautiful, counters the blackbird, if He did not
mean them to be loved? Nature made them for love, and God
made nature—and all He did is fitting. But the nightingale
says the thanks for all the beauty in Creation, including
woman's, is due not to the creature but to the Creator. The
blackbird says it would be foolish if love were a matter of
charity; and if virtue be contrary to vice, then love must be
a virtue—for its contrary is envy. God commanded each to
love his neighbour with all his heart—"And quho than ladeis
suetar nychbouris be?" This is raving, says the nightingale, for
a man may take such delight in his lady as to forget Him who
gave her such virtue, making a Heaven of her complexion—
though her hair shone like the beams of the sun, it should not
blind him to the perfect love. The blackbird then puts the
cultural case—love is a cause of honour, making men of cowards,
misers generous, lazy people diligent, vice virtue (partly of
Courtly Love theory—"love" in the "erdly" sense is synonymous with Courtly Love, since no other kind is recognised).
The contrary is true, says the nightingale: such vain love
blinds men, making them inconstant of mind, so drunk with
vainglory that they lose their intelligence, unconscious of all
danger until all honour is gone out of them, good repute,
possessions, and strength. Here the blackbird rather tamely
gives in—probably for no better reason than that the poem must
end somewhere, and in the triumph of the nightingale—
confessing its mistake:

> Blind ignorance me gaif sic hardines   99
>   To argone so agane the varite.

People should not be taken in the net of love set by the
Devil, but "luve the luve that did for his lufe de". Then
both birds sing together the most pious sentiments, flying up
through the branches: they console Dunbar, in memory, when
he can find no love.

T

This poem is another example of the difficulty of trying to confine Dunbar's work to easily-defined academic categories. Mackay Mackenzie, for example, includes it in poems headed "Allegories and Addresses". Even if we pass the identifying of personification of erotic love and divine love as blackbird and nightingale with "allegory", it remains to be said that the poem is also a fable, a debate, an example of aureation, a love poem, and uses the device of the double *ballade*: but finally and all the time it is, as I have "classified" it here, a religious poem. Dunbar's poems cannot, except in the most superficial and confusing way, be classified in terms of the "kinds". They can only be "classified", if the word is not a complete misnomer here, by their spiritual kinds. His work forms a spiritual order, loosely rather than tightly integrated, ranging from the adolescent fantasies of the courtly romantic poems to the deeply mature poems we are now considering. It is the aim of this work to try to suggest that much subtler order, which can only be apprehended by spiritual insight, hinted at, suggested—and therefore challenged, disagreed with, but must be thought about—never defined with certainty, never established once for all. The reality of his experience is too complex to be tidied up into categories, being as unconfinable by barriers as life itself: a truth which must apply also to any such intellectual conveniences I myself may be forced to have recourse to.

The *débat* form, rooted as it is in the deliberations of the Schoolmen, suits his mind very well—he is, after all, a highly intellectual poet—and he makes much of his opportunity to state two sides of an argument. The speech of the merle is as forceful and convincing as that of the nightingale: for no better reason than that, each being a "persona" of Dunbar, they are intellectually exactly matched. The logical processes work equally well for God and the Devil, truth and untruth, sense and nonsense. The proposition "All orbs are made of green cheese: the moon is an orb, therefore the moon is made of green cheese" is as logically defensible, formally, as any "true" one: the unreality is less obvious, but just as unreal, if one says "All birds have wings; kiwis are birds; therefore kiwis have wings". Given each its premises, its point of view, the merle and the nightingale argue equally well, to the delight of the reader until the forced ending, which cannot be shown to arise from any of the argument. The merle has erred through ignorance, that is, through false premises, not through illogical processes. This is a question of what is "real"; and the ideas of illusion and reality run through the poem, through both of these poems, as through so much of Dunbar's work—he is concerned with the true perception of the real from the illusory, and it is this that is the key to the spiritual order created by the poems: he is sifting experience.

But though he is sifting experience, this is not a private matter, nor even a merely personal one: he is sifting the human experience in general, partly through his own as an instance, partly through traditional material: his sieves are all traditional, and this poem is as rooted in tradition as most of his significant ones. Lydgate's "Chorle and the Bird" is probably its nearest ancestor, but the genre was common in the Middle Ages, beginning with French and Latin originals: the best known examples in Middle English are "The Owl and the Nightingale" and "The Thrush and the Nightingale". The use of aureation in the poem is another traditional feature, and here it is less obtrusive, more appropriate, and therefore better than anywhere else in Dunbar. The one flaw in the poem is inherent in its nature: the dice are loaded, the "debate" is not genuine but merely formal, the issues having been dogmatically decided beforehand. This is an evasion of reality, for the truth is that, like so many "either-or" questions, the answer is that both are partly right and the true answer is in a third view altogether—"both-plus-a-third". The real resolution of this debate, within its own terms, is Christian marriage, for in it the love of woman and the love of God are entirely compatible—indeed, are aspects of each other. Dunbar seems to include Christian marriage in the love of God, in some of the later stanzas, as Mr M. P. McDiarmid has pointed out to me: but the main trend of the poem, the insistence upon God "allone", and stanzas 5, 6, 7, and perhaps 8, persuade me that Dunbar is making the debate chiefly one of priestly and nunly celibacy versus Courtly Love. Dunbar is unlikely to have associated love and marriage at all, except as a desirable possibility. Love was habitually identified with *amour courtois*. Moreover, Dunbar, as usual, is personally implicated, and he himself was a celibate cleric. On Mr McDiarmid's side, however, is the fact that Church teaching would so include Christian marriage in divine love. It is a pity, in any case, that Dunbar did not develop this debate form,[13] a heritage from the Schoolmen, as Scottish poetry tends too easily to degenerate into slop.

Implicit in the poem is its significance for Dunbar's poetic development: if divine love is the true love, and Courtly Love the false, then the true poetry is religious, and that of *amour courtois*, of "Venus lawis", false. Dunbar's search for reality led ultimately, for him, to a re-affirmation of the traditional faith, the teachings of the Church, over against the heresy of *amour courtois*, which parodies the "trew" love.

> *Rorate celi desuper.*   I
> Hevins distill your balmy schouris,
> For now is rissin the bricht day ster,
> Fro the ros Mary, flour of flouris:
> The cleir Sone, quhome no clud devouris,
> Surminting Phebus in the est,
> Is cumin of his hevinly touris;
> *Et nobis Puer natus est.*

Thus opens the poem on the Nativity of Christ,[14] a traditional piece celebrating the festival of Christmas—but with its particular significance for Dunbar personally. Give praise to Him, O ye archangels, angels, dominions, thrones, powers, and various martyrs, and all you heavenly movements, star, planet, firmament, and sphere, fire, earth, air, and translucent water, let the highest and lowest of you give praise to Him who comes in such a humble manner. Rejoice, O sinners, and do penance, heartily thanking your Maker—for He whom you may not approach has very humbly come to you, to buy your souls with His blood and free you from the grip of the devil, and under no compulsion but that of His own mercy. Let all clergymen incline to Him and bow to that benevolent

---

[13] Mr A. D. Mackie's poem *The Young Man and the Young Nun* is an interesting twentieth-century sequel to Dunbar's.

[14] 79 ("Of the Nativitie of Christ").

Child, showing divine observance to Him who is King of Kings. Burn incense at His altar, read and sing in Holy Church with composed mind, honouring Him above all things.

> Celestiall fowlis in the are   33
>   Sing with your nottis upoun hicht;
> In firthis and in forestis fair
>   Be myrthfull now, at all your mycht,
>   For passit is your dully nycht,
>   Aurora hes the cluddis perst,
>   The son is rissin with gladsum lycht,
>   *Et nobis Puer natus est.*

Spring up now, flowers, from the root, turn yourselves naturally upward in honour of the blessed fruit who rose up from the rose Mary—spread your leaves out confidently and now at last take life from death in honour of that worthy Prince.

> Syng, hevin imperiall, most of hicht,   49
>   Regions of air mak armony;
> All fishe in flud and foull of flicht,
>   Be myrthfull and mak melody:
>   All *Gloria in excelcis* cry,
>   Hevin, erd, se, man, bird and best,
>   He that is crownit abone the sky
>   *Pro nobis Puer natus est.*

The refrain is from Isaiah ix. 6—"Unto us a child is born", and the poem shows a blend of Dunbar's higher styles; the aureate diction of "The Goldyn Targe", the laudatory rhetoric of the *ballade* on Bernard Stewart, the cataloguing of so many different poems, and something of the smooth sweet style of "Sweit rois of vertew":[15] but there is a brightness shining through it which is completely new, as if the dawn of hope of deliverance from winter and the "dully nycht" of evil was paralleled by his own deliverance from the nightmare of the court and its ways: the poem has also the note of joy in it that we find in a very different context in his exultant shout of "Welcum, my awin Lord Thesaurair!" Had he at last got his "kirk scant coverit with hadder", so infinitely preferable to his life at the court of James IV? We don't know—

---

[15] 49 ("To a Ladye").

there is no necessary connexion—but if the material order of the events are unconnected, the spiritual order is obvious and incontrovertible: and that is what matters. The poem is full of gladness, gladness at the rebirth of the year, the old pagan worship scoring the Christian theme, the worlds of nature and spirit united in a different vision of Woman—the "rois" Mary, the "flour of flouris". This superb poem is not unworthy of comparison with Milton's greater ode on the same subject, a salutary hymn to life, a strain of art which, though highly-wrought, is as universal as folk-song, and is in essence much older than Christianity itself.

A more specifically Christian poem, though still having overtones of the pagan cult of the dying God of the harvest, is "Amang thir Freiris",[16] the opening of which seems to suggest that Dunbar is now in a monastery, whether in retreat, or permanently, one does not know, but cannot help wondering whether the conflict written of in "This Nycht, befoir the Dawing Cleir",[17] ended in a victory for St Francis after all.

> Amang thir freiris within ane cloister,　　　　　　　1
> 　I enterit in ane oritorie,
> And knelit doun with ane pater noster,
> 　Befoir the michtie king of glorie,
> 　Haveing his passioun in memorie;
> 　　Syn to his mother I did inclyne,
> 　Hir halsing with ane *gaude flore*;
> 　And sudandlie I sleipit syne.

It seems to him (in dream) that Judas and many other Jews (it doesn't seem to occur to him that Jesus also was a Jew) took our Saviour, blessed Jesus, and thrust Him out with many pushes and shameful words, like a thief or traitor, threatening Him "O mankynd, for the luif of the". Falsely condemned before a judge, they spat in His face, struck and abused Him, and stripped Him of His clothes. They mocked Him, saying, if You are the Son of God tell us who struck You. In anger they bound Him to a pillar and scourged Him till the blood burst out at every vein (which would have rendered crucifixion

[16] 80 ("Of the Passioun of Christ").
[17] 4 ("How Dumbar wes Desyrd to be ane Freir").

superfluous), and at every stroke blood ran forth that might
have ransomed three worlds. Dunbar goes through the whole
agony of the robing with purple, crowning with thorns, bearing
of the cross, with such little touches of his own as that "His
feit with stanis was revin and scorde", and:

> The clayth that claif to his cleir syd   59
>   Thai raif away with ruggis rude
>   Quhill fersly followit flesche and blude . . .

Then he describes the nailing, adding that when they were
arising the cross,

> To gar his cruell pane exceid   75
>   Thai leit him fall doun with ane swak . . .

He dies between two thieves, but in doubt that He may be
still alive, they spear His side—thus Jesus endured to be
crucified and suffered death as a martyr.

> Methocht Compassioun, vode of feiris,   97
>   Than straik at me with mony ane stound,
> And for Contritioun, baithit in teiris,
>   My visage all in water drownd,
>   And Reuth into my eir ay rounde,
>   "For schame, allace, behald, man, how
>   Beft is with mony ane wound
>   Thy blissit Salvatour Jesu."

Then Remembrance came roughly, ceaselessly tugging at him,
throwing images of cross, nails, scourge, lance, and bloody
crown before his mind, so that Pain oppressed him with
Passion, and Pity struck at him continually, saying See how
Jews have treated your blessed Saviour "Chryst Jesu". Then
with happy greeting Grace passes him, saying, "ordain a
resting-place for Him who is so exhausted for you, and who
within three days shall bow low under your door-lintel"—
compare Death's speech to Dunbar in "In to thir Dirk and
Drublie Dayis":[18]

> Undir this lyntall sall thow lowt: 39
>   Thair is none other way besyde.

---

[18] 10 ("Meditatioun in Wyntir").

—"and be lodged in your house". Then at once Contrition ran after Confession, and Conscience accused me here and cast out many a poisonous sin; Repentance began to rise and pushed out the gates, Penance pacing up and down inside the house. Grace became Governor to keep the house in secure condition, always ready for our Saviour, until, early or late, He comes; Repentance spared no pain or penance to defend the house, with wet cheeks, at all times.

> For grit terrour of Chrystis deid   137
> The erde did trymill quhair I lay;
> Quhairthrow I waiknit in that steid
> With spreit halflingis in effray;
> Than wrayt I all without delay,
> Richt, heir as I have schawin to yow,
> Quhat me befell on Gud Fryday
> Befoir the Crosse of sweit Jesu.

The poem is brutal and crude in its insistence on the physical details of the Crucifixion, a sado-masochistic exercise which cannot be imaginatively responded to without sacrifice of sensitivity. There is an almost Hollywoodish vulgarity and grossness of sensibility in it, which needs some accounting for. That there was a streak of barbaric insensitivity in Dunbar has been noted already, in relation to such poems as "Lang Heff I Maed of Ladyes Quhytt,"[19] and "Madam, your Men Said Thai wald Ryd":[20] but these were not so much his own as called forth by the audience—it is the taste of the audience that is being met. Is this true here also? Villon in his "Ballade pour prier nostre Dame" refers to paintings of Heaven and Hell on church walls:

> Paradis peint, ou sont harpes et lus
> Et un enfer ou damnes sont boullus . . .

and there is other ample evidence that the visual arts were used forcefully to press the faithful into required frames of mind—friezes in churches, pageantry, plays, paintings, statuary, bas-reliefs, and above all, sensational crucifixes. There is a well-known painting of the Crucifixion by Grunewald

---

[19] 37 ("Of ane Blak-Moir").   [20] 31 ("To the Quene").

which is particularly gruesome in its painting of a scene of torture so appalling that the victim must have died much sooner than tradition alleges, under such treatment. This picture was painted specially for a hospital of syphilitics, [21] and the purpose of the exaggeration—if it be indeed exaggeration, for I may be wrong—seems to have been to impress the wretches there incarcerated that God Himself had endured an even greater suffering than their own appalling ones: the function of such art, in other words, is not mere sensation for sensation's sake, as in Hollywood films, but actually to relieve sufferings already so severe that nothing worse seems imaginable until something worse is in fact imaginatively created. But there is, as so often, no need to look any further than Dunbar's own poem for evidence: the poem is really in two parts, the first twelve stanzas dealing with the vision of the Crucifixion, and the last six dealing with the effect of the vision on Dunbar. In these last, we have the personifications set down above—Compassion, Contrition, Reuth, Remembrance, Pain, Pity, Grace, Confession, Repentance, Penance. These are the resulting effects of the vision, and it is safe to infer that therefore these results were also the intended ones, since the poem is traditional and contrived, deliberate, consciously controlled. It is also safe to infer that it must have taken a remarkable degree of suffering to impress Dunbar's audience, so inured to harsh sufferings were they themselves: barbarity and brutality were a usual part of life.

The anti-Semitism of ll. 9-16 jars on us today, but was obviously traditional material. Dunbar did not know, apparently, or was too dishonest to care, that Crucifixion was a Roman form of execution, never used by the Jews. Holy men were treated with great circumspection, to put it no higher, by the Jews, and the punishment for a provenly "false" prophet, as Yeshu of Nazareth certainly seemed to the Jewish Establishment of the time, was stoning. Jesus was condemned by the Sanhedrin as a "false" prophet because He blasphemously called Himself not merely another great prophet, but God. The significance of the freeing of Barabbas is that such arrogant blasphemy was deemed far worse than mere

[21] This was pointed out to me by Mr Sydney Goodsir Smith.

robbery: the one was a heinous sin, the other merely crime: and the Jews cared more about sin than crime.   The Church of Rome could not accept the fact of Roman guilt for the execution, but the great symbol of the Cross was given to the world only by ancient Rome, and could not have been given by any other culture.   Yet it has taken until the second half of this century for a Pope to acknowledge that the Jews are not entirely responsible for the Crucifixion.   Perhaps in another twenty centuries it may even be possible for a Pope to acknowledge that the Crucifixion was as much a Roman job as the butchering of William Wallace was an English one.

The poem has certain affinities with the Anglo-Saxon *Dream of the Rood*, which, describing the same events from the point of view of the animated Cross, makes a companion poem across the centuries: the older poem is by far the more sensitive and less brutal of the two.

The purpose of the above poem was to lead to salvation through exciting the feelings which would lead to confession, repentance, penance, and thus to ultimate delivery.   In "To The, O Mercifull Salviour, Jesus",[22] Dunbar sets out in verse just what this confession meant for a Catholic of his time:

> To The, O mercifull Salviour, Jesus,   I
>   My King, my Lord, and my Redemar sweit,
> Befoir thy bludy figor dolorus
>   I repent my synnys, with humill hairt contreit,
>   That evir I did unto this hour compleit,
>   Baith in werk, in word, and eik intent;
>   Falling on face, full law befoir thy feit,
>   I cry The mercy, and lasar to repent.

I confess myself to Thee, my sweet (favourite epithet for the revered—e.g., Sanct An, Sanct Francis) Saviour, committing myself to Thy supreme mercy, of the misuse of my five senses of hearing, seeing, tasting, touching, and smelling; of resisting, grieving, annoying, and rebelling against Thee, My God and almighty Lord.   With tears of remorse distilling from my eyes, I beg mercy of You, and leisure to repent.   I, a wretched sinner full of vice, confess myself also of the seven deadly

---

[22] 83 ("The Tabill of Confessioun").

sins—pride, anger, envy, avarice, lechery, gluttony, and sloth—throughout my life, for which I deserve to be destroyed. By Your five wounds have pity on me. I confess, too, that I have abused the seven deeds of corporal mercy, neither giving meat to the hungry, drink to the thirsty, nor visiting the sick, nor redeeming the prisoner, nor giving shelter to the homeless, nor clothing the naked, nor caring to bury the dead. Thou, who reckon mercy above all Thy works, I cry Thee mercy and leisure to repent. In the seven deeds of spiritual mercy, too, I have omitted to give my teaching to the ignorant, correction to sinners, counsel to the destitute, solace to the wretched outcasts, support of prayers to neighbours, to forgive neighbours' offences, and penitently to seek forgiveness of my own sins.

Lord, I have done very little reverence to Thy supremely renowned sacraments—Thy Holy Supper given in recompense of my sins, the holy penance of guilt, baptism, which washes away all my sins. In so far as I was negligent of these, with contrite heart and shedding tears I cry Thee mercy and leisure to repent.

> The Ten Commandis—ane God for till honour,   49
>   Nocht tane in vane his name, no sleyar to be,
> Fader and moder to wirschep at all hour,
>   To be no theif, the haly day to uphie,
>   Nychtbouris to lufe, fals witnes for to fle,
>   To leif adultre, to covet no manis rent;
>   Aganis thir preceptis culpable knaw I me;
>   I cry The mercy, and lasar to repent.

And wherever I have offended against the articles of truth—belief in God the Father, in Jesus, in Mary his Mother, and in the Crucifixion, Harrowing of Hell, and Resurrection from the dead to sit with the Father and judge the quick and the dead, I cry Thee mercy . . . I believe in the Holy Ghost, in the authority of the Church, the resurrection of the body, the salvation of those in state of grace—and I wholly renounce all those things in which I went astray before Thee, Lord and Judge of lands and sea. I, Lord, not being strong as a fortress, have sinned in hope, in faith, and in ardent charity, not having secured myself against vices with the four cardinal virtues—fortitude, prudence, temperance, and justice of deed, word, and intention, cast up my eyes to Thee, Christ Jesus . . .

I grievously regret also my offences against the seven commandments of the Church—to pay a tithe to it, eschew false oaths, keep holy festivals and fast-days, attend mass at the parish church on Sunday, make true confession to an ordained priest, and to take the sacrament once a year. Of my sins, too, against the Holy Ghost—putting off of repentance, sins against nature, inadequate confession of contrition, sinful reception of the sacraments, uncertainty of repentance and penance from the seven gifts sent me by the Holy Ghost, and deficiency in the six petitions of the Our Father, I cry Thee mercy. . . . I confess omitting to thank Thee out of gratitude or grace for having made me and bought my life with Thy death; failing to remember the space of this short life, the bliss of Heaven, the hideous enmity of Hell, to redeem my sins without further trespass; and to continuing always wayward in my intentions.

> I knaw me vicious, Lord, and richt culpable 105
>   In aithis sweiring, leising, and blaspheming,
> Off frustrat speiking in court, in kirk, and table,
>   In wordis vyle, in vaneteis expreming,
>   Preysing my self, and evill my nichtbouris deming,
>   And so in ydilnes my dayis haif spent;
>   Thow that was rent on rude for my redeming,
>   I cry The mercy and lasar to repent.

I have sinned in thinking lewd thoughts, extolling my mind in high exalted arrogance and folly, pride, derision, scorn, and vilification, presumption, disobedience, and contempt; in false vain-glory and negligent action. I have sinned also in theft and oppression (Dunbar?—theft, perhaps, but oppression?) in wrongful seizing and possessing of goods against good reason (again, Dunbar?), conscience, and discernment; in spending prodigally without care for the needs of the poor people (Dunbar?), in foul deceptions, in begetting false tales to bring honour low, and undermine treasure, land, and rents; and in excess of fleshly lust beyond measure (Dunbar?).

I confess myself of a dissembling mind, of hiding enmity
under a friendly face; of partial judgment and perverse
wilfulness; of flattering words and pretendings for material
needs; of falsely soliciting for unnecessary deliverance from
Council, Session, and Parliament, and for all manner of
wicked and guilty behaviour. I now purge myself of the guilt
incurred by keeping bad company, both knowingly and un-
knowingly, for criminal reasons; to deeds of felony, tyranny,
and vengeful cruelty. If I be culpable of hurt or homicide
in any way, action, advice, or consent, O dear Jesus—I cry
Thee mercy. . . . Although I do not have access to Thy precious
feet to kiss them as the Magdalene did when she craved mercy,
I shall weep tears like her for my misdeeds, and seek Thee
every morning at Thy grave—therefore forgive me as You
forgave her, seeing my heart penitent like hers. Before I
receive Thy precious body in my breast (this is the climax of
the whole poem, which is thus defined as a preparation for
Communion), I cry Thee mercy. . . . So that I may have You,
Jesus, always in mind, I ask that Your spirit shall so abound
in me that not a limb shall go unaffected in me, but fall in woe
at every wound, with Thee; that every stroke that ever stung
Your fair innocent flesh may pierce through my heart (see
the previously considered poem on the Passion), so that no
part of my body be whole.

> Off all thir synnis that I did heir expreme, 161
>   And als foryhet, to The, Lord, I me schryif,
> Appeling fra thy justice court extreme
>   Unto thy court of mercy exultyf;
>   Thow mak my schip in blissit port to arryif,
>   That sailit heir in stormis violent,
>   And saif me, Jesu, for thy woundis fyve
>   That cryis The mercy and lasar to repent.

One of the most frequently asked questions in literary
criticism is: "What did So-and-so believe?" Dante set out
what he believed in the whole of the *Comedy*—a hundred cantos:
and few poets since have set down so exactly what they believed
at all—or have been able to do so. Dunbar sets down the
core of his belief and ground of his whole mind and being in
one hundred and sixty-eight lines, and by so doing sets down

also the core of medieval belief—for the poem is, as usual, both personal and communal: he speaks for the congregation in general and himself in particular, for some of the sins he confesses to he was manifestly incapable of committing—there he speaks for others, though sharing their guilt in Christian manner. The set of integrated beliefs embodied in "To The, O Mercifull Salviour, Jesus", is the centre, but not, of course, the whole circle of his vision. Few poets rival Dunbar in sheer range and variety of poems: but at the core of the bulk of them is the application of the central Catholic doctrine of his time, as set out above, to various aspects of life. Through all his variety one has the sense of a unified personality and vision of life— an intellectual near-wholeness, tough and integral, always the same under the different appearances. There is nothing deliberately conscious in this—that would be impossible— but at the core of his being is a highly developed, highly complicated, yet completely (or as nearly so as is humanly likely) integrated body of intellectual belief and conviction colouring his vision of life in particulars and in general.

In the above poem he sets most of it down, for although it operates in him without effort, the consciousness of his complex structure of belief is always easily at hand—in the written doctrines of the Church. Dunbar is primarily a satirist and reformer—but he is never a revolutionary in the absolute sense: he is a true traditionalist in that he rebels, not against the tradition, but against its abuse. If, from our vantage-point in history, seeing what he could not see, we imagine we discern a more fundamental revolutionary implication behind his work—the satires of the court, for example— we must not make the mistake of thinking that he did so, too. He was essentially part of a continuing, perpetual, unending, uncompromising revolution which is the heart and life of that phenomenon which began two thousand years ago by the shores of Galilee, and is still called "Christianity". The essence of this vision of life, as of all truly religious visions, is communal: the furthering of the harmony of the community and its advancement is its chief concern. This is not to say communal as against personal—the distinction is totally unreal to the truly religious mind. There is no such thing as a person apart from a community, and a community is, by definition, a community of persons. The notion of individualism is a post-Reformation one: it would never have occurred to Dunbar, or any poet of his age or before it, to think of a split between the individual and society. Dunbar's, and their, unit of perception is not "I-not-them" but "I-in-them": not the individual against society, but the person-in-community. The two are as inseparable as the tree and the soil it grows in—indeed, they are not "two" but one, and this unity is the main concern of religion. The whole matter of this poem is to make conscious all the possible ways in which the "individual"—so-called, for the "individual" is a modern myth—can sin against community, against the commandment "Love thy neighbour as thyself" (because he *is* thyself).

The first value to be noted in this poem is the one most lacking in our own time—consciousness. However opinions may differ, today, on the question of sin or error, in detail, and in constitution, there can be no question at all that consciousness is desirable and necessary, if mankind is not to sink into the primeval swamp of undifferentiated sensation, of mere animality—which is anyhow impossible, for we are not our own masters, being neither responsible for our own creation nor for our own deaths. Confession is a means of maintaining awareness of human reality in the minds of the persons of the community, and as such, whatever creed-bias one may have, is an indubitable value of the highest possible importance. The passing of the habit of confession from large areas of human life in Europe is a major cause of the present loss of consciousness, leading to neuroses of all sorts. Psychotherapy is an attempt to meet the need thus created: but one which is founded on sand, having no grounding in an articulate and complete vision of life in all its height and depth, such as Catholicism has, or had, according to viewpoint, for the believer. It is beyond my competence here to enter into the vast problems raised by this poem, because they go far beyond poetry, involving one in religion, theology, philosophy, sociology, psychology—indeed, in everything relevant to human life. Yet it is impossible to do justice to this poem without some attempt to come to grips with its matter.

The main problem here is to try to separate what is universal from what is doctrinal—what is clearly of value to all mankind as a general thing from what is particular to Dunbar and his co-religionists. We have already asserted the universal value of consciousness as such; the problem now is what exactly should consciousness be *of*, in terms of the poem. This, for Dunbar, was laid down by the teaching of the Church, as far as is relevant to the rite of confession.

The first point of Dunbar's confession is clearly unexceptionable and universal: most men do in some degree, abuse the gifts of hearing, seeing, touching, tasting, and smelling. To review these matters regularly is an exercise in consciousness of unquestionable value.

His second point of confession is of the seven deadly sins in general—the dogma of Original Sin compels on believers the acceptance of guilt in some degree of all these as heritage, apart from personal abuses. Here we are on more difficult ground: the Church creates the sin, as the law creates the crime—are they obviously universally evil? Pride, for instance, has long been regarded as a virtue, not only in previous societies, but was in fact so among Dunbar's contemporaries. To what was Dunbar appealing in his panegyric on Lord Bernard Stewart but the pride of human worth? Yet, if one can accept that pride, as a sin, is an excess of self-respect, it is arguable that the true virtue valued by secular society is self-respect, and that pride is an abuse of the virtue. Similarly, while sexual desire is valuable, the excess of it called lust is universally condemned. A similar case may be made out for the remaining deadly sins—anger, avarice, sloth, gluttony, and envy. All of these are excesses of a human impulse not evil in itself—it is the abuse which is evil, and the name applies to the abuse; therefore it would seem that these points of consciousness have universal validity, quite apart from the question (inevitable today, but not in Dunbar's time) of one's total acceptance of Catholicism.

That the next point of his confession is also of universal validity seems to me to be clear—the seven deeds of corporal mercy. It is obviously true that people should, for their own and the community's good, feed the hungry (the truth is that there should not be any hungry, but that is another matter, involving techniques of social organisation impossible to the Middle Ages, though perfectly *possible* in our own time), visit the sick, slake the thirsty, help the prisoner, shelter the homeless, clothe the naked and dispose of the dead (but whether by burial is open to question). Yet all these involve some degree of sacrifice, if that be the word, on the part of each person so ministering: it is a communal necessity. That it was difficult in Dunbar's own time, with the rise of economic individualism savaging the old religious order, is evident from Dunbar's own poems—the satire on the merchants of Edinburgh, for example. But to the truly religious it involves no sacrifice really, since we are members one of another, and to do to "others" is to do to the "self" whether good or ill.

The fourth point, the seven deeds of spiritual mercy, also seem to be universal, though the question of particular belief does arise here and there. It is good to teach the ignorant (but what?), correct the erring (*if* they do err), counsel the destitute (something more practical would be needed, but is probably covered by the corporal mercies), support neighbours in "prayer" (this raises the question of belief, but as "moral" support, at least, is universally good), forgiving neighbours' offences, and seeking forgiveness for one's own sins.

The fifth point of confession is peculiarly Catholic, a matter of faith: the sacraments of the Church. Yet here, too, the universal mingles with the particular. Communion is a participation in the reality of being members one of another in the human race—a universal truth quite apart from the specific belief that this is so because we are also members of Christ, who is God, who is also Mankind. Baptism, on the other hand, would seem to be purely a matter of faith.

His sixth point is Judaic as well as Christian—the Ten Commandments—and some of these at least clearly are of universal validity beyond the faith. The One God is a matter of faith, and the keeping of His name, and keeping of the Sabbath (purely Judaic)—but the commandments dealing with murder, theft, respect for parents, covetousness, bearing false witness, loving neighbours, adultery, are all matters of universal validity. All such matters are self-evident—they

U

need no external authority to recommend them to human reason, which alone can show them plainly to be life-promoting, whereas their breach or neglect can be seen, as rationally, to be destructive. Catholicism itself has always insisted on this importance of reason (Dante was led by Virgil, the pagan, through two-thirds of his vision) as the necessary handmaid of religion—faith being a gift of grace added thereto for those who can receive it. Dunbar certainly, being no mystic, relied heavily on the element of reason, and we may be sure that his own is very much engaged here in this poem. The concept of "theft" here in "Thou shalt not steal" is not simply what we mean by theft today, an offence against the property of the "individual", but the religious one of taking more than your share from the community—theft as "sin", not merely as "crime".

The seven articles of the Creed form the material of the seventh point of his confession—belief in God the Father, Jesus the Son born of the Virgin, the Crucifixion, the Descent into Hell, the Resurrection on the Third Day, the Ascent into Heaven, and the Last Judgment. These are by definition matters of faith, though they are called articles of "truth". The important thing is that for Dunbar—and indeed historically —they are the ground on which all else rests. Without them, the rational side of Catholicism, with its many universal values, would not have been at all.

The eighth point of his confession is his failure to observe the seven cardinal virtues—the spiritual ones of faith, hope, and charity, and the moral ones of fortitude, prudence, temperance, and justice. These again would seem to have universal, self-evident validity, quite apart from their inclusion in the Catholic faith. Others might well be added to the list, but surely nothing could be taken away? The specific connotation of "faith" here of course is not universal: but faith itself is, whether it be in Gautama, Mahommed, or any other praeter-rational power of salvation, or even only in the "self" as courage. The moral values of course are Aristotelian rather than Christian, in derivation.

His ninth point is specifically Catholic—the seven commands of the Church—to pay a tithe to it as a first duty (a rather materialistic one for so spiritual a body), to eschew false oaths (universal enough), to keep festivals and fasts, to attend mass on Sunday, to attend the parish church, to make confession to a proper curate (what can the non-Catholic put in that all-important place?), and to take communion once a year.

His last point of confession is the vast list of particularised sins such as swearing, lying, blaspheming, gossiping, and so on—I have listed them above. It is impossible to believe— and unnecessary—that Dunbar is being personal here: only the Devil could achieve such depths of guilt. But being comprehensive, they cover as much as he can think of, not as his own actual, but as humanly possible guilt. He is at one with his community, the personal and the communal interlock, and he speaks not merely for himself but for all men. This is not only the mark of the truly religious, it is also the mark of the true poet, now unknown to the lost tribe of modern literati; and where seen, attacked by the swarm of egotistic anti-poets who disfigure the literature of our age.

The whole poem adds up to an immensely impressive instrument of consciousness, and argues a quite exalted state of culture of the mind. This is the true source of Dunbar's power, and at the core of the core is the belief that Yeshu of Nazareth, apotheosised as the Greek "Christos", was the perfect Man, the image of God, and that that is the human norm: a norm to which no man can attain, so that all men live in sin against their own perfect natures. This clash between the actual and the normal, between the fallen and the perfect is the source of the great dynamic spirituality which is the mainspring of the once-great Christian revolution—now long spent and moribund, and allowing itself to be used as a respectable front for economic forces which are totally anti-Christian, anti-religious (unless it be the pagan religion of Plutos-worship), anti-community, and ultimately anti-human and anti-God. What is most relevant here is that it was the main standard by which Dunbar satirised his time, the positive side of his vision, and the ultimate reality to which he came back after the long detour through the lunatic maunderings

of the Garden of the Rose, the terrible vision of the "Tretis",
the Hell of the court and town life, the comic defence against
insoluble problems, and the *Angst* of "I that in Heill wes".
This is where the golden targe of reason got him: and if we
today think we have a better "reality"—and it remains to
be seen—at least this was the best one available to Dunbar,
and even now, in its long decadence and decline, is still the
only complete vision of human life to have been evolved by
European civilisation.

The poem is, by its nature, a *tour de force*, but it does come
off as poetry. It stands as proof that a poem can embody a
highly complex system of intellectual and spiritual belief and
still be a poem. This is a hard lesson for the swarm of poeticules
now soiling the name of poetry with their pathetic clinging to
their spars of "originality" and their precious "personalities",
in the general wreck of a great communal poetic tradition—
the rats fleeing from the sinking ship. It is perhaps the last
great statement of the medieval phase of the Church,[23] and it
establishes once again that the Church of Rome, with all its
corruptions which gave the economic revolutionaries their
pseudoreligious excuse to overthrow it, was by far the greatest
cultural reality of the Middle Ages, and that our debt to it is
eternal and irrepayable: for it alone was the force which kept
alive the vision of the good human life, the consciousness of
real values in the ordinary world where might is right and the
only law is the law of the jungle. Its tragedy was, and is, that
it ceased to be, in its own phrase, *Ecclesia reformata semper
reformanda*.

This, then, is Dunbar's confession of faith. It is worth
noting that the only complete version of it is to be found in
the Howard MS.: the versions in Bannatyne and Maitland,
both post-Reformation, omit reference to prayer for dead
souls, the sacraments, mass, penance, confirmation, extreme
unction, tithes, and fasts.

There is another poem parallel to this one—"O Synful
Mann".[24] A shorter, and lesser poem, it deals with the forty
days fast of Lent.

[23] After Dante's *Commedia*, Chaucer's "The Parson's Tale," etc.
[24] 84 ("The Manere of Passing to Confessioun").

> O synfull man, thir ar the fourty dayis   i
>   That every man sulde wilfull pennence dre.
> Our Lord Jhesu, as haly writ sayis,
>   Fastit him self oure exampill to be.
>   Sen sic ane michty king and lord as he
>   To fast and pray was so obedient,
>   We synfull folk sulde be more deligent.

He goes on to exhort his hearers to make a good confession,
making conscious every sin, that it may be understood. No
leech can cure a wound until it be examined and made clean
in every part: and if one wound in twenty be left unhealed,
what use is it to cure the rest? So with confession—if there is
anything left unconscious or concealed, salvation will be lost.
A wise confessor can resolve every doubt and uncertainty, and
have complete power over your sins, but only if all is revealed—
otherwise the blind leads the blind. He enlarges this theme,
pressing home the need for an utter and complete confession—
this is entirely a matter of the sinner's own responsibility, for
the priest cannot know—"Thow knawis best quhair bindis
the thi scho". Confession should also be frequent—the account
seldom rendered is a very heavy one to pay—and one should
repent young, for there is small merit in repenting sins you are
too old to commit. The poem is a bit sententious, but is a fit
companion to "To The, O Mercifull Salviour".[25]
    He that loseth his life shall save it, and after the loss of life
in the confession of sins comes the resurrection from the dead:

> Don is a battell on the dragon blak,   i
>   Our campioun Chryst confountet hes his forse;
> The yettis of hell ar brokin with a crak,
>   The signe triumphall rasit is of the croce.
>   The divillis trymmillis with hiddous voce,
>   The saulis ar borrowit and to the blis can go,
>   Chryst with his blud our ransonis does indoce:
>   *Surrexit Dominus de sepulchro.*

The deadly dragon Lucifer is struck down, the cruel serpent
with the lethal sting (he seems to confuse snake and scorpion
here), the old cruel tiger with his bared teeth, having lain in

---

[25] 81 ("On the Resurrection of Christ").

wait for us so long, to grip us in his powerful claws. But the merciful Lord did not will it thus and caused him to fail of that prize.

> He for our saik that sufferit to be slane,   17
>   And lyk a lamb in sacrifice wes dicht,
> Is lyk a lyone rissin up agane,
>   And as gyane raxit him on hicht;
>   Sprungin is Aurora radius and bricht,
>   On loft is gone the glorious Appollo,
>   The blisfull day depairtit fro the nycht:
>   *Surrexit Dominus de sepulchro.*

The great victor who was wounded to death for our cause is risen on high, the sun, which had grown pale, now shines bright, and—darkness cleared away—our faith is re-established. The knell of mercy is sounded from the heavens and the Christians delivered from their sufferings, the Jews and their error confounded.

> The fo is chasit, the battell is done ceis,   33
>   The presone brokin, the jevellouris fleit and flemit,
> The weir is gon, confirmit is the peis,
>   The fetteris lowsit and the dungeoun temit,
>   The ransoun maid, the presoneris redemit.
>   The feild is win, ourcumin is the fo,
>   Dispulit of the tresur that he yemit.
>   *Surrexit Dominus de sepulchro.*

This is one of the noblest poems in the Scottish language, and the finest religious one. The technique is reminiscent of the panegyric on Bernard Stewart, but there the comparison ends. This is a heroic poem, the triumph of spring over winter, good over evil, health over disease, life over death, man over himself. As usual, it is at once personal and communal, original and traditional. The material is as old as the Easter hymns, but no pen but Dunbar's could have written this poem. The loud trumpet voluntary note is heard in him and in him alone—it is the product of the greatest technical mastery in the whole range of Scottish verse from Barbour to the present day, and of the most volatile temperament among Scottish poets. From the opening cannonade of the first incomparable

line to the last syllable of the last "*sepulchro*" there is nothing
we might add, nothing take away, without spoiling the poem.
The surge and power of it is language at its rare best, the might
of Teutonic rhythm asserting itself against the enfeebling
French corset, the spirit of Beowulf and Maldon transfiguring
the *ballade* stanza with its alliterative art.

In the first line we have the double plosive alliteration
"don is a battell on the dragon blak," and in the second a
throning of guttural cs in "campioun Chryst confountet,"
with the further semi-alliteration of "confoundet hes his forse."
The third line, one of the most powerful in poetry, has no need
of alliteration—"The yettis of hell ar brokin with a crak,"
yet there is a similar effect in the br and cr of "brokin with
a crak," and the three rolled rs and two kc sounds. There
is a tendency in the poem for every syllable to take on the
value of a stress, giving a spondaic effect, a massive aggression
breaking through the abstract pattern of the lines, the unstressed syllables of ordinary speech expanding like sails before
a great spiritual gale. The symphonic mass of the poem is
matched in English only by certain poems of Donne, Milton,
and Hopkins. This tendency of certain lines in a poem to
become longer than they are meant to be by taking on stress-
value on otherwise unstressed syllables is one of the surest
marks of greatness in poetry. Thus, in a Shakespeare sonnet,
the five-stress line may suddenly stretch out into a magnificent
seven:

> And with ˈold ˈwoes, ˌnew ˈwail my ˈdear ˈtime's ˈwaste.

This is so common a tendency in the last lines of Milton
sonnets as to be almost a characteristic:

> ˈI ˌwaked, ˈshe ˌfled, and ˈday ˌbrought ˈback my ˈnight . . .

> ˈThey ˈalso ˈserve who ˈonly ˈstand and ˈwait . . .

> ˈNew ˈpresbyter is but ˈold ˈpriest ˌwrit ˈlarge . . .

> And ˌwhen ˈGod ˈsends a ˈcheerful ˈhour, reˈfrains . . .

So in Dunbar's poem we have:

> Our ˈcampioun ˈChryst conˈfountet hes ˈhis ˈforse . . . 2

> The ˈsone that ˈwox ˈall ˈpaill ˌnow ˈschynnis ˈbricht . . . 27

But apart from this incremental *tendency*, the lines, almost entirely ten-syllabic, fall most easily into a four-stress pattern:

¹Don is a ¹battell on the ¹dragon ¹blak . . .		1
The ¹yettis of ¹hell ar ¹brokin with a ¹crak . . .		3
The ¹fetteris ¹¹lowsit and the ¹dungeoun ¹temit . . .		36
Sur¹rexit ¹Dominus de ¹sepul¹chro . . .		8
The ¹ransoun ¹maid, the ¹presoneris re¹demit,		37
The ¹feild is ¹win, our¹cumin is the ¹fo . . .		

More will be said on this subject in the chapter on Dunbar's metric. This poem is the one in which, of all his poems, Dunbar most clearly rises above his major rank and soars to the sublime. It is the highest point his spirit ever touched, and that means the highest point touched in Scottish poetry to this day. Another poem on this subject is found in the Bannatyne MS., and included in S.T.S. as by Dunbar. There is no authority for this attribution in the manuscript, and Mackenzie is right to exclude it from his edition: the more so because the absence of Dunbar's name beneath it in the MS. is reinforced by the poem's manifest inferiority.

A short religious poem may be quoted in its entirety:

Salviour, suppois my sensualitie   1
  Subject to syn hes maid my saule of sys,
Sum spark of lycht and spiritualitie
    Walkynnis my witt, and ressoun biddis me rys;
    My corrupt conscience askis, clips and cryis,
First grace, syn space, for to amend my mys,
    Substance with honour doing none suppryis,
Freyndis, prosperite, heir peax, syne hevynis blys.

The last four lines seem to anticipate Donne's style and manner. In his manuscript Maitland ascribes it to Dunbar.

Dunbar's poetry is much preoccupied with the image of woman—quite understandably, since she is life for man, even for celibate men. His vision of her has ranged from the *dame* of *amour courtois* romance to the horrific image of the Wedo. But the Church did not leave anything so vital and all-important (before the unbalanced masculine protest of the Reformation, that is) out of its scheme of things, but held before the faithful

the image of Mary, Mother of Jesus and wife of Joseph, as its
ideal. The last of Dunbar's poems now to be considered is,
very fittingly, his hymn of praise to her.

> Hale, sterne superne, hale in eterne,   I
>   In Godis sicht to schyne.
> Lucerne in derne for to discerne
>   Be glory and grace devyne,
> Hodiern, modern, sempitern
>   Angelicall regyne.
> Our tern inferne for to dispern
>   Helpe, rialest rosyne.
>   *Ave Maria, gracia plena,*
>   Hale, fresche floure femynyne.
> Yerne us, guberne, virgin matern,
>   Of reuth baith rute and ryne.

The paean goes one—Hail, young benign fresh flourishing
Alpha's (Christ's) dwelling-place, whose worthy offspring has
given us cause to sing before His tabernacle! All malign things
we thrust down by the sign of the Cross, and we pray this king
to bring us into His reign from the dark shadow of death.
Hail, Mary, mother and virgin, bright sun, by might of miracle
brightening our sadness! Hail, eastern star of day, light
among night's clouds emptying our darkness, conqueror of
fiends, unseen anchor, gentle nightingale, guide on the strait
and narrow way!

> Hale, qwene serene, Hale, most amene,   37
>   Haile, hevinlie hie emprys.
> Haile, schene unseyne with carnale eyne,
>   Haile, ros of paradys.
> Haile, clene, bedene, ay till conteyne,
>   Haile fair fresche flour delyce;
> Haile, grene daseyne, haile, fro the splene,
>   Of Jhesu genetrice.
>   *Ave Maria, gracia plena,*
>   Thow baire the prince of prys,
> Our teyne to meyne, and ga betweyne
>   As humile oratrice.

So it goes on for eighty-four lines, hailing her as queen of
heaven, adored by angels, great empress, shield against our

enemies, intercessor, mediator, saviouress, vicar of God, star, spice, lily-flower, imperial wall, place, beauty, triumphal hall, throne of God's excellence, heavenly power, royal hospital, ball of crystal, etc.:

> Imperiall wall, place palestrall 73
>   Of peirles pulcritud;
> Tryumphale hall, his trone regall,
>   Of Godis celsitud.
> Hospitall riall, the lord of all
>   Thy closet did include,
> Bricht ball cristall, ros virginall,
>   Fulfillit of angell fude.
>   *Ave Maria, gracia plena,*
>   Thy birth has with his blude
> Fra fall mortall, originall,
>   Us raunsound on the rude.

The carillon of joyful bells rings out from that benighted age down to our own, and out of time altogether. It is an astounding *tour de force*, unique in either Scots or English. The muscle-bound rhyming by which he gets his effect of a peal of bells, reminds us of a poem so much the opposite of this that we are astonished once again by the sheer spiritual range of Dunbar (apart from his poetic range), by the last three stanzas of his part of the "Flyting". The Scots Makars loved this kind of exuberant display of sheer virtuosity for its own sake, but none of them ever quite equalled this extraordinary volley. It is as near as Dunbar—that very classical and impure poet—ever came to "pure" poetry, the poetry of sheer lovely verbal noise for its own sake, with the intellectual content reduced to a minimum: intellectually, it is one tautology. In eighty-four lines he manages to say very much less than the few phrases of the Ave Maria itself: but how he says it! The Scots language has never produced anything quite so extravagantly exuberant".[26]

There is a similar poem, "Ros Mary",[27] often thought to be by Dunbar. As it is anonymous in the three manuscripts

[26] It is also one of his most successful examples of aureation—the Latinising is appropriate here.
[27] 87 (same title).

in which it appears, there is no authority for attributing it to
Dunbar at all, and certainly it is so corrupt and inferior that
nobody who cared for Dunbar's reputation would want to.
The material is traditional, Dunbar's contribution, in the poem
considered above, being that of his own sheer poetic genius,
and the freshness of his own personal sincerity in feeling an
old and conventional emotion completely anew in his own life.
And this is precisely what is missing, as well as even mere
poetic competence, in the "Ros Mary".

XIV

All My Ballattis under the Byrkis

D UNBAR was a highly conscious technician, a professional
verse-master,[1] as well as being a poet. This is worth
saying, because many good poets are not so: they work
by ear, by feeling, only half-consciously, upon a minimum of
technical know-how, in the theoretical sense. This does not
mean that they are "naives" or "primitives"—it simply
means that they have their own unformulated way of doing
what they do. Burns belonged rather to this type of practical
poet: Hopkins is a recent outstanding example of the opposite
type, a highly conscious and original metrist. Dunbar is
somewhere between the two, but nearer to Hopkins than to
Burns, in this particular. He was a man of learning and high
education—a clever and learned man as well as being a genius.
In " Schir, I Complane of Injuris",[2] he says:

> A refing sonne off rakyng Muris   2
> Hes magellit my making . . .

> That fulle dismemberit hes my meter . . .   8

> He hes indorsit myn indyting
> With versis off his awin hand wryting . . .   15

The word "making" shows his habitual thinking of his work
as an artefact rather than as an expression of personality or
utterance of a "message". The word "meter" shows his
consciousness of metric theory—though not which of many
theories he has in mind—as distinct from practice: and the
word "versis" shows at least his awareness of the Latin theory
of "verse", a turning, a measured, lined pattern. "Metre",
too, is derived from the Greek "metron", measure. These

---

[1] The problem of Dunbar's language is a problem for specialists; the reader is
referred to the Appendix (below, pp. 351 ff.), but Mackay Mackenzie's edition
includes a note on Middle Scots.

[2] 5 ("Complaint to the King aganis Mure").

are all the indications we have of what his metric principles were, in theory, as distinct from practice. Anything else we may posit of his metric must be derived from his practice as evidenced by the poems.

In a wider sense, of course, his "metric", which is the concern of this chapter, means simply his range of forms, the patterns in which his poems are composed; and a discussion of these will be the main subject here.

These "forms" of constant abstract patterning are of two chief kinds. The first of these kinds is the unrhymed alliterative stress-pattern native to the Teutonic languages: this kind I propose therefore to call "Teutonic". The second kind is the variety of lyric rhymed patterns of verse of more or less regular number of syllables, which is native to, or at least developed in, French and other Romance languages: this kind I propose to call, therefore, the "Romance" kind.

Dunbar has only one surviving poem in the Teutonic kind—"The Tretis of the Tua Marriit Wemen and the Wedo". All the rest of his work is in the Romance kind. M'Neill[3] makes the further useful subdivisions of the Romance kind into those in rhymed couplet form, and those in more complex stanzaic forms—which can themselves be further subdivided, when we come to them.

The alliterative line used in the "Tretis" is a development of the line of such Anglo-Saxon (I much prefer this term to "Old English", now fashionable, on the ground that it is more accurate: the latter is obscurantist, blurring an essential distinction between Angle and Saxon, and bringing in undesirable political connotations) poems as *Beowulf*. "The Tretis" has already been discussed at length, but here we must look at its versification. The basis of the verse is two hemistichs—always marked in the old poetry by a "caesura", so-called, which we will try to insert here—each of two main stresses, with a varying number of weaker syllables:

Aˌpon the ˈmidsummer ˈevin, ˈmirriest of ˈnichtis, 1
I ˈmuvit ˌfurth alˈlane, near as ˈmidnicht wes ˈpast . . .

[3] "Note on the Versification and Metres of Dunbar," in *The Poems of William Dunbar*, ed. Small, S.T.S., I. clxxii ff.

The alliteration here is only on the first and third stresses, although it varies throughout the poem.   In common with other alliterative poems of the period, both in Scots and English, it takes a free attitude to alliteration, compared with the old poetry—of *Beowulf*, in particular, in which the dominant convention of alliterating only and usually first, second, and third stresses, but never the fourth, with an occasional line with only one and three or two and three stressed, is scrupulously adhered to.   Dunbar sometimes has all four main stresses alliterating:

I ˈhard, ˌunder a ˈholyne,   ˈhevinlie grein ˈhewit . . .   12

Sometimes he alliterates also half-stressed or unstressed syllables, as in these:

Thair ˈdrank and ˌdid away ˈdule,   under ˈderne ˈbewis . . .   242

Sometimes he adds to the alliteration proper by having the alliterating syllable repeated also in the middle of a word, as in "midsummer" in the first line.   And sometimes he runs the alliteration on for two or more lines, as in the two opening ones, and in this:

All ˈgrathit into ˈgarlandis   of ˈfresche ˌgudlie ˈflouris,   18
So ˈglitterit as the ˈgowd   wer thair ˈglorius ˌgilt ˈtressis
Quhill ˌall the ˈgressis   did ˈgleme of the ˈglaid ˈhewis.

There is also double alliterating in the first of these lines, the one on **g** and the other on **f**.   Dunbar seems to work on the principle that as alliteration is a good thing, the more you have of it the better.   Compare that with the classical strictness of the Beowulf poet:

Ic þæt ˈˈlond-ˈbuende   ˈleode ˈmine
ˈSele ˈrædende   ˈsecgan ˈhyrde
þæt ˈhie geˈsawon   ˈswylce ˈtwegen
ˈMicle ˈmearc-ˌstapan   ˈmoras ˈhealdan
ˈEllor-ˈgaestas . . .

The piling up of alliteration in the "Tretis" can be very effective, however, giving a bubbling impression of high spirits, as in:

I ˌdrew in ˈderne to the ˌdyk to ˈdirkin eftir ˌmirthis   9
The ˈdew ˌdonkit the ˈdaill   and ˈdynnit the ˈfeulis.

The purpose of the alliteration in the Anglo-Saxon poetry was to bind together the two hemistichs, usually by alliterating the initial sound of the first stress of each hemistich, sometimes also the second stress of the first, but never the second stress of the second hemistich. In Dunbar, while it may serve this purpose, too, the consciousness of the hemistich as being the true unit of the verse is submerged, having been replaced by the Romance concept of the "line", the "versus", as the unit of metre: and his main use of it is for its sheer richness, its clattering, gossipy excitement. This suits his purpose in this poem admirably, and his choice of form here is admirable—a stroke of genius. In the two lines quoted above there is some question of where the main stress comes in each of the first hemistichs—I read it with the stress on "derne" in the first, and on "dew" in the second, but it could be read with the stress on "drew" in the first, and on "donkit" in the second, or a combination of these. It is even possible, though incorrect, to read each line as a five-stress: but each of the first hemistichs contains two full stresses and one half-stress. An accurate reading would probably be:

I ₁drew in ˈderne to the ˈdyk   to ˈdirkin eftir ˈmirthis,   9
The ˈdew ₁donkit the ˈdaill   and ˈdynnit the ˈfeulis.

This half-stress, or subsidiary stress, varying in degree of intensity from near full-stress to near-unstress, plays a much more important role in verse than is usually admitted—or was until this century—and particularly in "alliterative" verse (a misnomer, for the alliteration is not the essential ingredient, which is the two-stressed hemistich linked in couples *by* alliteration). The truth is that, as Scots and English (and no doubt other Teutonic languages) are stress languages, as distinct from syllabic (French), or temporal (Latin and Greek),[4] so the comparatively free-running subsidiary stress is the hallmark of verse in these languages, and a poet's sensitivity to it (and a reader's) is crucial.

Dunbar's delight in the extravagance of alliteration—is not his poem an extravaganza, at one level?—is typical of the virtuoso, or of the young poet revelling in his own power over

[4] Karl Shapiro, *Bibliography of Modern Prosody*, Baltimore 1948, intro.

beautiful noises. More importantly, it points to his expectation of a similar delight in his audience: he was writing for an audience which he knew would share his own highly cultivated love of poetry for its own sake as well as for its communication.

The success of this form is due to the fact that its rhythmic conventions are built on the true nature of the language it uses. Metre proper is a syllabic convention, most appropriate for such syllabic languages as French, whence, largely, it is derived. It is and has always been foreign to, and unassimilable in, English or Scots. This is so true that metrical theory—that everlasting debate in which nothing is ever settled—even proposes that the tension between the two elements, between the true nature of the language and the convention of metre, is the most important thing in poetry. This is a desperate view, much like saying that the tension between reality and unreality is the most important thing in life. The truth is that, as Manley Hopkins, among others, saw, all our poetry in the metrical convention has been miswritten, and the future depends on restoring the writing of poetry in our languages to its true basis—the stressed hemistich.[5] The beauties of our poetry in metre are in spite of that restriction, not because of it: still greater ones will emerge from bringing out the true nature of the language.

Dunbar's range in Romance metric is immense. Of these, the couplet is an early French form foreshadowed by the *Roman de Thebes* (*c.* 1150), and may be earlier.[6] Of the two types, Dunbar uses the five-stress or ten-syllabic only in "Now of Wemen this I Say for Me":[7]

> Wo wirth the fruct wald put the tre to nocht,   9
> And wo wirth him rycht so that sayis ocht . . .

---

[5] Professor D. A. Abercrombie, of the Phonetics Department, Edinburgh University, has concluded from phonetic studies of the living voice that this hemistich pattern is close to the natural movement of speech, whether verse or prose. His work is to be published soon, and should have a fruitful, perhaps even revolutionary effect on prosodic theory and practice. The experiments of Ezra Pound and other American poets, such as William Carlos Williams, seem to me to point in the right direction for the founding of a true English Prosody. Phonetics should have much influence in the future on matters of prosody.

[6] See also Schipper, *Altenglische Metrik*, Bonn 1881, p. 434.

[7] 45 ("In Prais of Wemen").

This couplet also is used as the basic verse of certain stanzaic poems—"This Nycht, befoir the Dawing Cleir",[8] being one. It will be more convenient to consider this couplet in these poems as they come up for consideration in place. The four-stress couplet Dunbar uses in four poems—five, if we hold that he wrote also the "Respontio Regis" to "Schir, Lat it Nevir in Toun be Tald".[9] These are: the relevant parts of "We that are here in Hevins Glory",[10] "Complane I Wald",[11] "Schir, Ye Have mony Servitouris",[12] and "Be Divers Wyis".[13] In the first of these, the purpose is chiefly comic, and in the others, it is satirical and plaintive. The measure had been already naturalised in Scots by Barbour in his *Brus*, and in the *Buik of Alexander*, whoever wrote it. Dunbar may have been as much influenced by these as by the French poets or by Chaucer. Barbour, of course, and the author of the *Alexander* poem probably, was influenced by French models, as was Chaucer. Dunbar would know the form also in Wyntoun's *Chronicles*. He seems usually to make the eight syllables his standard practice, as in "Schir, Ye Have mony Servitouris":[14]

> And thocht that I amang the laif   25
> Unworthy be ane place to haif,
> Or in that nummer to be tald,
> Als lang in mynd my wark sall hald,
> Als haill in everie circumstance,
> In forme, in mater, and substance,
> But wering or consumptioun,
> Roust, canker or corruptioun,
> As ony of thair werkis all,
> Suppois that my rewarde be small.

All these are eight-syllabic. But where it seems necessary, he will give only seven syllables:

> And all of thair craft cunning

---

[8] 4 ("How Dumbar wes Desyrd to be ane Freir").
[9] 22 ("The Petition of the Gray Horse, Auld Dunbar").
[10] 30 ("The Dregy of Dunbar").
[11] 19 ("Complaint to the King").
[12] 17 ("Remonstrance to the King").
[13] 29 ("Aganis the Solistaris in Court").
[14] 17 ("Remonstrance to the King").

X

—unless one were to argue that "thair" is meant, by licence, to have two syllables, unlike his normal practice. Elsewhere, he permits nine:

> Ane uthir sort, more miserabill,   37
> Thocht thai be nocht sa profitable,

and even ten or eleven, as in:

> Divinouris, rethoris, and philosophouris,   5
> Astrologis, artistis, and oratouris.

and other lines of catalogue. This would seem to make clear that he is still thinking in stresses, not in syllables, for in every case the lines have four stresses, if one allows the convention, common in Barbour, of stressing the final "-ing" of "cunning", which he clearly intends, for he rhymes it with "lawboring". In the regular lines, not only the stresses are regular, as in alliterative, and all Scots and English verse, but the weaker syllables are also regular. What we seem to be seeing here is a combination of the metric and alliterative techniques, the Romance and the Teutonic. It is most unlikely that Dunbar was thinking in terms of "feet" of the Greek sort—iambic, trochaic, and so on—for this pernicious plague in metrical theory entered poetics later in the sixteenth century: Thompson[15] dates it from about the publication of Tottel's *Miscellany* of 1557, "where the iambic metrical pattern makes its first unequivocal and dominant appearance in print in modern English".[16] But Thompson goes on to say that Dunbar "certainly" used it, which is precisely what I very much doubt. It seems to me that what emerges from Dunbar's practice *may* be misinterpreted as "iambic", but that what he is actually doing is combining elements of the Teutonic stress system with elements of the Romance syllabic one. The notion of applying Greek quantity terms to native poetry seems to date from the Italian and humanist influence— Puttenham being the first to give it critical utterance in 1587, though Gascoigne's *Instructions* foreshadow him.

In any case, there is no evidence that Dunbar thought in

---

[15] John Thompson, *The Founding of English Metre*, London 1961, p. 2.
[16] *Ibid.*

terms of quantity. What was going on in his verse, and in that of his Scots and English contemporaries, predecessors, and successors up to the great flowering of the Italian-influenced late Elizabethan poetry, was the resolution of two different traditions of measure in poetry—the Teutonic stress one, and the Romance syllabic. The former was the native tradition, the latter a product of the Norman conquest, and was due to the influence of the Norman ruling-class. To examine the results of this ruling-class influence on English poetry (and to a lesser extent on Scots) would take a book-length study in itself.

Dunbar's poems in stanzaic form are divisible into two main groups: those of which the lines are of equal length, and those of which the lines are of varying lengths. These two groups may be further subdivided into those which have a complete two-line refrain; those which have a complete one-line refrain; and those which have an incomplete, varying, one-line refrain. This is by no means exhaustive, but other occasional patterns are a variation on one or other of these types. Stanzas are usually of the same length, but in some poems, as in "Off Februar the Fyiftenc Nycht",[17] for example, the basic patterns are linked together in stanzas, or paragraphs, of differing length.

There are several types of stanza of equivalent lines without refrain. There is, for example, the five-line stanza of five-stress lines. In it are written four poems: "Sweit Rois of Vertew and of Gentilnes",[18] "This Nycht, befoir the Dawing Cleir",[19] "Lucina Schynnyng in Silence of the Nicht",[20] and "This Hinder Nicht, Half Sleiping as I lay".[21] In the five-line stanza of four-stress lines are: "Schir, at this Feist of Benefice",[22] "I Seik about this Warld Unstabille",[23] "In to thir Dirk and Drublie Dayis",[24] "My Heid Did Yak Yester Nicht",[25] and

---

[17] 57 ("The Dance of the Sevin Deadly Synnis").
[18] 49 ("To a Ladye").
[19] 4 ("How Dumbar wes Desyrd to be ane Freir").
[20] 39 ("The Birth of Antichrist").
[21] 60 ("The Dream").
[22] 11 ("Quhone Mony Benefices Vakit").
[23] 66 ("Of the Changes of Lyfe").
[24] 10 ("Meditatioun in Wyntir").
[25] 3 ("On His Heid-Ake").

"My Lordis of Chalker".[26] This pattern is of the type of the French rondel stanza,[27] of the first type, the fourth stanza of "Lucina" goes:

> Full mony ane man I turn unto the hicht   16
> And makis als mony full law to doun licht;
> Upon my staigis or that thow ascend
> Trest weill thy truble neir is at an end,
> Seing thir taikinis, quhairfoir thow merk thame rycht.

The last line is certainly eleven syllables, the first may be read as ten, counting "mony ane" as two: the rest are certainly ten syllables. Yet the old alliterative form shows under the surface, not only in the repetition of sounds as indicated (not to call it "alliteration" proper), but in the underlying presence of the old half-line:

> Full ˈmony ane ˈman   I ˈturne ˌunto the ˈhicht   16
> And ˈmakis als ˈmony   full ˈlaw to ˌdoun ˈlicht;
> Upˈon my ˈstaigis   ˈor that ˌthow aˈscend,
> ˈTrest weill thy ˈtruble   ˈneir ˌis at ane ˈend . . .[28]

What is really happening here is that half-stresses marked above (ˌ) are given the value of full stresses (ˈ) to fill out the pattern as a five-stress line—as we would now call it. A proper reading aloud would bring out the four-stress pattern marked above, with its half-stresses in the right place. This kind of thing can be shown all over verse in either Scots or English from the fifteenth century up to the present. An iambic reading of the first line would give:

> Full mo|ny ane man ‖ I turne | unto | the hicht . . .

which is nonsense: it "dismemberit hes my meter".

In the eight-syllable or four-stress type, the second-last stanza of "In to thir Dirk and Drubie Dayis" goes:

> For feir of this all day I drowp;   41
> No gold in kist nor wyne in cowp,

---

[26] 25 ("To the Lordis of the Kingis Chalker").
[27] E.g., Guest, *History of English Rhythms*, 1882, p. 644.
[28] Note, these are ten-syllabic couplets.

No ladeis bewtie, nor luiffis blys,
May lat me to remember this,
How glaid that ever I dyne or sowp.

If we try to bring out the half-line pattern of this, we get:

For ˈfeir of ˈthis	all ˈday I ˈdrowp,	41
No ˈgold in ˈkist	nor ˈwyne in ˈcowp,	
No ˈˈladeis ˈbewte	nor ˈˈluiffis ˈblys,	
May ˈˈlat ˈme	to reˈmember ˈthis	
How ˈglaid that ˈever	I ˈdyne or ˈsowp.	

What has happened here is that the half-stress is missing, the four full stresses standing starkly out—although, strictly, "this", in l. 4, and "ever", in l. 5 are really half-stresses with the weight of full ones conferred upon them only by the convention. Here we see at a glance why Dunbar is happiest in the shorter line stanza—the five-stress, so-called, line or "iambic pentameter", so-called, is difficult to handle because it almost invariably contains a half-stress, which is not catered for by the Greek theory as applied to our verse. The old four-stress line, properly so-called, is nearer to the pentameter than to the tetrameter: the line of blank verse, though it seems to have been suggested by Italian unrhymed verse (of Barberini and Trissino, for example), is the nearest thing to a development in metre of the old four-stress measure. This seems to me to be the reason why it achieved its paramount position in English verse, in the Elizabethan dramas and Miltonic epics.[29] The conflict between the two modes is less acute in the eight-syllable line than in the ten-syllable: and in less than eight syllables it is almost non-existent. Moreover, the old four-stress line and its blank verse successor are essentially heroic measures, best suited for narrative-dramatic poetry—and Dunbar was essentially a lyric poet. To argue against myself, his most perfect lyric is "Sweit Rois", which is in ten-syllabic lines: but these fall most easily into the old four-stress line:

ˈSweit ˌrois of ˈvertew	ˌand of ˈgentilnes	1
Deˈˈlytsum ˈˈlilie	of ˈeverie ˈˈlustyˌnes . . .	

---

[29] For discussion of this, see F. B. Gummere, *American Journal of Philology*, 1886 (vii), p. 46-78.

Another stanza of equal lines without refrain used by
Dunbar, is the so-called "Rhyme-Royal", or Chaucerian
stanza. Both names are misleading: the first has led to the
erroneous notion that it was called this because James I (of
Scots) used it in *The Kingis Quair*: and the second implies that
Chaucer invented it. In fact, the name of the stanza is a translation of the French "Chant-Royal".[30] Gascoigne mentions
it as "Rhythme royall . . . a verse of ten sillables, and seven
such verses make a staffe". Dunbar uses it in "The Thrissill
and the Rois",[31] "Quhat is this Lyfe",[32] and in the confession
poem "O Synfull Man".[33] Again, the lines tend to fall into
the old four-stress measure, as in "The Thrissil and the Rois":

In ˈbed at ˈmorrow	ˈsleiping ˌas I ˈlay	8
Me ˈthocht Aurˈora	with ˌhir ˈcrystall ˈene	
ˈIn at the ˈwindow	ˈlukit ˌby the ˈday	
And ˈhalsit ˈme	with ˈvisage ˌpaill and ˈgrene:	
On ˌquhois ˌhand a ˈlark	ˈsang ˌfro the ˈsplene,	
Aˈwalk, ˈluvaris,	ˈout of your ˈslomering,	
ˈSe how the ˌlusty ˈmorrow	ˌdois ˈup ˈspring.	

The last line has to be forced into the half-line pattern, being,
in fact, the one genuinely whole line in the seven—the others
are all made up of half-lines. One doesn't want to insist too
strongly on this, but merely to indicate a tendency, and to
bring out the two traditions in Dunbar's metric.

The ten-syllable octave without refrain is a noble form, and
it is surprising that of Dunbar's surviving work only the
ignoble "Flyting" uses it. In certain stanzas of that poem,
not only do we get extravagant alliteration and a semblance
of the old four-stress line, but every kind of poetic extravagance
is piled on, the syllables crowding far beyond the normal ten
to as much as fourteen or fifteen:

ˈMauch ˈmuttoun,	ˌbyt ˈbuttoun,	ˌpeillit ˈgluttoun,	ˌair to ˈHillhouse 241
ˈRank ˈbeggar,	ˌostir ˈdregar,	ˌfoule ˈflegar	ˌin the ˈflet;
ˈChitter ˈlilling,	ˌruch ˈrilling,	ˌlik ˈschilling	ˌin the ˈmillhouse,
ˈBaird re ˈhatour,	ˌthief of ˈnatour,	ˌfals ˈtratour,	ˌfeyndis ˈget. . . .

---

[30] See above, p. 47, n. 6.
[31] 55 (same title).
[32] 76 (same title).
[33] 84 ("The Maner of Passing to Confessioun").

The resources of both traditions are exploited here, as much as can be accommodated, and though pretty coarse fare, the verse is full of real and fine Scots words, and the thing has power and vitality.

The most elaborate of these stanzas used by Dunbar is that of nine five-stress lines. This is the form used in "The Goldyn Targe" and in it alone. It was used by Chaucer in *Queen Anelida and False Arcyte*, but is of French origin. Here again it is instructive to note the underlying four-stress alliterative pattern:

The ˈcristall ˈair,	the ˈsapher ˈfirmaˌment, 37
The ˈruby ˈskyes	ˌof the ˈorieˌnt,
Kest ˈberiall ˈbemes	on ˌemerant ˈbewis ˈgrene;
The ˈrosy ˈgarth	de ˈpaynt and ˈredo ˌlent, 40
With ˈpurpur, ˈazure,	ˈgold, and ˈgoulis ˌgent
Aˈrayed ˈwas,	by ˌdame ˈFlora the ˈquene.
So ˈnobiˌly	that ˈjoy was ˌfor to ˈsene;
The ˈroch aˈgain	the ˈrivir ˈresplenˌdent
As ˈlow enˈlumynit	ˌall the ˈlevis ˈschene. 45

All the lines except the second last fall quite easily into the old pattern, although ll. 38 and 43 are a bit forced in it. L. 39 is a standard alliterative line, as is the last line. L. 41 would probably be better read as "With purpur, azure, gold, and goulis gent": but at any level it is impure as an alliterative line, though not as two half-lines in the four-stress pattern.

The last of these stanzas of equal lines without refrain is the unique one of " I, Maister Andro Kennedy".[34] This is an octave of four-stress lines (eight syllables), but each alternate line is Latin. Here there is no question of an underlying half-line pattern: we get a solid, Latinate marching line:

> *In die mee sepulture*   97
> I will nane haif but our awne gyng,
> *Et duos rusticos de rure*
> Berand a barell on a styng;   100
> Drinkand and playand cop out, evin,
> *Sicut egomet solebam,*
> Singand and gretand with his stevin
> *Potum meum cum fletu miscebam.*

---

[34] 40 ("The Testament of Mr Andro Kennedy").

The Latin makes for wealth of feminine and double rhymes, and these in turn extend the line syllabically: thus, l. 97 has nine syllables, l. 98 eight, l. 99 nine, l. 100 eight, l. 101 nine, l. 102 eight, l. 103 nine, and l. 104 has ten syllables. The poem is strongly reminiscent of Villon.

I have given a complete stanza in each of these instances, so that the rhyme scheme may be easily seen. Rhyme came into the language along with metre, but there is no reason why it should not be used with the alliterative line—as indeed it is in such middle English poems as *Pearl*, although there the alliterative line is also counted syllabically:

In blys I se þe	blyþely blent
And I a man	al mornyf mate;
Ye take þeron	ful lyttel tente,
Þaz I hente	ofte harmez hate.

But it is a Romance development, not a Teutonic.

Dunbar used six stanzas (that we know of) having equal lines plus a refrain. Such poems, indeed, make up about two-thirds of his surviving known work. The refrain had great popularity, both in courtly and popular poetry, during the Middle Ages—and since. The device has a powerful mnemonic effect, and when used to express some weighty statement, takes on something of the "authority" of a proverb. Scots poetry is particularly fond of it, and this may be related to the Scottish love of proverb and heavy, solemn, or pithy and witty maxims. Dunbar is a master of the refrain, which can occasionally rise to the status of single-line poems—Villon's *"Mais ou sont les neiges d'antan"*, for example, and Dunbar's own *"Timor mortis conturbat me"*. Yet a refrain makes the rhyme-problem much more difficult for a poet, forcing him to keep finding new rhymes for his refrain, so that the longer the poem, the more impossible it becomes not to repeat yourself—a fault Dunbar by no means always escapes.[35] But this very fact is a stimulating challenge to a technical virtuoso. The power of *"Timor mortis"* of course derives from its religious weight in the service for the dead, but Dunbar's use of it makes it his own. In this poem we have a superb example of a metrical stanza which,

[35] It was acceptable in his time.

far from forcing the stress-nature of the language, as so often
happens in other poems, fits it at times with perfect closeness:

> No ˈstait in ˈerd ˌhere ˈstandis ˈsickir.   13
> As ˌwith the ˈwind ˈwavis the ˈwickir
> ˈWavis this ˈwarldis ˈvanitˌe.
> ˈTimor ˈmortis conˈturbat ˈme.

This perfection of correspondence between form and utterance
is the highest beauty of poetry—a fact which denies the notion
that poetry rises essentially from a tension between an abstract
metrical form and the language embodying it.   This point
seems to me so important that a slight digression may be
permissible here: it is very relevant to this chapter.   If one
takes, say, the opening of the twenty-third psalm as printed in
the Authorised Version, but following its natural form, one gets:

> The Lord is my shepherd—
> I shall not want.
>
> He maketh me to lie down in green pastures.
> He leadeth me beside the still waters.

This is, to my mind, poetic perfection, bringing out the natural
rhythmic beauty of English, the form and language in no point
at odds with each other.   Compare:

> The Lord's my shepherd, I shall not want,
>   He makes me down to lie
> In pastures green; He leadeth me
>   The quiet waters by.

The metrical version is doggerel, and doggerel is what too
easily becomes of Scots or English in the Romance metre.   The
first of these versions is a refined development of the old half-
line, four-stress verse; the second is the newer metrical system.

The excellence of "I that in Heill wes", especially the
stanza quoted above, is precisely that it so triumphantly over-
comes, subdues, the metrical form.   Yet even here, and especially in the best lines, lines two and three, the true rhythm of
the language does not conform to the four-stress accentuation
normal to such lines:

> As ˌwith the ˈwynd ˈwavis the ˈwickir,   14
> ˈWavis this ˈwarldis ˈvaniˌte.

seems to me to be the true reading of these lines. There are only three full stresses in each line. On the other hand, when reading aloud, I find myself tempted to read the first line not, as I would scan it at a glance on the page, but:

ˈNo ˈstait in ˈerd ₁here ˈstandis ˈsickir . . .   13

In other words, with five full stresses, and a half on the word "here".

Dunbar used this stanza also in ten other poems: "This Waverand Warldis Wretchidnes",[36] "Of Covetyce",[37] "Of Lentren in the First Mornyng",[38] "Telyouris and Sowtaris, Blist Be Ye",[39] "Thyne Awin Gude",[40] "Schir, for Your Grace",[41] "Welcom, My Awin Lord Thesaurair",[42] "Madame, Ye Heff a Dangerous Dog",[43] "He is Na Dog",[44] "In Hansill of this Guid New Yeir",[45] and "Welcum of Scotland to be Quene",[46] if that be by Dunbar. It is a very powerful little stanza, heroic in its stark elemental force, elegaic in its simplicity of statement, its solemnity.

The most popular of all these shorter stanzas is that of five four-stress lines (octosyllabic), with refrain. I think of it as the "discretioun" stanza, for the three poems "of discretion" are written in it: but there are about eighteen poems in it. These are: "Off Every Asking Followis Nocht",[47] "To Speik of Giftis or Almous Deidis",[48] "Eftir Geving I Speik of Taking",[49] "Quhome to Sall I Compleine Why Wo",[50] "Schir, Yit Remembir as of Befoir",[51] "Musing Allone this Hinder

<hr>

[36] 13 ("Of the Warldis Instabilitie").
[37] 67 (same title).
[38] 71 ("All Erdly Joy Returnis in Pane").
[39] 59 ("The Amendis to the Telyouris and Sowtaris").
[40] 72 ("Advice to Spend Anis Awin Gude").
[41] 18 ("To the King that He war Johne Thomosunis (*sic*) Man").
[42] 24 ("Welcome to the Lord Treasurer").
[43] 33 ("Of James Dog, Kepar of the Quenis Wardrop").
[44] 34 ("Of the Same James quhen He had Plesett Him").
[45] 26 ("A New Year's Gift to the King").
[46] 89 ("To the Princess Margaret").
[47] 14 ("Of Discretioun in Asking").
[48] 15 ("Of Discretioun in Geving").
[49] 16 ("Of Discretioun in Taking").
[50] 21 ("None may Assure in this Warld").
[51] 20 ("To the King").

Nicht",[52] "How sould I rewill Me",[53] "Full Oft I Mus",[54]
"Sanct Salvatour! Send Silver Sorrow",[55] "Madam, Your
Men Said Thai wald Ryd",[56] "He Hes Anewch that is Content",[57] "This Lang Lentern Makis Me Lene",[58] "Off Benefice, Schir, at Everie Feist",[59] "He that Hes Gold",[60] "Lang
Heff I Maed of Ladyes Quhytt",[61] and, though with much
play on internal rhyming, "Doverrit with Dreme".[62] In its
normal use, we have from "Off Everie Asking":

ǀSome ˌaskis ǀmair than he deǀservis,   11
ǀSum ˌaskis far ǁless than he ǀservis,
   Sum ǀschames to ǀask, as ǀbraidis of ǀme
And ǀall wiǀthout reǀward he ǀstervis:
   In ǀasking ˌsowld disǀcretioun ǀbe.

Here again we have a varying stress-pattern in verse which is
basically syllabic, and which the theorists of the "iambic"
school would read as iambic, with the usual rigmorole of
"modulations" into other non-existent "feet". In "Doverrit
with Dreme", however, Dunbar gives us one of his most daring
virtuoso performances, rhyming not only the lines, but, as if
to accentuate their existence and his own thinking in terms
of them, the half-lines as well:

Sa ǀmekle ǀtressone,   sa ǀmony ˌpartial ˌsawis,   26
Sa ǁlittle ǀressone   to ˌhelp the ǀcommoun ǀcawis,
That ǀall the ǁlawis   ar ˌnot ǀsett by ane ǀbene;
Sic ǀfenyeit ǀflawis   sa ǀmony ˌwastit ǀwawis
With ǀin this ǀland   wes ˌnevir ǀhard nor ǀsene.

Far from being one of his shorter poems, he keeps this up for
sixteen stanzas.[63] I have suggested elsewhere that the poem
might better be set out as a nine-line stanza rather than a five:
but the above example, is, I think, how Dunbar actually
thought of it. This is a highly intricate verse-pattern—too
much so, in my view, to permit a very deep view of the subject,
so that the thing becomes a mere catalogue with insufficient

[52] 8 ("Of Deming").   [53] 9 ("How sall I Governe Me").
[54] 69 ("Best to be Blyth").   [55] 1 ("To the King").
[56] 71 ("To the Quene").   [57] 70 ("Of Content").
[58] 46 ("The Twa Cummeris").   [59] 12 ("To the King").
[60] 2 ("Ane His Awin Enemy").   [61] 37 ("Of Ane Blak-Moir").
[62] 77 ("A General Satyre").   [63] Imperfectly in stanzas 1, 13, and 15.

comment—which makes great demands of the poet's technical resources. It is not merely the internal rhyming he has to cope with, but the fact that he also rhymes the half-lines of ll. 3 and 4 with the end-rhymes of ll. 1, 2, and 4; five rhymes on the same sound in each verse. This means also that the internal half-line rhyme of l. 4 must rhyme also with the end-rhyme, as shown above. This quick-step measure in the first four lines has the effect of adding to the power of the refrain line, which does not rhyme internally, but makes straight for the winning-post, like a runner in an obstacle race after the last obstacle has been successfully passed. It is precisely this kind of writing which underlines the name of "makar", reminding us that ποιητής meant originally just that, and had nothing to do with mystical inspiration, "genius", special spiritual quality, personality, or any other of the many things that the name "poet" has come to mean. These things, in so far as they are present at all—and they often are—are by-products of the one essential thing that makes a poet: a talent for making verse that sings, for bringing out the musics inherent in language.[64]   And by verse here I don't mean "metre", but any setting-out of poetic utterance in group-units of speech or song, as distinct from the run-on sentence structure of prose. Dunbar is the clearest example of this talent in Scottish poetry, and the most gifted with it, with the exception, in my view, of Robert Henrysoun, in whom the talent is less obvious, less displayed in virtuosity, but is more solid and weighty.[65]

Five pieces of seven-line stanzas with refrain, rhyming *a a b b c b c*, have come down to us from Dunbar. These are "Sic Tydingis Hard I at the Sessioun",[66] "This Hindir Nicht in Dumfermeling,"[67] "In Secreit Place this Hyndir Nicht",[68] "Sir Jhon Sinclair Begowthe to Dance",[69] and "Schir, I Complane of Injuris".[70]   The lines are all octosyllabic, and

---

[64] Without "something to say", of course, the talent is "lodged with him useless".

[65] Henrysoun is not more gifted generally as a metrist, but is underrated.

[66] 43 ("Tydingis fra the Sessioun").

[67] 27 ("The Wowing of the King . . . in Dumfermeling").

[68] 28 (same title).

[69] 32 ("Of a Dance in the Quenis Chalmer").

[70] 5 ("Complaint to the King aganis Mure").

two refrains alternate in "In Secreit Place". It is a swift, conversational form, as he uses it, with satiric and comic potentialities, which he exploits. It also has interesting dramatic possibilities, which he does not make the most of, his purpose rarely being dramatic, but which can be seen in, for instance, "Sic Tydingis Hard I":

> Ane murlandis man of uplandis mak   I
> At hame thus to his nychtbour spak,
>   "Quhat tydingis gossep, peax or weir?"
> The tothir rownit in his eir,
>   "I tell yow this undir confessioun,
> Bot laitly lichtit of my meir
>   I come of Edinburch fra the sessioun."

That "rownit", and the "undir confessioun" (a priest at confessioun is sworn to utter secrecy) are fine dramatic effects, setting the key to the whole: it is a pity that this treatment has to give way to a typical catalogue of vices, but one cannot imagine it in any other way—at least not at its length. I need not comment on the versification as such—the reader will see for himself that this is pretty straight syllabic measure, with the usual extra syllable here and there, but with little suggestion of the old pattern. But the pattern is not "iambic"—l. 4, for instance, has only three stresses, *if properly spoken*:[71] the same is true of l. 6, I suspect, though one might be induced to pass "of" as a stress in the context, and of l. 7, where "Edinburch" would be sounded more like "Embro", but definitely with no stress on "fra". In reading line one, moreover, I would give only a half-stress to "man", with only three full stresses in the line.

Dunbar makes considerable use of the ten-syllabic octave with refrain, mostly rhyming *a b a b b c b c*. There are twelve poems or more in this measure ascribed to Dunbar in the sources; and two or three are attributions, probably not by him at all. Definite ones are "Done is a Battell",[72] "Without Glaidnes",[73] "Be ye ane Luvar",[73a] "To the, Mercifull Salviour",[74] with

---

[71] Though Dunbar no doubt counted four.
[72] 81 ("On the Resurrection of Christ").
[73] 73 ("No Tressoun Availis without Glaidnes").
[73a] 68 ("Gude Counsale").
[74] 83 ("The Tabill of Confessioun").

alternating refrain "The Merle and the Nychtingaill",[75]
"The Ballade of Lord Bernard Stewart",[76] "Elegy on the Death
of Lord Bernard Stewart",[77] "Blyth Aberdeane",[78] "To Dwell
in Court",[79] and "O Wreche, be War".[80] Attributed are
"London, Thow art",[81] "We Lordis hes Chosin Us",[82] and
"Gladethe Thoue Queyne",[83] none of which I believe to be
by Dunbar. Some of these definitely fall easily into the old
half-line measure, despite[84] the ten-syllabic basis of the verse:

¹Don is a ¹battell	¹on the ¹dragon ¹blak, ɪ
Our ¹campioun ¹Chryst	con¹fountet ¹hes his ¹forse.
The ¹yettis of ¹hell	ar ¹brokin ¹with a ¹crak,
The ¹signe tri¹umphall	¹rasit ¹is of the ¹croce,
The ¹devillis ¹trymmillis	¹with ¹hidous ¹voce,
The ¹saulis ar ¹borrowit	¹and to the ¹blis can ¹go.
¹Chryst with his ¹bluid	our ¹ransonis ¹dois in ¹doce:
Sur¹rexit ¹Dominus de ¹sepul¹chro.	

In varying degree this applies to the whole poem, which is
thus seen as essentially composed of four-stress lines on the old
model, and not of "iambic pentameters". The letters set
above in bold type do not correspond exactly to a regular
alliterative scheme, but those that don't, do in fact have alliterative force in their respective lines: some of course are pure
alliteration, as in ll. ɪ and 6. There is a counterpoint also
between "umphall" and "mmillis", and the alliteration of l. 6
carries on into the "bluid" of l. 7 as shown above. In reading
aloud, however, the lines tend to lengthen into five and six
stresses, so great is the power of the poem.[85]
    In the four-stress (so-called) or octosyllabic form of the
eight-lined stanza with refrain, there are "Amang thir

[75] 63 (same title).
[76] 61 (same title).
[77] 62 (same title).
[78] 64 ("To Aberdein").
[79] 41 ("Rewl of Anis Self").
[80] 75 ("Of the Warldis Vanite").
[81] 88 ("To the City of London").
[82] 92 ("To the Governour in France").
[83] 90 (same title).
[84] And despite the fact that liturgical chant requires whole-line *reading*.
[85] See above, p. 301.

Freiris",[86] "Sen that I am a Presoneir",[87] "*Rorate celi desuper*",[88]
and "Memento, homo".[89] This gives a very different pattern:

|Sen that |I am a |preso|neir
Till |hir that |farest |is and |best,
I |me com|mend, fra |yeir till |yeir,
|In till hir |bandoun for to |rest.
I |govit |on that |gudli|est,
So |lang to |luk that I |tuk |lai|seir,
Quhill |I wes |tane with |outtin |test,
And |led |furth as a |preso|neir.

The actual rhythm tends to be three-stress, as in so much of
this type of verse (the so-called "iambic tetrameter"), and
indeed, line six is the only one which is, to my mind, really
four-stress, and which falls easily into the old half-line measure.

There are two poems of equal lines with refrain in which
the refrain is double. Both are six-line stanzas rhyming *a a a
b b b* : "Schir, Lat it Nevir in Toun be Tald",[90] and "Now
Culit is Dame Venus brand",[91] The line-base in each is octosyllabic, but here and there are traces of the old alliterative
measure:

|Quhen |I wes |yung and into |ply   7
And |wald |cast |gammaldis to the |sky,
|I had bene |bocht in |realmes |by,
  |Had I con|sentit to be |sauld.
  |Schir, lett it |nevir in |toun be |tauld
That |I suld |be ane |Yuillis |yauld.

L. 9 is a fair alliterative one, though not strictly in accordance
with the Anglo-Saxon rules. Similar lines occur in the other
poem, too, such as, from the first stanza, the line "In feynit
luve quhat foly bene".

The last of this *genre* of stanzas of equal lines with refrain,
though it really belongs apart, is the French triolet form. This
is not so much a stanza with refrain as refrain-type lines

---

[86] 80 ("Of the Passioun of Christ").
[87] 54 ("Bewty and the Presoneir").
[88] 79 ("Of the Nativitie of Christ").
[89] 74 ("Of Manis Mortalitie").
[90] 22 ("The Petition of the Gray Horse, Auld Dumbar").
[91] 52 (same title).

repeating within a small single-stanza poem consisting of eight lines of a basic four-syllables, rhyming *a b a b a b a b*: the first two lines are repeated as seventh and eighth, and the first as fourth. Dunbar uses this form in the responses of "We that ar Heir in Hevins Glory".[92] These are normally printed as four lines rhyming internally, but to bring out the form here is one of the three in triolet form:

> God and Sanct Geill 59
> Here yow convoy
> Baith sone and weill
> God and Sanct Geill.
> To sonce and seill
> Solace and joy,
> God and Sanct Geill
> Here yow convoy.

It would be ridiculous to make too much of this in terms of the old measure: but these are in fact half-lines, and when so regarded, the three-four couple above and the five-six couple make alliterative lines—the latter a perfect one: "To sonce and seill solace and joy".

The last variety of verse used by Dunbar is that of stanzas of lines of unequal length. The first of this type to notice is the tail-rhyme stanza, sometimes known as "versus caudatus", or "rime-couée". M'Neill[93] says it originated in the Latin lyrical poetry of the Church; and it passed through Latin popular poetry into the vernacular verse of France, England and Scotland, becoming very popular.[94] This is not, in itself, a stanza at all, but a device which can be used in many kinds of stanzaic construction. Here we are only concerned with what use we know Dunbar to have made of it. The simplest of his types is a six-line stanza divided into two parts, each with a couplet "head" of eight-syllabic lines rhyming *a a*, followed by a "neck" of "versus caudatus" of six syllables, followed by another couplet, the "body", to continue the metaphor, also of eight-syllabic verse rhyming *b b*—and ending

[92] 30 ("The Dregy of Dunbar").
[93] *The Poems of William Dunbar*, ed. Small, S.T.S., III., app. p. clxxxix.
[94] *The Poems of William Dunbar*, ed. Schipper, p. 353.

up with the tail proper in six syllables rhyming with the "neck"
line, this:

Head	{ Now lythis of ane gentill knycht	I
	{ Schir Thomas Norny, wyse and wycht,	
Neck	And full of chivalrie,	
Body	{ Quhais father wes ane Grand Keyne	
	{ His mither wes ane Farie Quene	
Tail	Gotten be sosserie.[95]	

The importance of this kind of line variation in Scots versification need not be stressed. It is found throughout Lyndsay's
Satyre of the Thrie Estaitis, in the two popular poems "Peblis to
the Play" and "Chrystis Kirk on the Grene", and in the
"standard Habbie" form which was the staple of our eighteenth-
century verse. Apart from the ballad, it seems to be the only
Romance form which became part of the popular and oral
tradition, in regular use.

The most famous Dunbar poem in a tailed stanza is "Off
Februar the Fyiftene Nycht" and its two sequels, "Than Cryd
Mahoun" and "Nixt that a Turnament wes Tryid".[96] Here
the basic three-line construct is built into various lengths, the
staple one being twelve lines, thus:

> Off Februar the fyiftene nycht   I
> Full lang befoir the dayis lycht
>   I lay in till ane trance,
> And then I saw baith hevin and hell;
> Me thocht amang the feyndis fell
>   Mahoun gart cry ane danse,
> Off schrewis that wer nevir schrevin
> Aganis the feist of Fasternis evin
>   To mak thair observance.
> He bad gallandis ga graith a gyiss
> And kast up gamountis in the skyiss
>   That last cam out of France.

The basic form here is the same as that of "Now Lythis of ane
Gentill Knycht" outlined above, only two stanzas of six are

[95] 35 ("Of Sir Thomas Norny").
[96] 57 ("The Dance of the Sevin Deidly Synnis"), ll. 1-108, 109-20, and 58
("The Sowtar and the Tailyouris War").

Y

linked together here by a quadruple *c c c c* rhyme in the tail-lines. Given this rhyming principle, there is no reason why it should not be built into stanzas as long as you can find a rhyme for, provided the paragraphing permits.

This form can be further elaborated by adding a third line to the couplet staple, making a triplet before the tail-line, and a total stanza pattern of eight lines. This is what Dunbar does in the "Fenyeit Freir":

> As yung Aurora, with crystall haile   I
> In orient schew hir visage paile,
> A sweving swyth did me assaile
>   Off sonis of Sathanis seid.
> Me thocht a Turk of Tartary
> Come throw the boundis of Barbary
> And lay forloppin in Lumbardy
>   Full lang in waithman weid.

This particular paragraph is built up for twenty-four lines, five fours, all rhyming with that first "seid". The swing from one line-length to another is a device which breaks up monotony, acts as a marker, has mnemonic value, pleases the ear, and enlivens the mind. The ballad alternating four and three has a similar effect, and so has the Burns stanza. Its main function would seem to be to break up a long narrative into small gobbets which, being self-contained, are more easily digestible by the listener.

A similar stanza, but with only two stresses, or a four-syllable basis, in the tail-lines, is found in "Quha will Behald of Luve the Chance":[97]

> Quha will behald of luve the chance   I
> With sweit dissavyng countenance,
> In quhais fair dissimulance
>   May non assure:
> Quhilk is begun with inconstance
> And endis nocht but variance,
> Scho haldis with continuance
>   No scherviture.

---

[97] 51 ("Inconstancy of Luve").

The same rhyme is sustained throughout the three octaves of
the poem, so that the form, as M'Neill points out[98] resembles
the old French virelay.

Another stanza of unequal lines is found in "Thir Ladyis
Fair".[99] In this one he uses a two-stanza couplet followed by
a tail-line of three (not four, as M'Neill says,[1]) in a stanza of
twelve lines rhyming *a a b a a b c c d c c d*:

> Thir ladyis fair   1
> That makis repair
> And in the court are kenned,
> Thre dayis thair
> They will do mair
> Ane mater for till end,
> Than thair guid men
> Can do in ten
> For ony craft thay can,
> Sa weill thay ken
> Quhat tyme and quhen
> Thair menes thay sowld mak than.

This, of course, can be thought of as a single four-stress line
internally rhyming, followed by a three: and indeed it is
usually printed that way. I have only set it out thus to bring
out the essential structure.

The last type of stanza to be considered is that using the
bob-and-wheel device. This device was a favourite in Scots
popular poetry from such early poems as "Peblis to the Play",
"Chrystis Kirk on the Grene", *The Pystill of Susan*, *The Book
of the Howlat*, and the anonymous "Kynd Kyttok", down to its
use in our time by Robert Garioch in "Of Embro to the Ploy".
Dunbar has nothing definitely known to be his in the forms
used in any of these above poems, but in "In Vice most
Vicius"[2] he uses a similar device:

> In vice most vicius he excellis   1
> That with the vice of tressone mellis;

---

98 *The Poems of William Dunbar*, ed. Small, S.T.S., iii. app., p. cxci.
99 48 ("Of the Ladyis Solistaris at Court").
1 *The Poems of William Dunbar*, ed. Small, S.T.S., iii, app., p. cxci.
2 36 ("Epetaphe for Donald Owre").

> Thocht he remissioun
> Haif for prodissioun
> Schame and suspissioun
> Ay with him dwellis.

This makes an unusual sextain, a couplet followed by a triplet (the former in four-stress lines, the latter in two-stress), and ending in a two-stress rhyming with the couplet, the scheme being *a a b b b a.*

In "Quhy will Ye, Merchantis of Renoun",[3] he has a similar device, giving this time a most unusual septain:

> Quhy will ye, merchantis of renoun   1
> Lat Edinburch your nobill toun
> For laik of reformatioun
>   The commone proffeit tyne and fame?
>   Think ye nocht schame
>   That ony uther regioun
>   Sall with dishonour hurt your name?

This poem belongs also in the refrain stanza type, for l. 5 is a refrain, and so is the word "name" in the last line: but the dip of l. 5 is of the "bob" type, and the following two lines have the effect of a "wheel". A similar use is made of "*Ave Maria, gracia plena*", in "Hale, Sterne Superne",[4] which has a twelve-line stanza built up of an octave of alternate fours and threes, followed by the rider "*Ave Maria, gracia plena*", then three lines in the original measure, the whole rhyming *a b a b a b a b*, blank, *b a b*, thus:

> Hale, sterne superne, hale in eterne,   1
>   In Godis sicht to schyne.
> Lucerne in derne for discerne
>   Be glory and grace devyne;
> Hodiern, mordern, sempitern,
>   Angelicall regyne.
> Our tern inferne for to dispern
>   Helpe, rialest rosyne.
>   *Ave Maria, gracia plena,*
>   Haile, fresche floure femynyne.
> Yerne us, guberne, virgin matern,
>   Of reuth baith rute and ryne.

---

[3] 44 ("To the Merchantis of Edinburgh").   [4] 82 ("Ane Ballat of Our Lady").

This kind of virtuosity is common in the Scottish medieval poets, but never is it more triumphant than here—one is reminded of the scene in Hugo's novel[5] where Quasimodo indulges in an orgy of bell-ringing in the tower of Notre Dame.

No Scottish poet, and perhaps no English one either, has used a greater range and variety of forms; and he matched them with as great a range of styles and dictions. No better technician ever wielded the pen in these islands: yet Dunbar is not in the highest rank. The ultimate lesson we take away from him is that, while this mastery of verse is the hallmark of the poet, technique is not enough. A poet ultimately is judged, not by his technical powers, but by what he says with them.

I have tried to bring out the influence of two different verse traditions, one of which is syllabically regular and non-stressed, the other syllabically irregular but stressed: and if I have exaggerated their distinction, at least I hope I have corrected the tendency to ignore this fact completely.

[5] *Notre Dame de Paris.*

XV

Als Lang in Mind My Wark Sall Hald

D UNBAR'S work, then, is a product of late fifteenth-century Scotland, in the main. In particular it is a product of the court of James IV. Behind it, in it, and exerting powerful influence upon it is the whole complex weight of the Middle Ages and their traditions: the rose and *amour courtois*, allegory, dream, the schoolmen, dialectic, the universities, theology, Boethius, Reynard, the *fabliaux*, aureation and Les Grands Rhétoriqueurs, the Troubadours and French lyric forms, Latin hymns and lyrics, the Goliards, minstrelsy and music, French culture in general (almost synonymous with "European"), sermon literature, law, women and marriage as seen by secular feudal theory and ecclesiastical-theological— the immense, colourful warp and woof of Medieval Christendom, of which the small kingdom of Scotland (traditionally a Celtic kingdom) was a region, a free and independent region not of England but of Europe.

Dunbar's allegorical poems are properly so described: they are not "allegories" at all in the strict sense, but poems in which allegorical elements conflict with a sensuous impressionism, a conflict of the abstract and intellectual with the concrete and sensuous, with the latter "realist" tendency the one most congenial to him and ultimately triumphant. Allegory proper is already dead, and the new poetry of "nature" is being born. Dunbar is not interested in intellectual depth—the true quality of allegory—but in spectacle, show, pageantry, the passing sensuous moment, the flash of sunlight upon hanging boughs reflected in the stream's clear water. His eye is not on the horizon, but on momentary detail, the sensuous impression. His allegorical personages are but shadows of shades; his allegorical structure shallow and vague. Dunbar reveals but little of the architectonic power of Henrysoun, much less of

Chaucer or Dante or Guillaume or Jean: but his eye is un-
surpassable. He is in these poems, in a strict sense, "superficial". The aureation used in these poems largely coincides
with the allegorical-pageant aspect, the impressionism usually
demanding simpler terms. These poems historically reflect
the emergence of the Renaissance from the medieval mind,
with extraordinary richness, the ample stanza form of most of
them the loom of a tapestry.

Dunbar's attitude to women is not to be seen in the aureate
poems of the rose tradition, but in the earthier poems on the
subject, the more satiric and comic ones such as "Thir Ladyis
Fair that Makis Repair",[1] "In Secreit Place this Hyndir
Nycht",[2] "This Lang Lentern Makis Me Lene"[3] and the
"Tretis".[4] In many of these he uses a light tripping measure
and handles it with consummate skill, with the virtuosity of a
dancer. He neither elevates woman too high in them, nor, as a
rule, sinks her too low down (the "Tretis" is an exception): she
is kept within human bounds. Among these poems the one
supreme lyric, "Sweit Rois of Vertew",[5] stands apart and is
unique in his and other Scottish poetry, the distilled drop of
the whole rose tradition. Mischief, ribaldry, demoniac humour
are rarely missing in the earthier poems on women, with a taint
of cynicism and even disgust by no means entirely absent, and
one suspects him of a certain disappointed resentment here
and there. As always, his laughter has a hard edge to it, his
humour is a bit grim and unsmiling, ungentle—unlike Henrysoun's. His attitude, in a word, is disrespectful, but not dishonourable. He is wild and irreverent, but never contemptuous or supercilious. Women are forces of nature obedient to
biological laws, not to moral or social ones invented by
men.

The centre of his work is poems of satiric force on various
aspects of town, church, and court life, poems such as "Ane
Murlandis Man of Uplandis Mak",[6] "Quhy will Ye, Merchantis

---

[1] 48 ("Of the Ladyis Solistaris at Court").
[2] 28 (same title).
[3] 46 ("The Twa Cummeris").
[4] 47 ("The Tretis of the Tua Mariit Wemen and the Wedo").
[5] 49 ("To a Ladye").
[6] 43 ("Tydingis fra the Sessioun").

of Renoun",[7] and the like. In these poems he is in the tradition
of medieval satire and complaint, of which perhaps Langland
is the great English exemplar; but the strain is European, not
merely English.   Dunbar here is an ecclesiastical moralist
chiefly lambasting the vices and follies of "the world" from a
conventional Catholic standpoint, but the note of more
personal resentment is never far distant.   Again, his mastery
of the variety of lyric forms he uses is the most salient feature
of his work: he not only "langage had at large" but also
"verse had at large".   Usury, profiteering at the expense of
the community, abuse of law, of ecclesiastical privilege, of
commercial privilege, all come under his flail.   Here, as
always, his use of the refrain has particularly telling effect—
"Within this land wes nevir hard nor sene": "And all for
caus of covetyce".   To this material he brings a new intensity,
a new virtuosity of short forms, a new personal commitment.

The bulk of this central poetry stems from and is aimed at
the life of the court of James IV.   Dunbar has no word to say
of the alleged greatness of James as a "Renaissance prince",
though he does here and there put in a word of personal
flattery noticing more kindly traits of the King.   But the main
weight of his witness here is devastating censure at times rising
to an almost hysterical note of warning and menace, as in
"Schir, Ye Have Mony Servitouris".[8]   His motives here are
often a mixture of envy, moral outrage, hurt pride, anxiety,
insecurity, and despair and depression.   No one can doubt
the personal suffering out of which he writes, its intensity, its
chronic nature.   He is a snob, egocentric, pessimistic, morbidly
sensitive—but finally it is his sense of values which is outraged
by what he sees at court, and by his own neglect.   This shakes
the very foundations of his world, exposing him to universal
anxiety—a deep religious dread and foreboding.   His sense of
class, his expectations of station, are outraged—but there is
something more.   No Gael though he was, the Scottish court
was traditionally a Celtic one.   This means that the bard or
fili of the court was traditionally second in rank only to the
King himself, whose chief counsellor he was, and whose follies

---

[7] 44 ("To the Merchantis of Edinburgh").
[8] 17 ("Remonstrance to the King").

or personal insults he denounced in the most vituperative verse, for he was by right the keeper of the King's conscience. James, however, treated him more as the King's convenience. In terms of Celtic tradition the wonder is not that Dunbar was so outspoken against the King, but that he was so mild. A Celtic bard would have called down Hell, fire, and brimstone on the head of any man who insulted his rank, king or commoner—and king and commoner walked in fear of his ire. This closeness to the King shows itself in Dunbar's work mainly only in the intimate tone of some of the more plaintive poems: a bard of the old school did not plead—he commanded. The tradition is seen in degeneracy in the relations of James[9] and Dunbar, allowing some of the most personal and human touches in his work, as "My Heid did Yak",[10] and "Schir, Lat it Nevir in Toun be Tald".[11]

The same command of a wide range of verse is seen in these poems, and in them, for the most part, his language is at its plainest and clearest, his tone at its simplest and most personal. The main undertone running beneath them is that he wanted to get away from the court altogether and into some humble (or not so humble) clerical post in which he would be able to practice freely his two crafts of priesthood and verse (this latter never overtly stated). His mastery of mood throughout is most impressive, whether he is ranting, pleading, reasoning, threatening, flattering, charming, wheedling, or making arch selfpitying but humorous appeals. No Scottish or English poet before him had such lyric mastery, such range, such force and assurance in a short span. In these he is the champion sprinter leaving the leisurely long-distince men far behind. In Damian he sees his chief enemy, the symbol of false values which is at the base of his own suffering at court, and on him, rather than on the King, who is the real culprit, he unleashes the venom of the outraged bard. No such demoniac power of imaginative vituperation has been seen before or since in the Scottish language, nor the English either. Only

---

[9] And it is also true that James is remarkably tolerant at so late a date, the Celtic tradition so far decayed.

[10] 3 ("On His Heid-Ake").

[11] 22 ("The Petition of the Gray Horse, Auld Dumbar").

in Gaelic might it be paralleled, but I don't personally know
of anything: and of course I except the deliberate scurrility
of the "Flyting"[12] from these remarks. This is no mere flyting,
though it draws heavily on the flyting tradition. Dunbar sees
that if Damian and his values triumph, the day of the poet is
over, and he throws all his armament into the attempt to
destroy him. The age of faith makes a last stand against the
encroaching age of magic, but not the least of its weapons is
sheer eldritch laughter. The two aspects of Scottish character
symbolised by Burns and Knox are both present in these
central poems of Dunbar.

But Dunbar's life at court was not entirely one of misery
and humiliation. In the company of the young Queen and
her entourage he knew some gayer, happier moments, and this
experience begot some of his finest poems—"Madame, Ye
Heff a Dangerous Dog",[13] "He is Na Dog",[14] and "Sir Jhon
Sinclair Begowthe to Danse",[15] for instance. These are exquisite little poems, like Flemish interiors, Dunbar at once at
his most natural and most artistic—the touch of humour, the
caustic wit, the impressionistic eye, the incomparable mastery
of verse and cadence, the sure-footed dancer, the master of
the precise word. These little poems, intimate and personal,
live for us as none of his aureate pageantry does. In them
history, the social reality of the court, speak out with their
own voice, though through that of the poet: and this is the
highest function of the poet's art, far superior and more lasting
than obscure metaphysical meanderings, the great cloudy
visions of romance, billowy, vast, and empty. But there are
also among these poems the ones in coarser—indeed in coarsest
vein, such as "Madam, Your Man Said Thai wald Ryd".[16]
They remind us that in Dunbar twisted and intertwined
strands of the most delicate sensibility and of the most coarse
brutality: so they do in many other poets and people, but
rarely so uninhibitedly as in Dunbar. This is as it should be,
and it is a difficult truth that there is no comedy, and little
humour even, without cruelty close by.

---

[12] 6 ("The Flyting of Dunbar and Kennedy"). [13] 33 ("Of James Dog...").
[14] 34 ("Of the Same James . . .").
[15] 32 ("Of a Dance in the Quenis Chalmer"). [16] 31 ("To the Quene").

This cruelty becomes itself the object and aim of the tradition of flyting, a tradition which, happily, time has allowed to sink down into the past.   It is a degradation of the art of poetry, of poets, and of the audience it is produced for: yet the technical virtuosity it demands of its poetic prize-fighters is remarkable, and much of Dunbar's greater work is incidentally indebted to the technical influence of the tradition.

This is particularly true of Dunbar's greatest poem, "The Tretis of the Tua Mariit Wemen and the Wedo".[17]   This poem weaves into its texture most of the main strands of Dunbar's work: romance, *amour courtois*, satire, complaint (though muted), ribald entertainment, comedy, flyting, nature impressionism, and much else.   The introduction and *finale* are "fine writing" in the romance tradition, in the courtly style of language: the main narration is in his plainer style, and much of his dialogue and characterisation in his most ribald and coarse vein.   The whole thing is a coarse joke mocking the high-flown courtly style, as of one who shows you a beautiful mossy stone in his garden, then lifts it to expose the creepy-crawly life underneath.   The energy and force of verse and language are superb, the characterisation hard-edged though running to extravagance—Dunbar was a master of extravaganza—the impressionism sharp as the comment running underneath the narration, the alliterative verse magnificently handled, its pace controlled and resilient, like a thoroughbred stallion, virility and verve the overriding quality of the whole poem.   I have perhaps overstressed the social content of this poem, and the reader may have to make allowance for my bias: but the social content is there, whether Dunbar specifically knew its significance or not.   A poet is never more a poet than when he creates beyond his own under-standing, and we pay him small respect in rejecting what is *donnée* beyond his intention.

Dunbar was a Master of Arts, an heir of the great medieval universities traditions.   This meant not only the sober dialectic of the schoolmen, the mystical piety of a Bernard, the theological subtlety and system of Aquinas, but also the ribald, bibulous humour of the Goliards, the wandering scholars who could

[17] 47 (same title).

sing *"Mihi est propositum in taberna mori"* on the same day, perhaps, as hearing a dissertation by Abelard. This is the spirit behind such poems as "I, Maister Andro Kennedy",[18] and even "This Hyndir Nycht in Dumfermeling",[19] "This Lang Lentern Makis Me Lene",[20] "Now Lythis of ane Gentill Knycht",[21] and "We that ar Heir".[22] This strain has unfortunately had more influence on subsequent poetry than certain others which might have been more beneficial, but it has been a fertile one. The note of extravagance is rarely far off, and that of harsh reality sounds deep and solid: the laughter is a defence against something often all too serious.

This serious reality is dominant in such poems as "I that in Heill wes and Gladnes"[23] with its tolling death knell refrain *"Timor mortis conturbat me"*, the note of universal lamentation for the mortality of the flesh and the ephemeral nature of human life—the note of *"Ubi sunt qui ante nos fuerunt"*, all flesh is grass, *vanitas vanitatum*, the dread of death, the great cosmic insecurity of man's position. Life is ane straucht wey to deid, the flesche is brukle, the Fend is sle: all erdly joy returnis in pane, there is nothing better to say of life than that it is illusion. Man must remember that he is but ash and to ash will return. In days of such dark moods one has no heart for songs, ballads, plays, and age waits beckoning at the door. Yet this very morbidity prompts a more stoical attitude, and it seems best to be blyth, content with things as they are: for treasure avails nothing without gladness. So he tries to stiffen himself and us. But the shadow of the death of even such heroes as Bernard Stewart falls across the light, and the disaster of Flodden plunges all in darkness: for but thy help this kyngrik is forlorn. All these poems[24] are sombre, even gloomy, some of them, and mostly in the quiet voice of his plain style, little given to the

[18] 40 ("The Testament of Mr. Andro Kennedy").
[19] 27 ("The Wowing of the King . . . in Dumfermeling").
[20] 46 ("The Twa Cummeris").
[21] 35 ("Of Sir Thomas Norny").
[22] 30 ("The Dregy of Dunbar").
[23] 7 ("Lament for the Makaris").
[24] 71 (All Erdly Joy Returnis in Pane"); (*"Memento, Homo, quod cinis es"*); 10 ("Meditatioun in Wyntir"); 69 ("Best to be Blyth"); 73 ("No Tressour Availis without Gleidnes"); 62 ("Elegy on the Death of Lord Bernard Stewart"); 65 ("Quhen the Governour Past in France").

pyrotechnic displays of virtuosity, but making even more play with the heavy flail of the refrain. In this mood Dunbar, the master of so many moods, speaks of his own sickness and fear of death; of the world-weariness and *Angst* of the fifteenth century; and of one of the eternal verities, the mortality of mankind. It is the mood for which he is best remembered— wrongly, in my view, for his best work is elsewhere than here.

Since nothing can spare us the ultimate fate of physical death, best is that we for deid dispone, eftir our deid that lif may we, and it is in the Church in which he was born and nurtured that he finds his solace from the dread of death, and it even affords him a triumphant victory over this black dragon, in the contemplation of the triumphal sign of the croce.[25] He may not be suited for the Franciscan marriage with Lady Poverty, and he has taught the laws of Venus,[26] but he can believe that all love is lost but upon God alone, and sing the fact in a superb poem of debate.[27] Thus he can sing the praise of Christ's nativity in *"Rorate Celi Desuper"*,[28] contemplate the gruesome details of the Crucifixion,[29] recount the articles of his faith seeking mercy and the leisure to repent:[30] and after repentance comes forgiveness, and he can cry in triumph Don is a battell (but only *a* battell) on the dragon blak, for our champion Christ has confounded his force. The bells of the Ave Maria ring out their joyous peal,[31] and the lost sheep is restored to the fold.

All this mass of complex, even conflicted experience is embodied in a correspondingly complex mass of verse form and a huge command of language and dictions, drawing upon the whole corpus of medieval lyric with incomparable range and skill.

While Dunbar's work cannot, for want of data, be dated chronologically, it forms a spiritual order which would not, in any case, be materially affected by any merely historical

[25] 81 ("On the Resurrection of Christ").
[26] 4 ("How Dumbar wes Desyrd to be ane Freir").
[27] 63 ("The Merle and the Nychtingaill").
[28] 79 ("Of the Nativitie of Christ").
[29] 80 ("Of the Passioun of Christ").
[30] 83 ("The Tabill of Confessioun").
[31] 82 ("Ane Ballat of Our Lady").

evidence that may yet come to hand, unless that evidence consisted of more poems definitely from his pen, and perhaps not even then. This spiritual order is not obvious; indeed, is very difficult to discern because of the nature of the poems. They are tied to occasions, conventions, festivals, moods, social and historical happenings—all things which seem to argue an almost chaotic existence in time. But if we look long enough and close enough, the mask of time wears thin, we begin to see through it, and all its surface distractions, to a timeless order underneath: an order of evaluated experience. It is comparatively easy to trace the development of a poet today—if he has any development—because we know enough, and because he is consciously "developing". But we do not know enough about Dunbar or his work, and he himself was quite unconscious of "development": his attitude to poetry is simply that of a professional makar of verses, with his eye on the immediate job in hand, not turned inward upon himself and his experience. But his experience keeps invading the poems, forcing itself willy-nilly on the work, so that a conventional piece, which might otherwise have been a dull enough pedestrian amble in verse, is charged with power and originality, with vehemence of utterance, cries of pain we do not expect, surprisingly direct remarks. The city of God keeps revealing itself through the lineaments of the city of Cecrops. Dunbar is the least Platonic of poets, but the numinous presence of the world of intelligent order that keeps breaking through his immensely, almost chaotically various world of appearance, is a testimony to Plato's vision the more valid for being the less intended.

The world of that appearance is the Scotland of James IV, the moral, social, political, and religious state of it: and in it, more particularly the town of Edinburgh, and most particularly the royal court. That world set a material limit to Dunbar's achievement: he was at once the poet and the prisoner of the court. His work has a shut-in, claustrophobic character in some ways, not of the man's temperament merely, but of his circumstances. His cries for a benefice are like the cries of a caged bird to be set free—and freedom, for him, meant the life of a priest of the Church. The "world" of intelligent "order" behind the appearance is a religious one. But the Church, too, set limits upon him, the most important of these being the prohibition against marriage. The note of deprivation sounds again and again in Dunbar. Firstly, we suspect, he was deprived of an inheritance within his own family. This is implied in the remark that he was brought up to believe (by his nurse—he never mentions his parents) that he would become a bishop. This means that he had no other "portion" of his own.[32] He was somehow deprived even of his expected bishopric, and not only that, but of even a small, country church, till he was old. This meant that he was deprived also of his independence; if he had even a mild inclination to the priesthood, he was deprived also of the satisfaction of useful routine work. And he was deprived of the opportunity to have a happy married and family life, by his clerical vows.

But if the court was a place of captivity to him, a gilded cage in a gilded age where he languished years-long on bird-seed and water, it also conditioned his work, and provided him with his forms. The courts of the time were much given to song and dance: the lyric was the staple of courtly enter-tainment, and lyric poems were mostly meant to be sung: music and poetry were wedded together in a song, and the longer forms, such as narrative and drama, had less importance. Bruce Pattison (speaking of the English court, it is true, but the term is applicable to any European court of the time) says: "Behind literary fashion were the court's interest in songs and the demand of the musical establishment for texts to sing.[33] When a poet of the time spoke of his "songs" and his "singing", he was not indulging in a poetic fiction—he meant what he said. The court was a *milieu* of lyric creation and performance, and a repository of lyric forms, which, having been invented (or the principles of their composition having been invented) by the troubadours, circulated and accumulated through all the castles and courts of Europe. The main theme of these lyrics was "love", and "love" meant "Courtly Love", or some derivative of it.

Dunbar found all this to his hand, with much else of French origin—romance, aureation, love-allegory, and a certain dream

---

[32] See also 20 ("To the King"), l. 76.
[33] Bruce Pattison, *Music and Poetry of the English Renaissance*, London 1948, p. 34.

ennui state hard to define but easily felt, a decadent upper-class languor. And from native sources he derived his language, his innate realistic tendencies, his wild intensity, humour, wit, the alliterative measure, and ultimately, his own genius in all its complexity. The court gave him his opportunity to explore and exploit lyric forms: this he did chiefly by turning them from musical to literary purposes. He rejected Courtly Love, the love-allegory, the high-flown dreaminess, the languor, the often vapid lyricism: but he accepted the forms and turned them to his own passionately critical purposes. Yet even this, while it gave him an opportunity to excel in lyric forms, worked against his use of larger and more important (from a literary point of view) forms: for narrative and drama are the chief forms in which a literature can express itself, whether in prose or verse. Only they are roomy enough to permit that large, all-embracing vision of life in its heights, depths, and in-betweens which is the ultimate and highest aim of literature. Lyric is, by its nature, a lesser form, and at its best belongs more to music than to literature as such: its virtues are an attainable perfection and an exquisite simplicity and beauty of utterance which is a pure delight: but, by its nature, it cannot contain a whole vision of life. It is, therefore, bitty, moody, transient, the butterfly-catcher of literature. Dunbar had to force it—as many great poets born to a predominantly lyric tradition have done—to do greater things than are proper to its nature (I cannot imagine "Schir, Ye Have Mony Servi-touris",[34] "Doverrit with Dreme",[35] or "The Flyting of Dunbar and Kennedy",[36] sung: yet they are all in what were originally "lyric" forms).

The wealth of lyric forms therefore were both a source of realisation of his genius and a limitation of it: Chaucer and Henrysoun, like Jean de Meun and Dante, before them, were better served by the narrative form in which they excelled, and Lyndsay, after Dunbar, was to find his freedom in it and in drama. Dunbar may have, most probably had, written works of larger nature that have not come down to us: but it is sufficient evidence of the truth of my contention that his greatest

---

[34] 17 ("Remonstrance to the King").
[35] 77 ("A General Satyre").   [36] 6 (same title).

work is the "Tretis", in which he escapes not only from lyric trammels, but even from metre and rhyme.

The Church gave him his education, his vision of life, and some of the forms in which he worked, derived from Latin, and Latin services: it was the Solveig from whose embracing love he set out on his pilgrimage, and to whose arms he returned in the end, having, like Gynt, tasted Hell.

Mention of Solveig brings one to the central fact of Dunbar's poetry: the preoccupation with woman. I say "woman" rather than "women", for although women are vitally present in his work, it is an image of woman (the reality behind the appearance) which he mostly seems to seek in them—as if they were the riddle of life, the vision of life itself, as if to be able to understand woman, to see her unity-in-variety, would be to see life itself "steadily and whole". The first image of woman—I speak spiritually, not temporally—he explores, is that of the *dame* of *amour courtois*, the dream-girl on her pedestal granting or withholding her favours from the grovelling slave, her *ami*, as she may choose, in a dream-world of perpetual May-morning, languishing in the garden of a sunny castle. This he rejects for the hollow sham it had become. Then he explores women as they really are, or, rather, more debased than they really are, with an element of disgust, arguing the lingering presence of the old ideal of the *dame* in the background: such women as in "This Lang Lentern Makis Me Lene",[37] "Thir Ladyis Fair",[38] and "Now of Wemen",[39] and such real women as the Queen and Musgrave: and finally, he sums up this vision of woman—the "anti-lady", we might call her—in the Wedo of the "Tretis".

The theme of fertility is running through all this, an undercurrent of Dunbar's work which surfaces from time to time: and in the Wedo he sees his image of the old goddess of the fertility cult. The *dame* of *amour courtois* was the "goddess" who presided over one heretical cult; in the Wedo he sees her opposite, the fertility goddess of the old pagan cult itself. This is his vision of Hell, and he moves up from it towards

[37] 46 ("The Twa Cummeris").
[38] 48 ("Of the Ladyis Solistaris at Court").
[39] 45 ("In Prais of Wemen").

Z

the light, which, for him, ends up with his vision of the Madonna. The image of the Catholic mother is his ultimate image of woman at once fertile and chaste—a mother of sons, wife of a humble man Joseph, and the vessel of divine life. In her he finds rest enough, and he shouts her praise with the exulta- tion of a condemned man who has won a reprieve. The fertility theme runs through the comedies—"I, Maister Andro Kennedy"[40] particularly—but, while it obviously is a real value, like the alcohol with which it is traditionally associated, the Bacchic wine, enough of it is salutary, too much is Hell.[41]

His vision of woman, whether of the *dame*, or of the Wedo, or of the Madonna, is always a religious one: and there is a profound sense in which these three dominant facets of woman are one. He sees all life in the vision of woman, and his religion is the religion of life. His religion, indeed, is his life, and his life is his religion: though in order to get to where he was (for he did not find religion after a long quest, as modern agnostics may do—it was there from the start), he had to go by the way he was not.

At court, he came nearest to peace and content—while still longing for his "kirk scant coverit with hadder"—in the presence and influence of the Queen. It is significant that she seems to have appreciated Dunbar, as his poems abundantly witness (most particularly "Schir, for Your Grace",[42] whereas the King preferred the scientific quack, Damian. Much of Dunbar's complaint and satire of his treatment at court is not merely personal to Dunbar: he is insulted in his poet-hood as well as his manhood by the gross distortion of values he finds there, and of which his genius was the victim. At the heart of his satire especially is the firm code of values which is inherent in all his poems and finds its fullest statement in "To The, O Mercifull Salviour",[43] Dunbar is to us the greatest man of his time and place because he deserved to be—this is itself the birthright of which he felt so deprived at court.

Illusion and reality play hide-and-seek in and out of his

---

[40] 40 ("The Testament of Mr. Andro Kennedy").
[41] The Tua Mariit Wemen and the Wedo are in revolt against the frustration of an evil marriage-system.
[42] 18 ("To the King that He was Johne Thomosunis (*sic*) Man").
[43] 83 ("The Tabill of Confessioun").

work, as they do in life: but for him, ultimately, and indeed all the time, illusion was the court and its life, so-called, and reality was the Church. His was not a monastic temperament, but he probably had a quite genuine inclination to the priesthood—as distinct from his vocation of poetry. Even his materialism was of the clerical sort: and by the end of his life he clearly was spiritually-centred. Materialism, after all, is only a problem when material want gets in the way of spiritual enrichment: when the mouth has been filled, the hands find work enough to be busy with: and work is prayer.

In all this, Dunbar was very much a man of his time: he transcends it, but only by taking as much of it into himself as his personal and formal limits allow and transforming it by the power of his own genius and spirit. In poetry, he inherited an abstract tradition of allegory and dream, already in retreat before a rising realism: and he came down heavily on the side of the concrete. But not so much that he entirely threw out the virtues of the older mode: he often achieves a rich synthesis of the two—as in "In to thir Dirk and Drublie Dayis"[44] and "This Hinder Nycht, Halff Sleiping as I Lay".[45]   His poetic achievement is mainly that he took the lyric forms he found at court and turned them from conventional songs into the thunderous trumpets of reform: that he sharpened the eye of Scottish poetry for the concrete, subtle detail in nature— he brought it a finer eye. He extended the whole range of Scottish verse by his still unrivalled mastery of lyric forms; he restored the native beat of the language in the "Tretis", but also combined it with metric practice in such poems as "Don is a Battell"—his supreme achievement in lyric form. In doing this, he subtilised and "firmed" the rhythm of Scottish verse, making it capable of a more sophisticated, complex, rhythmically varied song-speech than the great Henrysoun had left it. He brought Scottish poetry not only a finer eye, but a finer ear.

While his learning does not inform his work as much or as well as that of Henrysoun informs his, yet his practical intelligence as a makar—as distinct from ideas and learning, "intellectuality" in the academic sense—is unsurpassed in the whole range of Scottish poetry.

[44] 10 ("Meditatioun in Wyntir").   [45] 60 ("The Dream").

Linguistically, he extended the range of vocabulary in verse (having, in Lyndsay's famous phrase, "langage had at large"), not only in the direction of "aureation"[46]—a "sport"— nor simply in the opposite (though healthier) "sport" of scurrility, but in the plain measure of ordinary speech, being surpassed in this only by his great junior, Douglas. He brought not only a fine practical intellect to the making of poetry, but an even finer sensibility—he is the first "sensitive", though a tough one, in Scottish poetry.

He added to the social power of verse-application by intensifying the satiric element already present, but gentled by his great humour, in Henrysoun, making Lyndsay's work easier. He brought into his satire a greater social passion than any predecessor. This was at once a reforming trait and historically somewhat reactionary: he was reforming vices in legal, town and court life, and in marriage, from the point of view of his Catholic heritage, not from a "progressive" view of history: his denunciation of the capitalist sins would, for instance, seem "reactionary" to a Marxist—capitalism was the socially flowing tide. Dunbar is in much the same position in this regard as the greatest Catholic reformer of all—William Langland. Late medieval literature is full of such work: but in Dunbar it takes on a new intensity, a fresh imagery drawn from the social reality round about him, and an increased urgency mixed with a note almost of despair: the time for him is late.

His satire of the court denounces James's warped sense of values with astonishing candour—even more remarkable than Lyndsay's strictures on the fifth James in the next generation. Buchanan and Boece both witness Dunbar's truth againt James, the former calling him *ab literis incultus*, semi-illiterate, and the latter denouncing his "laik of letteris and virtew" and promotion of the worst types of hangers-on at court.[47] The bulk of Dunbar's work was satirical precisely because of the state of the court and country in which he lived.

He also added to poetry a new personal note in such poems

---

[46] I do not suggest that it is wholly bad in Dunbar—63 ("The Merle and the Nychtingaill") and 82 ("Ane Ballat of Our Lady") could not have been without aureation: but it was a dead-end.

[47] Mackay Mackenzie, intro., p. xvi.

as "My Heid Did Yak",[48] "Sir Jhon Sinclair Begowthe to
Dance",[49] "Madame, Ye Heff a Dangerous Dog",[50] "He is
Na Dog",[51] "Schir, Lat it Nevir in Toun be Tald",[52] and many
others. This was not entirely original: Henrysoun writes in
a similar vein in the opening stanzas of the *Testament of Cresseid*:
but as usual, Dunbar takes the line a stage further.

The bulk of his work reminds us yet again that, in an age
so benighted as to have lost sight of true values, to prefer and
promote the worst of men and activities and neglect poetry
and the arts, the main duty of a poet is simply to bear witness.
In this sense Dunbar was a poetic martyr, and like all martyrs,
he triumphs over his executioners: they are nameless, for the
most part, while he is part of mankind's universal heritage.

He was no democrat: that line runs past him from Henrysoun through Lyndsay to Fergusson and Burns: he was a snob
and a pseudo-aristocrat (socially, that is: humanly he was a
natural one). Yet Dunbar spoke out strongly about the rights
and wrongs of the exploited workers of his time, but it is the
peasantry he champions in this regard—the *bourgeois* master-
craftsmen and traders meet with no sympathy from him.

Above all, Dunbar was a makar not only in the sense of
being, but in the linguistic sense of making a valid and viable
literary dialect out of the varying speech of his people: aureation
was a mistaken attempt, at this level, in so far as it was not
simply a class fashion, another instance of the pseudo-aristocrat
"barbarian" (to use Arnold's phrase), in his love of ostentatious
display. He and his fellow-makars bequeathed to Scotland a
superb and homogeneous linguistic instrument, the destruction
of which was one of the worst blights of the Reformation.

Dunbar temperamentally fluctuated between a wild exultation and a deep depression. He was an extravert, as we
say now, objective mostly, in his work and in his life, gay,
sociable, a good talker, companionable, with a demoniac force
in his nature compelling him now to the heights and now to
the depths: he was, in fact, of that temperament which

[48] 3 ("On His Heid-Ake").
[49] 32 ("Of a Dance in the Quenis Chalmer").
[50] 33 ("Of James Dog . . .").
[51] 34 ("Of the Same James").
[52] 22 ("The Petition of the Gray Horse, Auld Dumbar").

psychology today would call "cyclothymic" or "manic-depressive": apparently very common in poets, for in Scots alone both Fergusson and Burns were of similar temperament, the former tragically so. It is typical of such poets that while they have a wonderful wealth of imagery and sensation, they are apt to be rather poor in leading-ideas, in the higher intellectual structures of poets of the opposite type—Dante, at best, Shelley, at a lower level. These two are introverts, "schizoid" or "psychasthenic", in the present jargon: the greatest contemporary example being the prose-poet James Joyce.

Dunbar is a hard man to get on with. I confess that I rather disliked him when I began this work: that I have had great difficulties of spiritual antipathy to overcome in my attempt to analyse his work and his mind. Let him now have the last, modest word:

> And thocht that I amang the laif　　　　　25
> Unworthy be ane place to haif,
> Or in their nummer to be tald,
> Als lang in mind my wark sall hald,
> Als haill in everie circumstance,
> In forme, in mater, and substance,
> Bot wering or consumptioun,
> Roust, canker, or corruptioun,
> As ony of thair werkis all—
> Suppois that my rewarde be small.[53]

---

[53] 17 ("Remonstrance to the King").

APPENDICES

APPENDICES

A NOTE ON MIDDLE SCOTS

The language used by Dunbar in his poems is now called "Middle Scots", or "Scots of the middle period", to distinguish it from "Early Scots" and "Modern Scots". The word "Scots" originally meant Gaelic, and was synonymous with "Erse", or "Irish". This was Dunbar's view, and he calls his own speech "Inglis", to distinguish it from "Scots", meaning Gaelic. Gavin Douglas was the first Makar to use the term "Scottis" for his own speech, to distinguish it from "Sudron", or English,[1] although Pedro de Ayala had mentioned the "Scottish language" in a letter dated July 1498. The problem was, of course, that when the kingdoms of the Picts and the Scots (Gaelic-speaking Celts from Ireland) were united under Kenneth MacAlpin, the Scots king, in 844, the term "Scots" was retained to describe the united kingdom, and gradually applied to the whole of what is now Scotland. Originally a Celtic kingdom, Scotland passed from Gaelic domination to that of the Anglic peoples of the south-eastern counties. This process was hastened by the influence of Margaret, the English princess who married Malcolm Canmore, King of Scotland, in 1607, when she fled from the Norman Conquest. Her own affinities were with the Lothian Angles, and at court she encouraged them and discouraged the Gaels, setting a precedent followed up by her sons in their own subsequent reigns. The Scottish nation which entered its period of trial in 1286 with the death of Alexander III was a loose union of Gaels (Scots proper), Welsh-speaking Britons, Normans, Galwegians, Flemings, Angles, and Norsemen. It took the Wars of Independence to hammer this assortment into some semblance of a homogeneous kingdom.

By the late fourteenth century, when John Barbour, who was patronised by the Crown, compiled his *Brus*, the Lothian tongue had become the language for popular literature, and even for some court records and other official and legal documents, as an alternative to Latin. This speech was, essentially, the Old Northumbrian spoken, with dialectal variations, on the East coast from the Humber to Aberdeen (of which Barbour was archdeacon). It was a very different tongue from that spoken in the great plain of England.

[1] *Eneados*, Prol. i, ll. 109-18.

The truth would seem to be that the speech of the south was dominated by the Saxon influence, and that of the north by the Anglian. Bede tells us:

> From the Saxons, that is from the land called Old Saxon, came the East Saxons, the South Saxons, and the West Saxons. And from Angeln came the East Angles, the Middle Angles, the Mercians, and *the whole race of the Northumbrians*.[2]

The Angles nearest to the Saxon kingdoms, especially during the great Saxon period, would be most influenced by the Saxon speech: the north would be comparatively uninfluenced. Dunbar's use of the word "Inglis", (or "Ynglis"), therefore, is not to be regarded merely as a form of the modern word "English". It meant something more like "Anglian", the speech of the Angles, the Northumbrains. In so far as, in Plantagenet times, Northumbria was considered to be part of the English kingdom, this gave rise to some confusion of loyalties for those "Northumbrians" who lived north of the Tweed—Dunbar's forebear Corspatrick among them. This comes out in the "Flyting", particularly in Kennedy's attack on Dunbar's descent from the traitor Corspatrick. To this day the term "English" is too overlarded with political significance to be of any value as a linguistic term, as is clear when we hear of "American English", "Australian English", and the like. By "Inglis" Dunbar certainly did not mean "English English"—he meant "Scottish English", or as Douglas, acknowledging the reality, called it, "Scottis".

By Barbour's time the northern tongue had emerged from the great grammatical change from an inflected to a non-inflected language, while the southern still retained, to a great extent, the declension of nouns, pronouns, and adjectives.[3] How this came about is somewhat obscure. Danish or Norse influence has been indicated, but the objection has been raised that the Anglian tongue itself had more Scandian features in it than the Germanic Saxon.[4] The influence of Gaelic, and perhaps of Cymric, may also have been a factor: but where so much remains in doubt and the linguistic specialists themselves seem to differ, the critic can only record the fact of this emergence, without delving into causes.

This emergent speech quickly developed characteristics which differentiated it even from the Old Northumbrian from which it

---

[2] *Historia ecclesiastica gentis anglorum*, Everyman edn., I, xv: my italics.
[3] J. A. H. Murray, *Dialect of the Southern Counties of Scotland*, 1873, p. 24.
[4] *Ibid.*

sprang, and with which it was, in its earliest phases, almost identical, so that it came to be properly called "Scots". In its early period, from about the late thirteenth century until about the middle of the fifteenth, it differed little from Northumbrian. The second period, for lack of better evidence, one thinks of as dating from about the time of James I's *Kingis Quair* until at least the seventeenth century. This "middle" period is the great age of Scots poetry, including the work of James I, Holland, Henrysoun, Dunbar, Hary, Douglas, Lyndsay, Scott, Montgomerie, Boyd, and many other poets, and the prose of Bellenden, Pitscottie, Boece, the anonymous author of *The Complaynt of Scotland*, Murdoch Nisbet's version of the New Testament, and much else. This period saw the establishment of a national literature (pioneered by Barbour in the "early" period, with Wyntoun following up) which ended for all time the identification of Scots with other "regional" dialects stemming from Anglo-Saxon. This is a historical fact which prevents Scots ever again being seen as a mere dialect, like the speech of Yorkshire, say, or Dorset. That which once has been for ever is. No amount of wishful political thinking by Unionists and Anglicisers can ever alter that basic reality, and treason against the Scottish tradition in European literature is not merely political and cultural treason against Scotland, but intellectual and spiritual treason against life.

The work of the middle period—we are not here concerned with modern Scots, dating from about the Ramsay publications of 1724 to the present day—was deeply rooted in European tradition, particularly in poetry, its major constituent. It is not true to say that whereas the early period of Barbour was "nationalist" in that it treated of the "Scottish matter", the middle period was "internationalist" (too often these days a euphemism, among the political enemies of Scotland, for "English"). Apart from the fact that in this period Blin Hary carried on the Barbour tradition in his epic-romance *Wallas*, the Middle Scots writers were all of them nationalist in a much deeper sense: they were nationalists in language. The medieval dominance of Latin, the *lingua franca*, had been breaking up all over Europe for some centuries, and the vernaculars were coming into their own as national languages capable of supporting a literature in their own right. Dante was the great Italian nationalist in this sense, making an ultimately united Italy almost inevitable by his decision to use the vernacular for his *Commedia*. The *Chanson de Roland* had already established French, and the great French tradition of poetry was in its high and incomparable flower —indeed, was rather faded—by this period. Chaucer had taken up the movement in England and done for the English language what Dante had already done for Italian: he too was a great nationalist, but again in language, not in matter. It was chiefly his influence—though that of Dante cannot be discounted—which inspired the Middle Scots poets to do for their own language and nation what Chaucer had done for his.

Chaucer's influence on Scottish poetry has been greatly and stupidly overrated: but his influence on Scottish nationalism has been as greatly and stupidly underrated. The Scots followed, not so much his work, as his example as a national poet making the great poetry of France and Italy part of the heritage of English. James I, Henrysoun, Dunbar, and Douglas did as much for Scotland —the latter making Scots the vehicle of the best translation of Virgil's *Aeneid* yet done in either Scots or English.

It was a great work, James[5] bringing over the *amour courtois* poetry of the "Rose" school, Henrysoun developing the narrative tradition of classical legend, Dunbar assimilating as many as possible of the vast wealth of lyric forms from French and Provençal, Douglas doing the foundation epic of Latin Europe. This is not to imply any deliberate policy on their part—it was part deliberate, part merely responding half-consciously to the needs of the nation and the time. The betrayal of their work began with the adoption of an English Bible by the Reformers and the defection of the King and his court to London in 1603; was advanced by the religious lunacies of destruction in the seventeenth century; and culminated in the sell-out of the nation to English pressure by the Scottish Parliament in 1707. Since then Scottish literature and language has led the life of guerilla warfare, outlawed, in occupied territory run by agents of the enemy.

The differences to be discerned between Early and Middle Scots are partly due to Celtic influences on both spoken and written forms; partly due to French influence under the impact of the Auld Alliance[6]: partly due to the influence of the *lingua franca*, Latin; and partly due to less obvious causes. Whatever the cause, the vowels *a*, *e*, *i*, *o*, *u*, and *ou* (*oo*) of the early period became (in written forms, of course) *ai*, *ay*, *ei*, *ey*, *yi*, *oi* *oy*; and *ui oui*, in the middle.[7] The use of silent *l* as a lengthening or diphthongising device crept in, as in *waltir* (wawtir), *chalmir* (chawmir), and *goldyn* (gowdin). There seems to be no marked grammatical

---

[5] The one truly "Chaucerian" poet—he was educated in England.

[6] Francisque-Michel, *A Critical Inquiry into the Scottish Language*, Edinburgh 1882, is worth study in this subject.

[7] Murray, *Dialects of the Southern Counties of Scotland*, p. 52.

influence of Gaelic in this period, and only a few vocabulary borrowings, such as *coronach, bard, Beltain, bannock, capyl,* and *car* (left, as in *car-handit*), although many more Gaelic words have been naturalised in the modern period.

The French influence may be said to have begun as early as David I's reign. His feudalising mind led him to encourage Norman influence; but it is during the two-and-a-half centuries from Bannockburn to the Reformation that the French influence was most keenly felt. Scotsmen studied and taught in Paris and other French (as in other European) centres; Scottish soldiers fought beside the French in French armies; and the Scottish court was rarely without French visitors. French universities influenced the newer Scottish ones; the house of Stewart was itself descended from the Norman family of Robert Bruce; and the feudal system itself was largely a Norman-French development. The Scottish legal system was founded on Roman and French (itself founded on Roman), and even the form of Protestantism adopted by the Scottish Reformers—anti-French Anglicisers though they were—was that of the Frenchman, Jean Calvin. So great was the commerce between the two countries that the wonder is, not that the French influence on the language and poetry was large, but that it was so small—due perhaps to the fact that the French influence was almost solely ruling-class in Scotland itself. Francophile accounts of the language tend—like that of Francisque-Michel mentioned above—to amplify the actual particular influence of the Auld Alliance by including in their lists of borrowings words which were general to Scottish and English dialects as a result of the Norman conquest: but this misleads not so much in the general as in the particular attribution of influence.[8]

The actual borrowings were extensive enough, however, and the influence affected not only diction but construction also. The use of *ane* instead of the older *a* is attributable, for example, to the French *un*. This characteristic middle Scots usage, with its "quaint" charm, has been thought to be of ancient date, older than the "English" use of *a*, with *an* before a vowel. In fact, the Acts of the Scottish Parliament from James I to James V show that instances of *ane* before a consonant were very rare before 1475, and only became regular after about 1500. The merest glance at literature of the early period will bear this out. It is doubtful whether *ane* was ever used in speech at all, as the indefinite article before a

---

[8] Here and elsewhere in this chapter I am indebted to work as yet unpublished by A. J. Aitken, Editor of the *Dictionary of the Older Scottish Tongue.*

consonant, from Barbour up to date.[9]　It was always, like aureation, a literary affectation without foundation in spoken language.[10] Murray points out an exceptional use of *ane* before *n* in Barbour ("ane narow plas", for instance), and links it with the later confusion of the article with the initial *n* of the noun deriving from the Old English.[11]　For example, *ane naeddre* is heard as *ae nedder* or the like, or *ane adder*—an adder.　A similar confusion is seen in the case of *that other* becoming *the tother*: *that ane* becoming *the tane*. But the rule of *a* before a consonant holds throughout the early period.

Another phenomenon attributable to French influence is the plural form given to certain pronouns and adjectives such as *quhilkis, saidis, uthiris, principallis*, and the like.　These correspond to the French *lesquels, lesdits, les autres*, and *principaux*.　Murray considers that they were perhaps first introduced in legal terminology, but became usual in literature of the middle period.[12]　There is no evidence that they ever were or became spoken forms.

In vocabulary, the French borrowings are too numerous to list exhaustively, but some typical ones are: *gloir, memoir, abailyement, arrace, ane* (ass), *compacience, covatyce, cure, enseinzie, fenester, garnisoun, gentrice, lawte, mallewgrus, perfurnis, pyssance, purpour, remeid, rewis, rounge, roy, syrurgeane, viage*.　Many of these words became redundant, or changed their form, but many passed into common use: *port, gean, corbie, ashet, gigot, houlet, dour, douce, causey, fash, baillie*, and *doole*, for example.　The number of French words found only in Scots and not in English is, however, very small.　Mr A. J. Aitken considers that the number is probably no greater than that of Gaelic ones.　Even these cannot with any certainty be attributed to the Auld Alliance, for it is possible that they, too, are from the earlier Norman period: but this is unlikely, since they would almost certainly show in English too.

The most striking linguistic influence on the Scots of the middle period is the Latin one.　This shows most clearly in the "aureation" of the language in certain poems.　Dunbar is the chief exemplar in this regard, but even he is much less addicted to it than those people who are taken in by it would have us believe: he used it very sparingly, for artificial courtly occasions mostly, but used it consummately well.　The fashion seems to have begun with the French *Grands Rhétoriqueurs*, was taken up in English by Lydgate, and

---

[9] Murray, *Dialects of the Southern Counties* of Scotland, p. 57.
[10] Grant and Main Dixon, *A Manual of Modern Scots*, Cambridge 1920, p. 75.
[11] Murray, *Dialects of the Southern Counties of Scotland*, p. 58.　　[12] *Ibid*.

to a lesser extent by Chaucer (too healthy a genius to spend much time on such a fashion), and James I in his somewhat Anglicised Scots. This fashion was not due directly to the *lingua franca*, whose influence was no less powerful in the early period of Barbour and Wyntoun: it was a passing French vogue which spread outward to other countries. The words themselves, the "aureate termis celicall", were certainly Latinate—but a decayed Latin. Among them are: *celicall, amene, decore, preclair, illustir, frustir, sempitern, matern, mellifluate, macul, habitakle, veir, lucerne, imperatrice, genitrice, vilipentioun, dispone, promove*, and many others familiar to readers of Dunbar. Some of them are seductive enough little witches for a susceptible poet to be taken in by them; but it is no matter for regret that so few of them ever passed into common speech. This has sometimes been attributed to the English usurpation of the place of literary Scots: but few of Lydgate's or Chaucer's aureate terms passed into common English speech either, therefore there must be more fundamental reasons for their failure to take root. Murray says well that the modern Scotsman finds Barbour, though more distant in time, closer to his own speech than the aureate style of Dunbar.[13] He might have added that he finds also the matter of Barbour closer to his experience of life than Dunbar in his courtly mood. Barbour, not Dunbar, is the true fountainhead of the Scottish tongue; and, linguistically speaking, Henrysoun and Douglas are purer streams of it than Dunbar: Douglas, indeed, is the highest point of the development of literary Scots, which rises to him and declines from him. But Barbour's *Brus* is the fountainhead of Scottish literature.

These were the chief, but by no means the only sources of difference between Scots of the early and Scots of the middle period. The basic Northumbrian of the early period already shows the influence here and there of southern forms, but these may be partly scribal, and certainly literary. The large Scandinavian influence on the early speech did not necessarily finish at any given date. The same may be said of the Flemish and Dutch influence, with even greater force. This is particularly true of technical terms during the great technical advances made in the Renaissance period, the fifteenth and sixteenth centuries especially. Much of the shipping terminology of this period is of Dutch or Flemish origin, due to the close trading connections between Scotland and the Netherlands. Among terms originally drawn form this trading influence are: *callant, groff, coft,* and *golf*.

---

[13] Murray, *Dialects of the Southern Counties of Scotland*, p. 61.

But there is yet another source of distinctive middle-period usage which gets less attention, perhaps because of its very nature. This is vocabulary of no known etymology at all—much of it probably coinage. This is more common in the popular literature of the period, and that part of the Makars' work closest to the popular, such as flytings and comic poems. Here we see the real creative language at work, creating out of itself without any external influence of a linguistic nature. Such words are: *gully, glowr, goif, pawk, gukkit, glaikit, cuif, daw, limmer, smaik, smy, bonny, canny,* and *scunner.*[14] There are many others, and they add greatly to a language already, as we have seen, immensely rich and various.

It is this richness and variety of language which is the most striking feature of Dunbar's poetry, and which was in David Lyndsay's mind when he mentions Dunbar as having "langage had at large". Dunbar was a master of Scots idiom and vocabulary at a time when they were at their fullest, and to the energy of his own passionate mind was added the verbal energy of a great literary language in the prime of youth. Dunbar's use of it, like his poetry, falls easily into three main categories which it is customary to call the "high", "middle", and "low" styles. I prefer to speak of "manner" rather than "style", which means too much to mean anything in particular: and we need adjectives a bit more accurate than "high", "middle", and "low". The so-called "high" manner is that used in the allegorical and romantic type of poems, and, being aimed chiefly at and produced for a court audience, is best described as the "courtly" manner. The poems of the so-called "middle" manner are mostly meditative, conversational, and moralistic poems, plain and unpretentious: they are best described as poems of the "plain" manner. Those in the so-called "low" manner are chiefly comic, satiric, and flyting poems aiming at or appealing to an audience which, while including the court, was more universal and popular. They are best described as poems in the "popular" manner.

It is significant that the Latin influence in the form of aureation is to be found chiefly in the poems in the courtly manner.[15] Here Dunbar is at the furthest possible remove from reality, his mind moving in a rarefied atmosphere of dream and allegory, immaterial, disembodied, and unreal. Yet even here his essential realism shows in his nature-description. The poems in the plain manner are

[14] Here again I am indebted to Mr A. J. Aitken's researches.

[15] The Latin influence on the religious poems is more appropriate and certainly more telling.

closest to the main current of literary Scots common to both verse and prose, from Barbour until, in verse at least, the present day. But it is in the poems in the popular manner that one finds the most interesting and significant linguistic features, for in them we find the greatest number of those words of "obscure origin", words that seem, like Topsy, to have just growed, and which are evidence of the vital creative power of the language. These earthy poems are not to be miscalled "realist"—it is in the plain manner that we find most reality—for they are full of extravagance and wild, eldritch fantasy, usually of a Rabelaisian kind. But they are full of that eternal peasant humour—earthy, crude, coarse—which vibrates with a vitality that is the eternal fountain from which human life rises and to which it returns for renewal.

The best-known poem in the courtly manner is "The Goldyn Targe". The best-known in the plain manner is "I that in Heill wes". And the poem which ought to be best-known in the popular manner,[16] though it weaves in strands of the other two manners also, is "The Tretis of the Tua Mariit Wemen and the Wedo". That this great poem has had so little recognition is a monument to the bad taste of past generations of poetry readers. The bulk of Dunbar's poems—and most of the best—are written in either the plain or the popular style. It is in them that we find the true poetry of speech, as distinct from stylised rhetoric.

But, in considering Dunbar we have to bear in mind that he was in fact a poet chiefly of court life—it is his main limitation, his lack of a national, international or universal *matter*, such as Barbour had, or of eternal human life such as Henrysoun, Lyndsay, and Burns had—and in this limitation he is the court's prisoner, not its bard. This of course is only relatively so: the religious poems and many of the satires do have a universal matter. But he lacks the all-in vision of life which is so manifest in Henrysoun. He is personal rather than impersonal, particular rather than universal, and ruling-class rather than national. He writes more as a James IV Scottish courtier than as a citizen of Europe.

[16] Admittedly it is stretching the term somewhat to call such a poem "popular": but it is, apart from the introduction and finale, nearer that than courtly or plain.

2 A

BIBLIOGRAPHICAL REVIEW

A. Textual Sources

MAITLAND FOLIO MS. Pepysian Library, Magdalene College, Cambridge. Collected by and/or for Sir Richard Maitland of Lethington, c. 1570-86. This contains 61 poems assigned to Dunbar, five of which are found only here, and two of which are complete only here. Although it is less comprehensive as a source of Scots medieval poetry than the Bannatyne, it has more of Dunbar's poems. Printed in *The Maitland Folio Manuscript*, ed. W. A. Craigie S.T.S., 2 vols., Edinburgh 1919-27.

REIDPETH MS. Cambridge University Library. Written between 1622 and 1623 by and/or for John Reidpeth. It contains 47 poems by Dunbar, eight of them not found elsewhere. This MS. seems to have been copied chiefly from the Maitland.

BANNATYNE MS. National Library of Scotland. Written by and/or for George Bannatyne "in tyme of pest", c. 1568. This is the most important source of Scottish medieval poetry, containing some 419 poems, divided into five parts according to theme. It has 60 poems by Dunbar, eight not found elsewhere, and two complete only here. The debt of Scottish poetry to Bannatyne has never been adequately acknowledged. Printed in *The Bannatyne Manuscript*, ed. W. Tod Ritchie, S.T.S., 4 vols., Edinburgh 1928.

ASLOAN MS. Auchinleck, Ayrshire; photostat copy, National Library of Scotland. Written by John Asloan c. 1515. It is badly damaged, probably half the poems missing. There are three poems by Dunbar, part of another, and one found only here. Printed in *The Asloan Manuscript*, ed. W. A. Craigie, S.T.S., 3 vols., Edinburgh 1922-3.

MAKULLOCH MS. Edinburgh University Library. Contains versions of Dunbar poems, but is of only minor importance for variant readings. Printed in pieces from *The Makulloch and the Gray Manuscripts* together with the Chapman and Myllar Prints, ed. G. Stevenson, S.T.S., Edinburgh 1918.

CHEPMAN AND MYLLAR PRINTS. Edinburgh 1508. This first work of printing in Scotland contains six poems by Dunbar and one attributed to him—"Kynd Kittok". Being the earliest known text, published in the author's lifetime, it has some claim to being authoritative, despite the lack of standardised orthography at the time. Dunbar is most likely to have overseen its publication. It also has importance for dating these poems, which must have been written before 1508. The poems are "The Goldyn Targe", "The Flyting", "The Tretis", "Lament quhen He wes Seik", "Andro Kennedy", and the "Ballade of Bernard Stewart". The only surviving copy is in the National Library of Scotland, Edinburgh. A photo-facsimile, ed. W. R. Beattie, was published in 1950.

ARUNDEL HOWARD MS., folio 161. British Museum. This contains 3 poems by Dunbar, one found only here.

ABERDEEN MINUTE BOOK OF SASINES, Vols. II, III, in MS. This contains copies of "The Twa Cummeris", by Dunbar, and "Gladethe Thoue, Queyne", which is anonymous, but attributed with great probability to Dunbar.

ROYAL MSS. No. 58, folio 15b. Appendix. British Museum.

B. Printed Editions

SELECT POEMS OF WILL. DUNBAR, Part First. Ed. R. Morison, Perth 1788. Another reprint from the Bannatyne MS.

CHRONICLE OF SCOTTISH POETRY from the thirteenth century to the Union of the Crowns. Ed. J. Sibbald, 4 vols., Edinburgh 1802. The first three volumes, containing 45 poems of Dunbar's, make the most comprehensive anthology of Scots poems of the period up to date, 1964. The fourth volume is a glossary which is in itself a work of Scots lexicography, with a long introduction discussing the terms Picti, Caledonii, and Scoti, which is still a valuable essay on the history of the Scots language. It is altogether a work of first rank and importance. He is particularly good on metric.

POEMS OF WILLIAM DUNBAR. Ed. D. Laing, 2 vols., Edinburgh 1834. This is the first collection of Dunbar's poems, and is therefore a pioneer work. A further edition in 1865 added some poems by minor makars as a supplement. It includes a memoir of the life, which begets some of the unjustifiable assumptions which still linger, although Baxter has shown how ill-grounded many of them are—e.g., that Dunbar wrote "London, Thou art of Tounes A per Se". He outlines poetry previous to Dunbar, considers Dunbar scholarship from Ramsay to Scott, and gives an outline of poetry up to Burns. He then gives us a critique of the poems with a biographical preamble. It is critically inadequate and outmoded, but he makes the valuable point that much of Dunbar, and perhaps his maturest work, may not have come down to us. His Appendix 1 discusses certain Dunbars, and Appendix 2 has a table of references to Dunbar in Public Records of Scotland. The worst that can be said against it is that it has put subsequent editors so much in its debt that errors by Laing have gone on being repeated ever since: which is no fault of Laing's. Most of the titles now given the poems, e.g., are Laing's and nowhere to be found in the sources, and many of the anonymous poems attributed without foundation to Dunbar owe their forged birth certificates to Laing and his uncritical followers. Not *all* Elizabethan plays were by Shakespeare.

TWO MARRIED WOMEN AND THE WIDOW, translated into English verse. Anon., Edinburgh 1840. Dunbar may have thought he wrote in Inglis, but here is the proof that he wrote in Scots. This is a translation into English heroic couplets, and the author modestly or timidly withholds his name. He need not have been so diffident, for the poem is no mean feat, though it may be a somewhat unnecessary one. A comparison with the original shows clearly the complete incompatibility of the Scots and English traditions—the one racy, earthy, realistic to the point of sub-realistic, the other stiff, rarefied, and sentimental.

LIFE AND POEMS OF DUNBAR. J. Paterson, Edinburgh 1860. This is a commentated edition of the poems with semi-modernised spelling. Paterson omits the best poem, the "Tretis", and other "more indelicate pieces", so we know just where we are. He thinks the "Tretis" has no merit, but quotes chunks of the less "indelicate" bits in his introduction to mark that he knows its existence, however regretfully. The book is uncritical and unscholarly. Paterson does, however, put up quite a good argument for dating the "Flyting" 1504, the year Kennedy took Glentig, possibly mentioned as his house by Dunbar. At least it could not have been before that date.

THE POEMS OF WILLIAM DUNBAR. Ed. John Small, S.T.S., 3 vols., 1884-93. With an introduction and appendices by Æ. J. G. MacKay (Small having died with the work incomplete), notes and a glossary by W. Gregor, and a note on the versification by G. P.

M'Neill. Still the standard text, although Schipper is more thorough in the matter of variants. Mackay Mackenzie has improved on it here and there, but fallen from it elsewhere. It is in any case the fullest annotated and glossed text, its introduction required reading, as are its notes, glossary, appendices, etc. These should be read with Baxter as corrective, and M. P. McDiarmid on Baxter, in *Scottish Historical Review*, xxxiii (1954), pp. 46-52, and compared with Mackenzie's. The introduction is full, but too speculative; its division of the poems into Allegorical, Narrative, Amatory, Comic, Laudatory, Vituperative, Precatory, Satirical, Moral, and Religious, is at once too much and too little; it is obscurantist in that it fails to put the weight where it belongs— on satire. The "kinds", e.g., overlap too much for the division to be precise: "The Tretis" belongs in several of his categories at once. MacKay's criticism is uneven, but he does stress the French influence more than the English, and above all argues for a native Scots one which was neither: and finally, and most convincingly, stresses Dunbar's own originality. It is, in any case, dated and a bit superficial, and at times a little daring—as when he compares Dunbar not only with Villon, but with Heine and Dürer. The appendices on references to Dunbar in the records on dating, on versification (dated and faulty), bibliography, and notes on the persons alluded to in the poems, are unexceptionably valuable. There is a facsimile of the tune and a stanza of "Welcum of Scotland to be Quene", and others of the opening of "The Goldyn Targe" as in Bannatyne and the C. & M. prints. Eleven attributions are also printed at the end. The notes, in volume 3, are still the fullest printed, as is the glossary. There is a special note also on relations between Scotland and Denmark (see "The Flyting"), 1488-1513. It is a great handicap to Dunbar studies that this standard work is not available, even in an abridged edition, to the general book-buying public.

THE POEMS OF WILLIAM DUNBAR. Ed. J. Schipper, Vienna 1892-4. A version was done also for the University of Edinburgh. The order reflects his theory of chronology, which is suspect, as is his re-ordering of the stanzas of the "Flyting". Schipper's orderly, organising mind invents order where it doesn't exist. Laing's view that the chronological presentation of Dunbar's poems is "obviously impracticable" is obviously true. But the great merit of the work is its exhaustive covering of variants, and, as sheer text, it is still the best edition yet made. It is curious to find such a scholar so unscholarly in places—his uncritical approach to authorship (e.g.,

"Kynd Kittok"). He also has an eye to received opinion. To generalise—his text is good, his opinions bad. Even textually, his conflating of texts to get the "best" is indefensible. His theory of order is ingenious but unscholarly; and to find such a mind shuffling such coin as "it must be", "it is likely that" when arguing for an attribution is lamentable. His order, in fact may be roughly close— but the point is, it may not, and we want something a bit more solid.

SELECTION FROM THE POEMS OF AN OLD MAKAR, adapted for modern readers. H. Haliburton (J. Logie Robertson), London 1895. This is a popularisation, now only a curiosity.

THE DUNBAR ANTHOLOGY, being an anthology of Dunbar and his contemporaries. Edward Arber, London 1901. This contains eight Dunbar poems and one attributed to him erroneously. It is of no importance to scholars, and emphasises the "wrong" Dunbar —the courtly rather than the satiric.

THE POEMS OF WILLIAM DUNBAR. Ed. H. B. Baildon, Cambridge 1907. This is a good critical and scholarly, popular, one-volume, edition of the poems, anticipating Mackay Mackenzie's. His comments are inadequate and conventional. One's impressions of the critical faculties of editors make one wonder at times why they think the stuff worth editing at all—or is it enough that they find other people do? Baildon has good notes on spelling, pronunciation, grammar, and metric. He is aware of the stress nature of Scots, as distinct from "feet". The text reproduces Schipper's order and dating, and therefore is something of a popularisation of Schipper, with that scholar's merits and demerits intact, if condensed. He sees through the myth of James IV's court as a "golden age" and describes it as a "selfish, coarse, and corrupt court", which is precisely what Dunbar says it was.

THE POEMS OF WILLIAM DUNBAR. Ed. W. Mackay Mackenzie, Edinburgh 1932. As there is no popular one-volume edition of the S.T.S. Dunbar, this is the standard obtainable text. The text itself is good, but the notes and glossary are hopelessly inadequate. The serious student needs to see it against the S.T.S. editions of Dunbar, and of the Bannatyne and Maitland MSS. He includes one minor poem which Small excludes ("Four Maner of Folkis ar Evill to Pleis"), but excludes poems which Small includes. Here and there he gives a better reading than Small. The introduction is critically inadequate and misleading—altogether a poor best.

SELECTED POEMS OF WILLIAM DUNBAR. Ed. Hugh MacDiarmid [C. M. Grieve], Glasgow 1955. This is a small selection of the poems, but a very good one. In his introduction, Hugh MacDiarmid whose injunction to his fellow-poets of the Scots Renaissance— "Not Burns—Dunbar"—has done much to revive appreciation of the Makars in the twentieth century, is in an unusually mild mood. He quotes John Speirs with approval, and rightly points out that Dunbar is as unlike Chaucer as a medieval poet could be. He claims that Dunbar is the best of all Scottish poets, and that this is why he has such importance for the Scots Renaissance. I cannot agree with this verdict. Henrysoun is a greater poet than Dunbar, and Lyndsay a greater satirist, while Douglas exceeds them all in wealth of language. But with these reservations, one can see that Dunbar has more temperamental affinities with MacDiarmid, and, most importantly, that there is an affinity of situations between them. Both (see below, *E. Periodicals*: Edwin Morgan) were born "under dawn's left hand"—Dunbar under the dawn of the Reformation, MacDiarmid under the dawn of socialism (which has not yet broken in Scotland), in an "age of transition". Dunbar's treatment by the establishment of his time was pussykin stuff compared with the abuse and neglect of MacDiarmid handed out by the medio-critics of our time. Both were men of exceptional passionate force and intelligence, and both lived by Scotland's motto—*Nemo me impune lacessit.*

WILLIAM DUNBAR, selected poems. Ed. James Kinsley, Clarendon Medieval and Tudor Series, Oxford 1958. This is a very good introductory volume, containing 44 poems and 2 attributions. It has a sound introduction and perspective—too kind to James IV— and commentaries by Pinkerton, John Merry Ross, Agnes Mure MacKenzie, W. L. Renwick, and C. S. Lewis. "The Tretis" is given only in an abridged form, a fact not sufficiently made clear to new readers. Kinsley stresses the French influence, particularly on form and technique, but he is equally insistent on the implied existence of a "vigorous national tradition in Scots". Douglas Young (see *E* below) points out that a possible Flemish influence might have been taken into account, but his criticism tends to ignore the space limitations of this small book. Kinsley points out, correctly, that the English influence tended to augment the aureation tendency—that is, the artificial. He says, also correctly, though it is by no means obvious, that this master of the kinds had scant respect for the proprieties *of* the kinds. This is why attempts to classify the poems by kinds inevitably fail—the kinds overlap, and the best poems fall into two or more "kinds". Kinsley correctly puts the emphasis where it belongs, on "The Tretis", the core of which is the old juxtaposition of appearance and reality. He says Dunbar's "eye seldom reached beyond the fringe, or his mind beneath the surface of that remote Stewart court which was his milieu". This is not quite true—his mind *did* see beneath the surface of the court. He also remarks, justly, that Dunbar shows no interest in philosophy or letters—the latter presumably in a theoretical or academic way, for his interest in poetry shouts from every line he ever wrote. But it is true, for instance, that Dunbar was much less of a scholar, and much less of a philosopher in temperament, than the learned and wise Henrysoun. He had a superb imagination, often eldrich, always passionate and powerful, full of wit and humour, and sheer energy of utterance—the mark of the true poet—embodied in a subtle technique of great range and power. It is, says Kinsley, essentially an art of the dance. This last is important. Some poets are painters, and some are singers or other sorts of musician, but Dunbar, was first and foremost a dancer. Hence his intricate and deft patterning, his sure-footedness and speed, his momentum, his gaiety, his occasional abandon, his fling and eldrich skreich, his occasional breathlessness and exhaustion. The directly relevant poems here are "Off Februar the Fyiftene Nicht", and "Schir Jhon Sinclair Begowthe to Dance". But the evidence is there chiefly in the mastery of a wide range of intricate stanzas, of *tempo di ballo*. Altogether, it is difficult to imagine—*pace* Douglas Young —a better critical introduction to Dunbar in such little space.

C. Literary Histories

THOMAS WARTON. *History of English Poetry*, 3 vols., 1774-81. His comments on Dunbar are now out of date.

DAVID IRVING. *History of Scottish Poetry*, Edinburgh 1861. A valuable book, superseded where Dunbar is concerned, but has an introductory chapter on Scottish poetry before the War of Independence, which is still valuable. The whole work is required reading for students of Scottish poetry.

WILLIAM SPALDING. *History of English Literature*, Edinburgh 1876. Too elementary for university use. Dunbar has one page, half of that—the better half—a quote from Irving.

B. TEN BRINK. *Geschichte der englischen Literatur*, 2 vols., Berlin 1877-93. The third vol. includes consideration of Dunbar. Of little interest today—he seems to know no medieval poet except Chaucer. Henrysoun gets no mention.

J. M. ROSS. *Scottish History and Literature to the Period of the Reformation*, Glasgow 1884. This is a good historical approach to Scottish literature. Ross makes the point that Dunbar was seven years older than Erasmus—too old to come under his influence. This is an interesting observation, as Dunbar's work suffers from the lack of what precisely the ideas of the Renaissance in Europe had to give it—a means of understanding and universalising his private experience of the evils in Scotland. A comparison with Lyndsay is instructive in this regard: Lyndsay takes the Renaissance and pre-Reformation ideas in his stride, giving his satire a structure and objectivity impossible to Dunbar. Ross sees Dunbar as an image of his time and place—a materialist spiritually corrupt, no reformer, devoid of social conscience. This is superficially convincing and partly true: but it is hoped that the present book goes some way to answer some of these charges, and give a deeper view of Dunbar, spiritually, reformatively, and socially. Ross is safer on the social and historical side than on the literary and much of Dunbar escapes him. He makes a rather debatable point in saying that Dunbar is the first Scot in whose literature we recognise distinctive features of national character: Barbour? Henrysoun? Blin Hary? "Anonymous"?

H. WALKER. *Three Centuries of Scottish Literature*, 2 vols., Glasgow 1892. Professor Walker's book is a valuable essay on the subject from Lyndsay to Scott. It falls outside our period really, but the chapter on Lyndsay is of interest to Dunbar students.

T. F. HENDERSON. *Scottish Vernacular Literature*, Edinburgh 1898, 1910. This is quite a good though very much dated volume, full of pre-MacDiarmid defeatism. Almost thirty years after Henderson sang the dirge over the auld leid, it sprang to astonishing life in a series of works unsurpassed since the sixteenth century, and is still the one major force in Scottish literature today, which shows sign of sinking back to mediocre anglicising among present-day poeticules. Henderson sees Dunbar as "naive and frank". Frank he may be, but naive? He sees the vernacular, so-called, as much better in the colloquial poems than in the courtly, the realist than the allegorical. He stresses the French influence and says that "human nature", whatever that may be, is the chief theme of

Dunbar. Villon, he says, is gayer—and he might have added sweeter, simpler, nobler but not subtler nor better. Henderson stresses Dunbar's originality and makes the shrewd remark that he was unacceptable to the Reformers, and hence fell into obscurity, while Lyndsay became the most popular poet before Burns.

G. GREGORY SMITH. *The Transition Period*, Edinburgh 1900. A valuable essay on the fifteenth century in European literature, of wide sweep and acute perception. The section on Dunbar is more useful for perspective than critical assessment.

J. H. MILLAR. *A Literary History of Scotland*, London 1903. This is still the standard work on the subject, though long out of date. The commentary on Dunbar is unexceptionable, but also undistinguished.

G. GREGORY SMITH. *Scottish Literature*, London 1919. This is a critical-historical study in an academic style of more leisurely and easy-going days, a little bit complacent, wispy, chatty, taking no risks and breaking no barriers. But it is a theoretical speculation on the subject by a scholar of real distinction, widely read, deeply interested, intelligent and responsive. He makes many wise observations and is both readable and stimulating—real merits always. Propounding the now-famous notion of the "Caledonian Antisyzygy", it is interesting theory rather than criticism.

G. GREGORY SMITH. "The Scottish Chaucerians," in *Cambridge History of English Literature*, Vol. II, 1932. A very inadequate and unsatisfactory work, much stiffer and more inhibited than the above, as if he were hill-climbing in his Sunday best. This is due partly, of course, to the difficulty of having to get too much into too little: but in such a case the unimportance of the unimportant should govern the whole, and that is precisely what is lacking. The result is shallow and pedestrian, dull, uninspiring, with too few percepts among too many words. His performance on Dunbar is lamentable. He seems to be so hypnotised by the notion of Dunbar as a "Scottish Chaucerian", trying to reconcile the irreconcilable without it ever occurring to him that the trouble is in his false premise. The result is rather like the man who complained:

> Last night as I went up the stair
> I met a man who wasn't there;
> He wasn't there again to-day—
> I wish to God he'd go away.

AGNES MURE MACKENZIE. *An Historical Survey of Scottish Literature to 1714*, London 1933. This is a valuable study. She makes the point that Dunbar was hampered both as priest and courtier, a man in his difficult position in his difficult time. (I confess that I had come to similar conclusions—a frequent experience during this work—before I read her book.) In this, she says, he was like his nearest English fellow-poet, John Dryden, who was of Scots ancestry. She gets the emphasis right—on the satires and comic poems, not the courtly. She says his "weariness" is attributable to his time. She remarks on the superiority of the "Tretis", and sees its link with "This Lang Lentern Makis me Lene". She says that "the favourite *bourgeois* emotion is disapproval". I suppose she means particularly Scottish *bourgeois*, rooted in Calvinist kill-joyism. I should have thought the main *bourgeois* emotion was a longing for mediocrity, fear of the extremely good, the better, the best, and a passion for the middling, comforting, compromising illusion—for fascidemocshcvism, a middle-class limbo, neither Heaven nor Hell—and certainly not Purgatory. The book is required reading, and the author is a fine writer with the true gift of being interesting and stimulating on just about everything.

W. L. RENWICK and H. ORTON. *The Beginnings of English Literature to Skelton*, 1509, London 1939. As its title suggests, this book is more concerned with English than with Scottish literature, but Professor Renwick, apart from his gifts as scholar and teacher, has a very fine critical sensibility, and his remarks on Dunbar and the Scots of the period are very shrewd and perceptive. The book has an excellent bibliography and is a first-rate text-book within its limits of space.

JOHN SPEIRS. *The Scots Literary Tradition*, London 1940. This work is a landmark, if a small one, in Scottish criticism. He annuls the unnatural marriage between Dunbar and Chaucer, that wish-thought of English literary imperialism, and shows that Dunbar, if he had read his Chaucer at all, had no notion of what he was really like—gamma-double-minus level—and went his own way regardless. He trounces aureation and puts the weight where it belongs, on the satiric and comic poems, as Mure MacKenzie had done in 1933. Much of what he says on Dunbar appeared in an article in *Scrutiny* in 1938 (see *E. Periodicals*, below). The main fault of this work is its brevity—a common complaint in Scottish literature, which could do with sheer bulk and roughage as much as anything—and one laments the lack of further major Scottish studies by this gifted critic. The book is directive rather than exploratory or demonstrative—a sketch for work not yet executed. Speirs sees not only the literary surface but, in the best traditions of Scottish criticism, the social and spiritual reality reflected in it. He points to the spiritual insecurity of the age, shows how it led to a morbid disillusionment which in turn begot a despairing Epicureanism, with aureation merely whiting the sepulchre, the whole life-impulse turning to a death-wish, and the great dance of death following the loss of faith. The truth of much of this comes out, I hope, in the present work: but Speirs misses, as others have missed until now, Dunbar's personal triumph, as I believe and have tried to show, over the black dragon of death, his own recovery of faith with at least the hope of personal salvation, whatever befell the age, at his end. The present work is, in fact, an attempt to take up the work of Dunbar criticism where Speirs left it for other fields of medieval study.

J. W. H. ATKINS. *English Literary Criticism: the Medieval Phase*, Cambridge 1943. A general work, of interest here chiefly on matters of theoretical and technical background.

E. K. CHAMBERS. *English Literature at the Close of the Middle Ages*, *Oxford History of English Literature*, Vol. II, 1945. Mainly of background interest here.

GEORGE KANE. *Middle English Literature*, Methuen 1951. Chiefly of interest for its work on romances, religious lyrics, with special reference to *Piers Plowman*.

C. S. LEWIS. *English Literature in the Sixteenth Century*, *Oxford History of English Literature*, Vol. III, 1954. This work contains an interesting discussion of Dunbar in the first chapter. It is in the style of an earlier age, a bit amateurish, leisurely, belles-lettrist—inadequate; but intelligent, independent, shrewd, enthusiastic, and very readable—the ultimate and vanishing grace. He scouts the "Chaucerian" libel, remarks on the inferiority of Skelton, and makes the telling point that "Hell" was joked about precisely because it was taken very seriously.

JAMES KINSLEY. *Scottish Poetry: A Critical Survey*, London 1955. This is one of the most important books on Scottish Literature published this century, simply because it was published at all—the only one of its kind, filling a too-long-felt need. But it is scarcely incisive enough, is too academic, in the bad sense of being "detached", instead of passionately committed to the salvation of an oppressed literature. Professor Kinsley himself contributes the chapter relevant to us here, on the makars, including Dunbar. This is much in the vein of his introduction to the *Selected Poems* (see above, *B. Printed Editions*): but, being less cramped, is that much fuller and better. Even more stress is laid on Dunbar's originality, and I entirely agree with his ultimate assessment—"He is an assured and independent inheritor of a European tradition far removed from Chaucer in temperament". Required reading.

KURT WITTIG. *The Scottish Tradition in Literature*, Edinburgh 1958. This is probably the best book on the subject since Gregory Smith's (reviewed above), but it is by no means comprehensive or trustworthy. Like the little girl, where it is good (e.g., on Barbour and Henrysoun), it is very, very good: but where it is bad (e.g., on Neil Gunn and the contemporary scene), it is horrid. It is a work of criticism rather than of history proper, and tends to make too much (O rare vice!) of Scottishness. Nationalism is as necessary to life as food and drink, but chauvinism is something else. The chapter on Dunbar is good without being remarkable, and adds little to Schipper's *tour-de-force* (see *F. Biography*, below). Wittig is in the tradition of Scottish criticism—acutely aware of the social background of literature, and knowing that literature cannot be judged apart from the higher values—a truth still to be learned by present English criticism, which is still too art-for-arty. He says that Dunbar's religion was fear-based, not always specifically Christian, and liturgical rather than theological or pious. Much of the truth of this has been brought out in the present work: but again, Wittig, like Speirs, misses the significance of the later poems. The Confession poems are as much theological and pious as they are liturgical, and "Don is a Battell" and "Hale, Sterne Superne!" are specifically Christian, as is "Amang thir Freiris, within ane Cloister". He has not—what critic has?—noticed the note of personal triumph in these poems, the passionate sincerity of religion in "Thow that in Hevin" (dated 1517), nor their link with a similar note of exultation in "Welcum, my awin Lord Thesaurair"; all of which argue his appointment to a benefice and subsequent recovery of his faith and serenity. He is good on Dunbar's originality, his welding of metre and subject, his realism of imagery and technical excellence. He is less convincing on the influence of Gaelic on this most anti-Gael of poets, and he says nothing at all—but who has?—about the fact that Dunbar's metric is largely derived from court song: a fact first pointed out to me by Professor W. L. Renwick, and which I am convinced is the truth. Wittig's book is nevertheless a landmark, though only a half-way one.

D. Commentaries

Æ. J. G. MACKAY. *William Dunbar, 1460-1520*, Edinburgh 1889. This is a reprint of his Introduction to the S.T.S. edition of Dunbar. It is still the fullest introduction to Dunbar studies, seeing him in his real historical and social perspective. But it must be seen in relation to such follow-up studies as those of Baxter (see under), Speirs, Kinsley, Janet M. Smith, Wittig, etc.

F. MEBUS. *Studien zu William Dunbar*, Brestlau 1902.

C. STEINBERGER. *Étude sur William Dunbar*, Paris 1908. A book of 180 pp. covering Dunbar's Scotland, his life, Scottish poetry, Dunbar's own poems, with a critical summary. Whole poems are printed with translations into French verse. It is a worthy effort, though a bit erratic. Nothing could be less true than that "toutefois la posterité sut rendre hommage au génie plus élevé de Dunbar". But she does see his satiric weight.

RACHEL ANNAND TAYLOR. *Dunbar*, London 1932. This book derives from Hugh MacDiarmid's direction to Scottish Renaissance poets: "Not Burns—Dunbar". Unfortunately, it is an attempt to debunk it. The result is a view of what Dunbar looks like if you think that Swinburne is a great poet. The work of a poet-scholar, it manages to be both bad poetry and bad scholarship. Yet there are things in it: she remarks on Dunbar's lack of the ballad "magic" (he was not a folk-poet); his lack of learning; his lack of metaphysical quality (a positive virtue, I should have thought, but she hadn't seen the craze for "metaphysical" escapism reach its present appalling dimensions, which threaten poetry with senile decay); his lack of mystical quality ("Don is a Battell"? "Hale, Sterne Superne"?); his eccentricity from the central folk-tradition (courtly limitation surely?); and his untypicalness—not necessarily a vice, one would have thought. All these are negatives. This negative debunking is written in prose of the richest purple—attar of roses mixed with a dash of vitriol. She shows no awareness of the fact that some of the poems "attributed" to Dunbar may not be by him—indeed, that there is no authority at all for such attribution, and much against. She says that Margaret Drummond (one of

James IV's paramours) died mysteriously at Stirling Castle; in fact she died at Drummond Castle. She declares that the author of the "Tretis" knew nothing about women. But she does say that the "Tretis" is "worth a hundred Golden Targes"; that Dunbar has a touch of *nostalgie de la boue*; and, most acutely of all, that his sensuality is mentalised. She denounces the cruelty of "Lang heff I Maed of Ladyes Quhytt", and the Queen's attitude to VD as reflected in the "libbin of the pockis" poem. She stigmatises Dunbar as a "bourgeois"—a dig at MacDiarmid, who is a proletarian and a Communist: anybody who can call Dunbar a *"bourgeois"* is purblind. Not only was he of the feudal (so-called) nobility, and a courtier, but his hatred of *bourgeois* values screams from poem after poem. He was a reactionary against the capitalist revolution then being born—he saw it, not as "progress", but as utter corruption and depravity; and that, morally, is precisely what it was. One wonders whether she had read Dunbar at all, or only a few chosen poems. She is right, however, in pointing out that Dunbar was only one of several major poets in and around his time. Her book serves generally to promote MacDiarmid's case.

JANET M. SMITH. *The French Background of Middle Scots Literature*, Edinburgh 1934. This is a thoroughly good and suggestive little study, bringing out the fact that the medieval Scots were so indebted to the French—like most Europeans of the time—that Scotland was almost a literary province of France. Indeed, the name "Europe", so far as poetry was concerned, was almost synonymous with what is now France, until the coming of Dante and other Italians. It is curious how English literature, which has been so quick and uncritical in claiming the medieval Scots as "Chaucerians", has never adequately acknowledged the fact of its own immense debt to French and Italian literature. Dr Smith ably acknowledges the debt of Scots to French literature in this period, and her book is required reading: indispensable.

J. W. BAXTER. *William Dunbar*, Edinburgh 1952. This work is a historical and biographical account of Dunbar and his work—the most exhaustive up to date. He has much to say on problems of authorship, editions, dating, and the like. He demolishes Smeaton (see *F. Biography*, below), blows away much wishful thinking about Dunbar's authorship of such poems as "Kynd Kittok" and various passages in the "Flyting" as historical evidence. Yet there seems to be no reference to Ayres's very important glossing of the Alathya-Eustis reference (see *E. Periodicals*, below). Matthew P. McDiarmid (see *F. Biography*, below) takes him very convincingly to task on two other points, himself contributing valuable new knowledge on the subject. But Baxter is required reading at any level.

E. Periodicals

F. R. OLIPHANT. Article in *Blackwood's Magazine*, CLIV (1893). Now of little interest, though he makes the interesting point that Dunbar has a range which at one end includes Spenser, and at the other Hogarth. The criticism is a bit shaky: was the bulk of Dunbar's work "ephemeral courtly truffles"? Was he a "strong careless genius"? He, too, has the Chaucer parrot stuck in his throat; and "it's time the claith wes owre the parrot."

A. S. NELSON. "William Dunbar," in *Gentleman's Magazine*, CCLXXXVII (1899). A popularising article of no academic interest.

H. M. AYRES. "Theodolus in Scots," in *Modern Philogoy* XV (1918). This is a very important discussion of the meaning of two lines of the "Flyting," as given in *The Poems of William Dunbar*, ed. Mackay Mackenzie:

> Insensuate sow, fals Eustase air,   321
> And knaw, kene scald, I hald of Alathya . . .

Mackenzie, in 1932, glossed "Alathya" correctly, but inadequately, as "truth", from Greek "aletheia". Of Eustase, he says: "probably the notorious Eustase the monk, outlaw, and magician, whose exploits are narrated in *Essays on . . . Literature, Popular Superstitions . . . of England in the Middle Ages*, by Thomas Wright, ii, pp. 121-46. Owing to the way he changed sides he is called traitor in English chronicles. He was killed in a naval engagement when bringing a French fleet over to help the barons against King John". Now, this ingenious explanation does great credit to the learned editor's breadth of reading; and he may be right. But this does not tell us why Eustase and Alathya should be so conspicuously contrasted. Mackenzie allows the English-hating Celt, Kennedy, as remarkable an interest in English history as his own. H. N. Ayres points to the *Ecloga Theoduli*, a widely-used medieval text-book. It is a debate between Alathya and Pseustis—Truth and Falsehood—the one meaning Orthodoxy and the other Heresy. They are referred to in Barclay's *Eclogues* as Alathya and "fals Sewstis". Barclay had already published his translation of *The Ship of Fools* in 1507, so it is possible that the *Eclogues* too were circulating about the time the

"Flyting" was written: but Kennedy may have got wind of "fals Sewstis" from some other source. The point that Ayres makes is that by appropriation of the initial "s" one gets "fals Eustis"—or Kennedy's "fals Eustase". In other words, Kennedy is accusing Dunbar of heresy—which he does also elsewhere. Ayres would seem to be right, and to have made a valuable contribution to scholarship by this article, published in 1918. Yet not only did Mackenzie miss it, apparently, but Bruce Dickins in the 1960 edition has not corrected him. I have already said that Baxter seems to have missed it: indeed, Ayres's important work has been entirely ignored, as far as I can ascertain, by Dunbar scholarship until now—surely a very strange matter. The importance of the point, apart from its textual value, is that it strengthens the case for believing that Dunbar was sympathetic to Lollardry (cp. "lamp Lollardorum"), and throws light on Kennedy's reading.

BRUCE DICKINS. (1) "Contributions to the Interpretation of Middle Scots Texts," a letter to *T.L.S.*, 21 Feb. 1924. A gloss of Aegeas in the "Flyting", l. 537, proconsul who martyred St Andrew. This was noted by Mackenzie in the 1932 edition. (2) *"Suggested Interpretation of a passage in the Flyting"*: another letter to *T.L.S.*, 10 July 1924, glossing l. 540, the word "throp" as Trophe, from Trophe, original of Troilus and Cryseide. Kennedy had read "Throp" as a name for Cryseide. Also noted by M. P. McDiarmid in 1932.

ANONYMOUS. An article on Dunbar in *T.L.S.*, 10 Apr. 1930. Apparently the B.B.C. commemorated in 1930 Dunbar's death, on the strength of Lyndsay's mentioning him as dead in the Papyngo poem of 1530. One excuse is as good as another, I suppose, and better than no notice. This article is a model of bad Dunbar writing. The author assumes that the poet was the man named in the St Andrews University lists; he says that Dunbar was conscientious only with regard to metre; he drivels on about Chaucer; he assumes that Dunbar wrote the London poem; he makes much of Dunbar's pro-Englishry and anti-Celticness; he assumes Dunbar wrote "Kynd Kittok"; ditto the "Droichis Pairt of the Play"; he states that the "Tretis" of the *three* mariit wemen and the wedo was *definitely* copied from the Wife of Bath: to which, of course it is inferior (probably because it was written in that uncouth language, Scots); he says that Dunbar's descriptive work was less accurate than that of his contemporaries (did he have Douglas's "Prologues" in mind?); he stresses the laureate fallacy, itself born

2 B

of the fallacy that Dunbar was the "rhymour of Scotland" mentioned in Henry VII's Privy Purse Expenses, 31 Dec. 1501 (he may have been, but the evidence is rather against, and in any case it is not proved): the only "influences" on Dunbar he alleges are the usual, largely mythical English ones. He makes one good and valid point, but rather obvious—a comparison of "Off Februar the Fyiftene Nycht" with the relevant scene in Marlowe's *Dr Faustus*. All in all, a vile article, English literary imperialism at its worst.

P. H. NICHOLS. (1) "William Dunbar as a Scottish Lydgatean", *PMLA*, XLVI (1931). This is a very good account of the correspondences between Dunbar's work and Lydgate's: but it too easily falls into the fallacy of *post-hoc, propter-hoc*. It still has to be demonstrated that Dunbar actually borrowed from Lydgate: a common source is more likely. The refrain of "*Timor mortis*", for instance, has a common source in the liturgy. The fact that Lydgate also wrote a *danse macabre*, a table of confession, and a poem of the Passion, does not mean that Dunbar got the germ of his own similar poems from him: these were the common stock-in-trade of clerical poets of the time. He is on firmer ground—and of strong literary interest—when he points out the remarkable recurrence of marine and lapidary images in both poets: but again, as he points out, they have (see also below, ISABEL HYDE) a common French ancestry. He concludes that Dunbar had more in common with Lydgate than with Chaucer—which I am prepared to concede. But Dunbar owed little to either, and Nichols fails to point out the most important matter of all—that Dunbar was a much better poet than Lydgate. (2) "Lydgate's Influence on the aureate terms of the Scottish Chaucerians," *PMLA*, XLVII (1932). This is a continuation of his study mentioned above. Much of my remarks on the above apply also to this study.

BRUCE DICKINS. A letter on the "Flyting," to *T.L.S.*, 14 Dec. 1935. This glosses "Puttidew" in l. 541. Professor Dickins says it refers to the legend of the Wandering Jew, who was said to have pushed Jesus of Nazareth when bearing the Cross. In French he was called "boute-dieu", the man who pushed God: hence the corruption in Scots, "puttidew". Dickins himself notes it in the 1960 edition.

C. F. BUHLER. "London, Thow art the Flowre of Cytes All", in *Review of English Studies*, XLII (1937). A scholarly review of the poem and its circumstances—a banquet given for Prince Arthur and Catherine of Aragon, in 1501. Buhler throws doubt on Dunbar's authorship, and is taken up by Baxter (see *D. Commentaries*, above), who attributes it to Fordun. Dunbar received his pension that year in Scotland on 20 Dec., so he could hardly have been in the English court by 31 Dec. the same year.

JOHN SPEIRS. "William Dunbar", in *Scrutiny*, VII (1938). This article is wrongly attributed to E. W. F. Tomlin in the Supplement to the *Cambridge Bibliography*. "It is my object in this paper to suggest that the core of his living achievement, that part of his achievement which we read *as if it were contemporary* (my italics), consists not of the ceremonial poems . . . but of the comic and satiric poems . . . the goliardic blasphemies . . . and the more acrid and radical satires that merge into the saturnine poems that give his work as a whole its dark cast." This opening sentence of Speirs' article puts our contemporary position better than I have seen it put elsewhere: it was the starting-point of the present book, which I hope bears out the truth of this contention, but adds a dimension missed by Speirs—the significance of the later religious poems, and the spiritual order created by the whole work in relation to Dunbar himself, as distinct from his age. Dunbar was not the "poet laureate" of James IV's court in that golden age of Scotland before Flodden: he was its vitriolic satirist, exposer of its vices, denouncer of its false values, and scourge of its king. Speirs makes the point, further brought out in the present work, that Dunbar's satire, at its best, is religious satire—written from a religious standpoint. He also makes the telling point—it is one of the main reasons why McDiarmid made his famous utterance—that whereas Burns' mind is uniquely Scottish, Dunbar's is European. This, too, has been brought out in the present work, I hope, for it has been my aim to see Dunbar in a European rather than an English, or even a purely Scottish, context. The significance of Speirs' remark in relation to Burns is that after the Treaty of Union of 1707, Scotland, always a European country, came to share England's isolation and insularity, lost her great European heritage, and gained only the unassimilable, eccentric English tradition.

BRUCE DICKINS. Letter to *T.L.S.*, 20 Jan. 1945. This letter discusses the "Flyting", l. 538. Dickins here makes the point that the Marcion mentioned is probably Marcion of Sinope, who started the Marcionite heresy, and not the emperor of that name. Noted in 1960 edition.

EDWIN MORGAN. "Dunbar and the Language of Poetry", in *Essays in Criticism*, XI (1952). This is a very perceptive little study, reminding one how good its author can be. He notes Dunbar's importation of the "syllabic verse of France" (not "imported" by Dunbar at all, who found it lying to his hand all round him in Scotland), and contrasts verse of stylised rhetorical language with the poetry of speech. Dunbar, he says, wrote "under dawn's left hand"—referring to the Reformation: some dawn—some left! But the point is taken and enlarged upon in the present work.

MATTHEW P. MCDIARMID. Review of Baxter in *Scottish Historical Review*, XXXIII (1954). This is a very scholarly work indeed by the distinguished editor of the S.T.S. edition of the poems of Robert Fergusson—the standard text. McDiarmid provides new information from the publications of the Scottish Records Society. From the protocol of James Young, no. 370, he quotes a statement made by the captain of the *Katering* (see "Flyting") on 20 Jul. 1490, about the interception of his ship by the French: from this Mr McDiarmid deduces that the poem probably dates from about that year. He states that Schir Jhon the Ros died in 1494, so that the "Flyting" must have been prior to that. This is in direct conflict with Schipper's contention that l. 154, referring to Kennedy's living in a "laithly luge that wes pliper menis" refers to Kennedy's buying Glentigh house in 1504, so the poem could not have been before that date (Ayres's reference to Barclay reinforces Schipper: see above). From the protocol book of John Foular, part 1, no. 543, he produces evidence of Dunbar as a witness to that document, described in it as "chaplain", on 13 Mar. 1508. He remarks in passing that there is no reason to suppose that Dunbar's pensions were for poetic services alone. All this is a contribution to Dunbar studies that goes far beyond the ordinary demands of reviewing: yet this original work of McDiarmid's has not been taken up by Professor Dickins in the 1960 edition of Mackenzie.

A. A. M. DUNCAN and M. P. MCDIARMID. "Notes and Comments on some wrongly-dated Entries in the Acts of the Lords of Council", in *Scottish Historical Review*, XXXIII (1954). This incidentally produces evidence that the Schir Jhon the Ros of Dunbar's "I that in Heill wes", and of the "Flyting", was Sir John Ross of Mountgreenan.

JAMES KINSLEY. "The Poverty of Scottish Literary Studies", in *Lines Review*, No. 10 (1955). This essay is not directly relevant to our author, but it and the discussion it provoked are of great importance to Scottish Studies.

R. L. C. LORIMER. "A Reply to Kinsley," *Lines Review*, Nos. 11-12 (1956). This essay takes up Professor Kinsley's article reviewed above, and discusses it with exceptional intelligence and knowledge of Scottish literary matters.

ISABEL HYDE. "Primary Sources and Associations of Dunbar's Aureate Imagery", in *Modern Language Review*, LI (1956). This is a defence of aureation, but not so much in terms of its diction as of its imagery—as the title implies. She traces the sources of such images as the Dragon, the harrowing of Hell, the pilgrimage (e.g., *vanitas vanitatum*), and Christ and Mary in common medieval stock. These are particularly the Bible and liturgy, the exegeses and commentaries, the Gospel of Nicodemus (apocryphal), the Bestiary, the Lapidary, and folk-sayings and proverbs or *sententiae*. This is only part of the story—she says nothing of sermons, for example, nor heraldry—but it is an important part, and the study is valuable. Its worst fault is its brevity: the subject could do with book-length treatment.

DOUGLAS YOUNG. Review of Kinsley's selection of the poems in *Scottish Historical Review*, XXXVIII (1959). A first-rate scholarly review, but a bit severe and less than fair: it is unreasonable to blame a man for not producing a book three times the length his publisher allows; and Kinsley, to meet Dr Young's demands, would have needed at least that. He points out that there is a need for critical apparatus and evaluation of textual sources; he expands on the inadequacy of glossing, noting, and attributing; he says editions should be compared with the *Dictionary of the Older Scottish Tongue* (but how—it is only half-finished: and where—for who can afford to buy it?): that Baildon and S.T.S. are better in respect of notes and such than Kinsley or Mackenzie (true, but space again). He makes the point that the Latin renaissance in Europe was in full spate in Dunbar's time; and this, he suggests, was an influence in the direction of aureation. He says there is "no reason for regarding Chaucer's classicising influence as more than a reinforcement of an international movement in which Scotland was by no means backward". Considering that Buchanan in the next generation was the greatest Latinist of his age in Europe, this point is sustained. He notes also the French and possible Gaelic influence, but draws attention to one which has been neglected—the Flemish. In this connexion he quotes Professor Renwick's note in the Kinsley selection, and Pinkerton, p. 128. But if Dr Young's scholarship makes us sit up and take notice, regretting once again that this best of living Scottish scholars is all but lost to Scottish Studies in Greek pastures, his literary criticism is apt to send us to sleep again: to describe Dunbar as "a master of *vers d'occasion*", as a summing-up, does not inspire confidence in the quality of the sensibility yoked with the excellent mind.

DENTON FOX. Essay in *Philosophical Quarterly*, No. 39 (1960). A valuable essay on some of the problems of dating Dunbar's poems.

F. Biography

DAVID IRVING. *The Lives of the Scottish Poets*, 2 vols., Edinburgh 1803, 1810. Superseded by the following work, in my view.

ANONYMOUS. *Lives of the Scottish Poets*, Society of Ancient Scots, 3 vols., London 1822. Though individual chapters are out of date, this work has not been surpassed up to date (1964). It contains the fullest account of Mark Alexander Boyd known to me, for example, though making no mention of his famous *Sonet*. The chapter on Dunbar (the articles are by various hands signed only by initials) is inadequate and out of date.

J. SCHIPPER. *William Dunbar, sein Leben und seine Gedichte*, Berlin 1884. This is a comprehensive study of the life, times, predecessors, and poetic position of Dunbar, with extensive verse translations of the poems into German. The critical chapter is a *tour de force*, and remains the standard critical introduction, for those who can get at it. It certainly has left its mark and is exhaustively thorough. This most distinguished of Dunbar scholars also attempts to arrange the poems in chronological order—a not-so-much brave as rash undertaking, and as I hope the present work brings out, has little bearing anyhow on the real order of the poems—the spiritual one.

W. H. O. SMEATON. *William Dunbar*, Edinburgh 1898. This work of fiction purporting to be scholarship is worse than worthless—it is dangerously misleading. Baxter (see *D. Commentaries* above) has demolished its unique "facts" once for all. Its continued lingering on the library shelves—not fiction ones either—is a mystery.

J. W. BAXTER. *William Dunbar*, 1952. (See *D. Commentaries* above.)

G. Records

ACCOUNTS OF THE LORD HIGH TREASURER OF SCOTLAND (1491-1513). Records Office, Register House, Edinburgh.

ACTA FACULTATIS ARTIUM S. ANDREAE. St Andrews University.

ANNALES UNIVERSITATIS GLASGUENSIS (Vol. I, 1451-58). Glasgow University.

ANNALES COLLEGI FACULTATIS ARTIUM IN UNIV. GLAS. (1451-55). Glasgow University.

COMPOTA THESAURARIORUM REGUM SCOTORUM (1485-92; 1500-2; 1502-4; 1504-6; 1506-7; 1511-12; 1512-13). H.M. General Register House, Edinburgh.

LIVRE DES CONCLUSIONS DE LA NATION D'ALLEMAGNE (1477-92). Paris Archives, No. 8.

LIVRE DES RECEVEURS DE LA NATION D'ALLEMAGNE (H2588). Archives Nationales, Bibliothèque Nationale, Paris.

LIVRE DES CONCLUSIONS DE LA NATION DE PICARDE (1476-83). Paris University Archives, No. 9.

PRIVY PURSE EXPENSES OF HENRY VII. British Museum, Add. MSS., No. 7099, year 1501.

PRIVY SEAL REGISTER (Vols. II, IX). H.M. General Register House, Edinburgh.

PUBLICATIONS OF SCOTTISH RECORDS SOCIETY. Protocol of James Young, No. 370, for 20 Jul. 1490; and protocol book of John Foular, Part 1, No. 543 for 13 Mar. 1508. Central Library, Scottish Section, Edinburgh—and elsewhere.

REGISTER OF THE FACULTY OF THEOLOGY. Paris University, Ms. 5657a (Latin), Bibliothèque Nationale, Paris.

REGISTRUM SECRETI SIGILLI REGUM SCOTORUM, Kols. II (1498-1504), IV (1508-13). H.M. General Register House, Edinburgh.

H. Language

J. KAUFMANN. *Traité de la langue du poète écossais William Dunbar* (*précédé d'une esquisse de sa vie et d'un choix de ses poèmes*). Bonn 1873.

This is a doctoral address of 107 pp., the bulk of which (pp. 47-107) is a close linguistic account of Dunbar's language. This is first-rate, but now somewhat dated—a book on the subject is long overdue. Required reading.

J. A. H. MURRAY. *Dialects of the Southern Counties of Scotland*, Edinburgh 1873. Still unsurpassed.

FRANCISQUE-MICHEL. *A Critical Inquiry into the Scottish Language*, Edinburgh 1882. He is a champion of the French influence, which he consequently over-rates: but the book is well worth study.

G. GREGORY SMITH. *Specimens of Middle Scots*, Edinburgh 1902.

JAMES COLVILLE. *Studies in Lowland Scots*, Edinburgh 1909.

WILLIAM GRANT and JAMES MAIN DIXON. *Manual of Modern Scots*, Cambridge 1921. A work in four parts, including two readers, one of prose and one of verse, the total some 500 pages—pretty comprehensive. Absolutely essential reading for anyone interested in any Scots linguistic study.

SIR JAMES WILSON. *Dialects of Central Scotland*, Oxford 1926.

ANGUS MCINTOSH. *Introduction to a Survey of Lowland Scots Dialects*, Edinburgh 1952.

DICTIONARY OF THE OLDER SCOTTISH TONGUE. Edd. Craigie and Aitken, Edinburgh (still in process). Comment on the importance of this work is superfluous. What must be said is that the ten or so volumes will be hard to get at for many students, and a one-volume edition should also be in hand.

SCOTTISH NATIONAL DICTIONARY. Ed. Murison, Edinburgh (also still in process). The above remarks apply also to this volume. These dictionaries can be expected to surpass such older works, well-known to students, as Jamieson's *Scottish Dictionary* and Warrack's *Scots Dialect Dictionary*.

I. Metric

J. SCHIPPER. *Altenglische Metrik*, 2 vols., Bonn 1882-8. A thorough account of the subject, but dated: Dunbar is one of the poets commented on.

F. B. GUMMERE. "A Discussion of the Old English and Metrical Systems, and their Interplay", in *American Journal of Philology*, 1886, pp. 46-78. A very interesting study, particularly relevant to the metric chapter of the present work.

H. B. BAILDON. "A Dissertation on the Rhymes in the Authentic Poems of Dunbar", in *Transactions of the Royal Society of Edinburgh*, xxxix (1899). This discussion of the rhymes is from a rather purist viewpoint—which we have little reason to believe was Dunbar's. To deduce corruption from the rhyming of "beme" with "quene", as Baildon does, is to multiply entities beyond necessity. It was commonly acceptable at the time, as was *rime riche*, and other "accidents"—assonance among them—not thought seemly in the Victorian era. The question of "authenticity" in Dunbar is still too problematical for anyone to use the word quite so confidently as Baildon does in the title: but he does admit in the text that an "authentic" text of Dunbar is impossible. It is well to remember that we do not have a single poem of Dunbar's known to be from his own hand and signed by himself. Baildon relies more confidently on modern Scots pronunciation as a key to Middle Scots than is justifiable. His attempts to deduce phonetic values from rhyme, therefore, are a bit shakily grounded. He asserts the supremacy of Schipper's text (and follows it and the chronology in his own edition). The paper is still of value —an important and painstaking phonetic study.

THOMAS S. OMOND. *A Study of Metre*, 1903. Still required reading on metric, but not particularly relevant to Dunbar.

GEORGE SAINTSBURY. *A History of English Prosody*, 1906. Professor Saintsbury's characteristically monumental study is now out of date, but still required reading.

P. F. BAUM. *Principles of English Versification*, Harvard 1922. A study of general value.

LASCELLES ABERCROMBIE. *Principles of English Prosody*, Part 1, London 1923. Still a valuable study.

KARL SHAPIRO. *Bibliography of Modern Prosody*, Baltimore 1948. A very useful guide, with a good introduction.

JOHN THOMPSON. *The Founding of English Metre*, London 1961. A discussion of the evolution of English metric from 1557 to the

Elizabethan high period. It has particular relevance to the metric chapter of the present work.

Acquaintance with the theories of Hopkins and Patmore is assumed here.

J. Bibliographies

WILLIAM GEDDIE. *A Bibliography of Middle Scots poets*, S.T.S., Edinburgh 1912. Fullest yet available.

F. W. BATESON. *The Cambridge Bibliography of English Literature*, 4 vols., Cambridge 1940.

GEORGE WATSON. Supplement to above, Cambridge 1957.

K. Miscellaneous

R. L. MACKIE. *King James the Fourth of Scotland*, Edinburgh 1958.

W. MACKAY MACKENZIE. *The Secret of Flodden*, Edinburgh 1931. Contains a prose translation of *La Rotta di Scocesi*, a contemporary Italian poem which tells of James's death by rashly trying to charge through to Surrey to capture him.

J. EVANS and M. S. SERJEANTSON. *Introduction to English Medieval Lapidaries*, E.E.T.S., CXC (1933).

WILLIAM CROFT DICKINSON. *Scotland from the Earliest Times to 1603*, Edinburgh 1961.

JOHN KNOX. *History of the Reformation in Scotland*, ed. Croft Dickinson, 2 vols., Edinburgh 1949. The Introduction is relevant here.

G. R. OWST. *Preaching in Medieval English, an Introduction to the Sermon Mss. of circa 1350-1540*, Cambridge 1926. Also, *Literature and the Pulpit in Medieval England*, Cambridge 1933.

J. PETER. *Complaint and Satire*, Oxford 1956.

C. S. LEWIS. *The Allegory of Love*, Oxford 1936.

R. M. WILSON. *The Lost Literature of Medieval England*, 1952.

J. E. SPINGARN. *A History of Literary Criticism in the Renaissance*, New York 1925.

BRUCE PATTISON. *Music and Poetry of the English Renaissance*, London 1948.

JOHN STEVENS. *Music and Poetry in the Early Tudor Court*, London 1961.

W. A. NEILSON. *The Origins and Sources of the Court of Love*, Harvard Studies, VI (1899).

W. G. DODD. *Courtly Love in Chaucer and Gower*, Harvard 1913.

R. H. TAWNEY. *Religion and the Rise of Capitalism*, 1937.

THOMAS JOHNSTON *A History of the Working Classes in Scotland*, Glasgow 1920 and 1946.

Index

Dunbar's poems are here cited by first lines. The titles given in brackets are mostly those used in *The Poems of William Dunbar*, ed. W. Mackay Mackenzie (Edinburgh 1932).